Arnulfo L. Oliveira Memorial Library

The World We Want

How and Why the Ideals
of the Enlightenment
Still Elude Us

ROBERT B. LOUDEN

OXFORD
UNIVERSITY PRESS

2007

OXFORD
UNIVERSITY PRESS

Oxford University Press, Inc., publishes works that further
Oxford University's objective of excellence
in research, scholarship, and education.

Oxford New York
Auckland   Cape Town   Dar es Salaam   Hong Kong   Karachi
Kuala Lumpur   Madrid   Melbourne   Mexico City   Nairobi
New Delhi   Shanghai   Taipei   Toronto

With offices in
Argentina   Austria   Brazil   Chile   Czech Republic   France   Greece
Guatemala   Hungary   Italy   Japan   Poland   Portugal   Singapore
South Korea   Switzerland   Thailand   Turkey   Ukraine   Vietnam

Copyright © 2007 by Oxford University Press, Inc.

Published by Oxford University Press, Inc.
198 Madison Avenue, New York, New York 10016

www.oup.com

Oxford is a registered trademark of Oxford University Press

Library of Congress Cataloging-in-Publication Data
Louden, Robert B., 1953–
The world we want : how and why the ideals
of the Enlightenment still elude us / Robert B. Louden.
    p. cm.
Includes bibliographical references and index.
ISBN 978-0-19-532137-1
1. Enlightenment.   I. Title.
B802.L68 2007
190—dc22   2006048075

9 8 7 6 5 4 3 2 1

Printed in the United States of America
on acid-free paper

Finally, for my parents,
Robert K. and Anne Z. Louden

Preface and Acknowledgments

T his is a book about two different pictures: a picture of a hoped-for future created by Enlightenment intellectuals slightly over two centuries ago, and a picture of our world at present. In drawing each picture I have aimed at accuracy of representation: in the case of the first picture, by looking carefully at what Enlightenment intellectuals from a number of different countries actually said about the future; in the case of the second, by examining the historical and statistical record. *That* the two resulting pictures are very different from each other I am confident I have established. This in itself may not be news to everyone, but some of the details concerning the extent of the gap did come as a shock to me, and I think that many readers will be surprised to learn that we have often not progressed as much as we think we have—indeed, that in certain central areas of human life things are actually worse now than they were two hundred years ago.

Why the two pictures are so different is much harder to substantiate, and here I am less confident of the particular answers I have offered. But if my explanations for why the ideals of the Enlightenment still elude us are rejected, I hope that in the future they will be replaced by more accurate explanations. Previous efforts in this area are clearly unsatisfactory, and at present we suffer from a lack of serious analysis of the causes behind our failure to realize ideals.

Unlike most philosophical critiques as well as defenses of the Enlightenment, the present study focuses extensively on the relevant historical and empirical record: first, by examining carefully what kind of future Enlightenment intellectuals actually advocated; second, by tracking the different legacies of their ideals. The result is a more note-laden text than I would have liked, but one that also (or so I hope) speaks clearly and accurately about a number of issues that contemporary authors have often treated in an obscure manner. At the same time, in my efforts both to explain why many Enlightenment ideals have still not been realized and to find strategies for grounding hope in unhopeful times, I have tried to include a more philosophical and theoretical dimension within what is often a fairly descriptive and empirical narrative.

The basic conception of Enlightenment ideals that I put forward in part I and evaluate in part II is often at odds with many recent portrayals of the Enlightenment. On my reading, the heart of the Enlightenment was not a misguided scientistic attempt to control human life by means of a technocratic state, but rather a morally motivated effort to expand human freedom and equality. And the Enlightenment strategies for promoting these goals of increased freedom and equality were consciously multidimensional and pragmatic: Enlightenment intellectuals advocated not just political reform, but religious, educational, economic, and legal reform as well, anticipating that progressive changes in one sphere would help trigger needed changes in others, and that cumulative effects would outweigh solitary ones.

However, the following study is by no means a mere encomium to the Enlightenment. For I believe I have also shown that several of the means they advocated toward their ends (means strongly endorsed by later generations) are inefficacious, that at least one of their central goals simply does not fit with human nature, and that several of their ideals display a disturbing pattern of devolving into distorted versions of themselves when attempts are made to realize them. At bottom, I seek to analyze and evaluate these ideals, to determine what is dead and what is living in them.

....

Many different institutions and individuals have helped me in writing this book, and now it is my pleasure to thank them. Initial reading and research on the project were supported by a National Endowment for the Humanities 2001 Summer Stipend, and by a University of Maine System Trustee Professorship in 2001–2. A first draft of part I was written during 2002–3, with the aid of a sabbatical leave from the University of Southern Maine and an American Philosophical Society (APS) Sabbatical Fellowship for the Humanities and Social Sciences. I am grateful to each of these institutions for their financial support. The APS Fellowship in particular enabled me to devote a full year of uninterrupted time to reading and writing. Founded by Benjamin Franklin in 1743 to help support "all philosophical experiments that let Light into the Nature of Things," the American Philosophical Society was the perfect scholarly organization from which to seek support for a writing project about the legacy of Enlightenment ideals. In this regard I would also like to warmly thank Karl Ameriks, Martha Nussbaum, and Allen Wood for their support in my Fellowship application, as well as for their steady encouragement over the years.

Earlier versions of several chapters were presented as invited lectures at Binghamton University, State University of New York, in February 2003, and at Rostock and Münster Universities in Germany in June 2003. I would particularly like to thank my hosts Melissa Zinkin, Niko Strobach, and Ludwig Siep for their hospitality, as well as members of each audience for raising a number of important issues that eventually led to improvements in my argument.

Three anonymous reviewers for Oxford University Press went well beyond the call of duty in evaluating two different versions of a not always robust manuscript, and I would like to thank them for urging me to be clearer and bolder in what I was trying to say.

During the time in which I worked on the manuscript, it was my good fortune to receive guest lecture invitations from a number of universities and scholarly organizations in parts of the world that I had never visited before. Although the specific focus of my lectures was Kant's moral philosophy, many of the broader themes of this book came up repeatedly during our discussions. For hospitality, friendship, helpful criticisms, and, yes, even occasional signs that the Enlightenment hope of a cosmopolitan community of the citizens of the earth is possible, I would like to particularly thank the following individuals, institutions, and organizations: Jens Timmermann, University of St. Andrews, Scotland (April 2002); Zeljko Loparic, Universidade Estadual de Campinas, Brazil, Brazilian Kant Society (June 2002); Maria Borges, Universidade Federal de Santa Catarina, Brazil (June 2002); Alan Thomas, University of Kent, England (March 2004); Heiner F. Klemme, Manfred Kuehn, and Dieter Schönecker, Philipps-Universität Marburg, Germany

(March 2004); Xiangdong Xu and Thomas Pogge, Peking University, China (May 2004); Isabell Ward and Graham Bird, University of Hertfordshire, England, UK Kant Society (March 2005); and Alix Cohen, Department of History and Philosophy and Science, University of Cambridge, England (March 2005).

Part of the challenge of this project involved not making a fool of myself when writing about disciplines in which I am not trained. For helpful advice and criticism in this regard I would like to thank several of my colleagues at the University of Southern Maine (USM): Richard J. Maiman (Political Science), Martin A. Rogoff (School of Law), and Michael Hillard (Economics). Thanks also to Robert McCauley at Emory University for discussion and criticism of the two religion chapters, as well as for advice on general methodological matters.

The library staff at USM has been especially helpful over the years in procuring research materials from other libraries and getting them to my base in Portland and for advice on research strategies. Special thanks to David Vardeman, interlibrary loan assistant; Zip Kellogg, reference librarian; and Loraine Ann Lowell, John F. Plante, and Robert M. Spencer, circulation assistants.

I have also explored some of the book's themes with undergraduates in my philosophy classes at USM in recent years. In particular, I would like to thank participants from my senior seminar in spring 2000 (Challenges to the Enlightenment), my senior seminar in fall 2005 (Hume), my Early Modern Philosophy classes in fall 2004 and spring 2006, and my Philosophy of Law classes in spring 2004 and fall 2006.

Finally, I would like to express my appreciation to the following individuals: Lawrence Simon (Bowdoin College) and other members of the Maine Ethics Reading Group, for prodding me to crawl out of my eighteenth-century fixation and confront more texts in contemporary philosophy (some specimens of which are employed in what follows); Beata Panagopoulos, head of technical services at the Kennedy School Library of Harvard University, for providing important research aid on an issue that had Mainers stuck; Ann Brushwein, software support specialist at USM, for doing amazing things to my computer disks that I still don't understand; Derek Phillips (University of Amsterdam), for encouraging me to keep my priorities straight; Peter Ohlin, my editor at Oxford University Press, for counseling both patience and perseverance; Aramis López, for help with the bibliography; and last but not least, Tama, Elizabeth, and Sarah, for putting up with my crankiness as I struggled to get the manuscript into shape.

Contents

Note on Citations
and Translations

Quotations from Kant's works are cited in the body of the text by volume and page number in *Kants gesammelte Schriften*, edited by the Royal Prussian (later German) Academy of Sciences (Berlin: Georg Reimer, later Walter de Gruyter, 1900–), except for quotations from the *Critique of Pure Reason*, which are cited by the customary use of the pagination of its first ("A") and second ("B") editions. When available, I use—with occasional modifications—the recent English translations in *The Cambridge Edition of the Works of Immanuel Kant*, general editors Paul Guyer and Allen W. Wood (Cambridge, UK: Cambridge University Press, 1992–). These traditional "Academy" volume and page numbers (and also the A and B pagination from the *Critique of Pure Reason*) are reprinted in the margins of most recent editions and translations of Kant's writings. I have also used the following shortened titles:

Anthropology   *Anthropology from a Pragmatic Point of View*

Conflict	*The Conflict of the Faculties*
Conjectural Beginning	*Conjectural Beginning of Human History*
Enlightenment	*An Answer to the Question: What Is Enlightenment?*
Groundwork	*Groundwork of the Metaphysics of Morals*
Judgment	*Critique of the Power of Judgment*
Morals	*The Metaphysics of Morals*
Peace	*Toward Perpetual Peace*
Pedagogy	*Lectures on Pedagogy*
Practical Reason	*Critique of Practical Reason*
Pure Reason	*Critique of Pure Reason*
Religion	*Religion within the Boundaries of Mere Reason*
Theory and Practice	*On the Common Saying: That May Be Correct in Theory, but It Is of No Use in Practice*
Universal History	*Idea for a Universal History with a Cosmopolitan Aim*

The World We Want

Introduction

The Enlightenment is the only historical period to be defined by a philosophical movement, and so philosophers can perhaps be excused for being a bit misty-eyed about it. However, Enlightenment philosophers were also more practical than many people realize. Ernst Cassirer, in his classic study *The Philosophy of the Enlightenment*, writes,

> The fundamental tendency and the main endeavor of the philosophy of the Enlightenment are not to observe life and to portray it in terms of reflective thought. This philosophy believes rather in an original spontaneity of thought; it attributes to thought not merely an imitative function but the power and the task of shaping life itself. Thought consists not only in analyzing and dissecting, but in actually bringing about the order of things which it conceives as necessary, so that by this act of fulfillment it may demonstrate its own reality and truth.[1]

3

In other words, Enlightenment philosophers also sought not merely to interpret the world but also to change it—indeed, they believed that it was their duty to do so. But although some of them were not shy in acknowledging that "Enlightenment is justly accused as the cause of revolutions,"[2] most Enlightenment intellectuals are correctly read as advocating peaceful change through free inquiry, public discussion, and institutional reform.

These latter strategies both overlap with and differ from "piecemeal social engineering." Piecemeal social engineering shares with its more radical utopian and authoritarian relatives a strong desire to improve the human condition through intentional societal development and change, but unlike them it is always constrained by respect for basic human rights and democratic processes.[3] At the same time, although commentators often claim to have located the origins of social engineering (piecemeal or otherwise) in the Enlightenment,[4] the term "social engineering" is itself out of place here. No application of any specific "engineering" technique to society was advocated by any major Enlightenment intellectual. Even if one defines "social engineering" more generically as the attempt to improve human society by means of "the scientific method," the label is still inappropriate (not to mention vague), for it is inaccurate to call Enlightenment social reform efforts "scientific." At bottom, their reform efforts were motivated by moral rather than scientific concerns: their goal was not an engineered society administered by a technocratic state, but increased freedom and equality for all human beings. What is appropriate is an acknowledgment that Enlightenment philosophers and intellectuals were strongly committed to "the task of shaping life itself" and "actually bringing about the order of things" which they conceived as necessary, believed that specific institutions and social practices play key roles in shaping human lives, were convinced that initiating certain fundamental changes in human institutions and social practices would facilitate a deeper moral transformation in human life, and held that it was humanity's duty to undertake these changes. Friends as well as foes of the Enlightenment tend to underappreciate these core commitments, plumping instead for sweeping statements and grandiose formulas that often have no demonstrable connection to anything Enlightenment intellectuals actually said or believed. Thus from one side we are informed that the Enlightenment's professed universalism was in fact merely a cloak for Western hegemony and cultural imperialism,[5] while from another we are comforted with the news that economic globalization and contemporary democratization represent the fulfillment of Enlightenment hopes.

Indeed, in many intellectual circles at present discussion of the Enlightenment has sunk to the level of derogatory clichés. The influential critics Max Horkheimer and Theodor Adorno, in *Dialectic of Enlightenment*, decreed that "Enlightenment is totalitarian" and that it ushered in "the administered world."[6] Similarly, Michel Foucault concluded that Enlightenment efforts at social reform have led not to increased freedom but to the carceral society, a condition where the individual is "the effect of a subjection," "the effect and instrument of a political anatomy."[7] Alasdair MacIntyre, in *After Virtue*, entered the fray later, proclaiming that "the Enlightenment Project of justifying morality" not only failed but "had to fail";[8] and soon countless critics joined the chorus, denouncing alleged Enlightenment sins of racism, Eurocentrism, sexism, and colonialism. These sins, alas, are sometimes all too real, but the present fixation on them has often obscured what is most important and compelling about the Enlightenment.

The present work is written from a much different perspective, one closer (in certain respects) to that of earlier scholars such as Cassirer, who, shortly before the Nazis exiled him from Germany, tried valiantly to silence the slogan of the "shallow Enlightenment" that was then also in vogue. "Instead of assuming a derogatory air," Cassirer wrote, "we must take courage and measure our powers against those of the age of Enlightenment, and thus find a proper adjustment.... We must find a way not only to see that age in its own shape but to release again those original forces which brought forth and molded this shape."[9] We today also need to find a way to see the Enlightenment in its own shape, as well as to try to recapture some sense of its hope for the future of humanity.

Although the connections may not be immediately apparent, this study is an outgrowth of my earlier books *Morality and Moral Theory: A Reappraisal and Reaffirmation* and *Kant's Impure Ethics: From Rational Beings to Human Beings*. In the latter work, I argued that an important and underexplored part of Kant's practical philosophy concerns the empirical study of human nature and culture, and that an integral aspect of Kant's empirical study of human beings deals with the influence of social and cultural institutions on human moral character. In the present project I am casting my net much more widely, in part because I have become convinced that the Kant I focused on in *Kant's Impure Ethics* is in some respects a less original Kant than I had earlier assumed. In arguing that the growth and spread of universal education, religious tolerance, republican government and the rule of law, free trade between nations, and the establishment of an international justice system would all jointly contribute to humanity's eventual moral transformation, Kant was clearly not a lone voice but part of a much larger intellectual ensemble. By means of his philosophy of history Kant injected more systematicity into these Enlightenment social reform projects, and in his practical philosophy (particularly in what he called "the second part of morals") he also gave them a more robust rationale. But the proposals themselves do not originate with him. Kant arrives on the intellectual scene toward the end of the Enlightenment, and— at least in his applied practical philosophy, if not in his theoretical—he is integrating a wide number of earlier proposals made by other writers working not only in Germany, but also in France, Britain, the United States, and elsewhere.[10]

In *Morality and Moral Theory*, I defended an alternative conception of moral theory, one that owes several debts to contemporary virtue ethics and antitheory criticisms of formalist programs in moral theory, but one that also (or so I argued) more accurately reflects the actual moral theories of Aristotle and Kant. My goal was both to demonstrate the present need for more empirically informed moral theories and to show that the best moral theories of the past were in fact more empirically informed than their contemporary commentators and critics often make them out to be.[11] The present work is not directly a contribution to ethical theory construction, though in its concern with applied issues of moral development and the challenges of translating moral ideals into reality, it does offer an indirect contribution to theory. Indeed, part of what intrigues me about Enlightenment philosophers and intellectuals is precisely the extent to which they were able to overcome foundational and methodological differences in philosophy and moral theory and to reach agreement on more concrete issues of social and cultural reform. But in the present study I do continue my earlier efforts to show that classical moral philosophers were very much concerned both with how to make their theories efficacious and with how to change the world. That they are seldom understood in this way at present is more a function of contemporary philosophical tastes and interests than of what they actually wrote.

In the present work I examine critically a widely shared Enlightenment strategy for the gradual realization of basic social and moral ideals. One of my goals is to demonstrate certain shortcomings of this strategy, and here I employ a two-pronged method that focuses on means as well as on ends. In some cases, the means employed toward the realization of the ends are shown to be ineffective; in other cases, the ends themselves are called into question. A second goal is simply to register accurately the large gap that exists between Enlightenment ideals and contemporary realities, a gap whose existence is often ignored or denied in many recent polemics about the Enlightenment. The pursuit of these two goals opens up additional questions as well: What are the causes of the large gap between Enlightenment ideals and present realities? How can we avoid past mistakes in this area? In cases where the means advocated by Enlightenment intellectuals are inefficacious, what more appropriate means for the realization of their ideals are available to us? And what remains in these ideals that we today need to recover and reassert?

The World We Want, while philosophically motivated, also involves a fair amount of historical and empirical research. The latter, though consciously mundane (my primary aim is not to uncover new facts, but to draw attention to, and then to reinterpret, certain well-established facts in making an argument about our failure to realize Enlightenment ideals), is needed at present. Philosophy, or at least the kind of philosophy undertaken here, "must involve more than abstract argument . . . it must engage itself in history. In this and other respects, philosophy cannot be too pure if it really wants to do what it sets out to do."[12] Certainly any philosophical assessment of the legacy of the Enlightenment should engage itself in history, though in fact few such assessments have actually done so.

I examine actual Enlightenment proposals for cultural and institutional change, with the benefit of two centuries' hindsight.[13] What specific proposals for cultural and institutional change did Enlightenment intellectuals put forward? How did they think their proposals were instrumental to the moral future they envisaged? To what extent are these proposals still appropriate to our own historical experience? How is our present world both similar to and different from the world they wanted? How and why do the ideals of the Enlightenment still elude us?

I do not intend to respond in detail to the attacks on Enlightenment ideals made by critics, in part because others have already done so, but also because, as noted earlier, most of these attacks are based on caricatures of Enlightenment ideals and are thus merely elaborate versions of a straw man argument. Rather, this study aims at an analysis and evaluation of the Enlightenment's actual goals, and also of the means advocated for achieving these goals. I believe that it is important at present to reexamine and rearticulate what the Enlightenment's hopes for the future actually were, in part because these hopes have often been distorted, and in part because by reflecting on them we are also led to give more thought to our own hopes for the future. Although I do endorse most of the Enlightenment's hopes (indeed, I believe that a strong majority of people do, once accurate versions of them are presented), in the present work I speak primarily not as an advocate of Enlightenment ideals but as an analyst and evaluator of them. What were these ideals? How and why have they still not been realized? Are better means toward the realization of these ideals available, and if so, what are they? What is still viable in these ideals, and what is not?

As a philosopher long intrigued by Kant, my own base of operations for approaching the Enlightenment is unavoidably Kantian. But in the present study considerable effort has been devoted to establishing clear points of contact and agreement between Kant's views and those of other important writers from the French, German, British, American, and sometimes even other Enlightenments. I remain partial toward the German Enlightenment, for "of all European variants of the Enlightenment, only the German one took up Enlightenment itself as a philosophical problem."[14] But I am also convinced—at least as regards the core ideals explored in the following pages—that substantial intellectual agreement existed between the different variants of the Enlightenment.

In stressing points of contact and agreement between different Enlightenments, I am conscious of the fact that my approach differs from that of many contemporary scholars, who tend to stress plurality and diversity over unity. G. J. A. Pocock, for instance, urges us to pluralize the Enlightenment "into a number of movements in both harmony and conflict with each other"; James Schmidt claims that "the very notion that there was a single thing called 'the Enlightenment' appears, more and more, to be an illusion."[15] On this central point, I side with Jonathan Israel: the currently fashionable claim

> that there was not one Enlightenment but rather an entire constellation or family of "Enlightenments" . . . encourages the tendency to study the subject within the context of "national history" which is decidedly the wrong framework for so international and pan-European a phenomenon. Worse still, it unacceptably ignores or overlooks the extent to which common impulses and concerns shaped the Enlightenment as a whole.[16]

At the same time, my stress on certain fundamental points of agreement between different Enlightenment intellectuals is not intended to support the claim that there was "a single thing called 'the Enlightenment.'" The international Enlightenment ideals with which this study is concerned by no means cancel out the existence of numerous conflicts, tensions, and divisions between different variants of the Enlightenment.

Nor should the intentionally broad scope of this study be confused either with surveys of "the" Enlightenment or its increasingly popular cousin, "the inflated Enlightenment," the latter of which has come to be "identified with all modernity, [and] with nearly everything subsumed under the name of Western civilization."[17] Many issues directly relevant to both the Enlightenment and modernity (not to mention Western civilization) are not examined at all in what follows. For example, this is a book not about "the intellectual foundations of modern culture,"[18] but about something a bit more modest and concrete. I am concerned with a widely shared Enlightenment strategy for moral reform, and I wish to determine what is living and dead in this strategy. Put differently, the specific themes explored in this work are themselves a function of the late eighteenth-century intellectual consensus that existed regarding the best means for the realization of desired ends.

At the same time, any serious analysis and assessment of these means and ends does entail that we move beyond influential platitudes that assert that the ethos of the Enlightenment amounts to simply endorsing an attitude of a "permanent critique of ourselves." For once we embrace this move we have created a hyperinflated Enlightenment that knows no temporal bounds: every philosophy student since Socrates who believes that "the unexamined life is not worth living" becomes an instantiation of the Enlightenment attitude. Contra Foucault, I do believe that some "faithfulness to doctrinal elements" is necessary: any significant investigation of the Enlightenment needs to investigate the specific means-ends story behind their hopes for the future.[19]

The method adopted in part I of this study is a simple and modest one, and it is important not to read too much into it. For each core theme introduced, I show that one finds expression and endorsement of it not only within the German Enlightenment (often, but not solely, established by means of Kant's texts), but also in the French, British, and American Enlightenments (and occasionally elsewhere as well). However, this is not an exhaustive study of any of these Enlightenments, nor of any of the authors whose works are cited. Rather, I focus on key expressions of a select core of social and moral ideals, and then indicate some level of the international support that existed for these ideals during the Enlightenment.

The specific fields of investigation chosen for this study are religion, education, economics, politics, and international relations. This list is intentionally selective and builds off of a similar investigation pursued in *Kant's Impure Ethics*. Although these five fields certainly do not exhaust Enlightenment intellectuals' interests in cultural and institutional change, they do, I believe, constitute their primary areas of concern. Within each of the five chapters in part I ("Then"), I focus on two or three core areas of agreement among Enlightenment intellectuals from different countries with respect to each relevant field of investigation. The aim, again, is not to show that there is one monolithic "Enlightenment Project" to praise or bash, but rather to indicate that, despite their numerous disagreements, Enlightenment intellectuals were surprisingly unified in their hopes for the future with regard to each of the five fields as well as in their commitments regarding the means needed for realizing these ideals.

In each of the five chapters of part II ("Now"), I examine the subsequent historical record, assessing to what extent the major changes and developments in each field do or do not correspond to those envisaged by Enlightenment theorists. In part II the post-Enlightenment historical record is also employed as a base for evaluating Enlightenment means and ends. In which cases does our own historical experience show that the means advocated toward Enlightenment ends have been ineffective? And in which cases does it suggest that the ends advocated simply do not fit with human nature? Finally, throughout part II as well as in my conclusion, I reassess the Enlightenment position in light of what has actually transpired over the past two hundred years in each field and offer what I believe are more accurate explanations than one finds elsewhere for why the ideals of the Enlightenment still elude us.

Three skeptical conclusions are reached in this study: (1) There is insufficient evidence to support the widespread Enlightenment assumption that external institutional change leads to desired internal attitudinal change. Moral transformation, if it is aided by institutional development, is much slower and more uneven within the human species than Enlightenment theorists assumed would be the case. (2) Several of the means advocated by Enlightenment theorists to realize their ideals—though strongly endorsed by later generations—have not led to their predicted results. The growth of free trade, for instance, has not reduced poverty between and within nations, nor has it brought about world peace. Similarly, the creation of an international commercial society and the explosive growth of education have not led to an engaged public sphere but rather to a privatized consumer culture. (3) At present—and this is due in part to the lack of predicted moral transformation summarized in the first point—insufficient numbers of people are strongly committed to Enlightenment ideals such as peace, elimination of poverty, reduction of inequality, and an engaged civic culture to make clear progress in realizing these ideals. The predicted extension and deepening of commitment to these ideals among the human population at large has not happened.

Again, though, my aims are also positive. At bottom, I seek to show what remains viable in Enlightenment ideals, and why we still have reason to hope that humanity may some day achieve those that survive scrutiny. My underlying goal is thus to present a reassessment, reenvisioning, and qualified defense of the moral and political ideals of the Enlightenment for our own time and place.

I

....

THEN

What had it been like to have convincing reasons for hope about the future of mankind? Were any of these reasons still valid? Could one any longer have such hopes after all the horrors of this century? Were his favourite thinkers just purveyors of dangerous illusions that blinded true believers and armed cynical manipulators with rationalist dogmas that had, ever since the Jacobin Terror, wreaked havoc upon mankind? Optimism, in short, was both his subject and his object.

—Steven Lukes, *The Curious Enlightenment of Professor Caritat*

I

....

Religion

Pure reason does not undermine religion, but rather its aberrations. You will lose prejudices and retain religion. The closer you bring religion to the light of reason, the more securely and durably it will be established for the future. Religion will not have to fear any attack by the understanding because the understanding approves of it, and if the understanding is its support, religion will become necessary and holy to the human race.

—Andreas Riem, *On Enlightenment: Is It and Could It Be Dangerous to the State, to Religion, or Dangerous in General? A Word to be Heeded by Princes, Statesmen, and Clergy* (1788)

The myth of the antireligious Enlightenment is still alive and well in many circles. According to sociologist of religion Mark Juergensmeyer, "Enlightenment modernity proclaimed the death of religion," and the alleged "reappearance" of religion in contemporary society has demonstrated the falsity of this proclamation.[1] Similarly, political theorist John Gray, in *Enlightenment's Wake*, points to the present "renaissance of particularisms, ethnic and religious" as the primary supporting data for his thesis that "we live today amid the dim ruins of the Enlightenment project"[2]—one implication being that the Enlightenment was fundamentally antireligious. According to Peter Gay, Enlightenment intellectuals were supposedly united by "a single passion... the passion to cure the spiritual malady that is religion, the germ of ignorance, barbarity, filth, and the basest self-hatred."[3] More recently, historian Jonathan Israel has summarized the essence of the Enlightenment tradition as consisting in "the philosophical rejection of revealed religion, miracles, and divine Providence, replacing the idea of salvation in the hereafter with a highest

good in the here and now."[4] And Gertrude Himmelfarb, while acknowledging that religion "was not the paramount enemy" in the Enlightenment
as it appeared in Britain and America, continues to defend the traditional
view that we find an "animus to religion" in the French Enlightenment.[5]

In this chapter, I wish to challenge the myth of the antireligious
Enlightenment[6] by presenting an account of Enlightenment religiosity, an
account anchored by three core ideas shared by a wide number of Enlightenment intellectuals from different countries.

The Unity Thesis

Most Enlightenment intellectuals were convinced that religion, if properly
reformed, could and should serve as a progressive force for the transformation of moral and social life—specifically, as a primary contributing factor
in the formation of a more cosmopolitan moral community. A key strategy
in their attempt to reform religion involves what I call the *unity thesis*, which
holds that all historical faiths are manifestations of one universal religion.
Leading representatives from many different aspects of the Enlightenment
share a commitment to the unity thesis. Lessing, for instance, expresses his
adherence to it repeatedly in his writings, the most famous example being
his parable of the rings (which he borrows from Boccaccio's *Decameron*) in
the play *Nathan the Wise* (1779). In Act III, scene vii, Nathan (who is
modeled on Lessing's friend Moses Mendelssohn)[7] addresses Saladin's
query concerning which of the three great religions (Judaism, Christianity,
Islam) is true by means of the following allegory. In the ancient East there
once lived a man who possessed a ring that had "the secret power to make
its possessor pleasing to God and man."[8] The ring was kept in the family for
generations, each bearer bequeathing it to his favorite son, until it was
passed on to the father of three sons, "all three of whom were equally
obedient to him, all three of whom he therefore loved equally." Not wishing
to favor one son over the others, the father hired an artist to make two exact
replicas of the original ring, so that upon his death he could present each
son with a ring. A quarrel soon broke out over who possessed the original
ring, but "the true ring was not provable ... almost as unprovable as the
true faith is to us now." Saladin interrupts Nathan's narrative at this point,
protesting, "The rings!—Don't play with me!—I thought the religions that
I named to you were certainly distinguishable." But, Nathan replies,
external differences notwithstanding, all of them are grounded on history,
written or oral, and "history must also be accepted only on trust and faith."

Returning to his allegory of the rings, Nathan relates that the three sons eventually appealed to a judge to settle their quarrel. But the judge too was unable to determine which of the three rings was the original, and so—since each son did in fact receive his ring from his father—he advised that each should try to prove the genuineness of his faith through the exercise of beneficence toward all people. And thus the task of religious believers everywhere is to demonstrate the genuineness of their faith through their conduct toward and relationships with other human beings. In this manner, Lessing's parable of the rings defends "a genuine religious pluralism, united by the common bond of universal humanity."[9]

French author Pierre Bayle, in his earlier *Philosophical Commentary on the Words of Jesus Christ* (1686–87), also advocates a version of Lessing's conclusion, albeit without quite endorsing the unity thesis: "If each religion adopted the spirit of tolerance that I recommend...the most that could happen would be honest rivalry in outdoing each other in piety, good conduct and knowledge; each religion would take pride in proving its favored share of God's love by exhibiting a firmer attachment to moral conduct."[10] And in the British deist tradition we find numerous expressions of the unity thesis. For instance, Lord Edward Herbert of Cherbury (1583–1648), the "father of deism," articulated a system of "Common Notions" within religion, a system that, "at least as it concerns theology, has been clearly accepted by every normal person, and does not require any further justification."[11] What he believed he had uncovered was the common thread that unites different historical faiths, a thread graspable by unaided reason. Amid the religious conflicts that had devastated modern Europe (and the desire to overcome these conflicts was itself a primary motive in developing the unity thesis), Herbert locates the following five Common Notions: "1) There is a Supreme God, 2) This deity ought to be worshipped, 3) The connection of moral virtue to piety is the most important part of religious practice, 4) Wickedness must be expiated by repentance, 5) There is reward or punishment after this life" (32–38). "Such then," he concludes, "are the Common Notions of which the true Catholic or universal church is built.... The only Catholic and uniform church is the doctrine of Common Notions which comprehends all places and all men" (40).

The American deist Thomas Paine provides one of the clearest and most radical expressions of the unity thesis. In *The Age of Reason* (1794), he rejects entirely the different historical faiths, on the ground that they are "no other than human inventions, set up to terrify and enslave mankind, and monopolize power and profit."[12] But beneath these various human distortions of religious faith—distortions caused not only by political and economic greed but also by variations in human languages and historical traditions—there is raw nature in all of its beauty and sublimity, God's creation, equally accessible to all:

> THE WORD OF GOD IS THE CREATION WE BEHOLD and it is in *this word*, which no human invention can counterfeit or alter, that God speaketh universally to man.... The Creation speaks a universal language, independently of human speech or human language, multiplied and various as they may be. It is an ever-existing original, which every man can read. It cannot be forged; it cannot be counterfeited; it cannot be lost; it cannot be altered; it cannot be suppressed. It does not depend upon the will of man whether it shall be published or not; it publishes itself from one end of the earth to the other. It preaches to all nations and to all worlds.... Search not the book called the Scripture, which any human hand might make, but the Scripture called the creation. (419, 420, 421)

France is often held to be the important exception to Enlightenment religiosity, with Voltaire's battle cry against the church, *Écrasez l'infâme* (Crush the infamous one), frequently being asked to carry the main burden of evidence. But at bottom Voltaire too embraces a clear deist faith that is very similar to Paine's universal religion of nature. In a letter to Frederick the Great (1770) he proclaims, "All nature cries aloud that He does exist: that there *is* a supreme intelligence, an immense power, an admirable order, and everything teaches us our own dependence on it."[13] Similarly, in an entry in his *Philosophical Dictionary*, he writes,

> Tonight I was in a meditative mood. I was absorbed in the contemplation of nature; I admired the immensity, the movements, the harmony of those infinite globes.... I admired still more the intelligence which directs these vast forces. I said to myself: "One must be blind not to be dazzled by this spectacle; one must be stupid not to recognize the author of it, one must be mad not to worship Him. What tribute of worship should I render Him? Should not this tribute be the same in the whole of space, since it is the same supreme power which reigns equally in all space?"[14]

Rousseau, too, in his vision of a nonsectarian civil religion that makes each citizen "love his duty," offers yet another Enlightenment endorsement of a universal natural religion of humanity. The various particular religions, he writes in *Emile* (1762), are to be regarded as so many salutary institutions which prescribe in each country a uniform manner of honoring God by public worship. These religions can all have their justifications in the climate, the government, the genius of the people, or some other local cause which makes one preferable to another, according to the time and place. I believe them all to be right as long as one serves God suitably. The essential worship is that of the heart. God does not reject its homage, if it is sincere, in whatever form it is offered to Him.[15]

Finally, in Kant we find an even bolder expression of the unity thesis: "There is only *one* (true) *religion*; but there can be various kinds of *faith*" (*Religion* 6: 107). The various historical faiths, on this view, are to be understood as humanly necessary vehicles for the transmission of pure religion. These vehicles can and will "differ according to differences of time and place," but if they are doing their jobs correctly they will all point to "one single *religion* holding for all human beings and in all times" (*Peace* 8: 367 n.). And the all-important moral content of this single religion is that of a universal "divine (ethical) state on earth" that will "one day enlighten the world and rule over it"—even though at present "the actual setting up of this state is still infinitely removed from us" (*Religion* 6: 122).

There are, of course, counterexamples to the claim that the Enlightenment was fundamentally religious, and the most significant ones are to be found in France. For instance, Baron d'Holbach proclaims in *Common Sense, or Natural Ideas Opposed to Supernatural* (1772), "Whoever will deign to consult common sense upon religious opinions . . . will easily perceive, that these opinions have no foundation; that all religion is an edifice in the air; that theology is only the ignorance of natural causes reduced to system; that it is a long tissue of chimeras and contradictions." But even Voltaire recoils at d'Holbach's audacity for asserting "that there is no God, without even having tried to prove its impossibility," and dismisses his writings as pernicious rant.[16] His rejection of d'Holbach's animosity toward religion was a representative reaction within Enlightenment culture. As others have noted, "Few *philosophes* held opinions as radical as d'Holbach's . . . [his] works were regarded as so materialist and anti-religious that they even shocked other radicals."[17]

Hume is the most significant eighteenth-century philosopher who poses a clear challenge to my thesis that the Enlightenment wanted to reform religion rather than to abolish it. But even he is closer to it than d'Holbach, in large part because his own skepticism prevents him from dogmatically asserting that there is no God. At the end of the *Dialogues Concerning Natural Religion* (1779), Philo, despite the devastating criticisms that he himself has leveled against many of the central tenets of natural theology, urges "a plain, philosophical assent to the proposition . . . *that the cause or causes of order in the universe probably bear some remote analogy to human intelligence.*" Admittedly, this is an extremely "attenuated deism"; Philo cautions readers that the proposition may "afford no inference that affects human life" or "be the source of any action or forbearance." But there remains room for genuine religious feeling even within it, a sense of wonder and awe at "so extraordinary and magnificent a question," provided that one does not slide into dogmatism and believe falsely that we have solid answers to all of our questions.[18]

So, while not all Enlightenment thinkers embraced the unity thesis, the majority of them did. And within the unity thesis we find a genuine religious commitment: the belief in a universal religion embracing all human beings. This is the distinctive core of Enlightenment religiosity, and it is a core that needs to be appreciated on its own terms as a sincerely held religious belief rather than rejected out of hand as yet another manifestation of the "shallow" Enlightenment.

The Morality Thesis

A second pervasive theme in Enlightenment religiosity is its conviction that the content and orientation of religion should be directed primarily toward *moral* concerns. Let us call this the *morality thesis*. The claim here is not that religion alone properly grounds or justifies morality; as is well known, many Enlightenment intellectuals explicitly reject this position. Rather, the morality thesis holds simply that religion's proper purpose is moral as opposed to theological. Different articulations of the morality thesis are readily available in a wide variety of Enlightenment texts. For instance, Benjamin Franklin, in summarizing "the fundamental principles of all sound religion" in a letter to Ezra Stiles in 1790, writes, "The most acceptable service we render to him [viz., God] is doing good to his other children."[19] Similarly (but, as usual, more radically), in laying out his "profession of faith" at the beginning of *The Age of Reason*, Tom Paine asserts that our religious duties consist simply "in doing justice, loving mercy, and endeavouring to make our fellow-creatures happy."[20] More traditional candidates for religious duty (surprisingly, even that of the duty to worship God) are conspicuously missing from Paine's list.

Kant is surprisingly close to Paine when he remarks in a 1775 letter to the Swiss theologian Johann Caspar Lavater that "to be righteous [*rechtschaffen zu sein*] is the sum of all religion" and that "all wooing of favors by the performing of rituals" would be strictly forbidden in a sound religion (10: 180). However, in his *Lectures on Pedagogy* (first presented in 1776–77), he allows that "the performing of rituals" has a legitimate, albeit subordinate place in religion, but if and only if it can be shown to contribute to the cause of morally good conduct:

> If religion is not combined with morality, then it becomes nothing more than currying favor. Singing praises, prayers, and going to church should only give the human being new strength, new courage for improvement, or they should be the expression of a heart inspired by the idea of duty. They are only preparations for good works, but not good works themselves, and one cannot please the highest being otherwise than by becoming a better human being. (9: 494)[21]

Similarly, in one of his moral philosophy lectures, Kant states, "Subjectively prayer is needed, not so that God, who is the recipient of it, should learn anything, and thereby be moved to grant it, but rather for our own sakes.... Prayers are indeed necessary for moral purposes, if they are to set up a moral disposition in us.... They serve to kindle morality in the innermost heart" (*Collins* 27: 323).[22] Throughout his writing career Kant maintained the view that all legitimate religious service must serve moral ends. As he states in his major work in religion, *Religion within the Boundaries of Mere Reason* (1793), "*Apart from good-life conduct, anything which the human being supposes he can do to become well-pleasing to God is mere religious delusion and counterfeit service of God*" (6: 170). "Good life conduct" (*guter Lebenswandel*) is held to be the "true goal" of religion, and the more progress human beings make toward this goal the more they will "be able to dispense with statutory articles altogether" (6: 175).

The development of Unitarianism provides yet another example of the strongly moralistic tendency of Enlightenment religiosity. Jesus is revered as *the* moral exemplar, but not as the second person of the Trinity. For Joseph Priestley, one of the founders of the new denomination, a key shift in outlook occurred when he became "fully persuaded that Christ was a man like ourselves."[23] Thomas Jefferson, spurred to write down his own views on the matter after receiving a pamphlet from Priestley, professes his own Unitarianism by stating that he ascribes to Jesus "every *human* excellence; and believing he never claimed any other.... The question of his being a member of the Godhead ... is foreign to the present view." Nevertheless, Jefferson continued, the "system of morals presented to us" by Jesus is "the most perfect and sublime that has ever been written."[24]

Articulations of the morality thesis among French Enlightenment writers are also plentiful. Perhaps the most famous example would again be Rousseau's nonsectarian civil religion, which holds "that in every country and in every sect the sum of the law is to love God above everything and one's neighbor as oneself; that no religion is exempt from the duties of morality; that nothing is truly essential other than these duties; that inner worship is the first of these duties; and that without faith no true virtue exists."[25]

As many of these citations indicate, Enlightenment intellectuals often linked the morality thesis to the unity thesis. When the two are joined together, the result is what may be called the *common morality thesis*. In other words, beneath the different historical faiths there lies a shared morality, a universal moral message. Key elements of this message include the following claims: All human beings are children of the same father; all human beings are moral equals; all human beings are morally obligated to treat each other justly and beneficently.

Here too, in the widespread Enlightenment concurrence with Lessing's conviction that the core message of religion is wholly contained within the command to "*love one another . . . this alone, if it is done, is enough, is sufficient and adequate,*"[26] a flattening tendency is present, one that many traditional religious believers strongly oppose. But the positive nature of the phenomenon again needs to be underscored and appreciated on its own terms. As Hume's Philo notes, "vulgar superstition" has had only "pernicious consequences on public affairs": "factions, civil wars, persecutions, subversions of government, oppression, slavery." We would be far better off, Cleanthes concurs, with a less inflammatory conception of religion: "The proper office of religion is to regulate the hearts of men, humanize their conduct."[27] Enlightenment religiosity was profoundly moralistic. In linking religion (a religion, again, that they believed was universal) directly to moral conduct and dispositions, Enlightenment intellectuals believed that they had found a powerful means for improving human conduct everywhere.

Toleration

Finally, toleration: "the characteristic and new religious idea" of the Enlightenment, an idea "which was possibly its most important legacy to succeeding centuries."[28] John Locke remains one of the most influential Enlightenment voices on the topic of religious toleration, despite the fact that his own theory of toleration does not seem especially tolerant by contemporary standards. "Those are not to be tolerated at all who deny the being of a God. Promises, covenants, and oaths, which are the bonds of human society, can have no hold upon an atheist. The taking away of God, though but even in thought, dissolves all."[29] Atheists are untrustworthy and hence subversive of the social order; to tolerate them would be political suicide. Even odder-sounding to contemporary ears is Locke's animus against Catholics: "That church can have no right to be tolerated by the magistrate which is constituted upon such a bottom that all those who enter into it do thereby *ipso facto* deliver themselves up to the protection and service of another prince" (51). Catholics ultimately owe allegiance to a foreign power (the pope), and thus civil magistrates cannot trust them either.

So Locke clearly does not defend anything close to a principle of *absolute* religious liberty, even though his English translator William Popple advocates precisely such a principle in the "To the Reader" note that precedes Locke's text.[30] Nevertheless, despite his significant restrictions on toleration (restrictions articulated toward the end of the text), Locke begins his *Letter* by proclaiming, "I esteem that toleration to be the chief characteristic mark of the true church" (13). It is this opening core conviction that toleration is the true sign of genuine religiosity that represents a milestone in religious thought. The conviction rests on two basic points. First, genuine faith comes only through free choice. The authorities can force people (for instance, as was often done, through torture) to *say* that they believe X and to externally behave *as if* they believe X, but such tactics can never guarantee that they have freely decided to believe X. Second, the church itself is understood to be "a free and voluntary society" (20), intended for the public worship of God and the salvation of souls. As a result, if church membership is to be truly free and voluntary, churches can coherently carry out their mission only through noncoercive means. "No force is here to be made use of upon any occasion whatsoever" (23).

A more radical theory of religious toleration was advocated by Pierre Bayle. On Bayle's view, religious believers (including magistrates) should tolerate each others' conflicting beliefs simply because in religious (as opposed to, say, mathematical) matters "it is impossible in our present condition to know with certainty...absolute truth."[31] Because absolute truth is humanly impossible in the religious sphere, "God is content to demand" from each person "that he seek the truth as diligently as possible and when he thinks he has found it that he cherish it and make it the rule of his life" (80). Bayle's argument thus extends the hand of toleration to a wider group of people than does Locke's—indeed, to *all* human beings who are *sincerely seeking the truth* and who then act consistently with their sincerely held beliefs.

Voltaire's position on toleration is also more radical than Locke's: "What is toleration? It is the prerogative of humanity. We are all steeped in weaknesses and errors: let us forgive one another's follies, it is the first law of nature.... We should tolerate each other because we are all weak, inconsistent, subject to mutability and to error."[32] In Voltaire's view, it is not even necessary to pass a Baylean sincerity test in order to be tolerated, in part because he doubts whether people can ever attain truth from within religious sects: "We know that every sect is a guarantee of error. There are no sects of geometricians, algebraists, arithmeticians, because all the propositions of geometry, algebra, arithmetic are true."[33] Here the blunt message is that because all members of all sects are companions in error, it behooves them to tolerate each other. However, elsewhere Voltaire presents a more positive argument for religious toleration, one that links up with his own commitment to the unity and morality theses discussed earlier: "It requires no great skill in argument or gift of eloquence to prove that Christians should tolerate each other. I will go further: I tell you, we ought to regard every man as our brother. What? The Turk, my brother? The Chinaman, my brother? The Jew and the Siamese as well? Yes, assuredly, for are we not all children of one Father and creatures of the same God?"[34] Underneath the guaranteed errors of religious sects there is a discernible common lineage shared by all human beings. But in most cases the appeal to toleration was itself made from within a religious position, albeit one that stressed shared beliefs rather than doctrinal differences. It is thus false to assert that "Enlightenment notions of tolerance are predicated on an indifference to existential or religious experience."[35] As Hume reminds readers in his essay "Of Superstition and Enthusiasm," it is the deists who are "friends to toleration" (and who, as we have seen, are by no means indifferent to religious experience), for they are "indifferent to any particular sect of *christians*."[36]

Finally, in Kant we find a theory of religious toleration that follows from his famous definition of enlightenment itself: "*Sapere aude!* Have courage to make use of your *own* understanding! is . . . the motto of enlightenment" (*Enlightenment* 8: 35). Our vocation as human beings is to cultivate our own rational capacities, and along with this vocation goes a moral responsibility to inquire into the reasons for our beliefs. But people cannot make use of their own understanding in religious matters unless freedom of belief is extended to the religious sphere. Indeed, as Kant remarks in a famous footnote in the first *Critique*, religion arouses a just suspicion against itself, and cannot lay claim to our unfeigned respect, unless and until its doctrines successfully withstand open and public scrutiny (A xi n.). Reflective human beings cannot take religious claims seriously until they are free to critically assess them. Toleration is therefore the true beginning of enlightenment, "the necessary social condition for people to use their own intellects to decide what they will believe. The Enlightenment's demand for toleration is thus the demand that people be given the opportunity to fulfill their deepest spiritual vocation: that of using their intellects to determine the faith they will live by."[37]

In sum, contrary to much contemporary wisdom, most Enlightenment intellectuals did not proclaim "the death of religion." On the contrary, religion occupied a much bigger space in Enlightenment thought than is generally recognized. In reaction against the religious violence of their own day, as well as in response to a growing awareness of "difference," Enlightenment intellectuals sought to develop a more pluralistic and less divisive concept of religion that would enable people to live in peace with one another. They advocated not "a rejection of religion, but merely a rejection of those features of religion that had led to so much suffering and warfare in the generations before."[38] And in rethinking religion, they sought also to forge a new concept of faith that would energize believers to work toward a more just and beneficent international order as well as to tolerate religious and cultural differences.

2

....

Education

The final destiny of the human race is moral
perfection. . . . How, then, are we to seek this perfection,
and from where is it to be hoped for? From nowhere else
but education.

—Kant, *Moralphilosophie Collins*

I t has long been recognized that education was a key element in
Enlightenment reform efforts. The communication and critical evaluation of ideas necessary for enlightenment could not be achieved by
people who lacked the ability to read, write, and think critically. But in
eighteenth-century Europe (not to mention elsewhere), most people did
lack the ability to read, write, and think critically. The "logic of the
Enlightenment" thus necessarily leads to education: if most people are
"not yet ready for autonomy, they must be *made* ready for it."[1]

Despite their widely different starting points and methodological
commitments, Enlightenment philosophers were united in their conviction
that education was of fundamental importance in human life. For Lockean
empiricists, who hold that the mind at birth is "like white paper, void of all
characters, without any *ideas*," education is the primary shaper of human
beings: "Of all the men we meet with, nine parts of ten are what they are,
good or evil, useful or not, by their education. 'Tis that which makes the

great difference in mankind."[2] In Locke's view, the preeminent place of education in human life stems from two facts: the experience-based nature of knowledge and the extreme malleability of human beings.[3] On the other hand, for Kant, who holds that knowledge has a strong *a priori* component, and who also acknowledges that many "germs" (*Keime*) and natural predispositions are already present in human beings at birth, it is the biological fact of human dependence that makes education necessary. Other animals "use their powers as soon as they have any in a regular manner," but "the human being is the only creature that must be educated" (*Pedagogy* 9: 445, 441). As a result, for both Kant and Locke, education "makes the great difference in mankind": "The human being can only become human through education. He is nothing except what education makes of him" (9: 443).

(Almost) Universal Education

Many earlier philosophers stressed the importance of education in human life, and some even made a case for *public* education.[4] But a hallmark of Enlightenment writing about education is its strong concern for the spreading and widespread diffusion of knowledge by means of universal public education schemes. As Jefferson announced at the beginning of his unsuccessful *Bill for the More General Diffusion of Knowledge* (1778), modern governments must find a way "to illuminate, as far as practicable, the minds of the people at large ... without regard to wealth, birth or other accidental condition or circumstance."[5] Similarly, Condorcet, in his 1791 article, *The Nature and Purpose of Public Instruction*, argued both that society had an obligation "to establish a system of public instruction that allows no talent to go unnoticed, offering it all the help heretofore reserved for the children of the wealthy," and that public instruction "must be the same for women as it is for men."[6] He opens his 1792 *Report on the General Organization of Public Instruction* with the following proclamation:

> To offer to all individuals of the human race the means of providing for their needs, of assuring their welfare, of knowing and exercising their rights, of understanding and fulfilling their obligations.
>
> To assure each one the facility of perfecting his skill, of rendering himself capable of the social functions to which he has the right to be called, of developing to the fullest extent those talents with which Nature has endowed him; and thereby to establish among all citizens

an actual equality, thus rendering real the political equality recognized by the law.

This should be the first aim of any national education; and, from such a point of view, this education is for the government an obligation of justice.[7]

Education, he concluded, "should be universal. That is to say, it should be within the reach of all classes of citizens."[8]

Of course, this is not to say that all Enlightenment theorists of education believed that everyone should receive the same education. Locke, for instance, warns readers near the beginning of *Some Thoughts Concerning Education*, "I have said *he* here because the principal aim of my discourse is how a young gentleman should be brought up from his infancy, which in all things, will not so perfectly suit the education of *daughters*" (§6). As Peter Gay notes, it never occurred to Locke "that every child should be educated or that all those to be educated should be educated alike. Locke believed that until the school system was reformed, a gentleman ought to have his son trained at home by a tutor."[9] Similarly, La Chalotais, in his influential *Essai d'éducation nationale* (Essay on National Education, 1763), was strongly averse to extending equal educational opportunities to the working class. To do so, he felt, would upset the social order:

> Even the common people wish to study; labourers and artisans send their children to the colleges in the smaller towns where it costs little to live, and when they have completed a course of useless studies which have taught them nothing except to disdain the calling of their fathers, they rush into cloisters, into the priesthood, they become officers of justice, and often subjects that are harmful to society. *Multorum manibus egent res humanæ, paucorum capita suffiiunt.* [The hands of many are needed for human affairs; but the heads of few are enough.]
>
> The Brothers of the Christian Doctrine, who are called *Ignorantins*, have appeared to complete the ruin of everything. They teach reading and writing to people who ought to learn only to draw and to handle the plane and the file, but who no longer wish to do so. They are the rivals or the successors of the Jesuits. The welfare of society requires that the education of the common people should not go beyond its occupations. Any man who looks beyond his trade will never work at it with courage and patience. It is hardly necessary that any of the common people should know how to read and write except

those who earn their living by these arts, or whom these arts help to earn their living.[10]

Rousseau, while declaring in his *Discourse on Political Economy* (1755) that public education is "one of the fundamental maxims of popular or legitimate government" and "certainly... the state's most important business,"[11] also emphasized later in *Emile, or, On Education* (1762) that men and women "ought not to have the same education":

> The quest for abstract and speculative truths, principles, and axioms in the sciences, for everything that tends to generalize ideas, is not within the competence of women. All their studies ought to be related to practice. It is for them to apply the principles man has found, and to make the observations which lead man to the establishment of principles. Regarding what is not immediately connected with their duties, all the reflections of women ought to be directed to the study of men or to the pleasing kinds of knowledge that have only taste as their aim; for, as regards works of genius, they are out of reach of women.[12]

Rousseau's position was later the central object of attack in Mary Wollstonecraft's *Vindication of the Rights of Woman* (1792). In arguing that "the whole tendency of female education ought to be directed to one point:—to render them pleasing," Rousseau "and most of the male writers who have followed his steps," Wollstonecraft noted, "have contributed to render women more artificial, weak characters, than they would otherwise have been; and consequently, more useless members of society." Books such as Rousseau's *Emile*, she continued, "tend, in my opinion, to degrade one half of the human species, and render women pleasing at the expence of every solid virtue."[13] But in her quest for educational equality for women, Wollstonecraft clearly appealed to basic Enlightenment principles: "The nature of reason must be the same in all ... [and] the inquiry is whether she have reason or not. If she have ... she was not created merely to be the solace of man, and the sexual should not destroy the human character.... If they [viz., women] be moral beings, let them have a chance to become intellectual."[14] However, the goal of a truly universal education system open to all people remained out of reach during the Enlightenment. While most educational reformers during this time did believe that everyone should be educated, they did not believe that everyone should be educated alike.[15]

The growing emphasis on *national* (or what today is often called "civic") education by writers such as La Chalotais and Rousseau also revealed a further tension within the Enlightenment ideal of universal education. How could the attempt to inculcate civic virtue be made consistent with Enlightenment commitments to human rights and tolerance for others? According to La Chalotais, education "should be of the State, by the State, and for the State": "I claim the right to demand for the Nation an education that will depend upon the State alone; because it belongs essentially to it, because every nation has an inalienable and imprescriptible right to instruct its members, and finally because the children of the State should be educated by members of the State."[16] Similarly, Rousseau, at the beginning of his chapter on education in *Considerations on the Government of Poland* (1772), writes, "It is education that must give souls a national formation, and direct their opinions and tastes in such a way that they will be patriotic by inclination, by passion, by necessity. When first he opens his eyes, an infant ought to see the fatherland, and up to the day of his death he ought never to see anything else."[17] To instill sufficient *amour de la patrie* in citizens, Rousseau advises that all subjects taught in Polish public schools (to be taught, of course, only by Polish teachers) must be imbued with a strongly nationalistic slant: students are to focus exclusively on Polish literature, Polish history, Polish law, and even Polish science.

An additional dividing point concerned the means by which universal education is best promoted. Should education be the exclusive business of the state, or should state education be merely one alternative among several? Here too there were strong differences of opinion. La Chalotais, as we saw, pressed for "an education that will depend on the State alone." Adam Smith, on the other hand, though strongly supportive of systems of education that would teach all the children of "common people" to "read, write, and account" before they had to start work, favored the model of Scottish parish schools, "where children may be taught for a reward so moderate, that even a common labourer may afford it; the master being partly, but not wholly paid by the publick; because, if he was wholly, or even principally paid by it, he would soon learn to neglect his business."[18] In Smith's view, the state should impose universal educational requirements and assist those individuals who need financial help in obtaining an education, but it should not maintain a monopoly over schools. The competition of the marketplace within the educational sphere will discourage teachers from "neglecting their business." Diderot also favored the use of market incentives in education. In his *Observations sur le Nakaz* (an extensive commentary on Catherine's proposed reforms for Russia), he writes, "Do you want lots of pupils and bad teachers? The state must pay the teachers. Do you want fewer pupils and excellent teachers? The teachers must be paid by the pupils."[19]

Kant, insofar as he believed that public education is "more advanta-geous" than private education and provides "the best model of the future citizen," is closer to La Chalotais (*Pedagogy* 9: 453, 454). However, his own argument in defense of public schools is, as one might expect, less nationalistic and more cosmopolitan. In his view, a public school setting open to all provides the best opportunity for future citizens to learn "restrictions through the rights of others" (9: 454),[20] that is, to learn to respect others and to accept the moral equality of all human beings. At the same time, he expressed concern that both private (or parent-controlled, insofar as they normally pay tuition) and public (state-controlled) systems of education were inherently too provincial and uncosmopolitan. In his view, education must be directed neither at parental nor national aims, but at the specieswide goal of human perfection:

> Parents usually care only that their children get on well in the world, and princes regard their subjects merely as instruments for their own designs. Parents care for the home, princes for the state. Neither have as their final end the best for the world and the perfection to which humanity is destined, and for which it also has the predisposition. However, the plan for education must be made in a cosmopolitan manner. (9: 448)[21]

But if states (not to mention parents, who "usually care only that their children get on well in the world") are footing the bill for education, how likely are they to accede to a cosmopolitan education scheme that attempts to teach children at an early age that "they must rejoice at the best for the world even if it is not to the advantage of their fatherland or to their own gain" (9: 499)? Here again we encounter one of the hardest roadblocks to universal education. Without strong international cooperation, education that is truly universal cannot become a reality.

Finally, there is the issue of compulsory schooling. Is the goal of universal education best promoted by *requiring* that children attend school, whether private or public? In part because the very idea of schooling itself was still something of a novelty, Enlightenment authors did not discuss compulsory schooling much. However, the following remarks of Jefferson are representative: "Is it a right or a duty in society to take care of their infant members in opposition to the will of the parent? . . . It is better to tolerate the rare instance of a parent refusing to let his child be educated, than to shock the common feelings and ideas by the forcible asportation and education of the infant against the will of the father."[22]

Although not all Enlightenment intellectuals who wrote on education themselves explicitly supported the ideal of a free public education that would be open to all, eventually this position, itself implicit in many of their own statements, did gain the upper hand. An underlying commitment to the universal diffusion of knowledge led later generations to gradually embrace Lessing's position that "education has its *goal* in the species [*Geschlecht*], no less than in the individual."[23]

Learning to Use One's Own Reason

The aim of education can no longer be to consecrate established opinions but, on the contrary, to subject them to free examination by succeeding generations that will be progressively more enlightened.

—Condorcet, *The Nature and Purpose of Public Instruction*

Enlightenment thinkers viewed education as a primary means for the diffusion of knowledge and the spreading of enlightenment. But whether schools could achieve this goal depended in no small measure on what was actually taught in them. What did Enlightenment theorists believe should be taught in the new public school systems that they were advocating? In what does an enlightened education consist? Here as elsewhere a wide variety of positions can be detected. At the same time, amid the diversity of views, a common thread is visible. Responding to a long history of religion-dominated educational schemes, Enlightenment educational reformers wanted future schools to impart objective and useful knowledge in nonauthoritarian settings that would encourage independent and critical reflection.

At one extreme stands Condorcet, in his stark assertion that "public education must be limited to instruction" (122)[24] and steer clear of the murky waters of education. By "instruction" was meant "the teaching of truths of fact and calculation"; by "education," the teaching of everything else—including "all political, moral, or religious opinions" (125). However, he did concede that "the teaching of the constitution of each country must form part of national instruction"—but if and only if "the constitution is regarded simply as a matter of fact" (131). Teachers can and should present the historical and political facts of their country's constitution: how it came into being, what rights and duties it extends to citizens, and so forth. But under no circumstances are they to "excite in its favor a blind enthusiasm which renders citizens incapable of judging it" (131); to do so would be to engage in a dogmatic exercise of political religion that exceeds the proper bounds of instruction.

Condorcet presents three important arguments in defense of limiting public education to instruction. First, the pluralism of modern societies itself precludes anything beyond this (122); there is not enough consensus once one moves beyond the realm of fact and calculation, and the different occupations of free citizens necessitate different kinds of training and specialization. Second, to go beyond instruction "would infringe upon the rights of parents"—parents have the right to teach religious values to their children; political authorities do not (124; cf. 126). Finally, when governments seek to impose their own values on students, they violate the latter group's own right to the freedom of opinion. An individual who does not decide for himself what to believe "is no longer a free man; he is the slave of his teachers" (125).

But once Condorcet himself confesses that "it is clear that opinions will be unavoidably intermixed with the truths that must be the object of instruction" (128), the unraveling of his radical curriculum proposal becomes evident. Even in mathematics, he notes, legitimate differences of opinion exist concerning the choice of demonstrations and methods to be used in proving theorems. In the physical sciences, progress will be stifled unless researchers, teachers, and students are encouraged to question assumed facts by exercising their own freedom of opinion. And in other fields there are even fewer facts and certain truths by which to form a solid basis of instruction. But here too, unless people are encouraged to exercise their freedom of opinion and to question alleged facts and truths, these disciplines will also become ossified (128–29). In every discipline, decisions need to be made regarding *which* facts to teach—decisions that are often influenced by "political, moral, and religious opinions."

Nevertheless, the general spirit of Condorcet's proposal is clear enough, even if the practical details of its implementation are not. Education should be about learning to think critically and independently, and one's thinking should be informed by the best currently available account of the facts. The latter should be determined by "the common reason of enlightened men" (130) (and women)—not by political or religious authorities.

Jefferson's curriculum proposals for elementary schools are not quite as astringent as Condorcet's; here we find no blunt proposal to steer clear of anything and everything that hints of indoctrination or opinion as opposed to empirical fact and logical inference. But both authors hold that religious indoctrination should form no part of elementary education, and that the focus of the curriculum should be on objective facts and the transmission of useful skills. Jefferson, for instance, advises, "Instead therefore of putting the Bible and Testament into the hands of the children, at an age when their judgments are not sufficiently matured for religious enquiries, their memories may be stored with the most useful facts from Grecian, Roman, European and American history."[25] A similar emphasis on fact over opinion is detectable in Jefferson's stress on teaching the three Rs. In all public elementary schools, he notes, "shall be taught reading, writing, and common arithmetick."[26]

However, Jefferson's rationale for focusing on reading, writing, and arithmetic is based not on a difficult-to-maintain distinction between objective instruction and subjective education but on the simple assumption that *everyone* needs a basic modicum of these skills, regardless of their station in life. In his *Report of the Commissioners for the University of Virginia* (1818), he summarizes the objects of primary education as follows:

> To give every citizen the information he needs for the transaction of his own business;
> To enable him to calculate for himself, and to express and preserve his ideas, his contracts and accounts, in writing;
> To improve, by reading, his morals and faculties;
> To understand his duties to his neighbors and country, and to discharge with competence the functions confided to him by either;
> To know his rights; to exercise with order and justice those he retains; to choose with discretion the fiduciary of those he delegates; and to notice their conduct with diligence, with candor, and judgment;
> And, in general, to observe with intelligence and faithfulness all the social relations under which he shall be placed.[27]

This same double stress on achieving independence and learning one's rights and duties as a citizen is also present in Condorcet. In his *Sketch for a Historical Picture of the Progress of the Human Mind* (1793; published posthumously in 1795) he writes,

> The degree of equality in education that we can reasonably hope to attain, but that which should be adequate, is that which excludes all dependence, either forced or voluntary.... By a suitable choice of syllabus and of methods of education, we can teach the citizen everything that he needs to know in order to be able to manage his household, administer his affairs, and employ his labor and

his faculties in freedom; to know his rights and to be able to exercise them; to be acquainted with his duties and fulfill them satisfactorily.[28]

Moral and political aims, at least of a suitably circumscribed sort, are also detectable in Jefferson's curriculum proposals. First, there is his view that education seeks to enable students to "know ambition under all its shapes."[29] An educated citizenry is the best defense against political tyranny and overly ambitious politicians. Here we also find the explanation for Jefferson's repeated stress on the place of history in the primary school curriculum. Jefferson agrees with Hume: history is the best teacher of human nature.[30] In Jefferson's view, the education to be gleaned from history is vastly superior to any that can be acquired by attending lectures on moral philosophy:

> Moral philosophy. I think it lost time to attend lectures in this branch. He who made us would have been a pitiful bungler if he had made rules of our moral conduct a matter of science. For one man of science, there are thousands who are not. What would have become of them? Man was destined for society. His morality therefore was to be formed to this object. He was endowed with a sense of right & wrong merely relative to this. This sense is as much a part of his nature as the sense of hearing, seeing, and feeling; it is the true foundation of morality, & not the & το καλον, truth, &c. as fanciful writers have imagined.[31]

The improvement of morals that education is to provide does not include inculcating a sense of right and wrong, for this sense is inborn. Rather, this innate sense needs merely to be exercised and improved through exposure to and reflection on relevant historical data.

Enlightenment curriculum proposals have often been criticized for their crass utilitarianism. Frederick Beiser, for instance, in defending romantic over Enlightenment ideals of education, writes, "The educational reforms of the late eighteenth century might be summarized in a single word: *utility* (*Nutzen*). The demand for utility meant that learning should be directly relevant to life, that it should be useful for human needs, showing people the means to happiness.... Without a doubt, there was no aspect of the ideology of the *Aufklärung* the romantics more despised than its utilitarianism."[32] However, when the charge of utilitarianism is placed in its proper historical context, it loses much of its sting. Yes, in comparison to the religion-oriented educational institutions and outlooks to which they were opposed, Enlightenment educational reformers certainly believed that education should have a more this-worldly focus. D'Alembert's *Encyclopedia* entry "School" (*Collège*), with its critique of the unwieldy curriculum taught in French schools and its debilitating effects on students, speaks directly to this point. After a young man has spent ten years in a French school, d'Alembert complains,

> he has only acquired a rather imperfect knowledge of a dead language and precepts of rhetoric and philosophy that he must try to forget; often his morals are corrupt with the deterioration of his health as the least of the consequences; the meaning of devotion is badly understood, but more frequently the knowledge of religion is so superficial that he succumbs to the first blasphemous conversation or to the first dangerous reading.[33]

To this extent, the *Nutzen* accusation is accurate. But Enlightenment educational reformers certainly did not want to turn education into a mere *Brotstudium*. Regarding Latin, for instance, d'Alembert adds, "I am quite far from disapproving the study of a language in which the Horaces and the Tacituses wrote; this study is absolutely necessary to know their admirable works, but I believe that we should limit ourselves to understanding them, and that the time spent doing papers in Latin is time wasted. This time would be better spent in learning the principles of one's own language."[34]

Similarly, Diderot, though he did not believe that all students should be required to study Greek and Latin, certainly did not disparage the classics. "It is impossible," he held, "to be a man of letters without a knowledge of Greek and, with still greater reason, without a knowledge of Latin. He must be intimately acquainted with Homer and Virgil, with Demosthenes and Cicero, if he wishes to excel."[35] In his view, "the learned languages, which are so difficult for all and useful to so few, should be postponed until a time when the mind is mature, and placed in the order of studies after a great many other subjects that are not only more generally useful, but also easier."[36]

The Enlightenment quest for an education that would be more practical and relevant to human needs was thus by no means intended to be detrimental to liberal learning. Peter Gay strikes a more balanced note when he remarks that Enlightenment educational reformers "saw the value of scientific training, but they loved liberal learning too much to discard it as useless or to patronize it as a mere luxury."[37]

The utilitarianism charge is even less convincing when interpreted as a critique of the moral orientation of Enlightenment educational reformers. The idea that the purpose of education is to show "people the means to happiness" is in fact foreign to most Enlightenment tracts on education. Rather, as we have seen, other goals such as acquiring knowledge of one's rights (Jefferson), subjecting established opinions to critical examination (Condorcet), and instilling civic values (La Chalotais) are stressed. None of these embraces either the idea that achieving happiness is the proper aim of education or that happiness should be the touchstone for all moral evaluation.

Finally, the related charge that Enlightenment reformers advocated an antireligious curriculum also loses much of its sting when placed in historical perspective. Yes, in comparison to the established curricula against which they were fighting, Enlightenment authors certainly did seek to de-emphasize religion's role in education. But contemporary readers will be surprised to see the extent to which religious education still remained an integral part of an enlightened education. La Chalotais, for instance, despite his well-known opposition to the Jesuit-dominated schools of his day, regarded religious instruction as fundamental: "Of all instruction, this is the most important."[38] And Locke held that to teach the foundation of virtue, "the first and most necessary of those endowments that belong to a man or to a gentleman," teachers must begin by imprinting on the student's mind "a true notion of *God*, as of the independent Supreme Being, Author and Maker of all things, from whom we receive all our good, who loves us and gives us all things."[39] Similarly, Rousseau, in his famous discussion of "Civil Religion" in *The Social Contract*, writes, "It is very important to the state that each citizen should have a religion which makes him love his duty."[40] At the same time (and this point holds for most Enlightenment authors on education), the religion to be taught must be a nonsectarian, reason-accessible deistic one that stresses "that in every country and in every sect the sum of the law is to love God above everything and one's neighbor as oneself; that no religion is exempt from the duties of morality."[41] Indeed, of the authors discussed in this chapter, only Condorcet insists that "religious opinions cannot form part of the common instruction" (*The Nature and Purpose of Public Instruction*, 127). And in his case, the logic of his own position entails not that religion must not be taught in public schools, but only that subjective opinions about religion must not be taught as objective truths.[42]

What curriculum proposals do we find in Kant, who believes that the human species' moral perfection is to be sought "from nowhere else but" education? Certainly proto-positivist qualms about separating objective instruction from subjective education (facts versus values) have no place here? Yes and no. On the one hand, moral education clearly receives pride of place in Kant's discussion of education—indeed, his discussion of pedagogy is largely a theory of moral education. The primary goal of education, in Kant's view, is the acquisition and development of morally good character.[43] However, Kant's understanding of what morality and moral character are also drives him away from any theory of education that hints of indoctrination or authoritarianism. The fundamental aim of Kantian education is indeed to "moralize" human beings, but moralization on Kant's view is achieved when people have acquired "the disposition to choose nothing but good ends. Good ends are those which are necessarily approved by everyone and which can be the simultaneous ends of everyone" (*Pedagogy* 9: 450). Moralized agents, in other words, have internalized the norms expressed in the different formulas of the categorical imperative. They have acquired deep-seated dispositions to act on universalizable maxims, to treat all people as ends in themselves rather than as means, and to regard everyone as a lawgiving member in a universal kingdom of ends.[44] But there is no specific list of dos and don'ts that students need to learn as part of this moral education. In his *Lectures on Pedagogy*, for instance, he notes, regarding moral education, that "everything is spoiled if one tries to ground . . . [it] on examples, threats, punishments, and so forth. One must see to it that the pupil acts from his own maxims, not from habit, that he not only does the good, but that he does it because it is good" (9: 475). The categorical imperative itself is not claimed to be "a new principle of all morality" (*Practical Reason* 5: 9 n.), but one with which "common human reason in its practical appraisals" already agrees (*Groundwork* 4: 402). The moral philosopher's task, in Kant's view, is not to drag in new principles from on high, but to analyze ordinary moral beliefs, to systematize them, and to articulate the underlying principles that tie them together. So although Kant does not accept the empiricist "moral sense" theory that Jefferson inherited from Scottish moralists such as Lord Kames (Kant, unlike Jefferson and Kames, does not believe that sound moral judgment is primarily a matter of feeling or sensation), both Kant and Jefferson agree that ordinary people do not need a moral theorist to inform them about matters of right and wrong. An understanding of such matters "already dwells in natural sound understanding and needs not so much to be taught as only to be clarified" (*Groundwork* 4: 397).

Because his focus is on moral education, Kant also does not offer much curricular advice in his *Lectures on Pedagogy*. At one point, he quickly

summarizes a recommended course of study for children by saying that it
should include reading and writing, languages, a bit of botany and "the
description of nature," geography, and mathematics (9: 474).[45] Here too
we find a common Enlightenment emphasis on imparting objective knowledge rather than inculcating subjective opinion. The child must "learn to
distinguish very well knowledge from mere opinion and belief. Thus one
prepares the way for a correct understanding and a *correct* taste rather than
a *fine* or *delicate* taste" (9: 474).[46]

Also, as we saw earlier, there is even less room for civic education and
the cultivation of patriotism in a Kantian curriculum than in a Jeffersonian
or Condorcetian one. Kant urges educators to stress "cosmopolitan dispositions" to students. Students must learn to "rejoice at the best for the
world even if it is not to the advantage of their fatherland or to their own
gain" (9: 499). In the *Lectures on Pedagogy* Kant makes no specific reference
to inculcating patriotic dispositions at all.[47] In his conviction that education
everywhere should be directed primarily at the specieswide goal of human
perfection rather than serve parental or national purposes, Kant was
influenced in particular by the German educational reformer Johann
Bernhard Basedow (1724–90), who founded the Philanthropin Institute
in Dessau in 1774. The opening of this experimental school, according to
one recent account, "marked a turning point in the history of education,
culture, and literature in Germany. Here for the first time the attempt was
made to develop and to practice an enlightened, interdenominational,
cosmopolitan, and tolerant education and culture which was in harmony
with children's nature."[48] The controversial experiment was short-lived
(the school closed in 1793; Basedow resigned as director after only two
years), but at one point Kant regarded it as "the greatest phenomenon that
has appeared in this century for the improvement of the perfection of
humanity, through it all schools in the world will acquire a different
form, and the human race will thereby be freed from the constraints of
the prevailing schooling" (*Friedländer* 25: 722–23).[49] Indeed, in 1776–77 he
even wrote two short fund-raising appeals for the struggling Institute,
encouraging "all teachers in private as well as in public school instruction
to use Basedow's writings" and all friends of humanity to subscribe "to the
monthly publication of the Dessau Educational Institute, under the title of
Educational Treatises."[50] Kant's strong endorsement of the Institute rested
on several factors: Basedow's commitment to a more Rousseauian child-
centered approach to teaching, to interdenominational religious instruction,
and to the teaching of foreign languages (including Latin) by conversation
and immersion all greatly appealed to him.[51] But above all, it was Basedow's

conviction that the primary goal of education was to prepare students to become "citizens of our world" that ensured Kant's fervent support.[52]

If the rationale of education is to spread enlightenment, this means that the curriculum taught in schools must itself prepare students to "have the courage to use their own reason."[53] This in turn requires a curriculum that emphasizes basic skill acquisition and the imparting of objective information rather than indoctrination. There is still ample room for imparting moral and religious messages in such a curriculum, but the messages must themselves be grounded in an informed public consensus based on fact and reason.

Enlightened Universities

Thus far we have looked only at Enlightenment curriculum proposals for the lower school levels. But what views did Enlightenment educational reformers put forward about college and university education, and what do their positions on higher education reveal about their more fundamental attitudes concerning the nature and purpose of education in general? It should be noted at the outset that Enlightenment reform efforts were focused more on primary rather than higher education, for two simple reasons: (1) Basic literacy had yet to be achieved in most countries. Achieving literacy was the top educational priority, and primary education was the appropriate means for achieving it. (2) European universities, many of which date back to the Middle Ages, were on the whole conservative, religiously oriented institutions that were strongly resistant to the Enlightenment spirit. Thomas Munck, for instance, in his analysis of the ways eighteenth-century educational institutions broadened the horizons of knowledge, writes,

> The older advanced institutions, the universities, largely failed to respond to the changing environment. They continued to provide traditional scholastic tuition (emphasising the classics, dialectics and rhetoric) for those pupils whose social status pointed towards careers in law and the church. However, with an antiquated curriculum, retention of Latin as the medium of instruction, and generally a total lack of research-based work, most universities had increasing difficulties identifying a clear educational role for themselves. French and English universities, in particular, were little more than social clubs for the sons of the rich.[54]

Surprisingly, even in Germany, where both the quantity as well as the quality of Enlightenment writing on the importance of education were extremely high, enrollment in universities actually declined significantly during the eighteenth century. According to Charles E. McClelland, in 1700 approximately nine thousand students attended the twenty-eight universities then existing in Germany, but by the 1760s this number had fallen to seven thousand. And by the end of the eighteenth century, "total enrollments at German universities had sunk to about 6,000 per year."[55] Adam Smith offers some insight into the sorry state of European universities during the eighteenth century when he observes that many of them had become nothing more than "sanctuaries in which exploded systems and obsolete prejudices found shelter and protection." According to his diagnosis, universities suffered from a plethora of maladies: they were essentially "ecclesiastical corporations; instituted for the education of churchmen," neglectful of their teaching duties, overly indulgent toward their faculty, resistant to reform, and objectionably insular.[56]

At the same time, many new colleges and universities were founded during the Enlightenment. For instance, by 1770 there were already nine colleges in colonial America, the first one (Harvard) having been founded in 1636.[57] However, each of these colleges was originally intended to serve a specific Protestant denomination and is thus closer to Smith's model of "ecclesiastical corporations; intended for the education of churchmen." None of them can be called direct products of Enlightenment educational reform. But several other modern universities do meet this description, and I turn now to them.

Jefferson and the University of Virginia

We wish to establish . . . an University on a plan so broad & liberal & modern, as to be worth patronizing with the public support, and be a temptation to the youth of other states to come and drink of the cup of knowledge & fraternize with us.

—Jefferson to Joseph Priestley,
January 18, 1800

Jefferson's plan for the University of Virginia was his lone success in the area of education, and one of which he was justifiably proud. Although the university did not begin admitting students until 1825, Jefferson's strong interest in college and university education dates back to at least 1779, and the University of Virginia is the best example of an American university strongly influenced by Enlightenment attitudes at its founding.[58] Jefferson wrote the founding document of the University (*Report of the Commissioners for the University of Virginia*, 1818), planned the organization and curriculum of the university, designed its first buildings, and served as its first rector.

Although he strongly supported universal public (but not compulsory) education at the primary school level, Jefferson's views about higher education were much more meritocratic. As we saw earlier, on his plan "all the free children, male and female," were to be guaranteed three years of free public schooling. After this point, those who wished to continue at their own expense could do so, and those who wished to continue but lacked the monetary means to do so were to be considered for a small pool of merit-based scholarships. Each year one poor boy "of the best and most promising genius and disposition" was to be chosen by the overseers of each of the different primary schools to go on to one of the regional "grammar" or secondary schools. After one or two years there, "the best genius" was again to be selected to attend for four more years, "and the residue dismissed." "By this means," Jefferson explained, in an often-criticized remark, "twenty of the best geniuses will be raked from the rubbish annually, and be instructed, at the public expence." After six years of secondary education, a final cut was to be made. The top half of the senior class, "who are to be chosen for the superiority of their parts and disposition," would be offered three-year college scholarships.[59]

However, one should not infer that all Enlightenment educational theorists endorsed Jefferson's position that a university education was for only the few geniuses who had been raked from the rubbish. An important counterexample is German writer Johann Adam Bergk (1769–1834), an energetic popularizer of Kant's work. In 1800 Bergk wrote an article entitled "Ueber die Einschränkung der Freiheit zu studieren durch den Staat" (On the Limitation of the Freedom to Study by the State), in which he argued that everyone should have unrestricted access to a university education. The duty of the state is to protect "the freedom of all according to the same laws"; to exclude potential students from universities because of their social origins, financial resources, or any other reason is inconsistent with this fundamental duty. "All right [*Recht*] rests on equality of action. What one citizen as such is allowed to do, all must be allowed to do."[60] Furthermore, when governments impose limitations on the number of university graduates they are also stifling the search for truth. Open competition and the free exchange of ideas are the best means of achieving maximum progress in the search for truth and new knowledge.

But to return to Jefferson: it is clear that he, like most of his contemporaries, believed that primary and college or university education should be designed for different groups of people, and that the different audience targets also entailed different educational aims. In the former case, the aim of education is to give all future citizens the information they need to transact their own affairs and lead independent lives, to be informed of their rights and duties, and to learn enough about human behavior so that they can "know ambition under all its shapes" and help protect their country against political tyranny. But in the latter case, the aim of education is

> To form the statesmen, legislators and judges, on whom the public prosperity and individual happiness are so much to depend;
>
> To expound the principles and structure of government, the laws which regulate the intercourse of nations . . . ;
>
> To harmonize and promote the interests of agriculture, manufactures and commerce, and by well informed views of political economy to give a free scope to the public industry;
>
> To develop the reasoning faculties of our youth, enlarge their minds, cultivate their morals . . . ;
>
> To enlighten them with mathematical and physical sciences, which advance the arts, which administer to the health, the subsistence, and comforts of human life;
>
> And, generally, to form them to habits of reflection and correct action, rendering them examples of virtue to others, and of happiness within themselves.[61]

Jefferson's conviction that the first goal of university education is to educate society's future leaders causes him to backslide a bit from the anti-indoctrination aspect of his primary education curriculum proposals. On March 4, 1825, the Board of Visitors of the University (of which Jefferson was a member) passed a resolution stressing the need "to pay especial attention to the principles of government which shall be inculcated . . . [in the University], and to provide that none shall be inculcated which are incompatible with those on which the Constitution of this State, and of the United States were genuinely based."[62] As a means of ensuring that political heresies not be propagated, the Board even provided a list of writings that "shall be used as the texts and documents" for appropriate courses within the University. The prescribed writings included political philosophy works by Locke and Sydney, the U.S. Declaration of Independence,

The Federalist, Washington's valedictory address, and even the 1799 Virginia resolution "on the subject of the alien and sedition laws."[63]

But while the academic freedom of professors teaching courses on "the subject of civil polity" would definitely be constrained by this resolution, the freedom of students to study what they wanted to study at the University of Virginia was much higher than at other universities during the early nineteenth century. In contrast to the required curriculum that students at Harvard and elsewhere faced during this time, Jefferson wrote, "We shall, on the contrary, allow them uncontrolled choice in the lectures they shall choose to attend, and require elementary qualifications only, and sufficient age."[64]

In his efforts to construct a distinctly modern university, Jefferson stressed that "some branches of science, formerly esteemed, may now be omitted; so may others now valued in Europe, but useless to us for ages to come." In his university curriculum proposals, pride of place is given to "the sciences which seem useful & practicable,"[65] though his educational plan is by no means narrowly vocational or anti–liberal arts. For instance, in his 1818 *Report of the Commissioners*, he recommended that one professorship be established in each of the following ten branches of learning: ancient languages, modern languages, pure mathematics, physico-mathematics (under which he included, among other disciplines, geography), physics (including chemistry), botany and zoology, anatomy and medicine, government (under which he included both history and the "Law of Nations" or international law), municipal law, and, finally, a tenth umbrella area consisting of ideology (cursorily defined later as "the doctrine of thought"), general grammar, ethics, rhetoric, belles lettres, and the fine arts.[66]

In addition to the modern emphases on natural, applied, and social sciences, a further respect in which Jefferson's curriculum shows its Enlightenment roots is in the area of religion. In the 1818 *Report*, he emphasized,

> In conformity with the principles of our Constitution, which places all sects of religion on an equal footing, . . . we have proposed no professor of divinity; and the . . . proofs of the being of a God, the creator, preserver, and supreme ruler of the universe, the author of all the relations of morality, and of the laws and obligations these infer, will be within the province of the professor of ethics; to which . . . a basis will be formed common to all sects.[67]

As a result, Virginia became the first nonsectarian American university. But nonsectarian was not supposed to mean antireligious. In a letter written in

1822, at a time when "the atmosphere of our country" was "unquestionably charged with a threatening cloud of fanaticism," Jefferson—in response to protestors at a meeting of the Board of Visitors who had complained that he was trying to establish "an institution, not merely of no religion, but against all religion"—issued an invitation to all religions to come to the campus and establish (at their own expense) "a professorship of their own tenets." His hope was that "by bringing the sects together, and mixing them with the mass of other students, we shall soften their asperities, liberalize and neutralize their prejudices, and make the general religion a religion of peace, reason, and morality."[68] Here too, in the quest for a universal religion of "peace, reason, and morality," we find other central Enlightenment ideals struggling to surface (see chapters 1 and 5). But as we will see in part II, the "threatening cloud of fanaticism" was to prove stronger.

Halle, Göttingen, Berlin

The roots of the modern university—particularly the effort to bring teaching and research activities into one institution—are widely conceded to lie in the German Enlightenment.[69] As noted earlier, the eighteenth century was a period of crisis for German universities: enrollments had declined severely, and some critics began to question whether the university system even had a future. R. Steven Turner writes,

> Fired by the Enlightenment's impatience with what it viewed as anachronistic institutions, representatives of this critical tradition began ... to attack the universities with a vehemence unprecedented in previous decades. They no longer attacked curriculum and methods alone, but also the most basic institutions of the universities: corporate government, the lecture, and the division into faculties. Occasionally critics even impugned the integrity of the professoriate as a professional group and with increasing frequency called for the outright abolition of the universities.[70]

At the same time, during the Enlightenment several new German universities were established that constitute important counterexamples to this general downward trend. The first one was the University of Halle, which opened in 1694. Influenced strongly by pietism, Halle introduced a number of important institutional changes that were gradually adopted elsewhere: vernacular lectures, a teacher-training program (initiated by August

Herman Francke, himself one of the leaders of the pietist movement), a progressive law faculty, stronger curricular emphasis on the natural sciences, and, at least for a while, a greater degree of academic freedom on theological matters. As Friedrich Paulsen notes, the academic freedom in particular "completely changed the character of the university. It ceased to be a school of traditional doctrine and became the workshop of original scientific research and the pioneer of truth, taking the lead in the whole domain of intellectual life."[71]

However, Halle's reputation as a progressive institution suffered severely after 1723, when the philosopher Christian Wolff was expelled by royal decree for having implied in a public lecture that it was possible for people to lead morally virtuous lives without the aid of religion.[72] After this point, attention in reformist circles turned gradually to another new university, founded in 1737 in Göttingen. Modeled in part on its rival in Halle (the leading figure in the planning for Göttingen, Privy Counselor Gerlach Adolf von Münchhausen, had himself been a law student at Halle), Göttingen adopted many of the pietist university's curricular and institutional innovations. But in a desire to avoid the *Hallesche Händel* (Halle quarrel) that had tarnished the latter institution after Wolff's expulsion, a stronger emphasis was placed on academic freedom. Göttingen's university statutes explicitly "forbade denunciations of teachers for 'heretical' opinions."[73] By this means, the political power of the theology faculty was weakened from the start.

Münchhausen also placed more emphasis on the philosophy faculty and contributed greatly to its gradual emergence as an equal partner with the three "higher" faculties of law, medicine, and theology. Traditionally, the "lower" faculty of philosophy, which comprised all of the arts and sciences,[74] served a merely preparatory role in European universities, coaching students who planned to eventually go on in the three lucrative professional fields. The long-standing dominance of the higher faculties also led some critics to complain that the universities were merely professional training schools. Within the broad scope of the philosophy faculty, Münchhausen stressed history, mathematics, and the natural sciences, in part as a way of attracting wealthy students who were headed for careers at court or in the diplomatic service. McClelland writes,

> Because nobles and wealthy students in general paid higher fees than the many ordinary "in-state" students (*Landeskinder*), Münchhausen deemed it necessary to attract a maximum of *Vornehme und Ausländer* (notables and foreigners) in order to bring money into the country

and help defray the cost of the university. Yet "academic mercantilism," ... as this system has been called, was not the only motive for attracting nobles and foreigners. Their presence would heighten the visibility of the new university and lend it some of their own social prestige. That, in turn, would attract other students.[75]

As part of his triple strategy for raising the social status, popularity, and wealth of the new university, Münchhausen also placed a special emphasis on the law faculty. Here he was particularly blunt: "That the legal faculty be filled with famous and excellent men is necessary above all, because that faculty must induce many rich and distinguished people to study in Göttingen."[76]

Faculty recruitment was another area of university life in which Münchhausen introduced noticeable changes. Higher salaries and perquisites (moving expenses, help with housing, access to an excellent library) were used as inducements to bring faculty to Göttingen, and greater emphasis was placed on faculty research and publication records. The latter in turn (as Münchhausen had hoped) contributed to increased visibility for the new university. Professors at other European universities in the eighteenth century experienced little if any pressure from the administration or their peers to publish. But a survey of publication records during this time shows that "the prestigious University of Göttingen presented a rather different situation, for its faculty as a whole published extensively during the second half of the 18th century. ... If by 1765 Göttingen could boast of being the most prestigious intellectual center in Germany outside of the Berlin Academy, it clearly owed this reputation largely to the publications of its faculty."[77]

Münchhausen's aims were unabashedly pragmatic: he wanted his university to teach modern subjects that he believed would attract members of affluent and worldly social classes to study at Göttingen rather than elsewhere. But in strengthening the arts and science faculty and curriculum, he also opened the door to other developments. One that is mentioned in nearly all histories of Göttingen's early days is the revival of classical scholarship under the leadership of Johann Matthias Gesner and his successor, Christian Gottlob Heyne. The combination of the increased use of vernacular languages for scholarly communication and publication and new secular curricula competing against older religious ones had led many people to predict the eventual demise of the study of Greek and Latin. But Gesner and Heyne were able to present "reasons convincing even to the enlightened for studying the classics, but for studying them in a different way." On their view, the classics were to be studied, not to impart eloquence by imitating surviving models of ancient Latin prose, but to cultivate the mind and "to train the taste, judgment, and intellect" of students.[78] The preferred vehicle for this cultivation was not the traditional lecture but the seminar: "small advanced classes in which original work is done by senior students under the guidance of the professor."[79]

The growth of neohumanism at Göttingen also contributed to the emphasis on *Bildung* or self-formation, championed in the writings of Wilhelm von Humboldt, Kant, Friedrich Schiller, and many others. "The true end of the human being," Humboldt declares in *The Limits of State Action* (1791–92), "is the highest and most proportional *Bildung* of his powers into a whole."[80] Humboldt, who played a lead role in the later founding of the University of Berlin (1810), "had come to Göttingen in the spring of 1788 ostensibly to study law and cameralism; but it was his participation in Heyne's famous philological seminar that shaped his future career as a scholar and educational reformer."[81]

"With the foundation of the University of Berlin," Paulsen writes, "a new chapter opens in the history of university teaching."[82] Building on the innovations of Halle and Göttingen, Berlin placed even stronger emphasis on academic freedom and original research. The principles necessary for the proper functioning of a university, Humboldt argued, "are isolation and freedom," and the state's job is to assure the university "an abundance (both as to strength and variety) of spiritual energy by its choice of men, and guarantee them their freedom to do their work."[83] However, his rationale for emphasizing research was driven not by a "publish or perish" mentality that depreciates the importance of teaching and pits professor against student, but by a broader conception of knowledge as necessarily open and unfinished, one that thus brings students and teachers together in pursuit of a larger common goal. Universities, Humboldt stressed—as opposed to primary and secondary schools—must "treat all knowledge [*Wissenschaft*] as a not yet wholly solved problem and therefore always remain in research [*immer im Forschen bleiben*], whereas schools take as their subject only the completed and agreed upon results of knowledge and teach these." This conception of knowledge as open rather than closed, he continued, "totally changes the relationship between teacher and student from what it was previously. The latter no longer exists for the sake of the former, both exist for the sake of learning [*Wissenschaft*]; therefore the teacher's occupation depends on the presence of his students."[84] Teachers and students work together as equal partners in pursuit of the common goal of discovering new knowledge, each developing their own powers in the process.

Berlin is also unique in the history of modern university education for having a (not always harmonious) chorus of original philosophical voices participate in its founding. Humboldt, who drafted several papers on education after being appointed minister of worship and public education in 1808, is traditionally regarded as the university's founder. But in the same year Friedrich Schleiermacher published *Occasional Thoughts on Universities in the German Sense: With an Appendix Regarding a University Soon to be Established*, and he too became a key voice in the planning of the university.[85] Johann Gottlieb Fichte, in his *Addresses to the German Nation* (first presented as public lectures in the amphitheater of the Berlin Academy in 1807–8), had argued in defense of a new system of education that would require the state to make "education universal throughout the length and breadth of its domain for every one of its future citizens without exception"; he was appointed dean of the philosophical faculty at the new university in 1810 and served briefly as first rector of the university. In 1807, Fichte wrote an essay (first published in 1817) entitled "Derivation of a Plan for an Institute of Higher Learning to Be Established in Berlin, Which Stands in Essential Relation to an Academy of Sciences," in which he argued that the government must provide financial support for all qualified students whose families cannot afford to pay tuition.[86] He, too, is properly regarded as one of the intellectual founders of the University of Berlin. Finally, Schelling's 1802 *Lectures on the Method of Academic Study* and Henrik Steffens's 1808–9 *Lectures on the Idea of Universities* are two additional important contributions to German university reform literature that also influenced the founding of Berlin.[87]

How do Jefferson's Enlightenment-influenced reform efforts in higher education compare with those of the Germans? The most obvious difference lies in Jefferson's lack of emphasis on faculty research and publication. But on this point, as is well known, more and more American institutions of higher learning adopted the German model once they began to establish graduate programs in the late nineteenth century.[88] On other key issues, we find solid agreement. Jefferson and the planners of Halle, Göttingen, and Berlin all stressed (1) a modern, secular curriculum that placed more weight on the arts and sciences and less on theology; (2) a learning environment that emphasized the importance of academic freedom—freedom for professors to teach and investigate what they wanted to teach and investigate, freedom for students to study what they wanted to study; and (3) instruction and communication in modern, vernacular languages, but (somewhat surprisingly) at the same time renewed support for the study of ancient Greek and Latin language, literature, and culture. In each of these three areas we find important Enlightenment legacies that have continued to exert a strong influence on subsequent developments in higher education.

3

....

Economics

*There is nothing which requires more to be illustrated
by philosophy than trade does.*

—Boswell, *The Life of Samuel Johnson*

Commercial Society

During the Enlightenment, a new kind of society arose—a commercial
society characterized, to be sure, by the self-interested pursuit of wealth and
the incessant "propensity to truck, barter, and exchange one thing for
another,"[1] but also one "in which dispute was to be replaced by conversation, inspiration by opinion, doctrine by polite manners, and the warlike
worlds of universal monarchy, wars of religion, feudal disorder and the
wars of ancient virtue, by a European republic of trading states."[2] Enlightenment philosophers, while not blind to the disruptive sides of this pro-
found transformation in human life,[3] were also its defenders. They
defended the new commercial society because they believed it represented
a better society—better morally, in the triple sense of being more just and
tending toward more liberty as well as more equality; better economically,
in the sense of producing more wealth and higher living standards; and
better in terms of its beneficial spillover effects. A vibrant commercial

society, they believed, had a tendency to raise the overall level of the arts and sciences, culture, and even the moral character of citizens.

The French *philosophes*, although not developing these themes systematically, articulated the core insights in their early admiration of England's developing commercial society. Voltaire, in his letter "On Trade" in the *Letters Concerning the English Nation* (1733), observes, "As trade enriched the citizens of England, so it contributed to their freedom, and this freedom on the other side extended to their commerce, whence arose the grandeur of the state."[4] Montesquieu, in *The Spirit of the Laws* (1748), writes, "Other nations have made the interests of commerce yield to those of politics; the English, on the contrary, have always made its political interests give way to the interests of its commerce. This is the people in the world who have best known how to take advantage of these three great things at the same time: religion, commerce, and liberty."[5] Similarly, Diderot praises the English Constitution for being "the most favorable to its commerce, the most appropriate to the development of genius, eloquence and all the faculties of the human mind."[6] Behind each of these passages lies the conviction that economic progress also engenders cultural, scientific, and even moral progress.

Hume, in his essays on economics, offers a more sustained defense of commercial society, one that in turn strongly influenced Smith.[7] In "Of Refinement in the Arts" (which was entitled "Of Luxury" in early editions of the essays published between 1752 and 1758), Hume argues that advances in industry and commerce are strongly linked to progress in the liberal arts: one cannot "be carried to perfection, without being accompanied, in some degree, with the other. The same age, which produces great philosophers and politicians, renowned generals and poets, usually abounds with skillful weavers, and ship-carpenters."[8] Improvements in the liberal arts in turn make people "more sociable": "Both sexes meet in an easy and sociable manner; and the tempers of men, as well as their behaviour, refine apace" (*RA*, 271). And increased sociability leads in turn to "an encrease of humanity": "Beside the improvements which they receive from knowledge and the liberal arts, it is impossible but they must feel an encrease of humanity, from the very habit of conversing together, and contributing to each other's pleasure and entertainment. Thus *industry, knowledge*, and *humanity*, are linked together by an indissoluble chain" (*RA*, 271). But the "indissoluble chain" extends still further. Advances in industry and the liberal arts also lead to reforms in government and political life, as well as higher standards of living for the majority of citizens:

> If we consider the matter in a proper light, we shall find, that a progress in the arts is rather favourable to liberty, and has a natural

tendency to preserve, if not produce, a free government.... Where luxury nourishes commerce and industry, the peasants, by a proper cultivation of the land, become rich and independent; while the tradesmen and merchants acquire a share of the property, and draw authority and consideration to that middling rank of men, who are the best and firmest basis of liberty. (*RA*, 277)[9]

The tendency toward social equality that results when peasants "become rich and independent" and "tradesmen and merchants acquire a share of property" is an additional benefit of commercial society that Hume emphasizes repeatedly. In "On Commerce," for instance, he asserts, "A too great disproportion among the citizens weakens any state. Every person, if possible, ought to enjoy the fruits of his labour, in a full possession of all the necessaries, and many of the conveniences of life. No one can doubt, but such an equality is most suitable to human nature, and diminishes much less from the *happiness* of the rich than it adds to that of the poor."[10]

Furthermore, once the effects of the "indissoluble chain" become visible in one nation, a similar progress occurs in neighboring countries as well, thus extending the chain further still. In "Of the Jealousy of Trade," for instance, Hume defends the following claim: "I will venture to assert, that the encrease of riches and commerce in any one nation, instead of hurting, commonly promotes the riches and commerce of all its neighbours."[11]

A central and controversial aspect of the Enlightenment defense of commercial society is its vindication of the pursuit of wealth and luxury. Here Enlightenment moralists clearly part ways with all of their predecessors: ancient Greek and Roman moral philosophers as well as Jewish and Christian authors regard luxury as a vice rather than a virtue. Cicero, for instance, writes in *De Officiis*, "If we will only bear in mind the superiority and dignity of our nature, we shall realize how wrong it is to abandon ourselves to excess and to live in luxury and voluptuousness, and how right it is to live in thrift, self-denial, simplicity, and sobriety" (I.xxx.106).[12] Hume's apologia for luxury (and his was only one of many) is not flat-footed; for instance, he does agree that "to be entirely occupied with the luxury of the table... without any relish for the pleasures of ambition, study, or conversation, is a mark of stupidity, and is incompatible with any vigour of temper or genius."[13] But he does defend what he calls "innocent" as opposed to "blameable" or "vicious" luxury. The "ages of refinement" (that is, of innocent luxury), he claims, "are both the happiest and most virtuous";[14] in making this claim he implies that the pursuit of innocent luxury is the most important underlying causal factor in all of the processes described earlier. The desire for luxury is not only a powerful engine that drives economic growth, but is also a motivating force that promotes the growth of the arts and sciences, deepens citizens' sense of humanity and morality, contributes to the improvement of government, and extends personal liberty.

Smith's defense of commercial society, as we have already seen, owes serious debts to Hume's—debts that Smith himself explicitly acknowledges.[15] Smith follows Hume in seeking to persuade readers that the pursuit of wealth and luxury, properly construed and constrained, is a virtue rather than a vice, and his arguments in defense of this alleged virtue are also quite similar to Hume's. For instance, like Hume, he believes that market economies that encourage commerce will gradually introduce "order and good government," increase the "liberty and security of individuals," and improve the material well-being of the working class to a point where the standard of living of "the very meanest person in a civilized country...exceeds that of many an African king" (*WN* III.iv.4, I.i.11).

However, this is not to say that their respective arguments on behalf of commercial society are identical. One important difference is that Smith offers a keener analysis of the causal factors that make possible the arrival and growth of commercial societies in human life. Here his own special gifts and abilities as a political economist become evident. Two key conditions that Smith highlights but that receive no mention at all by Hume are industrialization, "the invention of a great number of machines which facilitate and abridge labour, and enable one man to do the work of many," and the division of labor, "which occasions, in a well-governed society, that universal opulence which extends itself to the lowest ranks of the people" (*WN* I.i.5, 10).[16] The introduction of these two causal agents in the development of commercial society also enables Smith to present additional arguments on the latter's behalf. "The woolen coat, for example,...as coarse and rough as it may appear, is the produce of the joint labour of a great multitude of workmen" (*WN* I.i.11), and itself is a symbol of the diversity and vitality engendered by market economies. As Samuel Fleischacker notes, "Smith sees the effect of the division of labor on human personality as something to be embraced, not lamented. Commercial society is an intrinsic good because it is richly diverse, because it expresses, and enhances, the beauty of human differentiation.... Commercial society is *admirable*, says Smith, a flowering of the human spirit, and not merely something ploddingly peaceful and opulent."[17]

Finally, Smith's reputation as the patron saint of laissez-faire modern capitalism notwithstanding, he actually has more reservations concerning the arrival and growth of commercial society than does Hume. His strongest reservation, as noted earlier, concerns the dehumanization of workers that inevitably accompanies the division of labor. In "every improved and civilized society," Smith predicts, "the great body of the people" will, as a result of the progress of the division of labor, necessarily become "as stupid and ignorant as it is possible for a human creature to become"—"unless government takes some pains to prevent it" (*WN* V.i.f.50; cf. 61). His central hope is that universal education can overcome these debilitating effects. However, given his own experience as a student at Oxford University (where the greater part of the professors had "given up altogether even the pretence of teaching"; *WN* V.i.f.7), it is understandable if Smith does not always appear to be overly optimistic about education's transformative possibilities.

Kant

The French and British were not the only defenders of commercial society. Kant's remarks on this topic, though not nearly as extensive or systematic as either Hume's or Smith's, are equally positive. Like them, he sees freedom of commerce as part of a larger and more fundamental moral package of personal freedom and independence; like them, he sees the growth of economic as well as personal freedoms as contributing to desirable social and political reforms and the spread of enlightenment generally:

> Civil freedom cannot very well be infringed without feeling the disadvantage of it in all trades, especially in commerce, and thereby also the diminution of the powers of the state in its external relationships. But this freedom is gradually advancing. If one hinders the citizen who is seeking his welfare in any way he pleases, as long as it can subsist along with the freedom of others, then one constrains the vitality of all enterprise and with it, in turn, the powers of the whole. Hence the personal restrictions on the citizen's doing and refraining are removed more and more, and the general freedom of religion is ceded; and thus gradually arises, accompanied by delusions and whims, enlightenment, as a great good that must raise humankind even out of the selfish aims and aggrandizement on the part of its rulers, if only the latter understand their own advantage. (*Universal History* 8: 27–28)[18]

Like the Scottish moralists, Kant also defends the new commercial society over its feudal predecessor because of the independence and opportunities for material betterment that it grants to citizens:

> Every member of a commonwealth must be allowed to attain any level of rank within it (that can belong to a subject) to which his talent, his industry and his luck can take him; and his fellow subjects may not stand in his way by means of a hereditary prerogative (privileges [reserved] for a certain rank), so as to keep him and his descendants forever beneath the rank. (*Theory and Practice* 8: 292; cf. 293)[19]

Additionally, in his famous encomium to the *Handelsgeist* (spirit of commerce) in *Toward Perpetual Peace*, Kant remarks that this spirit "sooner or later takes hold of every nation," and that "the *power of money* may well be the most reliable of all the powers (means) subordinate to that of a state" (8: 368).[20] Kant and Smith both see human beings' incessant desire "to truck, barter, and exchange one thing for another" (*WN* I.ii.1) as a primary motivating force in the species' development. Further indications of Kant's endorsement of the role of commerce in human life include his account of "the history of freedom" in *Conjectural Beginning of Human History* via a familiar four-stage theory of development (hunting, pastoral life, agriculture, commerce) and his well-known claim that the self-interested actions generated by human beings' "unsociable sociability" often promote (contrary to their authors' intentions) the greater good of society (8: 109).[21]

Like Hume, Smith, and others, Kant also sees "industry, knowledge, and humanity" as being "linked together by an indissoluble chain." The growth of commerce and industry promote the development of the arts and sciences, and the latter in turn help prepare human beings for the deeper moral transformation that is their ultimate destiny: "Beautiful arts and sciences, which by means of a universally communicable pleasure and an elegance and refinement make human beings, if not morally better, at least better mannered for society, very much reduce the tyranny of sensible tendencies, and prepare human beings for a sovereignty in which reason alone shall have power" (*Judgment* 5: 433).[22]

Finally, Kant also parts ways with the ancients and offers a qualified defense of luxury as a welcome motor for economic, cultural, and even moral development. On the one hand, luxury "multiplies our needs" and "increases the enticements and attractions of inclinations," thus making it "hard to comply with morality." In this sense, "luxury is an incursion [*Einbruch*] upon morality." But luxury also promotes all the arts and sciences; it develops all the talents of man, and thus it seems as if this state is the destiny of the human being. It refines morality. . . . Luxury develops humanity to the highest degree of beauty. . . . By means of variety it enlarges our judgment, gives occupation to many human hands, and enlivens the whole of communal existence. In that respect, therefore, there can be no objection to luxury from the moral point of view, save only that there must be laws, not to restrict it, but to furnish guidance. (*Collins* 27: 397)[23]

In sum, major voices from different countries of the Enlightenment all offered defenses of the new commercial society. But their defense of freedom of commerce—under appropriate constraints of justice and, as we will see later, social welfare legislation—was also part of the much larger project of trying to foster morally decent societies.

"The Obvious and Simple System of Natural Liberty"

A network of moral values lay behind the Enlightenment defense of market economies, the most obvious member of which is personal freedom. As Peter Gay writes, "Fundamental values—Enlightenment values—were involved in the issue of economic freedom, most notably man's right to determine his own fate, his right to be treated not as a ward of a supremely wise government but as an autonomous being."[24] In invoking the concept of autonomy, some would argue that Gay is reading Smith through Kantian spectacles.[25] But it is very clear that the freedom of each citizen "to pursue his own interest his own way" (*WN* IV.ix.51) is central to Smith's basic conception of a just society. In a frequently cited passage, he states,

> It is the highest impertinence and presumption, . . . in kings and ministers, to pretend to watch over the œconomy of private people, and to restrain their expence, either by sumptuary laws, or by prohibiting the importation of foreign luxuries. They are themselves always, and without any exception, the greatest spendthrifts in the society. Let them look well after their own expence, and they may safely trust private people with theirs. (*WN* II.iii.36)

Gay, after quoting this same passage, adds, "Kant could have said the same thing."[26] Convincing readers that Kant *did* say the same thing is a major theme in Fleischacker's more recent study, *A Third Concept of Liberty: Judgment and Freedom in Kant and Adam Smith.* As Fleischacker sees it, "The most obvious connection between Kant and Smith is their shared antipathy toward political leaders who treat citizens like children."[27]

Indeed, Kant explicitly endorses Smith's antipaternalist credo in his *Anthropology*, noting that "people are condemned to permanent immaturity with regard to their own best interest" when heads of state believe falsely that "they understand better how to make their subjects happy than the subjects understand" (7: 209).[28] And the battle against immaturity (*Unmündigkeit*)— which Kant defines at the beginning of his essay "An Answer to the Question: What Is Enlightenment?" as the "inability to make use of one's own understanding without direction from another" (8: 35)—lies at the center of his own conception of enlightenment. But freedom and self-rule are not the only fundamental moral values behind what Smith calls "the obvious and simple system of natural liberty" (*WN* IV.ix.51). Included within this system (which is neither obvious nor simple) are also laws of justice. For Smith's endorsement of the view that every man should be "left perfectly free to pursue his own interest his own way" includes the following proviso: "as long as he does not violate the laws of justice" (*WN* IV.ix.51).

Unfortunately, in the *Wealth of Nations* Smith does not elaborate on the nature of these laws of justice. But we can acquire a basic picture of them by looking briefly at relevant passages from some of his other works. For instance, in the *Theory of the Moral Sentiments* (1759), he states clearly his position regarding the overriding importance of justice. Justice "is the main pillar that upholds the whole edifice" of human society. "If it is removed," Smith warns, "the immense fabric of human society . . . must in a moment crumble into atoms." "Society may subsist, though not in the most comfortable state, without beneficence; but the prevalence of injustice must utterly destroy it."[29] In *The Theory of Moral Sentiments* Smith is also prone to describe justice in narrow terms: "Mere justice is, upon most occasions, but a negative virtue, and only hinders us from hurting our neighbour. . . . We may often fulfil all the rules of justice by sitting still and doing nothing" (II.ii.1.9). However, there is also a positive side to the rules of justice. Justice also involves a sense of fair play in social and economic relationships, as determined by Smith's famous concept of the "impartial spectator." If a person is just, Smith holds,

> he would act so as that the impartial spectator may enter into the principles of his conduct. . . . In the race for wealth, and honours, and preferments, he may run as hard as he can, and strain every nerve and every muscle, in order to outstrip all his competitors. But if he should justle, or throw down any of them, the indulgence of the

spectators is entirely at an end. It is a violation of fair play, which they cannot admit of. (*TMS* II.ii.2.2)

In his *Lectures on Jurisprudence* (1762–64), an additional dimension of the laws of justice can be gleaned. Here Smith states that "the end proposed by justice is the maintaining men in what are called their perfect rights," that is, those rights "which we have a title to demand and if refused to compel an other to perform."[30] Each "perfect" right is thus correlative to a second-party "perfect" duty, and it is the government's responsibility to enforce the fulfillment of these duties.

Smith's insistence that the laws of justice must accompany the exercise of commercial liberty finds a parallel in Kant. For again, when Kant asserts the right of each citizen to seek his own welfare "in any way he pleases," he is quick to add the following qualification: "as long as it can subsist along with the freedom of others" (*Universal History* 8: 27). Here too a necessary background of fair play, equality of treatment, and respect for the rights of others is explicitly asserted in presenting the case for freedom of commerce.

But there is a further key area of moral value involved in the system of natural liberty, summarized by Smith as comprising "three duties of great importance, indeed, but plain and intelligible to common understanding" (*WN* IV.ix.51). Each of these three duties falls on the sovereign; they are governmental responsibilities toward citizens. Smith describes them as follows:

> First, the duty of protecting the society from the violence and invasion of other independent societies; secondly, the duty of protecting, as far as possible, every member of the society from the injustice or oppression of every member of it, or the duty of establishing an exact administration of justice; and thirdly, the duty of erecting and maintaining certain publick works and certain publick institutions, which it can never be for the interest of any individual, or small number of individuals, to erect and maintain; because the profit could never repay the expence to any individual or small number of individuals, though it may frequently do much more than repay it to a great society. (*WN* IV.ix.51; cf. V.i.c.1)

Two root assumptions lie behind each of these governmental duties: (1) liberty is part of a larger network of moral values, and (2) the values within this larger network form a hierarchy of values, the highest position of which is *not* always occupied by individual liberty. Smith invokes both assumptions on the rare but notable occasions when he defends protectionist policies. For instance, in discussing the state's duty to defend its citizens against foreign invasion, Smith argues that "when some particular sort of industry is necessary for the defence of the country," it is appropriate for the state to "lay some burden upon foreign, for the encouragement of domestic industry" (*WN* IV.ii.24, 23). His primary example is the Navigation Act of 1660, by means of which British shipping and navigation industries were aided by government policies that imposed a "double aliens duty" on all imported goods that arrived on non-British ships. Smith freely admits that "the act of navigation is not favourable to foreign commerce, or to the growth of that opulence which can arise from it." But he insists that "as defence . . . is of much more importance than opulence, the act of navigation is, perhaps, the wisest of all the commercial regulations of England" (*WN* IV.ii.30; cf. II. V.30, IV.v.a.27, 36). Additional acts of legislation designed to protect other domestic industries deemed necessary for national defense are also justifiable by means of these two assumptions, and they would also override the liberty of commerce.

Under the sovereign's second duty, the administration of justice— "protecting every member of the society from the injustice or oppression of every other member of it"—would create laws dealing with dishonesty, fraud, and violence, as well as regulations dealing with the enforcement of contracts. Here too government regulations designed to promote social justice will sometimes trump the exercise of natural liberty: "Such regulations may, no doubt, be considered as in some respect a violation of natural liberty. But those exertions of the natural liberty of a few individuals, which might endanger the security of the whole society, are, and ought to be, restrained by the laws of all governments; of the most free, as well as of the most despotical" (*WN* II.ii.94).

Finally, government's third duty: erecting and maintaining public works. Smith divides public works into two categories: "those for facilitating the commerce of the society, and those for promoting the instruction of the people" (*WN* V.i.c.2). Under the first category he includes the erection and maintenance of roads, bridges, canals, and harbors; however, a longer list that would include additional items such as transportation systems and communications networks is easily derivable from his definition. Under the second category, as we saw earlier (see chapter 2), Smith argues against state-directed systems of compulsory education but does hold that governments should establish universal education requirements for all citizens as well as assist those individuals who need financial help in obtaining education. Citizens in the new commercial and industrial societies need educational opportunities in order to overcome the dehumanizing effects of the division of labor, to be "less liable to the delusions of enthusiasm and superstition, which, among ignorant nations, frequently occasion the most dreadful disorders," and to become "more disposed to examine, and more capable of seeing through" questionable measures of government (*WN* V.i.f.61).

In Kant's discussions of political economy, we find a stronger emphasis on the need for social welfare provisions than we do in Smith. In the *Metaphysics of Morals* he argues that the sovereign has the right

> to impose taxes on the people for its own preservation, such as taxes to support organizations providing for the *poor, foundling homes* and *church organizations*, usually called charitable or pious institutions. . . .
> For reasons of state the government is . . . authorized to constrain the wealthy to provide the means of sustenance to those who are unable to provide for even their most necessary natural needs. The wealthy have acquired an obligation to the commonwealth, since they owe their existence to an act of submitting to its protection and care, which they need in order to live; on this obligation the state now bases its right to contribute what is theirs to maintaining their fellow citizens. (6: 326; cf. 367–79)

Some of these tax funds are to be used to provide income support for the poor, some for state-supported health care systems, other portions for universal public education. While scholars continue to debate the most appropriate way to integrate Kant's views on social welfare with his theory of right, it is clear that he, like Smith, was no champion of the night watchman state.[31]

In sum, another fundamental point of agreement stretching across national boundaries in the Enlightenment involves the moral values behind the defense of commercial society. Liberty is certainly one of these values, but liberty itself is sometimes trumped by principles of social justice and welfare.

International Trade

There is no place in the town which I love so much to
frequent as the Royal Exchange. . . . Sometimes I am
justled among a body of Armenians, sometimes I am
lost in a crowd of Jews; and sometimes make one in a
group of Dutchmen. I am a Dane, Swede, or Frenchman

at different times; or rather fancy myself like the old
philosopher, who upon being asked what countryman he
was, replied that he was a citizen of the world.

—Addison, "The Royal Exchange"

During the Enlightenment many technological improvements contributed
to the growth of trade between nations. In agriculture, new tools and
techniques produced greater efficiency and higher yields; in industry, the
introduction of labor-saving machines increased production rates. New
roads and canals were built to carry the growing trade between countries.
Advances in navigation brought the continents of the earth within regular
and easy reach of each other.[32] But governments were often more concerned with maintaining favorable balances of trade and with accumulat-
ing greater reserves of gold and silver, and they did not always encourage
trade with other nations. The dominant "commercial, or mercantile system" of economic policy, Smith complained, encouraged each nation "to
look with an invidious eye upon the prosperity of all the nations with which
it trades, and to consider their gain as its loss. Commerce, which ought
naturally to be, among nations, as among individuals, a bond of union and
friendship, has become the most fertile source of discord and animosity"
(*WN* IV.iii.c.9).

But it was Hume who first led the charge against the mercantilists'
"jealousy of trade." Unrestricted trade between nations brings mutual
benefits to all parties:

> Nothing is more usual, among states which have made some
> advances in commerce, than to look on the progress of their neigh-
> bours with a suspicious eye, to consider all trading states as their
> rivals, and to suppose that it is impossible for any of them to flourish,
> but at their expence. In opposition to this narrow and malignant
> opinion, I will venture to assert, that the encrease of riches and
> commerce in any one nation, instead of hurting, commonly promotes
> the riches and commerce of all its neighbours.[33]

Foreign trade has a stimulating effect on domestic economies, for once
people are presented with desirable imported goods, they will work harder
to acquire them, merchants will compete harder to bring them in at
affordable prices, and domestic manufacturers will work harder to match
the foreign competition. And when one country's economic situation

improves, neighboring countries are also propelled to work harder, for they will need to develop quality products of their own in order to engage in exchange. Likewise, foreign trade brings lower prices to consumers, while manufacturers benefit from lower prices on imported raw materials needed for production as well as from new markets for their goods. The country as a whole thus becomes richer. The economic advantages of foreign trade, Hume concludes, are so numerous and obvious, that rather than succumb to the petty jealousy of trade, we should rather rejoice in the prosperity of other nations: "I shall therefore venture to acknowledge, that, not only as a man, but as a BRITISH subject, I pray for the flourishing commerce of GERMANY, SPAIN, ITALY, and even FRANCE itself. I am at least certain, that GREAT BRITAIN, and all those nations, would flourish more, did their sovereigns and ministers adopt such enlarged and benevolent sentiments towards each other."[34]

Smith's later defense of free trade between nations owes important debts to claims that Hume makes in his essays on economics. Like Hume, he believes that different countries are by nature better suited to produce different goods and products, and that each country should concentrate on its natural strengths: "If a foreign country can supply us with a commodity cheaper than we ourselves can make it, better buy it of them with some part of the produce of our own industry, employed in a way in which we have some advantage" (*WN* IV.ii.12).[35] Similarly, Smith, like Hume, holds that free trade benefits not only consumers (by lowering prices), but also man- ufacturers. Manufacturers can import raw materials not available in their home countries, thus expanding their own operations and producing more goods. On the other hand, constraints on trade create higher prices, restrict the expansion and diversity of manufacturing (thus reducing the number of jobs), and also enable monopolies to develop for those goods that cannot be imported.

But behind these familiar economics- and efficiency-based arguments in defense of free trade lie *moral* arguments. Restrictions on trade are the result of paternalistic policies toward citizens—cases where government leaders treat people like children. Such policies are not only inefficient, Smith holds, they are also morally wrong: "To give the monopoly of the home-market to the produce of domestick industry, in any particular art or manufacture, is in some measure to direct private people in what manner they ought to employ their capitals, and must, in almost all cases, be either a useless or a hurtful regulation" (*WN* IV.ii.11). In addition to their objec- tionable paternalism, restrictions on trade are also morally wrong simply because they are unfair. They are examples of policies intentionally designed to benefit one group of citizens at the expense of another: "To hurt in any degree the interest of any one order of citizens, for no other purpose but to promote that of some other, is evidently contrary to that justice and equality of treatment which the sovereign owes to all different orders of his subjects" (*WN* IV.viii.30). It is not only consumers in the home country who are treated unfairly, but citizens of other countries as well: "To promote the little interest of one little order of men in one country, it hurts the interest of all other orders of men in that country, and of all men in all other countries" (*WN* IV.vii.c.60).

However, insofar as Hume and Smith both display occasional protectionist thinking, they also both raise moral concerns *against* free trade. Hume, for instance, in "Of the Balance of Trade," writes, "All taxes, however, upon foreign commodities, are not to be regarded as prejudicial or useless. . . . A tax on GERMAN linen encourages home manufactures, and thereby multiplies our people and industry. A tax on brandy encreases the sale of rum, and supports our southern colonies."[36] And Smith acknowledges that in certain small countries it will "sometimes be necessary to restrain the exportation of corn" (*WN* IV.v.b.39), that a moderate export "tax of five, or even of ten shillings" on wool is justifiable in Britain (*WN* IV.viii.31), and even that "subjecting all foreign manufactures to . . . moderate taxes" is justifiable (*WN* V.ii.k.32).[37] In other words, "the liberal system of free exportation and free importation" (*WN* IV.v.b.39) was never envisioned as an entirely free and unregulated market.

But the push for less restrictive trade polices between nations came not only from within the Scottish Enlightenment. In France, the physiocrats (from the Greek *phusis* and *kratos*, "rule of nature"), were also ardent campaigners for economic liberty. Although Smith rejected several key assumptions in the physiocrats' program, he was certainly sympathetic to founder François Quesnay's conviction that "complete liberty of trade should be maintained."[38] The Americans were also enthusiastic supporters of free trade. Benjamin Franklin, strongly influenced by his reading of Hume's "Jealousy of Trade," praises both the civilizing influences of free commerce between countries as well as its economic benefits:

> It seems a laudable wish, that all the Nations of the Earth were connected by a knowledge of each other, and a mutual exchange of benefits: but a Commercial Nation particularly should wish for a general Civilization of Mankind, since Trade is always carried on to much greater extent with People who have the arts and Conveniences of Life, than it can be with naked Savages.

I have seen so much Embarrassment and so little Advantage in all the Restraining and Compulsive Systems, that I feel myself strongly inclin'd to believe, that a State, which leaves all her Ports open to the World upon equal Terms, will, by that means, have foreign Commodities cheaper, sell its own Productions dearer, and be on the whole more prosperous.[39]

Jefferson, in his *Report on the Privileges and Restrictions on the Commerce of the United States in Foreign Countries* (1793), showed that he had read Smith well:

Instead of embarrassing commerce under piles of regulating laws, duties, and prohibitions, could it be relieved from all its shackles in all parts of the world, and could every country be employed in producing that which nature has best fitted it to produce, and each be free to exchange with others mutual surplusses for mutual wants, the greatest mass possible would then be produced of those things which contribute to human life and human happiness; the numbers of mankind would be increased, and their condition bettered.[40]

But the most enthusiastic American encomium to free trade between nations is Thomas Paine's. In part II of *The Rights of Man* (1792) he writes,

In all my publications, where the matter would admit, I have been an advocate for commerce, because I am a friend of its effects. It is a pacific system, operating to cordialize mankind, by rendering nations, as well as individuals, useful to each other.... If commerce were permitted to act to the universal extent it is capable, it would extirpate the system of war, and produce a revolution in the uncivilized state of governments. The invention of commerce has arisen since those governments began, and is the greatest approach towards universal civilization that has yet been made by any means not immediately flowing from moral principles.[41]

Here we find the ultimate moral argument behind the multiple Enlightenment campaigns for free trade: commerce not only civilizes people, "operating to cordialize mankind"; if universalized, it will eventually "extirpate the system of war" and bring world peace.

A key component in the Enlightenment claim that commerce would lead to peace was the critique of colonization and empire building. The desire to build up colonies was itself a major cause of war, and defenders of free trade attacked the cause in the hope that the effect would be less likely to appear. As usual, they deployed a mixture of both economic and moral arguments. Colonies are not cost-effective, Smith and others pointed out: "They have been a source of expence and not of revenue to their respective mother countries" (*WN* IV.vii.c.13).[42] And the very practice of colonization is unjust: it involves taking what does not belong to oneself and treating other people as means rather than ends. Examine Europe's commercial undertakings in Africa or in Asia, Condorcet noted, and you will witness a "murderous contempt for men of another color or creed."[43] No nation, Kant argued, has the right to found a colony by force: "Settlement may not take place by force but only by contract." Nor may Europeans use dishonest contracts in order "to found colonies by fraudulent purchase of their land, becoming owners of their land, making use of our superior force without regard for their first possession" (*Morals* 6: 353, 266). Ultimately, however, the Enlightenment hope that commerce would lead to peace rested on more than the critique of colonization and empire. Commerce, by civilizing people and creating bonds of union and friendship, would literally change people's characters. Over time, people would become less violent and destructive, less hateful and distrustful.

The commerce–peace connection was stressed by many Enlightenment authors, and certainly did not begin with Paine. English writer Nicholas Barbon, in his *Discourse of Trade* (1690), one of the best-known early tracts for freedom of trade, writes, "Another Benefit of *Trade*, is, That, it doth not only bring Plenty, but hath occasioned Peace."[44] Similarly, Montesquieu, in *The Spirit of the Laws* (1748), declared that "commerce is a cure for the most destructive prejudices" and that "peace is the natural effect of trade" (I.xx.1, 2; cf. 20). But the most famous and influential example is Kant. In *Toward Perpetual Peace* (1795), he predicts that the spirit of commerce "sooner or later takes hold of every nation" and "cannot coexist with war" (8: 368). War disrupts commerce and the economic as well as noneconomic benefits associated with it. Eventually, people will realize that their desire for the latter is stronger than their desire for the former, and they will demand that their government promote foreign policies that reflect this desire.

As is well known, Kant's linking of international commerce with world peace is part of a larger teleological story. On his view, "nature guarantees perpetual peace through the mechanism of human inclinations itself" (*Peace* 8: 368). Like Smith and other Enlightenment authors, he is convinced that social progress is often the unintended result of the actions of self-interested individuals. But in Kant's case, the main motor for progress is not an invisible hand but "the mechanism of human inclinations itself," or what he calls our "unsociable sociability" (*ungesellige Geselligkeit*): a bidirectional innate disposition that leads us both to associate with each other (sociability) but also to compete and fight against each other (unsociability). However, as a result of the latter,

> all talents come bit by bit to be developed, taste is formed, and even, through progress in enlightenment, a beginning is made toward the foundation of a way of thinking which can with time transform the rude natural predisposition to make moral distinctions into determinate practical principles and hence transform a *pathologically* compelled agreement to form a society finally into a *moral* whole. (*Universal History* 8: 21)

The activity of commerce—though driven by individuals' self-interested desires to better their own financial positions—nevertheless gradually forces enlightenment and, eventually, peace upon the peoples of the world. In asserting that the spirit of commerce itself gradually helps force enlightenment, Kant too endorses a version of Hume's proclamation that "*industry, knowledge,* and *humanity,* are linked together by an indissoluble chain." However, Kant extends the chain still further: world peace itself is an outcome of the growth of commerce and enlightenment. And in predicting that the spirit of commerce "sooner or later takes hold of every nation," he joins Smith, Franklin, Paine, and others in envisioning an expanding force that acts "to a universal extent" in drawing people closer together. All of this is part of "a hidden plan of nature" (*Universal History* 8: 27), albeit one that we also have "a duty to work toward" (*Peace* 8: 368).

4

....

Politics

Nationalism

Enlightenment thinkers are often accused of being blind to the significance of nationalism. According to philosopher Jonathan Glover, "The thinkers of the Enlightenment did not see the importance of... the contribution national loyalties make to our psychology"; historian Robert Darnton claims that Enlightenment philosophes refused "to respect boundaries, either of disciplines or of nations," and that "no one" in the Enlightenment Republic of Letters "conceived of the idea of nationalism."[1] Similarly, political theorist John Gray calls nationalism "easily the most powerful political phenomenon in the contemporary world" and touts it as yet another sign that the Enlightenment project is now exhausted and irrelevant.[2] But whether one examines political documents,[3] political events, or political philosophy from the Enlightenment, I believe the evidence supports the counterhypothesis that "nationalism was invented in the eighteenth century."[4] In the following discussion I excavate this underexplored

side of Enlightenment thought by analyzing a number of nationalist statements in Enlightenment political thought. While it is true that the most
ardent voices of late eighteenth-century nationalism are themselves not
always viewed as friends of the Enlightenment, this categorizing tendency
is itself partly a reflection of the question-begging assumption that the
Enlightenment is opposed to nationalism. At any rate, I shall also show
later that even the most canonical supporters of the Enlightenment themselves embraced a fundamentally nationalist message.

Rousseau

Rousseau's defense of nationalism is tied to his influential theory of sovereignty. In his view, "A legitimate political order must be based on the
general will, which is to say on the sovereignty of the people who compose
it."[5] Sovereignty resides not in monarchs or other political rulers but in the
people themselves. The former are merely representatives of the latter. As
he states in his *Discourse on Political Economy* (1755), "The first and most
important maxim of legitimate or popular government, that is to say, of a
government that has the good of the populace for its object, is . . . to follow
the general will in all things."[6] And in order for the general will to prevail,
the individual wills of citizens must conform to it as much as possible: "Do
you want the general will to be accomplished? Make all private wills be in
conformity to it" (171). The best way to promote this conformity to the
general will, in turn, is by *amour de la patrie*: love of the fatherland, patriotism. "Love of country is the most effective" means toward this goal (173),
and those cosmopolitans who assume that there somehow exists an infinite
supply of this *amour* that can then be spread limitlessly in all directions are
mistaken:

> The sentiment of humanity evaporates and weakens in being extend-
> ed over the entire world . . . we cannot be affected by the calamities in
> Tartary or Japan the way we are by those of a European people.
> Interest and commiseration must somehow be limited and restrained
> to be active. For since this inclination in us can be useful only to those
> with whom we have to live, it is a good thing that the humanity
> concentrated among fellow citizens takes on a new force through the
> habit of seeing each other and through the common interest that
> unites them. It is certain that the greatest miracles of virtue have been
> produced by the love of country. (173)

But what are the proper boundaries of the nation toward which citizens are to express their amour? What is a nation, and what are its identifying characteristics? In some of his writings, Rousseau toys with assigning this role to familiar material markers such as language and culture. In the opening sentence of his *Essay on the Origin of Language*, for instance, he writes, "Speech distinguishes man among the animals; language distinguishes nations from each other."[7] Similarly, in his sketch of human development in the *Second Discourse* (1755), he notes that human beings "slowly came together and united into different bands, eventually forming in each country a particular nation, unified by mores and characteristic features, not by regulations and laws, but by the same kind of life and foods and by the common influence of the climate" (143).

In both passages Rousseau implies that nations are prepolitical and exist long before the founding of civil society. However, his considered view is that nations are predominantly political, for these early prepolitical national groupings are fundamentally transformed and continuously shaped and molded by subsequent political factors.[8] Ultimately, national identity stems primarily from political influences and only secondarily from nonpolitical ones. This explicitly political conception of nationhood is highlighted in two short related essays, *Constitutional Project for Corsica* (1765) and *Considerations on the Government of Poland* (1772). In the former, Rousseau writes, "The first rule to be followed [in nation building] is the principle of national character; for each people has, or ought to have, a national character, if it did not, we should have to start by giving it one."[9] As an island that shares no borders with other countries, Corsica is relatively undistorted by foreign influences. Here nation builders can and should build upon the secure foundation provided by prepolitical influences such as language, culture, and food. However, people in less isolated countries of Western Europe are not so lucky; their distinctive national characters are being diluted and slowly erased by the homogenizing effects of international commerce. In the essay *Government of Poland*, Rousseau sounds an early warning against cultural globalization: "Today, no matter what people may say, there are no longer any Frenchmen, Germans, Spaniards, or even Englishmen; there are only Europeans. All have the same tastes, the same passions, the same manners, for no one has been shaped along national lines by peculiar institutions" (168). Nation builders in these countries cannot rely simply on prepolitical cultural factors but must adopt stronger measures in order to shape and sustain national character. In *Poland*, he warms up to this theme by referring collectively to "national institutions": "It is national institutions which can shape the genius, the character, the tastes, and the manners of a people; which give it an individuality of its own; which inspire it with that ardent love of country, based on ineradicable habits" (168). The primary institution on which he focuses is education. As we saw earlier (see chapter 2), Rousseauian education, unlike Kantian, is designed to serve nationalistic rather than cosmopolitan purposes: "It is education that must give souls a national formation, and direct their opinions and tastes in such a way that they will be patriotic by inclination, by passion, by necessity" (172). All subjects taught—literature, history, geography, government, even technology and science—are to be imbued with the same nationalistic slant:

> At twenty, a Pole ought not to be a man of any other sort; he ought to be a Pole. I wish that, when he learns to read, he should read about his own land; that at the age of ten he should be familiar with all its products, at twelve with all its provinces, highways, and towns; that at fifteen he should know its whole history, at sixteen all its laws; that in all Poland there should be no great action or famous man of which his heart and memory are not full, and of which he cannot give an account at a moment's notice. (172–73)

To ensure that citizens' souls receive the proper national formation, the state must strongly regulate all aspects of education: "The law ought to regulate the content, the order, and the form of their [viz., students'] studies" (173). And the teachers themselves must be not only moral exemplars but also committed nationalists: "They ought to have only Poles for teachers: Poles who are, if possible, married; who are all distinguished by moral character, probity, good sense, and attainments" (173).

At the same time, it should be noted that the nations Rousseau wants people to build are to be small, nonaggressive, nonexpansionist—indeed, isolationist—in character. To make Poles love their country, for instance, he advises Polish legislators to instill in citizens "a natural repugnance to mingling with foreigners" (170). Above all, legislators must avoid "the radical defect" of overreaching. The best states are always small states:

> The size of nations, the extent of states: this is the first and principal source of the misfortunes of the human race, and above all of the innumerable calamities that sap and destroy civilized peoples. Practically all small states, no matter whether they are republics or monarchies, prosper merely by reason of the fact that they are small; that all the citizens know and watch over one other; that the leaders can

see for themselves the evil that is being done, the good they have to do; and that their orders are carried out before their eyes.... Only God can govern the world; and it would require more than human capacities to govern great nations. (174)

It is for these reasons that some commentators have protested that Rousseau "did not advocate nationalism as we know it now, definitely not."[10] Clearly, most post-Rousseauian nations have not followed his advice to "keep it small." But his stress on both the importance of national character and the means of shaping it has certainly been heeded by nearly all subsequent nationalists.

Herder

Rousseau's nationalism is traditionally contrasted to Herder's, the former being tagged political nationalism, the latter cultural. With Rousseau, as we saw, national character is shaped primarily by political factors. Love of country is the outstanding expression of belonging to the nation, and a key legislative task is to promote those social and political institutions that will help instill the requisite amour de la patrie in citizens. Herderian cultural nationalism, on the other hand,

> considers the nation an organic unity whose supreme expression is the national culture—particularly the national language. For this sort of nationalism, politics is not an essential expression of the nation but only a means for ensuring independent and creative cultural expression in cases where the culture and the language are threatened. According to this conception, politics is a means rather than an end. The culture, rather than the manifestations of political will, is the focus of national identity.[11]

However, this contrast between Rousseauian political and Herderian cultural nationalism can be and has been overdone. Again, for Rousseau linguistic and cultural aspects of national identity do play significant roles. To give souls a proper national formation, citizens must be educated in the specific literature and history of their homeland, and legislators must strive to preserve their country's national customs. Similarly, to de-politicize Herder's nationalism is a mistake.[12] Isaiah Berlin, for instance, in attempting to make Herder more palatable to contemporary readers, insists that Herder's "national feeling was not political and never became so," that his "nationalism was never political," and that "nationality for him is purely and strictly a cultural attribute . . . he is interested, not in nationality but in cultures."[13] This is simply false. Herder does explicitly link nationality with self-government. In his *Letters for the Advancement of Humanity* (1793–97), for instance, he writes, "The *happiness of one single people* cannot be imposed on, talked onto, loaded onto the other and every other. The roses for the wreath of *freedom* must be picked by a people's own hands and grow up happily out of its own needs, out of its own desire and love."[14] And Herder's message of national liberation did find "a ready response among those cultural minorities of Europe struggling for political independence from long-established empires"[15]—not to mention cultural minorities outside of Europe. Furthermore, Herder views politics as an integral part of human life: "The human race has never been without government; it is as natural to it as its origin and as the grouping together of its members within families. As soon as there is a family there is a form of government."[16]

Herder's linking of nationality with self-government means both that he is opposed to imperialist ventures and that he wants each political state to express one (and only one) unique national character. Intermixing of nationalities must be avoided. In his *Ideas for a Philosophy of History of Humanity* (1784–91), he writes,

> The most natural state is . . . *one* nation [*ein Volk*], an extended family with one national character. . . . For a nation is as natural a plant as a family, only with more branches. Nothing, therefore, is more manifestly contrary to the purpose of political government than the unnatural enlargement of states, the wild mixing of various races and nationalities [*die wilde Vermischung der Menschen-Gattungen und Nationen*][17] under one sceptre. . . . Such states are but patched-up contraptions, fragile machines, appropriately called state-*machines*, for they are wholly devoid of inner life, and their component parts are connected through mechanical contrivances instead of bonds of sentiment. Like Trojan horses these machines are pieced together . . . they are bereft of national character . . . lifeless monstrosities.[18]

Herder's organic model of politics and nationhood does not sit well with modern realities of multiethnic states. On his view, all efforts to build multiethnic nations are "doomed from the very outset."[19] His advice to the cultural minorities who reside within the artificial boundaries of such "lifeless monstrosities" is to secede and form their own autonomous nation-states.

But although Herder's nationalism is clearly not apolitical, it remains the case that it is primarily cultural and only secondarily political. Consider first his concept of "nation": "Every distinct community is a *nation*, having its own national culture as it has its own language."[20] For Herder, nations are defined first and foremost as linguistic and cultural entities. And each nation is a natural, organic entity ("a nation is as natural a plant as a family"), whose borders are not to be reconfigured by human meddlers: "Whom nature separated by language, customs, character, let no man artificially join together by chemistry."[21] Within each national organism there is an inherent, unique, creative power, the expression of which is its indigenous culture. And each national culture is to be preserved, valued, and respected on its own terms: "All comparison is unprofitable," because "each nation has its centre of happiness within itself."[22] Like Rousseau, Herder also fears a future in which a single global culture has smothered local traditions. In *Yet Another Philosophy of History* (1774), he protests against "the so-called Enlightenment and culture of the world" as envisioned by cosmopolitan intellectuals:

> "Ways of living and mores!" How wretchedly primitive was the age in which nationality and national character still existed; and, with it, hatred and hostility towards the foreigner, self-centered parochialism, prejudice, attachment to the soil where one was born and in which one was buried; a native mentality, a narrow span of ideas—eternal barbarism! With us, thank God, national character is no more! We love each and every one, or rather, we can dispense with love; for we simply *get on* with one another, being all equally polite, well-mannered and even-tempered. To be sure, we no longer have a fatherland or any kinship feelings; instead, we are all philanthropic citizens of the world. The princes speak French, and soon everybody will follow their example; and, then, behold, perfect bliss: the golden age, when all the world will speak one tongue, one universal language, is dawning again! There will be one flock and one shepherd! National cultures, where are you?[23]

Second, Herder's approach to politics itself is essentially cultural. He is no friend of artificial "state-machines": they are "lifeless monstrosities," inherently dehumanizing. And because Herder thinks government is as natural as the family ("as soon as there is a family there is a form of government"), he has no need for political theory abstractions such as the social contract and sovereignty. In *Ideas for a Philosophy of History* he writes,

> Since we are told by the political scientist that every well constituted
> state must be a machine regulated only by the will of one, can there
> conceivably be any greater bliss than to serve in this machine as an
> unthinking component? What, indeed, can be more satisfying than to
> be whirled round all our lives on Ixion's wheel, contrary to our better
> knowledge and conscience, with no comfort other than that of being
> relieved of the exercise of our free and self-determining mind in order to
> find happiness in functioning as insensible cogs in a perfect machine?[24]

As others have noted, ultimately Herder's own political vision is closer to
the communitarian anarchism of a Proudhon or Kropotkin.[25]

However, as was also the case with Rousseau, there are tenable
aspects of Herder's nationalism that distinguish it from later darker nationalisms. Again, he is adamantly opposed to "the unnatural enlargement of
states": no state has the right either to impose itself on minority ethnic
groups within its boundaries or to engage in acts of aggression against
neighboring peoples. Herder's nationalism is a liberal nationalism based on
the universal right to national self-determination.[26]

There is also an important internationalist dimension to Herder's
political thought, albeit one that differs in several respects from liberal
Enlightenment cosmopolitanism. In his view, the future world envisioned
by certain Enlightenment intellectuals—a world in which everyone has
become a philanthropic citizen of the world but in which no one belongs to
a fatherland or has any kinship feelings—would be an unnatural world of
"paper-culture."[27] At the same time, he is strongly committed to principles
of national diversity and mutual recognition. Each nation has its own
unique contribution to make to human history, based on its own specific
national character. In *Ideas*, he summarizes the "principal law" that he
believes is operative in history as follows: "*Everywhere on our earth, that which
can be will come to be, partly in keeping with the location and needs of the place, partly
according to the circumstances and opportunities of the time, partly in line with the innate
or developing character of the peoples.*"[28] For Herder, the flourishing of ethnically
and culturally diverse national communities is itself a necessary part of the
realization of the ideal of humanity (*Humanität*). In *Letters Concerning the
Advancement of Humanity*, he asserts that we do not bring humanity "with us
ready-made into the world; but, in this world, it is to be a goal of our
strivings, the sum of our endeavors.... Humanity is the treasure and the
yield of all human efforts."[29]

Humanität for Herder denotes a collective human achievement, the
end point of human history, a process in which the development of diverse

national characteristics plays an integral role. We are to regard the earth itself "as a garden, where here the one and there the other human national plant... [flowers] in keeping with its own formation and nature."[30] As Ergang notes, "Each national plant has its allotted place in this garden and also its characteristic beauty and its peculiar fragrance."[31] For Herder, achieving Humanität thus involves not the overcoming of nationalism but rather a process that can be realized only in and through free organic national development. And again, it is not possible to rank the different cultural contributions of nations on a single scale:

> Let one have no pet tribe, no favorite people on the earth....In that period when everything was taking form, nature developed the form of the *human type* as manifoldly as her workshop required and allowed....The original form, the *prototype of humanity* hence lies not in a single nation of a single region of the earth; it is the abstracted concept from all exemplars of human nature in both hemispheres. The *Cherokee* and the *Huswana*, the *Mongol* and the *Gonaqua*, are as much letters in the great word of our species as the most civilized Englishman or French-man....The culture of humanity...shoots forth everywhere.[32]

However, in the final analysis Herder's vision of international politics as a peaceful garden of flourishing national plants "cannot be described as other than exceedingly naïve."[33] He offers no specific proposals for resolving conflicts among nations because he thinks properly constituted nations never fight each other: "Cabinets may deceive each other, political machines may be moved against each other until the one blows the other to pieces. *Fatherlands* do not move against each other in that way; they lie peacefully beside each other, and support each other as families."[34] But families have of course been known to fight each other, and peace among nations cannot be secured through a faulty argument by analogy.

Fichte

Fichte rounds out the trinity of late eighteenth-century authors who are traditionally regarded as founding fathers of modern nationalism. But caution needs to be exercised when calling him a defender of nationalism. First of all, at least in his early writings, we often find explicit affirmations of cosmopolitanism and negative assessments of patriotism and nationalist sentiment. In *The Vocation of Man* (1800), for instance, Fichte declares, "It is the vocation [*Bestimmung*] of our species to unite itself into one single body, all the parts of which shall be thoroughly known to each other, and all possessed of similar culture."[35] Similarly, in *Some Lectures Concerning the Scholar's Vocation* (1794), when discussing man's vocation in society, he defines "society" simply as "the relationship in which rational beings stand to one another," and then proceeds to describe the state merely as a transitional tool to be used to further the ends of society: "The state is ... only a *means for establishing a perfect society*, a means which exists only under specific circumstances. Like all those human institutions which are mere means, the state aims at abolishing itself. *The goal of all government is to make government superfluous.*"[36] And in *A Contribution toward Correcting the Public's Judgment of the French Revolution* (1793), he implies that most people (sovereigns and professional geographers excluded) do not take questions of nationality seriously:

> You fear for us the subjection by a foreign power, and to secure us against this misfortune, you prefer to subject us yourselves? Do not be so confident that we regard the situation in the same way you do. It is easy to believe that you prefer to subject us yourselves than to leave it to somebody else; but what we cannot understand is why we should prefer it so much.... Do you think that the German artisan and peasant are very much interested whether a Lorrainese or Alsatian artist and peasant from now on finds his town or village in the geographic handbooks in the chapter on the German Reich and no longer in the chapter on France, and that he will throw away his chisel and his plow to see this brought about?[37]

Second, in the early 1800s, when Fichte begins to praise nations rather than to condemn them, he still does not ascribe any intrinsic value to them. Rather, he views nations instrumentally as culture carriers, and temporary ones at that. One nation carries the cultural torch for a while, and then passes it on to another. The fate of individual nations themselves is of no vital concern; what matters is the growth and spread of human culture. In his lectures on the *Characteristics of the Present Age* (1804–5) he asks,

> What is the fatherland of the truly educated Christian European? In general it is Europe, in particular it is in each age that European state which stands at the height of culture.... Let the earth-born, who accept the soil, the river, and the mountain as their fatherland, remain citizens of the fallen state; they retain what they wanted and what makes them happy: the sun-loving spirit will be drawn irresistibly and

will turn to where light and justice exist. And in this cosmopolitan understanding [*in diesem Weltbürgersinne*] we can remain perfectly calm about the actions and fates of states, for ourselves and for our descendants, to the end of time.[38]

Fichte's "cosmopolitan patriotism"—his view that particular nations have value as temporary promoters of culture and human perfection, and that one should strive to help one's nation contribute toward this universal goal and take pride in it when it does so (in effect, an early version of "think globally, act locally")—was expressed most succinctly in the first of his *Patriotic Dialogues* (1806). The interlocutor designated as B states,

> Cosmopolitanism is the will that the purpose of life and of man be attained in all humanity. Patriotism is the will that this purpose be attained first of all in that nation of which we are members, and the wish that this light may radiate from this nation over all mankind.... Every dominant will... can only become active in its surroundings.... Thus every cosmopolite necessarily, through his limitation by a nation, becomes a patriot.

He continues a bit later:

> The patriot desires that humanity's goal be reached first of all in that nation of which he is a member. In our times that goal can be promoted only by science [*Wissenschaft*]. Thus science and its widest possible dissemination in our time must be the immediate goal of humanity, and no other goal can or should be set for it.... Only the German can desire this, because only he, through his possession of science and the given capacity of understanding it, can know that this is the immediate goal of humanity. This goal is the only possible patriotic one. Thus only the German can be a patriot. He alone, while serving his nation, can work for humanity as well.[39]

Fichte reiterates the same basic message at the conclusion of his better-known *Addresses to the German Nation* (1807–8): "If there is truth in what has been expounded in these addresses, then are you [Germans] of all modern peoples the one in whom the seed of human perfection most unmistakably lies, and to whom the lead in its development is committed."[40] The German people are humanity's best hope. In these *Addresses*—public lectures delivered in Berlin when the city was occupied by Napoleon's troops, at a time when Germany was not yet a unified state but only a loose confederation of principalities—several Herderian themes appear, the most fundamental of which is the connection between language and nationality. For both Herder and Fichte, nations are shared language communities, and all such communities have the right to self-governance. Fichte states, "It is true beyond doubt that, wherever a separate language is found, there a separate nation [*Nation*] exists, which has the right to take independent charge of its affairs and to govern itself" (184).

Like Herder, Fichte also views the political machinery of the state merely as a vehicle for the promotion of the nation's culture. His nationalism too is thus more cultural than political: "The state is not something which is primary and which exists for its own sake, but is merely the means to the higher purpose of the eternal, regular, and continuous development of what is purely human in this nation" (125).

Also, both Herder and Fichte define peoples linguistically and culturally rather than racially. On Fichte's view, "We call those human beings whose organs of speech are influenced by the same external conditions, who live together, and who develop their language in continuous communication with each other a people [*ein Volk*]" (49). At the same time, both authors are (linguistic and cultural) segregationists: different *Völker* should not mix with each other. If the distinctive qualities of nations "are dulled by being mixed and rubbed together [*durch Vermischung und Verreibung abgestumpft*], the flatness that results will bring about a separation from spiritual nature, and this in its turn will cause all men to be fused together in their uniform and collective destruction" (198).

Just as Herder opposes the *wilde Vermischung* of different races and nationalities under one scepter and the disappearance of "national cultures," so Fichte rejects the tidings of those writers who proclaim "the new universal monarchy that is beginning" and the "grinding together [*Zerreibung*] of all the germs of what is human in humanity" (198). Both authors advise people to focus on the development of their own specific national culture: "Only when each people, left to itself, develops and forms itself in accordance with its very peculiar quality...then, and then only, does the manifestation of divinity appear in its true mirror as it ought be" (197–98).

One major difference between Herderian and Fichtean nationalism concerns the latter's hierarchical ranking of cultures. Even here, though, Fichte's justification for ranking is itself based on quasi-Herderian speculations concerning the purity levels of different language communities. On Fichte's view, the more foreign words that are incorporated into a given language, the more impure that language becomes. And when a language community uses an impure language, it loses its distinct national identity as well as the ability to make original contributions to culture and science. According to Fichte, the German people "alone, above all other European nations," possesses a pure and uncontaminated language; the Germans alone have "retained and developed the original language of the ancestral stock," while others have "adopted a foreign language and gradually reshaped it" (45, 47). This reshaping leads to cultural atrophy. The German, Fichte holds, "speaks a language which has been alive ever since it first issued from the force of nature"; other European peoples "speak a language which has movement on the surface only but is dead at the root" (58–59; cf. 62). And because the German language is alive, its native speakers are uniquely situated (provided they stay vigilant and maintain their language purity) to make creative and original contributions to human culture. Great poetry, for instance, can be created only from language that is alive: "It is quite impossible for a dead language to have poetry in this higher sense.... Only a living language can have such poetry" (68). Non-Germans, with their impure languages, lack a true culture. "The German spirit, on the other hand, will open up new shafts and bring the light of day into their abysses, and hurl up rocky masses of thought, out of which ages to come will build their dwellings" (73). And so the Germans become an elect people, an *Urvolk*: "Only the German— the original man who has not become dead in an arbitrary organization— really has a people and is entitled to count on one ... he alone is capable of real and rational love for his nation" (111, cf. 107, 92). At the same time, in keeping with the spirit of cosmopolitan patriotism, the Germans' mission is to carry the cultural torch for all of humanity: their endeavors "will be characterized by a spirit that is not narrow and exclusive, but universal and cosmopolitan" (99).[41]

But who is a German? One of the more curious contradictions in the *Addresses* occurs in the following passage:

> Whoever believes in spirituality and in the freedom of this spirituality, and who wills the eternal development of this spirituality by freedom, wherever he may have been born and whatever language he speaks, is of our kind [*ist unsers Geschlechts*]; he is one of us [*es gehört uns an*], and will come over to our side. Whoever believes in stagnation, retrogression, ... wherever he may have been born and whatever language he speaks, is non-German, and a stranger to us. (108)

Throughout most of the lectures, Germans are identified by their native language and homeland; they are people "whose organs of speech are influenced by the same external conditions, who live together, and who develop their language in continuous communication with each other" (49). But in the preceding passage they are identified simply by their love of "spirituality" and their commitment to its spreading. Employing these latter identity criteria make it easier for many people to be Germans, and also provides some support for the claim "that Fichte is not a prophet of *völkisch* German nationalism."[42] But because he has also violated "the most fundamental of all principles,"[43] the principle of contradiction, ultimately Fichte's theory of nationalism falls apart.

Humean, Kantian, and Other Enlightenment Nationalisms

Rousseau, Herder, and Fichte are the most familiar and ardent eighteenth-century advocates of nationalism. But to marginalize their message (as many do) by labeling it simply as a Counter-Enlightenment or proto-Romantic protest against mainstream Enlightenment political thinking is a mistake. Most Enlightenment intellectuals, their reputations as cosmopolitans notwithstanding, defended principles of state sovereignty and self-determination.[44] Indeed, the tensions between nationalist and cosmopolitan commitments were not generally evident to them, for they saw no conflict between love of country and love of humanity. The following remark by Andrew Vincent concerning Kant also holds generally for the majority of Enlightenment authors: "Kant's apparent cosmopolitanism is not, in itself, anti- or post-nationalist. Despite Kant's subsequent cosmopolitan reputation, nationalism, in its first European blush (before it had colonized European states), was not perceived to be anti-cosmopolitan. This was something that liberal nationalists, from Mazzini to the present day, have always tried to trade on."[45]

To be sure, the fervent appeals to linguistic and cultural nationalism that one finds in Rousseau and especially Herder and Fichte are not as evident in other Enlightenment writers. A clear contrast here is Hume, who holds that "a nation is nothing but a collection of individuals," and who conceives of nation-states as arising from "the accidents of battles, negociations, and marriages."[46] For Hume, the nation-state is "a necessary but strictly utilitarian political device" for the efficient distribution of justice, not an organic unity resting on shared language and culture. As he announces at the beginning of his essay "Of the Origin of Government," "We are, therefore, to look upon the vast apparatus of our government, as having ultimately no other object or purpose but the distribution of justice.... Kings and parliaments, fleets and armies, officers of the court and revenue, ambassadors, ministers, and privy-counsellors, are all subordinate in their end to this part of administration."[47]

Still, it is important to take note of these more moderate Enlightenment nationalisms. The most significant case is Kant, who for many is the exemplar of Enlightenment cosmopolitanism. At the conclusion of *Theory and Practice* (1793), he does express hope that "a universal state of nations" (*ein allgemeiner Völkerstaat*) will be ushered in (8: 313). But by the time *Perpetual Peace* appears in 1795, he has dropped his commitment to the idea of a world republic and replaced it with that of "the *negative* surrogate" of a voluntary league of sovereign nations (8: 357). Independent states, he now warns, "are not to be fused into a single state" (8: 354). The most plausible explanation for this shift lies in Kant's explicit conviction, articulated at the beginning of *Perpetual Peace*, that states are themselves inherently moral and legal persons possessing the right to autonomy.[48] The Second Preliminary Article for perpetual peace, for instance, is essentially an autonomy of states principle, and holds that "no independently existing state (whether large or small) shall be acquired by another state through inheritance, exchange, purchase or donation" (8: 344). In his comment on this article, Kant writes, "For a state is not (like the land on which it resides) property [*eine Habe*] (*patrimonium*). It is a society of human beings that no one other than itself can command or dispose of. Like a trunk, it has its own roots; and to annex it to another state as a graft is to do away with its existence as a moral person and to make a moral person into a thing" (8: 344).

Here we are close to precisely the same sort of organic, transcendental talk about the unity of the nation-state (a state "has its own roots") that is traditionally associated with Fichte as well as later nationalists—talk that understandably frightens many. But there are also some key differences. For Kant, a state (*Staat*) is not the same as a nation (*Nation*) or people (*Volk*). A state is not to be identified by linguistic, cultural, or ethnic criteria, but by political ones. In the *Metaphysics of Morals* (1797), he writes, "A *state* (*civitas*) is a union of a multitude of human beings brought under laws of right" (6: 313). According to this view, states come into being through the free consent of their members: "The act by which a people forms itself into a state is the *original* contract" (6: 315).[49] Furthermore, not all peoples form states. Some peoples remain in the state of nature and do not choose to make the crucial transition to the civil state. Such peoples, Kant holds, "do not constitute states, but only tribes" (*Völkerschaften*; 6: 343). Once a sovereign state exists, it possesses moral and legal rights of autonomy. But unless and until a people chooses to form a political union "under laws of right," it does not possess this right.[50]

Kant does appear to regard the terms Volk and Nation as synonyms. This can be gleaned from his discussions of national character in the various versions of his anthropology lectures—material that, as Vincent notes, sometimes "is just deeply cranky."[51] In his own published version of these lectures,

Anthropology from a Pragmatic Point of View (1798), the relevant section is entitled
"Der Charakter des Volks" (7: 311). But in several of the analogous sections
that are recorded in student and auditor transcriptions of Kant's annual
lecture course in anthropology, the word "Nation" (rather than "Volk")
appears. In the *Collins* lectures (1772–73), for instance, the relevant section
is entitled "Vom National Charackter" (25: 232); in the *Menschenkunde* (1781–
82), "Charackter der Nationen" (25: 1181); and in *Mrongovius* (1784–85),
"Capitel vom Character der Nationen" (25: 1398). In still other anthropology
transcriptions, "*Völker*" rather than "*Nationen*" appears in the section title, for
example, *Parow* (1772–73; 25: 450) and *Friedländer* (1775–76; 25: 654). Finally,
even in his own 1798 *Anthropology*, Kant moves casually from subheads like
"Die französische Nation" (7: 313) to "Das englische Volk" (7: 314).

However, for Kant (and here he differs from Rousseau, Herder, and
Fichte) *Volks/Nationalcharakter* is not primarily a cultural phenomenon.
Rather, it lies deeper within biology. In *Friedländer*, for instance, he states
that the determination of a people's character "must not be taken from
contingent matters, for example, from religion." Rather, that which is
"uniform, which has yet remained an essential component among all the
variations of the people, must be picked out. That which is characteristic
refers here to what is *distinctive* in regard to the mind of the entire people"
(25: 654–55). Similarly, in the 1798 *Anthropology*, he refers to the national
character of England and France as being "innate" (*angeboren*) and "unchangeable" (*unveränderlich*; 7: 312).[52]

The United States of America—"the world's greatest artificial nation,"
but also the one that "has the most vivid personality, and the greatest ability
to inspire love and hatred among those who encounter it"[53]—is often put
forward as the paradigm of political or civic nationalism. Here we find a
nation formed by commitment to shared political ideals rather than common
descent, language, religion, or culture. This artificial nation arose largely
because America was from the start a melting pot that drew in people from
different countries. In his *Letters from an American Farmer* (1782), French-born
author J. Hector St. John Crèvecoeur (speaking through the fiction of
"Farmer James" of Pennsylvania) writes,

> What then is the American, this new man? He is neither an European,
> or the descendant of an European: hence that strange mixture of
> blood, which you will find in no other country. I could point to you a
> family, whose grandfather was an Englishman, whose wife was Dutch,
> whose son married a French woman, and whose present four sons have
> now four wives of different nations. He is an American, who, leaving

behind him all his ancient prejudices and manners, receives new ones from the mode of life he has embraced, the new government he obeys, and the new rank he holds. He becomes an American by being received in the broad lap of our great *Alma Mater* [fostering mother]. Here individuals of all nations are melted into a new race of men, whose labours and posterity will one day cause great changes in the world.[54]

Enlightenment intellectuals associated with the founding of the United States such as Jefferson, Franklin, and Paine were themselves strong supporters of this civic nationalism. Jefferson, for instance, in a letter to Joseph Priestley of June 19, 1802, writes, "It is certain that written constitutions may be violated in moments of passion or delusion, yet they furnish a text to which those who are watchful may again rally and recall the people; they fix too for the people the principles of their political creed."[55] Similarly, Paine, in the last number of *The American Crisis*, notes, "Our citizenship in the United States is our national character. Our citizenship in any particular state is only our local distinction. By the latter we are known at home, by the former to the world. Our great title is AMERICANS—our inferior one varies with the place."[56]

Along with this appeal to shared political ideals as a way of grounding nationalism went a defense of the universal right of emigration. Membership in a nation-state was to be an act of individual choice, not the result of linguistic, cultural, or ethnic identity. Franklin, in *On a Proposed Act to Prevent Emigration* (1773), asks, "God has given to the Beasts of the Forest and to the Birds of the Air a Right when their Subsistence fails in one Country, to migrate into another, where they can get a more comfortable Living; and shall Man be denied a Privilege enjoyed by the Brutes, merely to gratify a few avaricious Landlords?"[57] Similarly, Jefferson, in *A Summary View of the Rights of British America* (1774), proclaims that British settlers in America "possessed a right which nature has given to all men, of departing from the country in which chance, not choice, has placed them, of going in quest of new habitations, and of there establishing new societies, under such laws and regulations as to them shall seem most likely to promote public happiness."[58]

At the same time, these early American nationalists—like most European Enlightenment nationalists—saw no conflict between cosmopolitan and nationalist commitments. Paine, in his *Letter to the Abbé Raynal* (1782), writes, "The true idea of a great nation, is that which extends and promotes the principles of universal society; whose mind rises above the atmosphere of local thoughts, and considers mankind, of whatever nation or profession they may be, as the work of one Creator. The rage for conquest has had its fashion, and its day. Why may not the amiable virtues have the same?"[59] Paine's nimble prose may seem merely to mask two "radically incompatible" points of view,[60] but he and his compatriots clearly believed that the nationalist ideals they were fighting for were also

> in a great measure the cause of all mankind. . . . The sun never shined on a cause of greater worth. 'Tis not the affair of a city, a country, a province, or a kingdom, but of a continent—of at least one eighth part of the habitable globe. 'Tis not the concern of a day, a year, or an age; posterity are virtually involved in the contest, and will be more or less affected, even to the end of time, by the proceedings now.[61]

Franklin and Jefferson also intentionally echo Paine's language in letters—Franklin declaring " 'tis a Common Observation here [viz., in Paris], that our Cause is *the Cause of all Mankind*"; Jefferson that "it is impossible not to be sensible that we are acting for all Mankind."[62] But in virtue of what was the American cause a universal cause? A key part of the answer lay in the right to self-government, itself the core of every nationalist's creed. Jefferson writes, "Every man, and every body of men on earth, possesses the right of self-government. They receive it with their being from the hand of nature. Individuals exercise it by their single will; collections of men by that of their majority; for the law of the *majority* is the natural law of every society of men."[63]

In sum, contrary to contemporary wisdom, Enlightenment intellectuals *did* deal with difference,[64] and their myriad articulations of nationalism are one indication of this. But while the ideology of modern nationalism was itself born in the Enlightenment, most Enlightenment nationalists saw no conflict between cosmopolitan and nationalist commitments. Their vision of a future in which humanity would be "cosmopolitically united" (Kant, *Anthropology*, 7: 333) was also one in which sovereign nation-states would continue to play an integral role.

Republicanism

Fraud lurks in generals. There is not a more unintelligible word in the English language than republicanism.

—John Adams to Mercy Otis Warren,
August 8, 1807

In conjunction with the growing popularity of the idea of each people's right to self-government, the Enlightenment also witnessed a surge of popular opinion in favor of representative government, popular sovereignty, the rule of law, and the separation of government powers. These ideals were often expressed compactly, if oddly (at least to contemporary ears), under the rubric of "republicanism." And just as the tension between Enlightenment nationalist sentiments and cosmopolitan ideals was considerably softened by the liberal tone of the former, so Enlightenment republicanism, at least in most of its guises, was also made to fit with liberalism. For it was a predominantly liberal republicanism.[65]

Etymologically as well as historically, a republic is simply a political order devoted to the public good. Thus Cicero writes in his *Republic* that "the commonwealth is the people's affair" (*res publica*), and Plato stresses in his *Republic* (*Politeia*) that the ideal commonwealth aims at the happiness not of one particular group within the *polis*, but of the whole.[66] To help ensure that the commonwealth *is* the peoples' affair, political power in a republic must be shared by different groups. But historically, this power-sharing requirement within republics proved to be compatible with different styles of government; in the classical republican model of mixed government, there could be monarchic republics, aristocratic republics, and democratic republics. It was not until the late eighteenth century that republicanism came "to be associated exclusively with the cause of popular sovereignty and majoritarianism, and applied to large commercially-oriented nations (as distinct from the urban polities of the Renaissance or ancient Rome and Greece)."[67]

Montesquieu, in *The Spirit of the Laws*, argued that republican government was suitable only for small states: "It is natural for a republic to have only a small territory; otherwise it cannot long subsist. . . . In an extensive republic the public good is sacrificed to a thousand private views."[68] Rousseau likewise held that the best republic was a small republic. In his *Considerations on the Government of Poland*, for instance, he writes, "The first reform you need is a change in the extent of your country. Your vast provinces will never permit you to enjoy the strict administration of small republics. Begin by contracting your boundaries, if you wish to reform your government."[69] But as larger nation-states became the political norm in the Enlightenment, republican ideology increasingly was applied to them.

For Paine, republicanism was virtually synonymous with representative government. In his discussion in part II of *The Rights of Man* (1792), he begins by echoing Cicero, but soon injects a strongly antimonarchical message:

What is a called a *republic* is not any *particular form* of government. It is
wholly characteristical of the purport, matter, or object for which
government ought to be instituted, and on which it is to be employed,
res-publica, the public affairs, or the public good; or, literally translated, the *public thing*. It is a word of good original, referring to what
ought to be the character and business of government; and in this
sense it is naturally opposed to the word *monarchy*, which has a base
original signification.[70]

While acknowledging that "various forms of government have
affected to style themselves republics," Paine insists that "the government
of America, which is wholly on the system of representation, is the only real
republic in character and practice that now exists."[71] He reaches his
conclusion by a process of elimination, first, by accepting Rousseau's
point that a republic "cannot be extensive on the simple democratic
form" (participatory democracy is not feasible in large states). Next, monarchy is ruled out, for in practice it is humanly impossible for one individual
to possess enough knowledge to understand the public good in an extensive
republic. The aristocratic form of government is in a slightly better position, since power here resides in a group of people rather than in a single
individual. But this option too is defective, for "there is still no security for
the right use and application" of the rulers' abilities. This leaves "what is
now called the representative" as the only remaining form of government
suitable for a modern republic. However, since democracy alone "affords
the true data from which government on a large scale can begin," the
appropriate form of the modern republic will be "representation engrafted
upon democracy."[72] But even Paine's democratic republicanism stopped
short of simple majoritarianism. The will of the majority cannot be allowed
to override the rights of minorities; in a just republic, civil power "cannot be
applied to invade the natural rights which are retained in the individual."[73]

James Madison, in his famous contributions to *The Federalist Papers*
(1788), also accepted the conventional wisdom that participatory democracy "must be confined to a small spot," while urging readers to accept "the
experiment of an extended republic."[74] Like Adams, Paine, and Jefferson,
Madison too criticizes "the extreme inaccuracy with which the term
[republic] has been used in political disquisitions," and then proceeds to
define republics in terms of popular sovereignty and the representative
form of government: "We may define a republic to be . . . a government
which derives all its powers directly or indirectly from the great body of the
people, and is administered by persons holding their offices during pleasure

for a limited period, or during good behavior."[75] Or, as he remarks more tersely in *Federalist* No. 10, "A republic, by which I mean a government in which the scheme of representation takes place."[76]

For Madison, the scheme of representation was more than a technical device for achieving government among large populations. He believed it would also help better articulate the true public interest and "guard against the confusion of a multitude." Elected representatives, he held, would serve to

> refine and enlarge the public views by passing them through the medium of a chosen body of citizens, whose wisdom may best discern the true interest of their country and whose patriotism and love of justice will be least likely to sacrifice it to temporary or partial considerations. Under such a regulation it may well happen that the public voice, pronounced by the representatives of the people, will be more consonant to the public good than if pronounced by the people themselves, convened for the purpose.[77]

But his most famous argument in defense of the scheme of representation is that it would serve as a "cure for the mischiefs of faction." The cure for factions argument stands in tension with the prior "purifier of interests" argument, for behind the former lies a skepticism as to whether *any* human being (regardless of the extent of his or her wisdom, patriotism, and love of justice) can be counted on to articulate and promote the common good. In Madison's view, the civic virtue of classical republicanism is not an attainable ideal for human beings. "By a faction," he writes, "I understand a number of citizens, whether amounting to a majority or minority of the whole, who are united and actuated by some common impulse of passion, or of interest, adverse to the rights of other citizens, or to the permanent and aggregate interests of the community."[78] Unfortunately, the causes of faction are "sown in the nature of man"[79]—we are all fallible beings who act out of self-interest, and in whom reason is a weaker force than passion. So rather than attempt the impossible task of removing the causes of faction, Madison settles on a more manageable second course: controlling its effects. How is the latter to be achieved?

The easiest case is when the faction constitutes a minority. Here it will simply be voted down; the majority will be able "to defeat its sinister views by regular vote."[80] The more difficult case is when the majority itself constitutes a faction. Although an extended republic can offer no strict guarantees against the formation of such a faction (for again, the causes of faction are sown into human nature), it does offer the best defense against majoritarian factions, for the following three reasons: (1) In a large republic, the number of representatives will be smaller in proportion to the number of citizens than in a small one. It is thus less likely that a majority faction will effectively exercise its voice in a large republic than in a small one. (2) Because candidates for office in a large republic will be elected by a greater number of citizens than in a small one, it will be more difficult for corrupt politicians to get elected in the former than in the latter, for they will need to persuade a greater number of voters. (3) The larger the republic, the greater the number of competing interests that are present. In a large republic, it will therefore be more difficult for a majority faction to gain control and stifle minority rights. The competing interest groups will, so to speak, cancel each other out, or at least weaken each other's effectiveness.

Some of Madison's premises are challengeable. In 3, for instance, the sheer size of a republic bears no necessary relation to the number of competing interests present within it. Depending on the circumstances, large populations can be relatively harmonious, small ones acrimonious. But if his arguments are prefaced with a qualification along the lines of "In real life, this is more likely to be the case than not," the conclusions are plausible. Madison no doubt assumed that his readers would insert the necessary qualifications.

In Germany, Kant also was a strong defender of republicanism. His "first definitive article for perpetual peace" reads, "The civil constitution in every state shall be republican" (*Peace* 8: 349). For Kant, a republican state is defined in part as one that rests on the consent of the governed, and one in which citizens themselves ultimately make the laws. Republican regimes hold out the best prospects for peace, he believes, because in such states the consent of the citizens is required in order to declare war, and such consent is not likely to be forthcoming. Ordinary citizens "will be very hesitant to begin such a bad game, since they would have to decide to take upon themselves all the hardships of war (such as themselves doing the fighting and paying the costs of war from their own belongings)" (8: 350).[81]

But there is more to Kantian republicanism than the idea of popular rule. Another key ingredient is the separation of powers. "*Republicanism*," he stresses, "is the political principle of separation of the executive power (the government) from the legislative power" (8: 352). Democracy, as Kant and most Enlightenment authors understood it, lacks this separation of powers and is a form of government in which the same people who make the laws also interpret and apply them. The result is a kind of despotism or mob rule where, in the absence of constitutional safeguards to protect minority rights, the majority is always able to exert its will and (due to human self-interest) may also easily exempt itself from the law.[82] Protection of minority rights is thus a third key element in Kant's conception of republicanism. In the *Metaphysics of Morals*, for instance, he writes, "Any true republic is and can only be a *system representing* the people, in order to protect its rights in its name, by all the citizens united and acting through their delegates (deputies)" (6: 341; cf. 8: 352).[83]

The ideal of the rule of law also forms part of Kant's concept of republicanism. The republican constitution, he holds, "is the only enduring political constitution, in which the *law* itself rules and depends on no particular person. It is the final end of all public right, the only condition in which each individual can be assigned *conclusively* what is his" (*Morals* 6: 341). Ultimately, a republican constitution on Kant's view is the only political constitution that accords with the idea of right, for it alone respects the freedom, equality, and independence of all citizens (see *Theory and Practice* 8: 290; *Peace* 8: 350, 366). As a result, all states have a duty to reform themselves and work toward the achievement of republican ideals. All states "are under obligation to change the kind of government gradually and continually so that it harmonizes *in its effect* with the only constitution that accords with right, that of a pure republic" (6: 340).

....

At least among laypeople, the term "republic" is not much used at present to refer to the preceding constellation of political ideals. It has been super-seded by "democracy"—though using the latter term to refer to the same group of concepts that had earlier been referred to by the umbrella term "republic" is equally as confusing (and even more likely to upset language purists). But once we dig beneath the surface of each term and locate their common referents, the growing popularity over the past two hundred years of the ideals referred to is not hard to fathom.

5

....

International Relations

longside the growing nationalist sentiment and emerging modern
state system of the era, and in response to the most horrific wars
ever witnessed on European soil, scores of Enlightenment authors
responded to the challenge of establishing a peaceful international order.
Broadly speaking, their proposed solutions took one of two basic forms,
though aspects of both forms were often present in specific individual
proposals: first, a *political* strategy, which called on states to form an
international federation, engage in arbitration to settle disputes, and
apply sanctions (including, when necessary, collective military force) to
uphold the federation's decisions; second, a *legal* strategy, which sought
to bring all states under one universal legal order in order to bring war
itself within the bounds of law. In this chapter I examine and evaluate
some of the central Enlightenment examples of each of these two
strategies.

Peace through Federation

Crucé

The most impressive seventeenth-century plan to achieve peace through federation was unfortunately one that did not (and even today does not) attract much attention. In 1623, the French monk Émeric Crucé (ca. 1590–1648) published *Le nouveau Cynée* (The New Cyneas), the first modern proposal to substitute "international arbitration for war as the court of last resort for nations."[1] Crucé's plan was unique for its time in advocating not just a federation of Christian states of Europe, but a federation of all nations of the known world: Persia, China, Japan, the Ottoman Empire, Russia, Morocco, Ethiopia, the East and West Indies were all invited to join. Additionally, he proposed that the "Sultan of the Turks" be given first rank in the world council under the purely formal chairmanship of the Catholic pope—ahead of all the sovereigns of Europe.[2]

Crucé's project also stands out among its seventeenth-century peers in advocating peace as a primary goal rather than as a side effect of political ambition. F. H. Hinsley writes,

> The principal feature of the *Nouveau Cynée* is that it did not advocate peace solely or primarily as the by-product of the solution to some political problem—the launching of a crusade, the defence of Europe against the Turk, the reconstruction of a new Empire. It conceived of political advantages as being the consequence of establishing peace. The political advantages it had in mind were the growth of religious toleration, the freedom and expansion of world trade, the abatement of poverty, the reduction of taxation, as well as the consolidation of the power of the prince; and by peace it meant universal peace.[3]

Behind Crucé's proposal lay the simple but sincere ideal of a common humanity, a belief that all human beings are "men like ourselves, formed in the same mould, and by the same workman, capable of reasoning, and of the moral virtues that can make them worthy of friendship and admiration, if one does not allow one's self to be prejudiced by obstinacy and presumption."[4] If we could successfully disclose this fact of common humanity and separate it from the distorting influences of politics, religion, local traditions, race, and ethnicity, we would then realize that universal peace is obtainable:

Why should I, a Frenchman, wish harm to an Englishman, a Spaniard, or a Hindoo? I cannot wish it when I consider that they are men like me, that I am subject like them to error and sin and that all nations are bound together by a natural and consequently indestructible tie, which ensures that a man cannot consider another a stranger. . . . I will say the same as regards the religions which so arouse men's passions, and set them against one another, so that when a Christian meets a Jew or a Mohammedan, he thinks he is contaminated by their presence and imagines he sees a demon.[5]

Critics may complain that the way Crucé's world council was to achieve and maintain peace was "unformulated and imprecise,"[6] and everyone may smile at the naïveté of his view of human nature and politics (two criticisms that apply to many of the Enlightenment proposals to be examined). But it is hard not to admire the boldness of Crucé's plan.

Sully

Sully's *Grand Design of Henry IV*, first published in 1638, was—in large part because of its association with the popular king Henry IV of France—a much more influential Enlightenment peace project. Maximilien de Béthune, duc de Sully (1559–1641), was finance minister under Henry, and after the king's assassination in 1610 he retired to work on his memoirs, which he revised several times over the years. The particular version of the *Grand Design* (which Sully attributes to the well-liked king, though he himself is undoubtedly its author) that exerted the most influence constitutes the last chapter of a posthumously published edition of his *Memoirs*, issued in 1745 and edited by the Abbé de l'Ecluse des Loges. Chapter 30 of the 1745 edition of the *Memoirs* is entitled "Wherein is discussed the Political Scheme, commonly called the Grand Design of Henry IV."[7]

In this text, Sully writes ambitiously of the king's plan "of a political system, by which all Europe might be regulated and governed as one great family" (25). The key ingredient in the plan was to be the creation of a "general council, representing all the states of Europe." This general council, Sully explained, would consist of a "certain number of commissaries, ministers, or plenipotentiaries from all the governments of the Christian republic, who were to be constantly assembled as a senate, to deliberate on any affairs which might occur; to discuss the different interests, pacify the quarrels, clear up and determine all the civil, political, and religious affairs of Europe, whether within itself or with its neighbours" (42). Additionally, each member state would be required "to contribute, in proportion to their several abilities, towards the support of the forces and all the other incidental expenses which the success of such an enterprise might require" (34).

The provincialism of Sully's Eurocentric proposal pales in comparison to the global reach of Crucé's earlier plan. But an even graver defect concerns its underlying political motives. Empire rather than peace was the ultimate goal. As Leibniz noted, "One can suspect him of having the overthrow of the House of Austria more in view than the establishment of a society of sovereigns."[8]

Penn

English Quaker and founder of the colony of Pennsylvania, William Penn (1644–1718) also put forward a proposal for a European federation of peace. In his 1693–94 work, *An Essay towards the Present and Future Peace of Europe by the Establishment of an European Dyet, Parliament, or Estates,* Penn proposed that the "Sovereign Princes of Europe" agree "to meet Yearly, or once in Two or Three Years at farthest," to create a "Sovereign Assembly" before which "all Differences depending between one Sovereign and another, that can not be made up by private Embassies" would be adjudicated. Furthermore, if any of the sovereigns of Europe

> shall refuse to submit their claim or Pretensions to them, or to abide and perform the Judgment thereof, and seek their Remedy by Arms, or delay their Compliance beyond the Time prefixt in their Resolutions, all the other Soveraignties, United as One Strength, shall compel the Submission and Performance of the Sentence, with Damages to the Suffering Party, and Charges to the Soveraignties that obliged their Submission.[9]

Like Sully (whose plan influenced his; see n. 9), Penn proposed an international federation confined to Christian Europe, a federation whose members would agree to enter arbitration to resolve their differences, and one that included sanctions for noncompliance. However, Penn's proposal was clearly superior to Sully's insofar as the "search for peace was firmly placed above the cause of Christendom against the infidel and above the goal of predominance in Europe."[10] The federation idea was now invoked as a means toward the goal of peace, rather than as a way to shift the European balance of power in France's favor. Unlike Sully, Penn was not intent on recasting the political map of Europe; rather, he respected the existing boundaries of sovereign states. Indeed, he was well aware that the issue of national sovereignty would be a fundamental objection to his proposal for a European parliament. He responded to this objection by arguing that states would "remain as Soveraign at Home as ever they were. Neither their Power over their People, nor the usual Revenue they pay them, is diminished" (13).

Saint-Pierre

The most well-known peace through federation tract of the early eighteenth century—one that influenced many later proposals, including Kant's—was Charles Irénée Castel de Saint-Pierre's (1658–1743). Influenced by Sully's *Grand Design* but unaware of both Crucé and Penn, Saint-Pierre based the first edition of his work, *Mémoire pour rendre la paix perpétuelle en Europe* (1712),[11] in part on his own experience as secretary to the French diplomat Melchior de Polignac at the complicated negotiations that resulted in the Treaty of Utrecht (1713), a process involving eleven separate treaties that finally brought the twelve-year War of the Spanish Succession to an end. Despite widespread ridicule and opposition, Saint-Pierre continued to seek acceptance of his position for years to come. In 1713 a revised, two-volume edition was printed at Utrecht under the title *Projet pour rendre la paix perpétuelle en Europe.*[12] A third volume was added in 1717 under the title *Le Projet de traité pour rendre la paix perpétuelle entre souverains chretiens.* In 1729 Saint-Pierre published his *Abrégé du Projet de Paix Perpétuelle*, and in 1738 a new edition appeared.[13]

Saint-Pierre begins the 1712 *Mémoire* with the following observation: "Having seen with my own eyes... all the evils that war causes... I resolved to investigate the original sources of the evil... by ascertaining whether or not it was possible to find practical ways to end all their [viz., Europe's] future disputes *without declaring war*, and thereby establishing permanent peace between them" (356–57). His chief proposal for ending disputes was "a permanent machinery for arbitration" between all of the European "Christian states," to be created when their sovereigns "sign a treaty of union, and set up a permanent congress." In effect, the congress itself (consisting of one representative from each state, regardless of size) was also to function as the arbitration board. By signing the treaty of union, each member state of the newly created "European Union" also agreed that "each would keep exactly to their mutual agreements, that trade would never be disrupted,... that all future disputes would be ended *without declaring war* through arbitration," and that each would "be satisfied with what they possessed currently" (356–57, 362)—that is, to respect existing geopolitical boundaries. However, if arbitration proved unsuccessful in resolving disputes, collective force would be applied. The proposed congress, he added, must be "ready to use force to restrain the party wishing to renege on his promise" (359); it must be a "*form of association strong enough and determined enough to punish infringements*" (361).[14]

In the 1738 edition of his *Abrégé* Saint-Pierre advocates the same basic scenario, but further details are added. This later version of the *Projet* centers on the signing of a treaty consisting of five articles. Article I requires signatories to respect present geopolitical boundaries as established by "*the latest treaties.*"[15] Article II provides for necessary revenues: financial support for an international army as well as for the maintenance of the permanent congress. "Each Ally shall contribute, in proportion to the actual revenues and charges of his state, to the security and to the common expenses of the grand alliance" (26). Article III spells out a two-step method of dispute resolution. In cases of disputes between states, members must first agree to enter voluntary mediation. If this does not work, the second step is mandatory arbitration. In both cases, members of the congress who are not parties in the dispute are to function collectively as a third party whose responsibility is to resolve the dispute. In signing the third Article, Saint-Pierre notes,

> the grand Allies have renounced, and renounce for ever, for themselves and for their successors, resort to arms in order to terminate their differences present and future, and agree henceforth always to adopt the method of conciliation by mediation of the rest of the grand Allies in the place of the general assembly, or in case this mediation should not be successful, they agree to abide by the judgment which shall by rendered by the Plenipotentiaries of the other Allies permanently assembled. (27)

Article IV provides for the additional deterrent of force, should arbitration fail:

> If any one among the Allies refuse to execute the judgments or the regulations of the grand alliance, negotiate treaties contrary thereto, make preparations for war, the grand alliance will arm, and will proceed against him until he shall execute the said judgments or rules, or give security to make good the harm caused by his hostilities, and to repay the cost of the war according to the estimate of the Commissioners of the grand alliance. (28–29)

Finally, Article V provides for the establishment and modification of agreements between member states. A simple "plurality of votes" is required for new agreements to take effect, whereas "the unanimous consent of all the Allies" is needed to initiate any changes in the five fundamental articles (29).

Though Saint-Pierre's plan still lacked the global scope of Cruce's earlier proposal, it was the most detailed and comprehensive peace through federation project of the early eighteenth century. But while even his most severe critics did not doubt his sincerity, in the end the plan attracted little support. Perhaps the most telling objection was its political naïveté. As Frederick the Great quipped to Voltaire, "The thing is most practicable; for its success all that is lacking is the consent of Europe and a few similar trifles."[16]

Rousseau

Strictly speaking, Rousseau's name does not belong in a discussion of Enlightenment authors who advocated peace through federation. His own nationalist commitments, his preference for small, self-sufficient, and insular political communities, his opposition to cosmopolitanism and cultural globalization—in these and other ways, Rousseau stands apart from liberal Enlightenment views about international relations. But despite his numerous criticisms of Enlightenment peace plans, he was also inadvertently one of their greatest popularizers. For, as it turns out, "Saint-Pierre is largely known second hand: the *Projet de paix perpétuelle* has been almost as a rule read only in the 'extract' prepared by Rousseau."[17]

In book 9 of his *Confessions*, Rousseau relates the story of how he became associated with Saint-Pierre's writings. Although he met briefly with Saint-Pierre "two or three times in his old age," the abbé had been dead more than a decade before Rousseau was invited to undertake the difficult job of editing and condensing "twenty-three volumes, diffuse, confused, full of prolixities, repetitions, and narrow or false views, amongst which it was necessary to fish out some few that were great and lofty, which gave one the courage to endure the painful task."[18] In large part because his own writing style and basic outlook differed so strongly from Saint-Pierre's, Rousseau finally decided "to present the author's and my own ideas separately. . . . My work, therefore, was to be composed of two entirely separate parts. The one was intended to explain . . . the different schemes of the author; in the other, which was not intended to appear until the first had produced its effect, I should have brought my judgment to bear upon these same schemes."[19]

But there was still the thorny problem of what to select from the twenty-three volumes for the special two-prong treatment. Here he notes, "I made my first attempt upon the 'Paix perpétuelle,' the most important and elaborate of all the works which made up the collection."[20] Rousseau's *Abstract* and *Judgment* of *la Paix perpétuelle* were both written in 1756, but they were published over twenty years apart: the *Abstract* in 1761, the *Judgment* posthumously in 1782. However, the differences between *Abstract* and *Judgment* are not always as clear-cut as Rousseau leads readers to believe they would be: he does not always succeed in presenting Saint-Pierre's ideas and his own separately. As C. E. Vaughan notes, when composing the *Abstract* Rousseau "treated his materials with the freest hand.... Except as regards the mere kernel of the Project, there is much more of Rousseau than of Saint-Pierre in the whole statement."[21]

And Rousseau, unlike Saint-Pierre, is no proponent of peace through federation. As he states bluntly in the *Judgment*, "Without doubt, Perpetual Peace is at present an absurd dream."[22] But while his own views on international relations have often been criticized for their inconsistency and lack of detail,[23] several of his own criticisms of Saint-Pierre's plan are telling premonitions of what would later become standard objections to international federation proposals. Near the beginning of his *Judgment*, for instance, he notes that powerful princes will oppose the introduction of a federation of nations and seek to "prevent its establishment" (99; see also 131). Leaders of powerful (and even not so powerful) states view federation schemes as intrusions on national sovereignty—encroachments on the presumed rights of states both to wage war and to be the final judges of their own internal affairs. Even in the *Abstract*, Rousseau observes (without explicitly noting his own disagreements with Saint-Pierre) that for such a federation to achieve its goal of establishing perpetual peace, much stronger incentives both to join the Union and then to adhere to its decisions would be needed than Saint-Pierre and others realized:

> It is necessary that the Confederation should be so general that no considerable Power would refuse to join it; that it should have a judicial tribunal with power to establish laws and regulations binding on all its members; that it should have an enforcing and coercive power to constrain each state to submit to the common counsels.... Finally, ... it should be firm and enduring, so that its members should be prevented from detaching themselves from it at will the moment they think they see their own particular interest running contrary to the general interest. (43)

In other words, a truly effective international federation of peace would need to be one that all states joined, that refused the right of secession, and that had the right (and power) to always compel members to do its collective bidding. But this would require, among other things, that states relinquish their cherished right to national sovereignty.

Finally, in the *Judgment*, Rousseau expresses the straightforward reservation that idealistic plans such as Saint-Pierre's simply don't square with human nature. From both a moral and a rational perspective, he admits, perpetual peace makes sense: "If ever a moral truth was demonstrated, it seems to me it is the general and special utility of this project. The advantages which would accrue to every prince, to every people and to the whole of Europe, from its practical adoption, are immense, obvious, undeniable" (97). But unfortunately, in real life considerations of morality and reason are not what motivate most people to act: "If, in spite of all this, this project is not carried into execution, it is not because it is chimerical, it is because men are crazy and because to be sane in the midst of madmen is a sort of folly" (95).

However, though Rousseau clearly rejects the Enlightenment optimism that forecasts an end to war through the growth of reason and the establishment of an international federation, he suffers no illusions about the nobility of war. When we close the lofty books on law and ethics and look at the world around us, we see "nations groaning under yokes of iron, the human race crushed by a handful of oppressors, . . . fires and flames, the countryside deserted, towns pillaged, . . . a scene of murder, ten thousand butchered men, the dead piled in heaps, the dying trampled under horses' hooves, everywhere the face of death and agony. . . . Whose stomach would not be turned by these sad subjects?"[24] Regrettably, these gruesome scenes have recurred countless times in subsequent years. And still we are no closer to peace.

Kant

The spirit that breathes in the Kantian essay Perpetual Peace *must benefit every friend of justice, and even our most distant progeny will admire in this monument the elevated frame of mind of the venerable sage.*

—Friedrich Schlegel, *Essay on the Concept of Republicanism Occasioned by the Kantian Tract "Perpetual Peace"* (1796)

Much more has been written (especially by philosophers)[25] about Kant's peace through federation proposal than all of the plans discussed thus far. In part, this is because his work on international relations is more multidimensional, enigmatic, and theoretically ambitious than that of his predecessors, thus lending itself to a variety of readings and applications.[26] Although Kant refers briefly to Saint-Pierre and Rousseau several times in presenting his own peace plan (the title of his essay *Toward Perpetual Peace* clearly stems from Saint-Pierre), his casual references leave it unclear as to whether he had actually read any of Saint-Pierre's own versions of the *Projet* or only Rousseau's *Extrait*. In either case, he definitely owes some debts to each author. At the same time, a look at the key differences between Saint-Pierre/Rousseau's peace project and that of Kant will enable us to better appreciate the unique character of the latter. Briefly, the major differences may be summarized as follows.

First, although he occasionally leans (at least *qua* philosopher) toward the even stronger universalism of a world-state,[27] on the whole Kant is a stronger supporter of state sovereignty than are earlier peace through federation advocates. A universal "state of nations" (*Völkerstaat*), though "correct *in thesi*" (*Peace* 8: 357), is neither a realistic nor a desirable option. States are proud of their sovereignty and "do not at all want" to submerge themselves into a single global state; the latter alternative "is still more dangerous to freedom" than the omnidirectional violence that it seeks to replace, since it may lead "to the most fearful despotism" (*Theory and Practice* 8: 311). Thus a voluntary league of nations (*Völkerbund*) is to be preferred over one all-consuming *Völkerstaat*: sovereign states "are not to be fused into a single state" (*Peace* 8: 354; cf. 8: 367).

Second, even though Kant frequently uses phrases such as "league of nations," "federalism of free states," "permanent congress of states," and "association of states" to describe what he is advocating, he in fact offers readers no solid details concerning what form such an organization should take, where and when it would meet, how exactly it would resolve disagreements between members, and so on. As Michael Doyle notes, "Although Kant obliquely refers to various classical interstate confederations and modern diplomatic congresses, he develops no systematic organizational embodiment of this treaty. . . . He appears to have in mind a mutual nonaggression pact, perhaps a collective security agreement, and the cosmopolitan law set forth in the third definite article [of *Perpetual Peace*]."[28] Many readers regard this second difference as an unintentional but obvious weakness. However, Allen Wood argues plausibly that it is in fact a strength resulting from Kant's direct appeal to ordinary citizens: "Kant's project is purely *philosophical*; its articles have an unrestrictedly cosmopolitan intent and are presented as commands of each individual's own reason."[29] Although scholars continue to debate the exact details of Kant's position (a position that itself underwent modifications over time), what he appears to have advocated is the initial establishment of a small, voluntary league of nations without coercive powers ("This league does not aim to acquire any power of the state"; 8: 356), one that would then expand gradually into a stronger worldwide federation of states with at least some coercive authority at the federal level.[30] On this reading, Kant's peace plan is initially much more modest than that of earlier Enlightenment authors, but eventually stronger.

Third, Kant universalizes Saint-Pierre's proposal. He advocates not just a congress of European states, but—eventually—"a *federalism* that should gradually extend over all states" (*sich allmählich über alle Staaten erstrecken*; 8: 356; cf. 357). The global scope of Kant's proposal echoes Cruce's earlier ambitious plan (with which Kant was unfamiliar), but its cautious gradualism distinguishes it from all earlier federation schemes. Here he has a dual aim. First, he is attempting to address the incentive issue raised by Frederick the Great, Rousseau, and many others. Non-member states will *want* to join the federation once they witness the benefits (peace, economic prosperity) that accrue to member states. Second, the gradualism of the plan makes it more viable than its predecessors. The goal is to take some concrete steps "*toward* [*zum*] perpetual peace," not to instantly realize it.

Fourth, in addressing all enlightened citizens of the world rather than simply princes and rulers of Europe, Kant also appeals to universal principles of "cosmopolitan right" (8: 357) that are binding on all human beings collectively. In linking his proposal with principles of international right, he is invoking a second strategy toward peace (see "Peace through Law," below), thereby relieving some of the pressure placed on the first—a federation of sovereign states. In appealing to this second means, he is trying to put traditional natural law theories to new use (even while dismissing Grotius, Pufendorf, and Vattel as "only sorry comforters" whose code "has not the slightest *lawful* force . . . since states as such are not subject to a common external constraint"; 8: 355).

Fifth, there is the famous "republicanism requirement" enunciated in the "first definitive article for perpetual peace": "The civil constitution in every state shall be republican" (8: 349; cf. *Morals* 6: 354). Here as elsewhere, Kant is attempting both to deflate some of the utopianism and to inject some needed psychological realism into peace through federation discussions. By allowing only republican regimes into the federation, peace between member states stands a much better chance of being realized. For

> when the consent of the citizens of a state is required in order to decide whether there shall be war or not (and it cannot be otherwise in this constitution), there is nothing more natural than that they will be very hesitant to begin such a bad game, since they would have to decide to take upon themselves all the hardships of war (such as themselves doing the fighting and paying the costs of the war from their own belongings, painfully making good the devastation it leaves behind, and finally—to make the cup of troubles overflow—a burden of debt that embitters peace itself, and that can never be paid off because of new wars always impending). (8: 350; cf. *Conflict* 7: 90 n.)[31]

In short, wars are much less likely to be started by democracies than by nondemocracies, simply because ordinary citizens will not readily give governments their consent to wage war.

Sixth and finally (and this is the biggest single difference between Kant's peace proposal and its Enlightenment predecessors), there is the overarching philosophy of history in which it is wrapped. Nature itself, he proclaims in *Idea for a Universal History with a Cosmopolitan Aim*, has "as its highest aim a universal *cosmopolitan condition*, as the womb in which all original predispositions of the human species will be developed" (8: 28; cf. *Anthropology* 7: 334, 331). Ultimately, "the guarantee [*Garantie*] of perpetual peace" is "nothing less than the great artist nature (*natura daedala rerum*) from whose mechanical course purposiveness shines forth visibly, letting concord arise by means of discord between human beings even against their own will" (*Peace* 8: 360).

By means of this teleological account of history which posits both a universal cosmopolitan condition and world peace as its end point "whether we will it or not" (8: 365), Kant is able to integrate the political and legal dimensions of his peace proposal within a larger story of human cultural and institutional development—a story that in turn is tied to a specific biological and psychological account of human nature. All of these latter phenomena, he holds, collectively contribute to the formation of the former. At bottom, Kant's philosophy of history is a theory about the movement over time from the necessity of nature to the morality of freedom within the human species—an account of humanity's "external" progress (improvements in visible cultural and social institutions), which itself serves as a preparation for "inner" moral change. History, he holds, concerns "the transition from the crudity of a merely animal creature into humanity, from the go-cart of instinct to the guidance of reason—in a word, from the guardianship of nature into the condition of freedom" (*Conjectural Beginning* 8: 115; cf. *Universal History* 8: 21).

Broadly speaking, Kant's philosophy of history is part of a larger Enlightenment belief in progress. However, his own assumption of progress is not as heavy-handed or naïve as that of other Enlightenment authors. Among other things, he explicitly rejects confident claims of linear progress. For at any moment, humanity may regress: "No one can guarantee that now, this very moment, with regard to the physical disposition of our species, the epoch of its decline would not be liable to occur.... For we are dealing with beings that act freely, to whom, it is true, what they *ought* to do may be *dictated* in advance, but of whom it may not be *predicted* what they will do" (*Conflict* 7: 83).

Kant's recognition that the epoch of our decline may occur at any moment would seem to conflict with his claim that nature *guarantees* the arrival of a cosmopolitan condition and peace. However, his considered view is that the guarantee is somewhat less than ironclad. As he writes in the *Metaphysics of Morals* (1797), perpetual peace is "a task based on duty" (6: 350; cf. *Peace* 8: 368). In earlier texts, he also stresses that human attitudes will need to change before people (especially politicians) will willingly endorse the radical idea of a universal federation of nations. A major portion of the "task based on duty" thus needs to be carried out on the educational front (see *Collins* 27: 470–71).

But to return to "the great artist nature": What are the means of progress, the instruments employed by nature to achieve its goals with respect to the human species? First and foremost, there is our "unsociable sociability," a bidirectional inclination rooted in human nature that leads us both to form associations with one another but also to compete against one another. As a result of human beings' competitive nature, their insatiable desire for power and status,

> all talents come bit by bit to be developed, taste is formed.... Without these qualities of unsociability... all talents would... remain eternally hidden in their germs; human beings, as good-natured as the sheep they tended, would give their existence hardly any greater worth than that of their domesticated beasts.... Thanks be to nature, therefore, for the incompatibility, for the spiteful competitive vanity, for the insatiable desire to possess or even to dominate! For without them all of the excellent natural predispositions in humanity would eternally slumber undeveloped. (*Universal History* 8: 21)

Like Smith, Kant is thus convinced that social progress is often the result of the unintentional behavior of self-interested individuals. But Kant's invisible hand is much larger than Smith's, for human unsociability is held to be the central driving force behind the development of *all* branches of human culture, art, science, and politics—including the hoped-for transformation into a united cosmopolitan condition: "All culture and art that adorn humanity, and the most beautiful social order, are the fruits of unsociability" (*Universal History* 8: 22).

Once Kant's project for perpetual peace is situated within his philosophy of history, both the scope and feasibility of the project increase greatly. Education, religion, the arts and sciences, culture, and commerce are all given strong supporting roles—along with politics, war, and international law—in humanity's progress toward a universal cosmopolitan condition. While earlier Enlightenment writers lack Kant's complex philosophy of history, to the extent that they share his basic views about the important roles that educational, religious, economic, political, and legal reform must play if humanity is to progress morally, they are all ultimately in basic agreement with one another. Kant's philosophy of history is thus itself a bold attempt to systematize and bring theoretical integrity to Enlightenment hopes for humanity's future. And in anchoring his account in "the mechanism of human inclinations itself," he is also trying to provide some empirical assurance for these hopes, "an assurance that is admittedly not adequate for *predicting*" when peace will come, "but that is still enough for practical purposes and makes it a duty to work toward this (not merely chimerical) end" (*Peace* 8: 368).

Both the quantity[32] and the quality of these Enlightenment peace through federation proposals are impressive, albeit underappreciated, achievements—achievements rendered even more extraordinary when one considers the fact that the authors of the proposals often reached their similar conclusions entirely independently of one another. Here as elsewhere, Enlightenment intellectuals were surprisingly unified in their thinking about basic cultural and institutional reform.

Peace through Law

*Throughout the Christian world I observed a lack of
restraint in relation to war, such as even barbarous
races should be ashamed of; I observed that men rush*

*forth to arms for slight causes, or no cause at all, and
that when arms have once been taken up there is no
longer any respect for law, divine or human.*

—Grotius, *The Law of War and Peace*

The second major strategy for achieving peace put forward by Enlightenment intellectuals was primarily a legal rather than a political one, and
involved efforts to bring all states under a single legal order by means of
which states could resolve their differences peacefully. Although not a new
strategy—it builds on the tradition of natural law, a tradition that achieved
its most influential formulation in the late Middle Ages under Aquinas, but
whose roots lie much further back in ancient Greek philosophy[33]—the
peace through law strategy of the Enlightenment is vitally important. At
bottom, it is the story of the birth of international law in the modern sense
of the term.

This second approach is not as directly pacifist as the first, for part of
its mission was to show which wars are sanctioned by the common rules
and which are not—which wars are just, which unjust. However, this
difference, though real, is one of degree rather than kind. For nearly all
the federation proposals examined earlier endorsed war as a way of establishing peace only when other options would not work. Also, the just war
theory associated with the peace through law approach, while certainly not
seeking to abolish war completely (some wars are morally and legally
justified, others are not), does have both a pacifying intent and effect.
Part of its aim in distinguishing just wars from unjust wars is to reduce
the number of wars being fought; conflicts that fall into the latter category
are not sanctioned by international law, and are thus illegitimate undertakings.[34] Both the federation and law approaches share the underlying
assumption that war is to be undertaken only as a last resort, when other
avenues of resolution have failed. War, Grotius admonishes, "*is not to be
undertaken, unless of necessity,*" and it "*is not to be undertaken save from a most weighty
cause at a most opportune time.*"[35] When war is undertaken of necessity, the
principles of *jus in bello*—justice in war—hold that war must never be fought
in such a way as to constitute a greater evil than the evil it was intended to
remedy. Finally, both approaches hold that war is waged so that peace may
be secured (cf. *JBP* III.xxv.2).

The two approaches are also by no means mutually exclusive; aspects
of each strategy were often present in specific proposals. Grotius, for
instance, briefly discusses the role of arbitration, both as a means of

avoiding recourse to war and as a way of facilitating the ending of wars undertaken (*JBP* II.xxiii.8, III.xx.46–48). He also points out that "*war may be obviated by a conference*" (*JBP* II.xxiii.7), an insight Saint-Pierre would later use "as the motto for his *Projet.*"[36] Some of the federation theorists examined earlier also included appeals to international law within their own peace proposals. Kant, for instance, stresses that the idea of a community "of all nations on the earth that can come into relations affecting one another is not a philanthropic (ethical) principle but a principle *having to do with rights*" (*ein rechtliches Prinzip*; *Morals* 6: 352). This appeal to what he calls "*das Weltbürgerrecht (ius cosmopoliticum)*"—cosmopolitan right or "world citizen's law"—is clearly a reference to one type of international law, as is his application of the more traditional *Völkerrecht* (law of nations) in *Perpetual Peace* (8: 354). So the difference between the two approaches, though real, was ultimately one of degree rather than of kind. Each group occasionally employed the tools of the other.

Law of Nature, Law of Nations

In a footnote to *An Introduction to the Principles of Morals and Legislation* (1780), Bentham writes, "The word *international*, it must be acknowledged, is a new one; though, it is hoped, sufficiently analogous and intelligible. It is calculated to express, in a more significant way, the branch of law which goes commonly under the name of the *law of nations*."[37] Bentham's proposal to replace "law of nations" with "international law" did eventually catch on, but the emergence of international law within Enlightenment thought involved not merely the simple replacement of one term by another but rather a rethinking of how the law of nations (*ius gentium*, *droit des gens*, *Völkerrecht*) did or did not fit with the complex tradition of natural law.

Natural law—the belief that there exist rationally ascertainable norms governing the behavior of all people—is essentially a philosophical doctrine that (as is the case with philosophy generally) came increasingly under the wing of theology during the Middle Ages. On the other hand, the origins of our second term, "the law of nations," lie in ancient Roman legal practice rather than in philosophy. In 242 B.C., Rome's increased contacts with foreign powers led to the creation of a new praetor or magistrate position, whose specific charge was to deal with lawsuits involving foreign parties.[38] The body of customary laws governing relations between members of different peoples eventually was referred to as *ius gentium*—in distinction to *ius civile* or civil law, laws that each people has given to itself and that are specific to each community.

Despite the fundamentally different origins of these two bodies of law, over the centuries legal theorists repeatedly drew connections between *ius naturale* and *ius gentium*, primarily because of their shared universal scope. The Roman jurist Gaius, for instance, writes in his *Institutes* (A.D. 161), "Those laws which each people has given itself are peculiar to each city and are called the civil laws [*ius civile*]. . . . But what natural reason dictates to all men and is most equally observed among them is called the law of nations, as that which is practised by all mankind."[39] However, other writers argued that there are fundamental differences between natural law and the law of nations. Francisco Suárez (1548–1618), the last great advocate of the Catholic theory of natural law, while acknowledging that ius gentium "has a close affinity with the natural law,"[40] also held that the two types of law differ in four basic ways. First, the precepts of ius gentium, unlike those of natural law, "are dependent upon the intervention of human free will and of moral expediency rather than that of necessity" (II.xvii.9, cf. II.xix.2). Second, ius gentium, unlike ius naturale, does not forbid evil acts on the ground that they are inherently evil; rather, it "renders acts evil by prohibiting them" (II.xix.2). Third, ius gentium is subject to change in ways that natural law is not: "*Ius gentium* cannot be immutable to the same degree as the natural law" (II.xix.2). And fourth, ius gentium, unlike natural law, "is not observed always, and by all nations, but as a general rule, and by almost all" (II.xix.2). But consensus on this matter was very slow in coming, and positions opposed to Suarez's also appeared later. Hobbes, for instance, though at bottom a radical critic of natural law ("the laws of nature . . . are not properly laws"), also reverted to a position very close to Gaius's when he proclaimed that "the law of nations, and the law of nature, is the same thing."[41]

In short, strong disagreement about the relation between natural law and the law of nations (in addition to discord over the proper definitions of each type of law) was a hallmark of discussion from the very beginning. But this disagreement is itself a primary contributor to the emergence of international law.

Grotius

Although the popular claim that Grotius is "the father of international law" has proved difficult to sustain, what is less debatable is that he was instrumental in developing a distinctively *modern* theory of natural law.[42] Among other things, Grotius was the first Protestant to make a substantial contribution to natural law theory, and this itself is a sign that he succeeded in shifting the discipline away from its more familiar association with Thomist scholasticism. But what makes Grotius's approach to natural law theory modern? Some have pointed to the alleged secularism in his often-cited remark, "What we have been saying would have a degree of validity even if we should concede that which cannot be conceded without the utmost wickedness, that there is no God, or that the affairs of men are of no concern to Him" (*JBP* §11). But as other commentators have noted, this dictum can in fact be traced back to earlier writers, and at any rate Grotius is by no means trying to detach natural law from God.[43] Indeed, he goes on to argue in the very next section that God's existence is presupposed by natural law: "The law of nature of which we have spoken, . . . proceeding as it does from the essential traits implanted in man, can nevertheless rightly be attributed to God, because of His having willed that such traits exist in us" (§12).

A more promising answer lies in the strong emphasis on natural rights that we find in Grotius's conception of natural law. For instance, in addressing the question "What is Law?" near the beginning of *The Law of War and Peace*, he says that one meaning of law refers to "a moral quality of a person, making it possible to have or do something lawfully" (I.i.4). Similarly, in the prolegomena he states that law's "essence lies in leaving to another that which belongs to him, or in fulfilling our obligations to him" (§10). Whether such claims entitle us to infer, as Richard Tuck would have it, that Grotius treated "the law of nature as totally to do with the maintenance of other people's rights" is doubtful.[44] For Grotius emphasizes that this rights-based sense of law is just *one* of several different meanings of law (I.i.3–4). Still, the stress on natural rights does provide an important part of the answer to the question "What makes Grotius's account of natural law modern?" For it gives natural law theory an individualist, liberating element that medieval natural law thought lacks.

Another part of the answer lies in what J. B. Schneewind calls "the Grotian problematic."[45] In his early work *The Law of Prizes* (1606, first published in its entirety in 1864), Grotius employs natural law principles as a means of resolving rights disputes between warring parties of different religions. His basic strategy, also employed later in *The Law of War and Peace*, is to appeal "to certain fundamental conceptions which are beyond question, so that no one can deny them without doing violence to himself" (*JBP*, Pro. §39). The fundamental conceptions appealed to—self-preservation, self-defense, ownership—are ones to which, Grotius argues, even radical skeptics must consent. Whether or not his argument succeeds, the attempt to find ways to maintain social order in the face of conflict—ways that can gain consensus among reasonable people of different religious faiths and political orientations—signals a new understanding of natural law, one designed to fit modern realities.

But what of Adam Smith's claim (which has been repeated by many later writers) that Grotius was "the first who attempted to give the world any thing like a system of those principles which ought to run through, and be the foundation of the laws of all nations"?[46] The degree of systematicity in Grotius's account of the law of nations has been the subject of ongoing debate. In the opening section of the prolegomena, he announces that he intends to treat, "in a comprehensive and systematic manner," "that body of law...which is concerned with the mutual relations among states or rulers of states, whether derived from nature or established by divine ordinances, or having its origin in custom and tacit agreement." Here he implies that the law of nations has three sources: natural law, divine law, and human custom and agreement. But how are these three sources related to one another? Is each an independent source of the law of nations? Are the three sources hierarchically ranked? Which source (if any) is predominant? Grotius does not resolve these fundamental questions.

To further complicate matters, later he does imply that the sole source of the law of nations is consent or agreement. In prolegomena §40, he contrasts "the principles of nature" with "common consent," adding, "The former points to the law of nature; the latter, to the law of nations." This consent-based analysis of the law of nations reappears repeatedly in later parts of *The Law of War and Peace*. At I.i.14, for instance, Grotius states that "the law which is broader in scope than municipal law is the law of nations; that is the law which has received its obligatory force from the will of all nations, or of many nations." And at II.xviii.4, in his discussion of the law relating to embassies, he asserts that the law of nations "does not certainly arise from definite reasons, as the law of nature does, but takes its forms according to the will of nations."

In these passages, Grotius's account of the law of nations echoes Suárez's. Both authors ground the law of nations more in consent, custom, and human choice than in nature or necessity. But not everyone was happy with this softer notion of ius gentium. Jean Barbeyrac, whose 1724 French translation of Grotius's text first brought *De Jure Belli ac Pacis* to the attention of many eighteenth-century readers in Europe (an anonymous English translation of Barbeyrac's edition appeared in 1738),[47] pointedly criticizes Grotius's weaker consent-based account of the law of nations in his own extensive notes that accompany his translation. "Our author," he complains, is committed to a merely "arbitrary law of nations," one that is "basically just a custom observed by a number of nations, although there is no element of obligation *per se* in this custom."[48] States may and do unilaterally renounce customary practices, when perceived necessity or even convenience dictates. Something stronger than the consent of nations is needed to ground the important rights and duties that are the subject of Grotius's study.

But perhaps Grotius does after all provide the stronger foundation that Barbeyrac claims is needed. For like Suárez, he also holds that the primary difference between municipal (or civil) law and the law of nations is that the latter has universal scope (I.i.14; cf. Suárez, II.xix.1). This would seem to make Grotius's law of nations (as Suárez would put it) "human and positive." However, because on Grotius's view municipal law and the law of nations differ by degree only, what he asserts concerning the relationship between natural law and municipal law also applies to the relationship between natural law and the law of nations. In prolegomena §15, he states, "Since it is a rule of the law of nature to abide by pacts . . . out of this source the bodies of municipal law have arisen." Similarly, in prolegomena §16 he writes, "The mother of municipal law is that obligation which arises from mutual consent; and since this obligation derives its force from the law of nature, nature may be considered, so to say, the great-grandmother of municipal law." Thus, on Grotius's view, the law of nature is the source of the law of nations.

In the end, Grotius does want to indicate the origins of the law of nations within natural law to a greater extent than Suárez did. At the same time, he does not elucidate the practical implications of this alleged genealogical relationship between the laws of nature and of nations. In cases of conflict between the two types of law, which one takes priority and why? How distinct is ius gentium from natural law? Grotius does not have clear and consistent answers to these questions.[49] The merit of his claim to be the first writer to treat that body of law "which is concerned with the mutual relations among states . . . in a comprehensive and systematic manner" thus rests more on the detail and wide range of his discussion of ius gentium than to the clarity, originality, or precision of his own conception of international law.

Pufendorf

Samuel Pufendorf (1632–94), another central figure in Enlightenment discussions of natural law, was appointed by Karl Ludwig, elector of the Palatinate, as "the first incumbent of the new chair of the Law of Nature and of Nations" at the University of Heidelberg one year after the publication of his first work, *Elementa Jurispsrudentiae Universalis* (*Elements of Universal Jurisprudence*, 1660).[50] Pufendorf's major work is the enormous *De Jure Nature et Gentium* (*On the Law of Nature and Nations*, 1672, translated into French by Barbeyrac in 1707). A shorter student compendium of its main ideas was published in 1674 under the title *De Officio Hominis et Civis* (*On the Duties of Man and Citizen*).

As concerns the relation between natural law and the law of nations, Pufendorf sides with Hobbes. There is no law among nations except natural law—the same natural law that governs individuals in the state of nature. In *De Jure Nature et Gentium*, Pufendorf cites approvingly from Hobbes's *De Cive* XIV.4, where Hobbes states that the precepts of natural law and the law of nations "are the same." Pufendorf then adds, "To this statement we ... fully subscribe. Nor do we feel that there is any other voluntary or positive law of nations which has the force of a law, properly so called, such as binds nations as if it proceeded from a superior."[51] International law for Pufendorf is thus merely a branch of natural law. However, he also holds (departing here from Hobbes) that sovereign states, regardless of their size or political power, have equal rights in the international area. In the *Leviathan*, Hobbes had argued that individuals are roughly equal in the state of nature "in the faculties of the body, and mind." Pufendorf explicitly transfers this equality in the state of nature from individuals to states:

> Liberty is something that all men have equally who have it at all, and it is not divided into degrees which have equally who have it at all, and it is not divided into degrees which are distinguished by extent and resources. Therefore, although one sovereign's kingdom may stretch out six hundred miles and another's but a hundred, yet the latter holds the same sovereignty in his little realm as the other does in his larger, nor does the latter attain the end of established states any less than the former. (*JNG* VIII.iv.18)[52]

In doing so, he also translates Hobbes's notion of a natural equality of individuals based on physical strength and cunning into a legal equality between sovereign states. Pufendorf's doctrine of the legal equality of sovereign states in turn becomes a central postulate in many later international law documents.

However, when he articulates the character and basis of natural law itself, Pufendorf moves away from Hobbes and toward Grotius. Both

Grotius and Pufendorf place a great deal of weight on sociability as a basic feature of human nature, and hence as a basis of natural law. But in Pufendorf's case, sociability is held not to be inconsistent with self-interest or self-preservation, so that a kind of reconciliation between Hobbes and Grotius is reached. As Pufendorf notes, "It should, first of all, be observed that self-love and a sociable attitude should by no means be opposed to each other, but rather that their tendencies should be restrained in such a way that the latter be not checked or destroyed by the former" (II.iii.16). He brings Hobbesian self-preservation and Grotian sociability together to form the basis of natural law in the following passage:

> It is easy to find the basis of natural law. It is quite clear that man is an animal extremely desirous of his own preservation, in himself exposed to want, unable to exist without the help of his fellow-creatures, fitted in a remarkable way to contribute to the common good, and yet at all times malicious, petulant, and easily irritated, as well as quick and powerful to do injury. For such an animal to live and enjoy the good things that in this world attend to his condition, it is necessary that he be sociable, that is, be willing to join himself with others like him, and conduct himself towards them in such a way that, far from having any cause to do him harm, they may feel that there is reason to preserve and increase his good fortune. (II.iii.15)[53]

Pufendorf's commitment to sociability renders his conception of the state of nature and its laws quite un-Hobbesian. On his view, "Man cannot avoid inclining naturally to peace ... the natural state of men, even when considered apart from commonwealths, is not one of war, but of peace" (II.ii.9). Additionally, Pufendorf's natural laws are not Hobbesian principles of prudence that are "not properly laws" but rather dictates of reason that are to be understood as commands issued by a supreme sovereign—a sovereign whose existence all "men of discernment" acknowledge:

> If these dictates of reason are to have the force of law, there is need of a higher principle. ... It must, therefore, under all circumstances be maintained that the obligation of natural law is of God, the creator and final governor of mankind, who by His authority has bound men, His creatures, to observe it. And this assertion can be proved by the light of reason. Inasmuch as it has long been established by men of discernment ... we now assume that God is the maker and controller of this universe. (II.iii.20)[54]

Still, many resisted the "naturalist" position that the law of nations was merely a division of natural law, in part because of its counterintuitive implications. Pufendorf had tried to show that all legitimate precepts actually observed among nations are deducible from natural law. But this led him to conclude that significant examples of what are commonly regarded as international law don't count as law at all. Regarding treaties, for instance, he wrote, "Special agreements of two or more peoples, usually defined by leagues and agreements of peace . . . do not properly fall under the term of laws. . . . They no more form part of law than do agreements between individual citizens belong to the body of their civil law" (II.iii.23). This conclusion was roundly rejected by the next wave of Enlightenment natural law theorists.

Rachel and Zouche

In opposition to Pufendorf, Hobbes, and others who viewed the law of nations simply as a branch of natural law were those who held that there exists "a distinct Law of Nations, clearly marked off from the Law of Nature."[55] These so-called positivists[56] argued that the law of nations itself constitutes an independent type of law based simply on custom and agreements between states, one not reducible to either civil or natural law. In developing a view of international law that rested on actual state practice, they were able both to sidestep interminable debates about the definition and details of natural law as well as to anticipate later developments in international relations theory.

The most prominent exponent of the positivist position was Samuel Rachel (1628–91), a professor of the law of nature and of nations at the University of Kiel who also served briefly as a diplomat in the service of the Duke of Schleswig-Holstein-Gottorp. In his *De Jure Naturae et Gentium Dissertationes* (*Dissertations on the Law of Nature and of Nations*, 1676), Rachel strongly criticizes both Hobbes and Pufendorf. His attack on Hobbes is global ("Never, I must confess, have I lighted on any writer who has put before the world views more foolish or more foul"; I.cix), but part of his rage is reserved for Hobbes's denial that there exists a distinct law of nations independent of natural law: "The classification of Hobbes, who holds that one kind of Natural Law is of Men and the other of States, the latter being commonly called Law of Nations, is obviously inept" (II.xciv). Similarly, in critiquing Pufendorf, Rachel accuses him of being nothing more than "a slave to his hypothesis, which is that there is no Law of Nations" (II.cii).

In presenting his own contrasting position in defense of the independent status of the law of nations, Rachel acknowledged an explicit debt to the earlier writings of Richard Zouche (1590–1660):

> This view has also the support of the English jurist Richard Zouche, who, in his book entitled *Jus inter gentes* (part I, § I), makes the Law of Nations twofold: one part he derives from a common assent; and of the other he says, "Furthermore, besides common customs, anything upon which single nations agree with other single nations, for example by compacts, conventions, and treaties, must also be deemed to be law between nations." (II.xii)

Zouche, Regius professor of civil law at Oxford, focused on what he called "law *between* nations" (*ius inter gentes*) as opposed to the "law *of* nations" (*ius gentium*). In his book *Iuris et Iudicii Fecialis, sive, iuris Inter Gentes, et Quaestionum de Eodem Explicatio* (*An Exposition of Fecial Law and Procedure, or of Law between Nations, and Questions concerning the Same*, 1650), from which Rachel cites at II.xii, Zouche defines law between nations as "the law which is observed in common between princes or peoples of different nations."[57] The traditional term "law of nations," Zouche adds, is ambiguous, and can refer either to law between nations or civil laws that are common to a plurality of nations. Rachel, somewhat confusingly, follows Zouche's stress on law between nations, but in doing so he also holds on to the traditional term "law of nations."

In arguing for his view that there is "a distinct Law of Nations, clearly marked off from the Law of Nature," Rachel begins (II.xc) by citing the central opposition texts (Hobbes, *De Cive* XIV.4; Pufendorf, *De Jure Naturae et Gentium* II.iii.23),[58] and then launches his own defense. First, he argues that the law of nations, though not promulgated by a supersovereign who keeps states in awe, nevertheless deserves to be called law. The agreements of sovereigns themselves constitute a legitimate source of law:

> Although I freely grant to Pufendorf that the Law of Nations does not issue in the form of laws of the sort that are decreed by a superior, yet the Law of Nations does not for that reason fall to the ground. Granted that, according to the received mode of speech, Law especially means a rule of human conduct imposed by a law-giver upon his subjects, still pacts are not on that account to be barred from all Law, and not even from Law properly so called. . . . Even if, then, one free Nation is not the superior of another, and one can not lay down

Law specially so called for another, yet if they choose to bind themselves by pacts, they are reciprocally bound just as if by true Law.
(II.xci)

Second, he accuses his opponents of confusing the remote and proximate causes of obligations to obey rules. In the case of civil law, the proximate
cause is the will of the sovereign; in the case of pacts, the proximate cause is
"the free will and consent of the parties thereto" (II.xcii). However, in both
cases the remote cause of the obligation to obey can be tracked to "the
following rules of Natural Law: Obedience must be rendered to the Civil
Majesty, and to law-givers issuing just and regular enactments; Good faith
must be observed" (II.xcii). If one ignores proximate causes and refers only
to remote causes, then even civil law disappears, and only natural law
remains—an absurd conclusion. Furthermore, Hobbes and those who
follow him are guilty of a glaring inconsistency when they define civil law
in terms of its proximate cause of obligation, and then refuse to extend the
same courtesy to pacts between sovereigns.[59]

Finally, Rachel submits that we also

have the proof—and none better or stronger can be had—afforded
by the confession of so large a number of Nations that never hesitate
to appeal to a Law of Nations. For whenever one of them complains
that it has been injured by another, the question is debated not always
of an infringement of the Law of Nature, but of the Law of Nations.
What folly it would be, then, for those who appeal to a Law of
Nations, and who claim that they and others are bound by its
obligation, to try to deny its operation. (II.xcvii)

The Law of Nations exists as an obvious empirical fact: states appeal to
treaties and custom constantly in trying to resolve international disputes.
To deny its existence is absurd.

Still, when all is said and done, Rachel does acknowledge the force of
Hobbes's infamous claim that "where there is no common power, there is
no law." To remedy this defect in his own program, he proposes a world
court. States, Rachel suggests, should

erect of their own motion, by common agreement, a College of
Fecials[60] wherein, as a necessary first step, controversies which have
arisen between States should be cognized and argued and decided, in
such sort that nothing save necessity would open the way to war, it

being undertaken only against those who have declined to obey a judgment rendered, or who in other ways have shown contumacy towards the authority and decrees of this College. (II.cxix)

In proposing the creation of a College of Fecials (one whose "utility would be unsurpassed"; II.cxix) to help enforce the law of nations, Rachel thus links his own project to a key ingredient found in many of the peace through federation proposals discussed earlier.

Wolff

In the mid-eighteenth century, Christian Wolff (1679–1754) developed a conceptually ambitious theory of international law that represents an important middle position between the naturalism of Pufendorf and the positivism of Rachel. In his 1749 work *Jus gentium methodo scientifica pertractatum* (*The Law of Nations Treated According to a Scientific Method*), Wolff argued that international law originates in the law of nature, but then develops a life of its own. There is on his view a "natural" or "necessary" law of nations, which was "originally nothing except the law of nature applied to nations."[61] But because "the nature of a nation is not the same" as that of a human individual (§ 3R), the principles of the law of nature do not always apply to nations in the same manner in which they apply to individuals. Natural law, to a certain extent, "can be changed by the act of nations voluntarily" (§ 3R). By means of the distinction between *necessary* and *voluntary* laws of nations, Wolff is thus able both to ground his theory of international law within traditional natural law doctrine as well as to leave space for its subsequent development outside of natural law. And by means of the additional contrast between *stipulative* and *customary* laws of nations, he is able to extend his treatment of international law outside of natural law still further. For unlike necessary and voluntary laws of nations, these latter two types of international law are both particular as opposed to universal: they rest merely on the explicit or even tacit consent of individual nations that have made agreements with one another.

Wolff's treatise on the law of nations was originally intended as a supplement to his eight-volume work, *Jus naturae, methodo scientifica pertractatum* (*The Law of Nature Treated According to a Scientific Method*, 1740–48), and was written after his triumphant return to the University of Halle, following an eighteen-year exile at the University of Marburg. His attempt to treat international law "according to a scientific method" means, among other things, that in comparison with other Enlightenment natural law theorists, he is not terribly concerned either with previous works in legal theory or with actual legal practice. As he writes toward the end of his preface, "We do not follow the mass of jurists.... We admit as true only what is inferred as a necessary consequence from previous conclusions, but we do not invent doubtful principles.... The method by which we have determined to present the law of nature and nations and which we use in our philosophy... requires truth without colouring and childish conceit."[62]

Like Hobbes, Wolff begins from a hypothetical state of nature, applying the law of nature to individuals and states alike. However, his conception of natural law is quite un-Hobbesian. Like Pufendorf and Grotius, Wolff stresses the drive toward sociability and mutual assistance within human nature; additionally, his own commitment to perfectionism in ethics strongly influences his views regarding the purpose of human society: "The purpose of natural society, and consequently of that society which nature herself has established among men, is to give mutual assistance in perfecting itself and its condition ... consequently the promotion of the common good by its combined powers" (§ 8).[63]

A key element in Wolff's theory of international law is his famous hypothesis of the *civitas maxima*, the universal state that is made up of all nations: "All nations are understood to have come together into a state, whose separate members are separate nations, or individual states" (§ 9). The civitas maxima is understood to have been formed by a "quasi-agreement" (§ 9R) analogous to the social contract by which particular *civitates* or states are formed. And just as each state develops laws with respect to the things that concern its citizens, so the purpose of the civitas maxima is to promote the common good of all nations by means of cooperation under rules that express their joint will and consent: "The laws of the supreme state likewise ought to prescribe the means by which its good is maintained" (§ 11).

All states are moral equals in the civitas maxima: "By nature all nations are equal the one to the other.... Just as the tallest man is no more a man than the dwarf, so also a nation, however small, is no less a nation than the greatest nation. Therefore, since the moral equality of men has no relation to the size of their bodies, the moral equality of nations also has no relation to the number of men of which they are composed" (§ 16, 16R).

And because all members are moral equals, the form of government adapted by the civitas maxima is to be a democratic one employing the simple principle of majority rule (§ 19, 20). Adherence to the principle of majority rule implies also that "some sovereignty over individual nations belongs to nations as a whole" (§ 15). But how (in 1749) could one actually determine the majority will of all nations? Because "all the nations scattered throughout the whole world cannot assemble together, as is self-evident, that must be taken to be the will of all nations which they are bound to agree upon, if following the leadership of nature they use right reason" (§ 20). The majority will of nations is thus to be inferred from principles of natural law in accordance with right reason, also taking into account the nature and purpose of the supreme state.

Finally, a hypothetical ruler of the civitas maxima must also be assumed, one who is to be considered as reflecting the will of all nations "following the leadership of nature" and in accordance with "the right use of reason" (§ 21). The voluntary law of nations, which is common to all nations, is thus to be understood as that law which reflects the will of an imagined world sovereign, who in turn represents the presumed collective will of the majority of member states (cf. § 22). But (again) this universal voluntary law of nations must also be distinguished from both stipulative and customary laws of nations, both of which rest on particular agreements between states.

Wolff's civitas maxima is thus thoroughly hypothetical—a philosophical construct reflecting (what he believes is) the internal logic of international law. Unlike, say, Saint-Pierre, he is not putting forward a proposal for the actual reconstruction of the political world. Both the universal state and its ruler are expressly acknowledged to be fictions. But as Wolff also notes, "Fictions are advantageously allowed in every kind of science, for the purpose of eliciting truths as well as for proving them" (§ 21R). Accordingly, the employment of such fictions constitutes an integral part of Wolff's own scientific method. Commentators who view Wolff either as striving toward "the realization of the Law of Nations" or as arguing that nations must as a matter of fact form "some kind of global political entity"[64] fail to recognize the fundamental role of advantageous fictions in his system.

Vattel

Finally, Emerich de Vattel (1714–67), a Swiss jurist and diplomat, whose influential 1758 work *Le Droit du Gens, ou Principes de la Loi Naturelle, appliqués à la Conduite et aux Affaires des Nations et des Souverains* (*The Law of Nations, or the Principles of Natural Law, applied to the Conduct and to the Affairs of Nations and of Sovereigns*) represents the last major Enlightenment contribution to the natural law tradition. In his preface, Vattel gives pride of place to Wolff. "This great philosopher," Vattel declares, is the only theorist to have correctly grasped how and why "the precepts of the natural law with respect to individuals ought, by reason of the character of that very law, to be changed and modified when being applied to States. . . . Hence he concluded that the Law of Nations should be treated as a distinct system, a task which he has successfully performed."[65] To support his claim, Vattel then cites a lengthy passage from the beginning of the preface to Wolff's *Jus gentium methodo scientifica pertractatum*, where Wolff states that while "the Law of Nations is certainly connected with the Law of Nature," because "the nature and essence" of nations differ from that of individual human beings, the Law of Nations is thus "not the same at all points as the natural law" that "controls the actions of individuals" and therefore requires "a separate treatment as being a law peculiar to Nations" (7a). Following Wolff, Vattel views international law as being rooted in natural law. But (also in agreement with Wolff) because states are inherently different from individuals, he holds that once natural law is applied to nations, it takes on a life of its own.

Vattel's debts to Wolff are thus considerable. Indeed, in his preface he states that at first his goal was merely to serve as a popularizer of Wolff's complex system (here he may well have had Barbeyrac's treatments of Grotius and Pufendorf in mind). "I resolved," he writes, "to facilitate for a wider circle of readers a knowledge of the brilliant ideas contained in" Wolff's work and to make his theory "accessible to cultured people in a more attractive form" (7a–8a). But after several attempts, he concluded, "If I was to reach the circle of readers I had in mind I should have to compose a new work quite different from the one before me" (8a). The book that Vattel actually did write should thus not be construed merely as a popularization of Wolff's theory of international law, but rather as a work that, though based on the definitions and general principles first presented by "that great master," "the noted philosopher of Halle" (8a), aims to make an original contribution to the law of nations.

How then does Vattel's own theory differ from Wolff's? In his preface, he notes three disagreements. First, in a nod to the growing republican spirit of the age, he rejects Wolff's endorsement (see Wolff, § 871, 982) of patrimonial kingdoms—territorial units inherited from one's father: "I do not even acknowledge the term, which I consider at once revolting, untrue, and dangerous in the effects it may produce upon the minds of sovereigns" (8a). Second, he rejects Wolff's position that "it is not by nature illegal to use poisoned bullets or arrows" to destroy an enemy in time of war (§ 878). "This conclusion," Vattel protests, "shocks me and I deeply regret finding it in the work of so great a man" (9a).

The third and most fundamental disagreement concerns Wolff's derivation of the voluntary law of nations from the hypothesis of the civitas maxima. Vattel writes,

> From the outset it will be seen that I differ entirely from Mr. Wolff in the foundation I lay for that division of the Law of Nations which we term *voluntary*. Mr. Wolff deduces it from the idea of a sort of great republic (*Civitas Maxima*) set up by nature herself, of which all the Nations of the world are members. To his mind, the *voluntary* Law of Nations acts as the civil law of this great republic. This idea does not satisfy me, and I find the fiction of such a republic neither reasonable nor well enough founded to deduce therefrom the rules of a Law of Nations at once universal in character, and necessarily accepted by sovereign States. It is essential to every civil society (*Civitas*) that each member should yield certain of his rights to the general body, and that there should be some authority capable of giving commands, prescribing laws, and compelling those who refuse to obey. Such an idea is not to be thought of as between Nations. Each independent State claims to be, and actually is, independent of all others. (9a)

Vattel's perspective on the law of nations thus stresses state sovereignty to a much greater degree than Wolff's. States, Vattel holds, can and do get along very well without forming a civitas maxima; the idea of a universal federation of nations is "not so necessary to them as the State itself is to individuals" in the state of nature (10a).

Nevertheless, the differences between Wolff and Vattel regarding this third point are smaller than Vattel and some of his commentators claim. For Wolff's civitas maxima, again, is a philosophical construct employed to help derive the voluntary law of nations. He is not actually proposing that sovereign nations come together to form an international society or a world-state. Rather, he is asking, "What laws *would* nations consent to *if* they were so united?" Vattel's own basic derivation of the voluntary law of nations, even though it does not make use of "the fiction of such a republic," is quite similar to Wolff's. For instance, later in *Le Droit des Gens*, he writes, "What we call the voluntary Law of Nations consists in the rules of conduct, of external law, to which the natural law obliges Nations to consent; so that we rightly presume their consent, without seeking any record of it" (III.xii.§ 192). Insofar as Vattel and Wolff both derive the voluntary law of nations from the "presumed consent" of nations (cf. Vattel, introduction § 27; Wolff, § 22), they are pursuing similar projects. In both cases, the voluntary law of nations is arrived at inferentially by asking "What is it reasonable to suppose that nations would consent to, given the laws of nature and the character and purpose of sovereign states?"[66]

By all accounts, Vattel was extremely successful in making his Wolffian-inspired theory "accessible to cultured people in a more attractive form." Between 1759 and 1863, "there were twenty French editions of… [*Le Droit des Gens*], with ten translations in England between 1759 and 1834, and eighteen translations or reprints in the United States up to 1872. In the same period Grotius appeared in only one further edition and translation."[67] In the United States, his reputation quickly eclipsed that of all other Enlightenment natural law theorists. Charles Nussbaum reports that Vattel's work "became a textbook in American colleges, and after the establishment of the Republic, the favorite authority in American theory of International law." As support for the latter claim, he refers to a study of American legal cases decided from 1789 to 1820 in which Vattel was cited or quoted more than five times as often as either Grotius or Pufendorf.[68]

But again, Vattel's work is also the last mainstream effort in which international law is identified with natural law. "From the late eighteenth century onwards, international law is usually understood to be positive, not natural, law. It is positive not in being enacted by a superior but in being jointly willed by states, who bind themselves explicitly through treaties or implicitly through customary international law."[69] While natural law has by no means disappeared entirely from the intellectual horizon, it has ceased to play a defining role in discussions of contemporary international law.[70] At least within legal (if not philosophical) circles, theorists have become less interested in trying to deduce the law of nations from the abstract dictates of "nature" and "reason," and more convinced that the correct way to proceed is to examine empirically how states have actually regulated their dealings through treaties and customary practices.[71] As for "the law of nations" and its linguistic relatives (ius gentium, droit des gens, Völkerrecht), by the late nineteenth century Bentham's term "international law" had for all practical purposes replaced them. Today the former terms rarely appear outside of scholarly contexts. But the latter term seems only to have inherited, rather than to have resolved or cast off, the inherent difficulties, controversies, and ambiguities of the former.

II

....

NOW

*Our age is enlightened; that is to say, such knowledge
has been discovered and publicly disseminated as
would suffice to correct at least our practical principles.
The spirit of free inquiry has dissipated those false
conceptions which for so long barred the approach to
truth, and undermined the foundations upon which
fanaticism and deception had raised their throne.
Reason has purged herself of both the illusions of the
senses and the delusions of sophistry, and philosophy
itself, which first seduced us from our allegiance to
Nature, is now in loud and urgent tones calling us back
to her bosom. How is it, then, that we still remain
barbarians?*

—Friedrich Schiller, *On the Aesthetic Education
of Man* (1795)

S hortly before his death in 1794, Condorcet wrote, "Our hopes for the
future condition of the human race can be subsumed under three
important heads: the abolition of inequality between nations, the
progress of equality within nations, and the true perfection of mankind."[1]
While this simple declaration gives the lie to the many critics who continue
to assert that Enlightenment ideals are "little more than an imperialist
masquerade aimed at subduing the rest of the world under the pretense of
promoting universality,"[2] it also serves as a stark reminder of how poorly
we today have fared in achieving the Enlightenment's hopes for the future.
For as others have noted, "History...has ratified none of these forecasts."[3]
The signs of this failure are unfortunately almost equally evident when we

examine the legacy of the longer but often more modest list of Enlightenment hopes for the future analyzed in part I of this study.

Briefly, in part II I have three central aims. My first aim is simply to
document clearly how far we today are from having realized the central
Enlightenment ideals examined earlier. This sad conclusion remains
true even when we substitute my somewhat "softer" Enlightenment (an
Enlightenment that was not antireligious, not technocratic and obsessively
rationalistic, not antinationalistic) for the more canonical "harder" Enlightenment that is traditionally employed as a norm in such equations. Indeed,
in several key areas the empirical evidence clearly shows that we have
actually regressed rather than progressed. In other words, contrary to
popular wisdom, in certain fundamental areas of human life things are
worse now than they were two hundred years ago. Any complacency or
pride on this matter—regardless of whether it assumes either that the
Enlightenment's most important promissory notes are being paid off, or
that we are somehow "beyond" its concerns now—is thus unwarranted
and sorely out of place. Drawing attention to the enormous gap that often
exists between Enlightenment ideals and current realities is not in itself an
esoteric task, and some readers may question its intellectual significance.
I believe that it is important to provide an accurate inventory of this gap,
simply because its very existence is persistently denied or ignored by
numerous critics on both the left and the right.

Clearly, there are different ways of judging the success or failure of
Enlightenment ideals, depending on, among other things, which ideals one
selects. Nearly half a century ago, Alfred Cobban, in his lucid assessment,
In Search of Humanity: The Role of the Enlightenment in Modern History (1960),
while stressing that he was judging "the Enlightenment by something more
modest than world-wide success," found vindication of Enlightenment
ideals in "the progress of scientific knowledge and technological invention,"
the increased "toleration of religious, and even irreligious, opinion," the
lessening of restrictions on "freedom of thought and expression," and the
greater acceptance of "liberal political ideals," along with its consequent
reduction of "the arbitrary element in government."[4] But he also noted a
growing "contemporary malaise," one that he attributed in part to "the fact
of war and the menace of nuclear destruction," but even more to what he
called "a new kind of tribalism" that has led to "an ethical recession from
the standards of the Enlightenment."[5]

The present assessment offers somewhat different conclusions, in part
because I have focused on different ideals. I have not concentrated on "the
progress of scientific knowledge and technological invention," primarily

because I believe that science and technology are not what are most important about the Enlightenment. The rise of modern science predates the Enlightenment and was itself a precipitating cause of it. The heart of the Enlightenment project was not at all a misguided scientistic attempt to control human life—"not social engineering carried out under the aegis of a technocratic state"[6]—but rather a morally motivated effort to expand human freedom and equality. Because the present assessment starts from the latter assumption, I believe it is also a mistake to judge the Enlightenment "by something more modest than world-wide success." The Enlightenment's core commitment to cosmopolitanism necessitates that it be judged in terms of its global impact. All of its key hopes for the future concerned the human species as a whole, not favored groups within it.

Additionally, I believe that an accurate assessment requires us to focus on the means–ends relationship in Enlightenment ideals. Several of the ideals that are featured prominently in Cobban's assessment—freedom of thought, liberal political ideals, and the rule of law, for instance—were not valued by Enlightenment intellectuals simply as ends in themselves, but because they were believed to be what Kant called "a great step . . . *toward* morality" (*Peace* 8: 376n). In other words, they were believed to be means toward (or at least favorable conditions for) the moralization of humanity. A new moral disposition to respect all human beings was supposedly being facilitated by democratic institutions and the rule of law, and the "propensity and calling to *think* freely" and to make "*public use* of one's reason" was supposedly being facilitated by the right to freedom of expression (*Enlightenment* 8: 41, 38). To talk about the success or failure of the Enlightenment without taking into account what its advocates ultimately hoped to achieve by means of their institutional reforms is to adopt a perspective very foreign to their own, one that cuts off veins and arteries from the heart of their program and then praises the former after they have been detached from the latter.

My second aim is to explain why Enlightenment ideals have not been realized. Showing *why* something has not been achieved is always more difficult than showing *that* it is has not been achieved, and here I admit at the start that I am more confident of having achieved success with regard to my first aim than with my second. But if my answers to the more difficult *why* question are rejected, it is to be hoped that more skillful investigators will continue this particular line of inquiry and offer us better answers in the future. At present, we are sorely in need of more and better analyses and evaluations of the causes of the gap between Enlightenment ideals and present realities. For the effort to realize these ideals remains modernity's most significant social reform project, and all subsequent ones need to learn from its mistakes.

As noted earlier, this study concerns not just the Enlightenment's ends but also its means. One reason for this double focus on means and ends is simply that I believe that a strong majority of people, when presented with accurate descriptions of what these ends are, do support most (but not all; see below) of them. (However, the degree and level of this support is admittedly another matter, which I turn to in a moment.) Who does not wish to see a reduction of poverty between and within nations, a lessening of religious hatred, educated and civically engaged citizens, the growth of democracy, and peace rather than war? (Somewhat less rhetorically and more to the point: while there are undoubtedly some who reject these goals, this is not the book for them—if indeed any is.) However, sometimes the problem is not with the ends themselves but with the means that have been chosen to realize these ends. I believe, and try to demonstrate in what follows (see, in particular, my discussion of contemporary economics in chapter 8), that in several central cases the historical evidence shows that the means advocated by Enlightenment intellectuals to realize their ideals have proven to be ineffective. As a result—for those of us who continue to embrace these ideals—attention must now be focused on finding more efficacious means for realizing them.

But there is one important caveat. Enlightenment intellectuals believed strongly that external institutional development would lead to inner moral transformation. Humanity would become moralized through and by means of the growth of education, participation in democratic polities dedicated to the rule of law, free trade between nations, and the establishment of an effective international justice system. In the process of becoming moralized, support for Enlightenment ideals would itself become stronger and more widespread across the human species. However, I believe the empirical evidence also shows that the connection between external institutional development and internal moral development is itself not as straightforward as Enlightenment intellectuals assumed. Here as well, the root of the problem is that inefficacious—or at least questionable—means have been chosen to realize ends. But in this particular case the advocacy of inefficacious or questionable means has had a much wider and more detrimental impact on all of the remaining Enlightenment ideals. For at present, meaningful support for Enlightenment ideals generally is much weaker, particularly in the United States, than Enlightenment intellectuals predicted would be the case. Two major causes for this present lack of support, I believe, are that Enlightenment assumptions about how to achieve moralization, as well as assumptions about what moralization itself consists in, have not been vindicated. But even more fundamentally, failure to achieve the central goal of moralization has itself contributed to a widespread retraction or boomerang effect: the remaining Enlightenment ideals are no longer energetically supported by sufficient numbers of people.

My third and final aim does concern Enlightenment ends rather than means. Although I do reject all versions of instrumentalism that hold "that there is no rational deliberation of ends, but only of means,"[7] I do believe that more epistemologically modest and justifiable methods for evaluating ends are needed. One such method that I borrow (ironically) from Hume involves using human experience itself as a way to assess ends.[8] Which Enlightenment ideals have been endorsed by subsequent generations, and which have been resisted or rejected? In the latter cases, what reassessments of these ideals are therefore in order? Here I employ a commonsense *principle of psychological and historical realism* to attempt a difficult salvaging operation: in those cases where we encounter two centuries of steady resistance to Enlightenment ideals, it is reasonable to infer that the ideals themselves are at least in need of amendment, if not outright dismissal. Human nature and human history should be taken into account in assessing and evaluating ideals. At bottom, I am advocating here a version of "ought implies can": if experience shows that people cannot do something, it is futile to tell them that they ought to do it. This particular way of assessing Enlightenment ideals is pursued most prominently in my opening discussion of contemporary religion (chapter 6), but it should be kept in mind throughout part II.

However, sometimes my assessment of Enlightenment ideals in the light of subsequent history goes in the other direction: toward endorsement and renewed commitment rather than amendment or rejection. Here an additional simple test involving what I call the *principle of continued need and importance* is employed. If the threshold of the human psychological and historical realism test is not unambiguously met, and if additional independent arguments for the continued need and importance of the ideal in question can be made, then the results of the salvaging operation will lead to greater recovery of and recommitment to the original rather than loss or dismissal. This latter version of the salvaging operation is first employed in my discussion of contemporary education (chapter 7), but it too should be kept in mind throughout the following discussion. Needless to say, both versions of this salvaging operation involve a complex process of weighing competing considerations that are very difficult to measure on any single scale, and hence it is unrealistic to expect that objective certainty can be achieved by means of this method.

Yet another strategy for assessing Enlightenment ends involves articulating simple cases of mistaken identity, that is, pointing out instances where what initially appears to be the achievement of an Enlightenment ideal by subsequent generations is in reality something quite different. In these cases, the ideal realized is the same as the original in name only—the underlying reality is quite different. This particular strategy is employed most clearly in my discussion of the fate of post-Enlightenment nationalism in chapter 9. However, milder versions of it are also made use of in my analysis of contemporary international institutions in chapter 10, as well as in the examination of education in chapter 7. In the case of these "mistaken identity ideals," further assessment of the original Enlightenment ideals (once they are separated out from their contemporary counterfeits) by means of both the principle of psychological and historical realism and the principle of continued need and importance is then called for.

The troubling question that Schiller posed over two hundred years ago remains relevant today, and it is still in need of a convincing answer. Indeed, on my reading, the inquiries that I am pursuing in part II are simply mundane variations on his fundamental theme. But here as well (recall my earlier response to Cobban), part of the issue concerns the particular ideals on which one focuses. In what follows I am not primarily concerned with advances in technology, with the spirit of free inquiry, or with science's rejection of superstition (though of course these too are all part of the Enlightenment), but rather with other ideals, such as the reduction of poverty, the lessening of hatred, and the possibility of peace. How and why, after more than two hundred years, have we still failed to realize these Enlightenment ideals? Where, and in what ways, have we fallen short in realizing them? What does our own experience tell us about the appropriateness of these goals? Why—despite, but to a certain extent also because of, the progress of the Enlightenment—have we not done better in creating the world that Enlightenment intellectuals wanted? How is it that we still remain barbarians? This is what I attempt to answer.

6

....

Religion

We have to regain the belief in moral regeneration, in the moral future of mankind. We have to regain this belief in the face of and in spite of the egoism of nations and the materialism of classes. The true living God cannot breathe except in social morality and cosmopolitan humanity.

—Hermann Cohen, "Address to the World Congress for Free Christianity and Religious Progress" (1913)

The "Resurgence" of Religion

Intellectuals (particularly those who see themselves as heirs of the Enlightenment) have often asserted that religion and modernity are necessarily incompatible. But the evidence at present suggests that the case for the "secularization thesis"—in either its hard version as the death of religion or in its soft version as religion's marginalization—is no longer tenable. Important counterexamples to the thesis are prevalent, not only in the United States, where church attendance and affiliation to religious bodies remain very high, but also in Latin America and, more recently, Eastern Europe and Russia.[1] Indeed, according to some observers, the late twentieth-century revival of religion "has pervaded every continent, every civilization, and virtually every country."[2]

   Seeing the counterexamples mount, contemporary intellectuals have scurried to rethink the relationship between religion and modernity. However, their work has not been easy, for the most influential theories of modernity are anchored in an assumption of the decline of religion. As one sociologist of religion notes, "It would be difficult to think of a phenomenon that caught Western students of religion more by surprise than the world-wide resurgence of religion . . . that occurred with increasing visibility from the late 1970s onward."[3] Although the number of religionists (followers of any religion) fell from 99.8 percent of the world population in 1900 to 81.1 percent in 1970, by 2000 it had rebounded to 84.8 percent. And the numbers are expected to increase still further over the next fifty years, whereas the number of nonreligionists—who increased from 0.2 percent of the world in 1900 to 18.9 percent in 1970, but then fell rapidly to 15.2 percent by 2000—is expected to continue to decline.[4]

However, if, as I argued in part I, the Enlightenment was fundamentally religious rather than antireligious (albeit religious in ways that sometimes clash with earlier as well as later conceptions of what "being religious" means), then the sheer persistence of religion in modernity would neither surprise nor dismay Enlightenment intellectuals. But the *specific shapes* that religion has assumed since the Enlightenment are another story, and to this story I now turn. This is an enormous topic, and due to considerations of space I restrict myself here to a few observations and comments concerning the shape of contemporary religiosity with respect to the three identifying characteristics of Enlightenment religiosity discussed earlier. Afterward, I use these observations and comments to support the following claim: the spirit of Enlightenment religiosity, suitably tempered by two hundred years' hindsight, has much to offer us at present.

The Unity Thesis

*And to-day, through the penetrating power of commerce
and science, something like a world culture begins to
appear. With it, the question is bound to arise whether a
world religion is not a necessary accompaniment of
world culture, and if so, what sort of religion it must be.*

—William Ernest Hocking, *Living Religions and
a World Faith* (1940)

First, as regards the unity thesis, the vast majority of post-Enlightenment religious practitioners have clearly rejected the Enlightenment conviction that all historical faiths are manifestations of one universal religion.

Granted, one can find occasional post-Enlightenment flickers of this conviction, for example, in Baha'ism, a late nineteenth-century offshoot of Islam that originated in Iran and that tries to synthesize basic themes of Judaism, Christianity, and Islam by downplaying their theological differences;[5] or in John Dewey's book *A Common Faith*, in which he defends the "religious" over "religion," by which he means a faith not confined to sect, class, or race, one defined simply and solely in terms of human allegiance to ideals.[6] Broadly speaking, post-Enlightenment approaches to religious unity can be divided into two groups: "the conservative program of integrating or harmonizing the living religions and the radical program of creating a humanistic world religion more or less from scratch."[7] However, none of these flickers has ever gained many followers, and some of them also depart from the Enlightenment unity thesis in significant ways. In the case of Baha'ism, for instance, universality is reached not through common reason and natural religion, but by syncretizing rival revelation claims. In Dewey's case, we have moved into the paradoxical territory of a faith without God that still wants to call itself religious—something that has severely limited appeal for traditional religious believers.

Contemporary scholars of religion have also developed a substantial body of theological and philosophical work on religious diversity and pluralism that is in certain respects reminiscent of the unity thesis. John Hick, for instance, in *An Interpretation of Religion: Human Responses to the Transcendent* (1989) and related writings, defends "the pluralistic hypothesis" that "the great post-axial faiths constitute different ways of experiencing, conceiving, and living in relation to an ultimate divine Reality which transcends all our varied versions of it."[8] On Hick's view, Hinduism, Buddhism, Judaism, Christianity, and Islam are all to be regarded "as alternative soteriological 'spaces' within which, or 'ways' along which, men and women can find salvation/liberation/ultimate fulfillment."[9] More recently (and much more modestly), Paul J. Griffiths, in *Problems of Religious Diversity* (2001), has defended the thesis of "open inclusivism," by which is meant the view that religious believers should be open to the possibility that religions other than their own may teach truths not already explicitly taught or understood by their own religion.[10] Similarly, Schubert M. Ogden, in *Is There Only One True Religion or Are There Many?* (1992), rejects religious exclusivism (that is, the view that true religious claims are to be found only in one's own religion) on the grounds that "there would be no way, even in principle, of ever verifying it in terms of common human experience and reason, since no human experience could show that God has not given or cannot give the possibility of salvation in some other way."[11]

Post-Enlightenment scholars of comparative religion, by downplaying truth-claims and issues of theological content and focusing on individual experiential aspects of religion, have also presented influential briefs for a quasi-unity thesis among the world's religions. Prominent examples here include William James's definition of religion as "the feelings, acts, and experiences of individual men in their solitude, in so far as they apprehend themselves to stand in relation to whatever they may consider the divine" and Rudolf Otto's "idea of the holy."[12] However, such an approach stops well short of the Enlightenment unity thesis. It does not assert that all religious believers share the same theological beliefs, but merely that they experience similar feelings.

But while this theoretical work does in several respects represent an advance over Enlightenment discussions of religious unity (for instance, in its greater understanding and appreciation of Eastern religions, as well as in the greater variety and sophistication of its formulations of religious unity), its actual impact on present mainstream religious practice is negligible. At present, it is clear that a conviction concerning the underlying unity of religion does not carry anything close to the widespread intellectual support that it had during the Enlightenment.

The most telling objection to the unity thesis and to the spirit of Enlightenment religiosity generally has been the unexpected growth of numerous fundamentalisms and evangelical sects, and the related decline, or at least shrinkage, of more liberal religious outlooks. Within present-day Christianity, which represents approximately 33 percent of the world population and is still the largest single religious group (though it is losing ground to Islam, whose members reproduce at a greater rate), the largest annual growth rates are found among Pentecostals (8.1 percent), followed by Evangelicals (5.4 percent). Roman Catholics, at 1.3 percent, are actually 1.1 percent behind the annual growth rate of humanity (1.4 percent) and are thus declining rather than growing. Unitarianism—a sect that, perhaps more than any other, embodies the spirit of Enlightenment religiosity—saw its membership decline by nearly 20 percent between 1970 and 1995.[13] This dual phenomenon of marked religious growth from the side of fundamentalism and evangelicalism and of shrinkage from the side of more liberal sects has occurred not only within Christianity (the West's current obsession with Islamic fundamentalism notwithstanding, the term "fundamentalism" is actually homegrown on American soil, and developed out of early twentieth-century evangelic Protestantism),[14] but within Islam, Judaism, and elsewhere as well. In their "yearning for a more dynamic and critical faith, one that would stand in judgment over the modern world, not lend it support," as well as in their quest for "an authentic experience with the divine, genuine spiritual solace and a clear understanding of the one path to salvation,"[15] contemporary evangelicals as well as fundamentalists of all persuasions represent a clear rejection of Enlightenment religiosity. As Samuel Huntington notes, once one looks at a few of the details behind the late twentieth-century global resurgence of religion, it becomes evident that "a universal religion is only slightly more likely to emerge than is a universal language."[16]

At the same time, while the recent global revival of (certain kinds of) religion did catch many scholars off guard, there were signs even within the Enlightenment that the unity thesis was going to be a hard sell. For insofar as all varieties of fundamentalism and evangelicalism seek to return to the fundamentals of faith and to recapture the vibrancy of spiritual life, we can look at earlier "revival" efforts that emphasize raw faith, trust in revelation, and personal witness to religious experience—several significant examples of which occur within the Enlightenment—as themselves being proto-fundamentalisms and -evangelicalisms. Three of the most important of these Enlightenment revival efforts are pietism, Methodism, and the Great Awakening. But notable Enlightenment examples can also be found outside of Protestantism, for instance, in Judaism, Hasidism, and in Catholicism, Jansenism. In each of these revivalist movements we find a protest against the allegedly objectifying, abstract, and impersonal methods of Enlightenment natural theology. This protest was perhaps best summarized by the Counter-Enlightenment critic Johann Georg Hamann, who rejected the Enlightenment as merely "cold, unfruitful moonlight" and pinpointed its central failure on an overreliance on a conception of reason that is "independent of all tradition and custom and belief in them," one also divorced from natural language, whose only credentials are "tradition and usage."[17]

The Morality Thesis

Certainly one can point to multiple connecting points (or at least *perceived* connecting points) between religion and morality in post-Enlightenment religious practice. Mundane examples here include the continuing conviction on the part of most laypeople that any satisfactory morality must be grounded in religion, the resultant moral education that parents expect their children to receive from exposure to religious tradition, as well as the specific moral causes that contemporary religious believers advocate as a result of their religious commitments. But these perceived religion–morality connections are not at all the same as those advocated by Enlightenment intellectuals who subscribed to the morality thesis. First of all, the latter group's radical reduction of religion to morality—their claim that religious activities are of instrumental value only, that is, must serve merely as means toward moral ends—is entirely absent in contemporary mainstream religion. A much greater emphasis on prayer, worship, and ritual as themselves being integral to religious life is evident at present. Most contemporary religious believers do not view such activities as mere moral instruments, or what Kant called "preparation for good works." Second, the *kinds* of moral causes advocated by contemporary religious believers are quite different from what Enlightenment theorists had in mind in propounding the morality thesis. For them, the moral causes and commitments engendered by religion centered on "good works" and beneficence toward others—on what Jefferson, in presenting his case for the superiority of the moral "doctrines of Jesus compared with those of others" called "inculcating universal philanthropy, not only to kindred and friends, to neighbors and countrymen, but to all mankind, gathering all into one family."[18] But with contemporary religionists, particularly those of a fundamentalist bent, the favored moral concerns are local, particularistic, and nationalistic.

However, at least on the theoretical front, post-Enlightenment developments regarding the *common morality thesis* (a subsidiary thesis, I suggested earlier, that follows from the combination of the unity and morality theses) appear more promising. Hick's pluralistic hypothesis, for instance, includes the following assertion: "The fundamental moral claim is . . . to treat others as having the same moral value as myself. This is in effect a transcription of the Golden Rule found in the Hindu, Buddhist, Confucian, Taoist, Zoroastrian, Jain, and Christian scriptures, and in the Jewish *Talmud* and the Muslim *Hadith*."[19] Many other scholars have also argued that versions of a golden rule ethic are present in and fundamental to all of the major religious traditions.[20] Such claims do not of course embrace the more radical components of the morality thesis, for instance, its commitment to reduce religion to morality. But to the extent that contemporary theorists and scholars of religion do agree that the major religious traditions share a common moral outlook, one that stresses that all human beings possess equal moral worth and must be treated accordingly, we can say that the common morality thesis has fared much better than either the unity thesis or the morality thesis. The problem now is to make this scholarly consensus efficacious: to find ways to make actions fit words.[21]

Toleration

Given the frequent affirmations of pluralism, diversity, and multicultural-ism that one finds in many societies at present, toleration would seem to be one Enlightenment value that has clearly taken root and thrived in post-Enlightenment cultures. And I do concur that modernity's track record with respect to toleration is stronger than it is with either of the other two hallmarks of Enlightenment religiosity discussed in chapter 1. But several qualifying remarks are also in order regarding toleration. First, the con-temporary emphasis on tolerating and respecting difference departs in several key respects from Enlightenment appeals to toleration. For instance, the primary *object* of toleration has shifted. At present, it is more differences of race, gender, political belief, and what philosophers call "views of the good" that constitute the bulk of the appeals to tolerance, whereas in the Enlightenment appeals to tolerance were primarily appeals to religious tolerance. Although both types of appeal to tolerate and respect difference (religious as well as secular) can ultimately be linked together by an underlying principle of equal liberty, this more principled and unqualified commitment to openness was not yet fully present and explicit in most Enlightenment defenses of toleration.[22] Second, the *arguments* for toleration have shifted. During the Enlightenment, toleration was justified by appeals to the fallibility of our beliefs (Voltaire, Bayle), respect for autonomy (Kant), the impossibility of coercing genuine religious belief (Locke, Kant), and the danger of civil strife (Locke and many others). Behind each (save but one)[23] there was an assumption that there is a truth to be found, and that toleration is a necessary precondition for finding it. However, today the value of diversity itself serves as the primary ground for appeals to toleration. No underlying assumption about a true belief waiting to be found (if only we grant people the freedom to seek it) is present. But for many, this shift in perspective will merely be welcomed as an overdue acknowledgment of Nietzsche's dictum that the idea of there even being " 'truth' at this level refers to all sorts of things which today we call 'fantasies' [*Einbildungen*]."[24] Finally, the relatively strong endorsement at present of the Enlightenment value of toleration (the above differences between Enlightenment and contemporary conceptions of toleration notwithstanding) cannot erase the dual facts that there still exist an appalling number of hate crimes committed in many of the same contemporary societies that advocate tolerance and diversity, and that outside of these societies we often find not even a pretense of toleration but rather official endorsement of hate toward others. Intolerance is still alive and well in the contemporary world, and many of us have still not managed to follow Voltaire's advice "to regard every man as our brother."

Splitting the Difference

Of the five focal areas of Enlightenment concern examined in part I of this study, religion has fared the worst in the contemporary world. The dominant modes of religious practice at present are very different from what Enlightenment religious reformers hoped the future would bring. In the other fundamental areas of Enlightenment concern investigated in part I—education, economics, politics, and international relations—modernity has embraced at least some of the Enlightenment reformers' ideals. However, since the Enlightenment, "religion has come to constitute itself far more often as a center of resistance to Enlightenment ideals and values. Much of popular religion now sees itself as 'correcting' the 'one-sidedness' of modern Enlightenment culture by privileging what is irrational and parochial, defending tradition, authority, and superstition."[25]

The most common response to this development is one of skepticism, and it comes in two different versions. However, both versions endorse the same conclusion: the Enlightenment has nothing to offer contemporary religious practice. Skeptics (mostly, but not entirely) on the right who embrace one or another variety of popular religion at present are inclined to say, as did their Counter-Enlightenment forebears, that the Enlightenment radically misunderstood religion. As a result, they think that the Enlightenment has nothing to offer contemporary religion. On the other hand, secular skeptics (mostly, but not entirely) on the left who often view themselves as the heirs of the Enlightenment are dismayed at the contemporary resurgence of religion and believe that humanity is moving in the wrong direction. But because they read the Enlightenment as a secular, antireligious movement, they too hold that the Enlightenment has nothing to offer contemporary religious practice.

I believe that both of these skeptical responses are incorrect in their shared conclusion, though I do accept at least one assumption on each side. I share with skeptics on the right the assumption that most religious believers do not find the thin gruel of Enlightenment religiosity spiritually satisfying. Two hundred years of post-Enlightenment religious history has convinced me that most religious believers want a more personal, richer religious experience, one that is definitely not "carefully cleansed of everything miraculous and mysterious."[26] But I also share with skeptics on the left a strong antipathy toward the kind of religiosity that is enjoying a revival at present: one that, even in its mildest versions, preaches an objectionable exclusionism and in its stronger versions, hatred and violence as well.

Again, though, I believe both sides err in thinking that the Enlightenment has nothing to offer contemporary religious practice. In my view, the spirit of Enlightenment religiosity, tempered by two hundred years' hindsight, has much to offer us at present. We need to find a way to split the difference between Enlightenment religious thought and contemporary religious practice. In making this claim, I mean first to offer a simple argument by analogy. In response to the religious wars of their day as well as a growing awareness of different cultures and religions, Enlightenment intellectuals undertook to rethink religion. The same basic conditions that led to this earlier reconceptualization of religion are again present today, and a similar response is also needed today.

But how similar? To what extent and degree can the spirit of Enlightenment religiosity actually help us today? What is needed, and what I believe is possible, is not a wholesale return to Enlightenment religiosity, but rather a critical and selective appropriation of some of its key attitudes and methods. In other words, what I am advocating in the area of Enlightenment religious ideals is a revisioning, a salvaging of what still seems sound in the face of two centuries of human interaction with (and often resistance to) these ideals. First, we need to retrieve the simple conviction that religion is not completely impermeable to common reason: we need to (re)convince ourselves that members of different faiths can rationally communicate with each other on at least some basic points of religious belief. The multiple outbursts of religious violence that we have experienced in recent years are a blunt omen that much contemporary religion—particularly in its fundamentalist forms—is generating much heat but little light. Contemporary religion, as Juergensmeyer notes on the last page of his study of the global rise of religious terrorism, "needs the temper of rationality and fair play that Enlightenment values give to civil society."[27]

Second, and related, we need to acquire a qualified reappreciation for at least some of the methodological assumptions of natural theology (a theological orientation that of course does not begin in, and is not unique to, eighteenth-century Enlightenment Europe). Most Enlightenment intellectuals approached religion from within the purview of natural theology. They sought to discover truths about religion, morality, and God, using only common methods of reasoning and data that are widely accepted and available to everyone. As is well known, post-Enlightenment criticisms of natural theology are legion. Schleiermacher, for instance, complains that natural religion is only a "meager and lean religion" containing "infinite ambiguity" but "no determinate form, no truly individual presentation of religion." "This contentless, formless thing," he concludes, is "the negation of everything positive and characteristic in religion," and is merely the product "of an age whose hobbyhorse was a lamentable generality and an empty sobriety, which, more than everything else, works against true cultivation [*wahre Bildung*] in all things."[28] On the view advocated here, natural theology should not be regarded as the last word in religion, but neither should it be viewed as "the negation of everything positive and characteristic in religion." Rather, it should be viewed as a constructive way of achieving both *minimal consensus* among and intellectual respect for different religious faiths. (The content and form for which it strives are, so to speak, intentionally modest, so as to achieve maximal agreement.) Other approaches to religion that devalue the universal communicability of reason and objective empirical data are inherently limited by their particularity and are thus not up to the task of cross-cultural understanding.[29] To put the point in Rawlsian terminology: the method of natural theology, suitably moderated and updated, can and should be employed to try to achieve an "overlapping consensus" in religion.[30]

How much consensus will be achieved by such an approach? This is an empirical question that cannot be answered unless and until people employ the method in good faith. But it seems safe to say both that any consensus achieved will be much more modest than Enlightenment intellectuals strove for and that a more modest consensus is all that is in fact needed for purposes of defusing religious violence and promoting mutual respect between people of different religious faiths. For such purposes, it is not necessary that people become convinced that the world's religions speak with a single voice on complex theological matters. Strict adherence to the full *content* of the unity thesis (viz., the claim that all historical faiths are manifestations of one universal religion), in other words, is not itself necessary to achieve these goals. A single world faith is neither desirable nor necessary. Rather, it is enough if people retrieve some of the *methodological spirit* behind the unity thesis—particularly the conviction that basic religious convictions can be articulated and discussed by means of common reason and the perspective of natural religion. To borrow the language of Enlightenment clergyman Andreas Riem, we need to reconvince ourselves that "reason does not undermine religion, but rather its aberrations," and that in applying reason to religion we can "lose prejudices and retain religion."[31] Nor is commitment to the complete moralization of religion necessary. The stance that believers within the major religious traditions take on the status and role of ritual and sacrament within their own faith bears no necessary connection to the goals of defusing religious violence and promoting mutual respect between different faiths.[32] What is necessary here is simply that religious believers of all persuasions begin to pay more than lip service to the common morality thesis. Finally, Voltaire's message of universal tolerance needs to be energetically reaffirmed by religious leaders of all persuasions in the contemporary world so that all religious believers really do come to regard every man as their brother.

Insofar as religion continues to be the primary shaper of people's moral beliefs, and insofar as religion's message at present is predominantly antiuniversalist and exclusionist, the moral world that Enlightenment intellectuals pursued—a world where "a violation of rights on *one* place of the earth is felt in *all*" (*Peace* 8: 360)—is still a very long way off. The internal attitudinal changes that are necessary to cope successfully with an external environment that is becoming increasingly globalized are not being fostered effectively by contemporary religion. Most people will not succeed in "thinking and feeling beyond the nation"[33] unless and until contemporary religions adopt a more cosmopolitan stance and preach a more universalistic message. For contemporary religions to do so while still maintaining their individual identities and historical traditions admittedly will require a difficult balancing act. That they must nevertheless attempt to do so—if peace is ever to have a chance—is the conclusion to which humanity's post-Enlightenment experience points.

7

··

Education

A Schooled World

Historical and international statistics about education are plentiful at present, at least when one focuses on fundamental issues such as enrollment figures and graduation rates over time. However, a word of caution is in order before taking a brief look at some of them. B. R. Mitchell notes, "Of all the subjects on which statistical material exists, probably none shows less uniformity, both over time and between countries, than education."[1] Major causes for this lack of uniformity include the following: definitions as to what constitutes a primary school, a secondary school, and a university vary from country to country; educational institutions themselves often change considerably over time within each country, thus sliding in and out of definitional parameters; international statistics concerning enrollment are not gathered in a consistent manner; and curricula and graduation requirements vary from region to region, and also change over time.

Nevertheless, when one first looks at these statistics, however variable and inconsistent they may be, it is impossible not to come away without a firm sense that education is one key area of human life where Enlightenment thinkers have received a good portion of what they wanted. Enlightenment authors wanted a future world in which illiteracy would be wiped out via universal schooling, and this is more or less the world that we now have.

"More or less" because literacy and school attendance rates still vary enormously from region to region. From 1996 to 2002, for instance, 97 percent of the children in industrialized countries attended primary school, but only 59 percent of the children in sub-Saharan Africa did so. And of course school attendance alone does not guarantee literacy. The total adult literacy rate in 2000 was still only 85 percent. Finally, there remain significant gender and wealth gaps in present literacy rates. While the male adult literacy rate in 2000 was 92 percent, for females it was only 77 percent. And while the adult total literacy rate in industrialized countries was 97 percent, in the least developed countries it was only 48 percent.[2] Within the sphere of education, Condorcet's hopes for "the abolition of inequality between nations, the progress of equality within each nation"[3] have still not come to pass.

Nevertheless, the enormity of the changes in this area of human life over the past two centuries cannot be easily dismissed. The world of the Enlightenment was definitely not a schooled world. Although numerous arguments for universal education had been made by the end of the eighteenth century, public elementary and secondary schools were at this time still a rarity. Parents who could afford to send their children to private (usually religiously affiliated) educational institutions or to bring private tutors into their own homes often (but not always) did so. Schooling was not yet compulsory; it was essentially an option for the well-to-do. In the United States, for instance, the first compulsory school attendance law was not passed until 1852, in the state of Massachusetts. And this law required only that children between the ages of eight and fourteen attend school for twelve weeks each year.

Similar sea changes are evident in higher education. Access to higher education has increased sharply over the past two hundred years. "Throughout the Western world, universities today educate some 40–50 percent of young adults,"[4] whereas in the Enlightenment only about 1 percent of young (male) adults in the Western world even attended a college or university. In the United States, for instance, one author estimates that "perhaps one out of every thousand colonists in 1775 had been to college at some time or other."[5] And most of these colonial college students never completed a degree. By 1776, 4,773 baccalaureate degrees had been conferred by the nine colonial American colleges, at which time there were three thousand living graduates of these institutions. Over the next quarter-century, another 4,371 degrees were conferred, bringing the total to 9,144 in 1800. Harvard, Yale, and Princeton together account for almost three-fourths of all the degrees conferred in America in the seventeenth and eighteenth centuries.[6] In Enlightenment Europe, university enrollment rates were a bit higher: "As many as 2–3 percent of young men were able to enrol in university faculties during the early seventeenth century, a figure not equalled again until the early twentieth century."[7] At the same time, as was also the case in colonial America, the dropout rate was very high; for instance, half of the students enrolled at Cambridge University between 1590 and 1640 never finished.[8]

And now? At present the U.S. higher education system (which has grown to over thirty-five hundred institutions) educates about 14.5 million students, and 27 percent of the U.S. population ages twenty-five to sixty-four has completed at least a BA degree.[9] Statistics regarding university degree completion in Europe also reveal impressive growth, albeit on a more modest scale. At present, 13 percent of the German population ages twenty-five to sixty-four has completed a first university degree or *Diplom* (which generally requires five to six years and is closer to a U.S. master's degree). For the United Kingdom the figure is 17 percent; for France it is 11 percent.[10] Although much is made of the "unparalleled experiment" in the United States to extend "to a greater degree than all other nations" the benefits of higher education "to all citizens, whatever their class, race, sex, ethnicity, or religion,"[11] it should also be noted that many countries at present have higher college and university graduation rates than the United States. In a recent country-by-country comparison of the "number of bachelor's degree recipients per 100 persons of the theoretical age of graduation," Finland (33.9), the Netherlands (33.5), New Zealand (37.3), Norway (33.9), and the United Kingdom (36.8) all came out ahead of the United States (33.2).[12] But the broader global picture is clear: "The total numbers of higher education students worldwide have grown exponentially in recent decades—from 51 million in 1980 to 82 million in 1995, an increase of 61 percent. The numbers now [2003] top 90 million."[13]

Women's access to higher education has also increased enormously over the past two hundred years. During the Enlightenment, women were not even allowed to attend colleges or universities; what little education they managed to acquire outside of these institutions was usually about conduct and little else. In the United States, Oberlin College inaugurated coeducational higher education for women in 1837, when it enrolled four female freshmen.[14] In 1869–70, over 81 percent of the bachelor's degrees awarded in the United States were still conferred on men. But by 1981–82, slightly over 50 percent of U.S. bachelor's degrees awarded went to women, and the percentage of bachelor's degrees awarded to women has increased annually since then.[15] In other words, for over twenty-five years, more women have been graduating from U.S. colleges and universities than have men. At least within the United States, it would appear that Wollstonecraft's goal of educational equality for women has been achieved—indeed, surpassed.

At the same time, the exponential growth of higher education is very unevenly distributed among nations. It has occurred only in wealthy countries; in poorer countries the percentage of students attending colleges and universities at present is virtually identical to what it was for European males during the Enlightenment. Data gathered by the World Bank confirm that "college enrollment rates are especially low in poor countries, where only about 3 percent of college-age youth have an opportunity to enroll in college or some type of vocational program. . . . By contrast, nearly 40 percent of college-age people in wealthy countries enroll in college or vocational school programs."[16] In the crucial area of education, the Enlightenment hope that the future would bring a gradual spreading of opportunities and benefits to all of the peoples of the world has not come to pass.

Another area of concern is the recent trend toward privatization of higher education in wealthy countries. Since the early 1980s, federal and state support for higher education in the United States has decreased steadily, forcing colleges and universities to become more dependent on tuition and private revenue sources.[17] Similarly, in the European Union (where public funding has long been the main source of funding for universities, and where the principle of free higher education for qualified applicants has been a key component of the social democratic model) student fees have been introduced. For instance, starting in 2006, universities in England began charging full-time undergraduates up to £3,000 per annum in course fees. These "top up" fees, though modest by American standards, do represent a clear step back from public funding of higher education. Whether this current privatization trend in higher education will eventually metastasize into an endorsement of La Chalotais's position that educational opportunities should not be extended to the working class is doubtful. But it does represent a clear departure from the opposing German Enlightenment ideals of Fichte and Bergk, both of whom argued in defense of free higher education for all qualified applicants.

Accurate statistics on primary and secondary school attendance during the Enlightenment are not easy to come by, but it is possible to sketch a rough picture. In eighteenth-century Europe, "areas where half or more of the school-age children [ages six to twelve] received instruction at some stage during the year were educationally advanced. A fifth to a third represents an average achievement; less than 10 percent can be seen as the bottom of the range with figures close to 1 percent by no means unknown even in 1800."[18] Examples at the top of this range include Brandenburg-Prussia, "where attendance in the second half of the eighteenth century ran at 50 percent or more depending on the local area"; Vienna, where in 1770 only 42 percent "received no education at all"; and the more urban areas of England, Scotland, and France. Eastern and central Europe, on the other hand, were at the low end. For instance, "even after reforms had led to a major expansion of schools in the last two decades of the eighteenth century, Russia had less than half of 1 percent of its school age population under instruction in 1807."[19]

For colonial America, accurate primary school attendance figures are even harder to obtain. Systematic provision for publicly supported schools did exist in parts of New England, but even here "the statutory requirements were not always enforced."[20] The Massachusetts School Law of 1647, for instance (which sought to counteract "one chiefe project of that ould deluder, Satan, to keepe men from the knowledge of the Scriptures"), stipulated that "every township in this jurisdiction, after the Lord hath increased them to the number of 50 householders, shall then forthwith appoint one within their towne to teach all children as shall resort to him to write and reade. . . . And it is further ordered, that where any towne shall increase to the number of 100 families or householders, they shall set up a grammar schoole."[21]

When the areas outside of New England are included (and when all races are included), school attendance rates in colonial America were certainly much lower than the corresponding figures for the areas of eighteenth-century western Europe referred to earlier. Lawrence Cremin, for instance, estimates that, of the white population living in late eighteenth-century America, "well under half were likely to have had any formal schooling, and that sporadically and intermittently."[22] But the picture changes dramatically once widespread compulsory schooling legislation takes effect in the late nineteenth century. In 1870, only 2 percent of

U.S. seventeen-year-olds were high school graduates; by 1970, 76 percent of them were.[23] In 1900, only half of the U.S. population "five to nineteen years old were enrolled in school; by 1950, this proportion had increased to nearly eight in ten (and by 1990 to more than nine in ten)." At present, 87 percent of the U.S. population ages twenty-five to sixty-four has completed at least an upper secondary education.[24] Current upper secondary education completion rates for populations in other G-8 countries are also impressive. For instance, in Canada the figure is 79 percent; in Germany and Japan, 81 percent. But for non-G-8 countries, the figures are much lower: Portugal, 21 percent; Brazil, 34 percent; Indonesia, 22 percent; Tunisia, 8 percent.[25]

Although notable disparities between rich and poor still exist, the Enlightenment's biggest success in the field of education has been in convincing future generations to make school and university education more accessible to vastly larger numbers of people. However, as I argue below, a schooled (or even a colleged and universitied) world does not necessarily translate into a world where people have acquired the courage to use their own understanding, much less a world of morally good people.

Education for What?

It is quite clear that there are many more educational institutions on our planet than there were two hundred years ago; that a much higher percentage of human beings are attending schools, colleges, and universities than was the case two hundred years ago; and that Enlightenment intellectuals deserve much of the credit for both of these developments. But once we set aside the optimistic pile of statistics trotted out earlier, the picture is not as pretty. For the widespread growth of and accessibility to educational institutions over the past two centuries has not brought about the two most fundamental transformations that Enlightenment authors believed education would bring to human life. The first transformation was intellectual and civic. Education, they believed, would create not just an informed citizenry but a critical public: citizens who, in Kant's famous formulation, had acquired the courage to make use of their own understanding and who would consistently exercise this courage in public, presenting and defending their views before others, subjecting all authority— political, religious, scientific—to critical scrutiny, and speaking freely on all matters. The second transformation (though in the end it was held to be interconnected with the first) was moral. For Kant and many other

Enlightenment authors, the final destiny of the human race is moral perfection, and we are to seek this perfection "from nowhere else but education" (*Collins* 27: 471).

We enter now a nether region where educational statisticians seldom tread, in part because of difficulties in defining precisely what it is that one is trying to measure, in part because we are concerned not just with observable behavior but ultimately with internal attitudes and beliefs, in part because contemporary governments and policy organizations do not place a high priority on issues of intellectual and moral transformation. (This is not where the money is.) Solid data are lacking, but I believe it is evident that although the goal of intellectual and civic transformation still strikes a responsive chord among a shrinking cadre of liberal arts professors, few students and parents at present place a priority on this goal or view education as the means of achieving it. As a result, the goal of an enlightened public sphere is not what presently drives education at any level; it is not what most people want from education. And as for the second goal, moral transformation, it lacks substantial numbers of defenders even within the present professoriate, much less within the population at large.

Increasingly, at all levels, education is valued merely as a *Brotstudium*. As we saw earlier, the romantics' critique of Enlightenment educational reforms as a crass demand for utility and real-world relevance was one-sided and reductionistic and missed what was most compelling about the Enlightenment educational vision. Most educational reformers in the Enlightenment were strongly supportive of liberal education and even of the importance of (the reading, if not the writing and speaking of) ancient Greek and Latin. They did not believe that good education must always pass a test of practical relevance or usefulness, or that it should necessarily serve as a means to happiness. At the same time, precisely because Enlightenment educational reformers valued education largely for its possibilities of intellectual, civic, and moral transformation, they were not advocates of pure liberal education. They would disagree vehemently with Cardinal Newman's famous definition of "liberal knowledge" in *The Idea of a University* (1853): "That alone is liberal knowledge which stands on its own pretensions, which is independent of sequel, expects no complement, refuses to be *informed* (as it is called) by any end, or absorbed into any art, in order duly to present itself to our contemplation."[26] Enlightenment education is not independent of sequel, it does expect a complement, and it is informed by an end. However, it is also plain that the fundamental goals that informed Enlightenment education (the intellectual, civic, and

moral transformation of human beings) have receded far into the background of contemporary educational concerns, while the utilitarian and
pragmatic dimensions of Enlightenment education, which for Enlightenment thinkers were of only secondary importance, have now achieved
dominance. As one critic remarks, the tremendous international growth
of education over the past half century is driven primarily not by beliefs
about the intellectual, civic, and moral transformation capabilities of education, but "above all by expectations that during coming decades perhaps
half of all jobs in the postindustrial turbocapitalist economies will require a
minimum of sixteen years' schooling and training."[27]

Granted, the Enlightenment belief that education would produce
morally good people presents an easy target for critics. When Locke tells
us that "of all the men we meet with, nine parts of ten are what they are,
good or evil, ... by their education,"[28] something seems very wrong with
the numbers. The easy counterexamples of educated but evil people, and of
uneducated but morally good people, seem not to have occurred to him.
Nor should two centuries of sharp increases of education at all levels be
required in order to prove the commonsense observation that there is no
necessary connection between education and moral goodness.[29]

But once the bald assertion of a necessary connection between education and moral goodness is abandoned, are we thereby forced to also give
up any and all views that assert that education should have *some* influence
on a person's moral outlook? And if we do think that education should have
some influence on a person's moral outlook, what *kind* of an influence?
Although the moralizing thrust of Enlightenment education was explicitly
not an attempt to inculcate a rigid moral code in students, certain basic
moral attitudes were stressed repeatedly. One specific moral outlook that
many Enlightenment authors hoped to cultivate through education was
cosmopolitanism. This goal, as we saw earlier, was particularly prevalent
among intellectuals in the German Enlightenment. Basedow, for instance,
held that the primary aim of education is to prepare students to become
"citizens of our world"[30] rather than of a specific principality or state. And
Kant stressed that the correct plan for education "must be made in a
cosmopolitan manner," urging teachers to stress "philanthropy toward
others and then also cosmopolitan dispositions" in their lessons, so that
students would eventually come to "rejoice at the best for the world even if
it is not to the advantage of their fatherland or to their own gain" (*Pedagogy*
9: 499). Enlightenment pleas for cosmopolitan education were based in
part on the level-headed premise that an internal transformation of moral
attitudes was needed to accompany the external transformation of the

human social environment that was already taking place due to economic and technological changes if the globalizing tendencies of the latter were to be embraced rather than resisted.

Many American colleges and universities at present do strive to offer curricula aimed at promoting world citizenship and "cultivating humanity" in their students,[31] but no hard data exist to support the claim that such curricula are successful in achieving their aim. Certainly there is no guarantee that students who receive an education intended to inculcate cosmopolitan dispositions will actually develop such dispositions and act consistently from them. Some people are resolutely selfish, and no amount of exposure to a world-citizen model of education is going to change them. Educators can only try to inculcate cosmopolitan dispositions, and then hope for the best—acting on the highly plausible assumption that the habits of thought, reflection, and emotional response human beings learn when young usually (but not necessarily always) influence their moral orientations as adults.

A second specific moral attitude that Enlightenment reformers tied to education was increased civic participation. Educated citizens, Jefferson believed, would learn to "know ambition under all its shapes"; their knowledge of human history would enable them to prevent ambitious politicians from degenerating into tyrants, and their understanding of the importance of their rights as citizens would motivate them to do so. They would be "guardians of their own liberty."[32] For Rousseau, public education is "the state's most important business,"[33] for it is through education that souls receive "a national formation" and become "patriotic by inclination, by passion, by necessity."[34] (However, as we saw earlier, these nationalist goals often stand in tension with the internationalist goals of a cosmopolitan education, which further complicates matters.)

Insofar as the concept of "civic participation" denotes observable behavior patterns in addition to internal attitudes, it should be possible to test empirically, albeit roughly, what impact educational curricula concerned with civic participation actually have on their students. To what extent, if any, have two centuries of (nearly) universal education actually increased civic participation? One recent study entitled *Citizenship and Education in Twenty-Eight Countries: Civic Knowledge and Engagement at Age Fourteen* (2001) addresses at least part of our question. Described as "the largest and most rigorous study of civic education ever conducted internationally," it involved "representative samples consisting of 90,000 14-year-old students in 28 countries." Included in the study is a table on "Students' Reports on Expected Political Activities as an Adult." Some key findings include the following: 85 percent of U.S. fourteen-year-olds reported that they expect to vote in national elections, as did a strong proportion of fourteen-year-olds elsewhere (the voting figures range from a high of 91 percent in Denmark and Hungary to a low of 55 percent in Switzerland). Nearly three in five U.S. fourteen-year-olds (59 percent) expect to collect money for a social cause, 50 percent plan to collect signatures for a petition, and 39 percent expect to participate in a nonviolent protest march. High and low figures on the "collect money for social cause" question are 85 percent (Chile) and 28 percent (Czech Republic); on the petition question, 75 percent (Columbia) and 27 percent (Finland); and on the protest march question, 86 percent (Cyprus) and 21 percent (Finland).[35]

Although the responses of U.S. fourteen-year-olds do not represent the highest scores on any of the civic participation questions asked in the survey, they are nevertheless impressive—particularly when compared with the actual civic participation figures of their future adult selves. What causes the drastic diminution of civic zeal in American individuals between adolescence and adulthood, and does modern education itself have something to do with it? Social critics from Tocqueville on have often commented on adult Americans' retreat into domesticity. Alan Ryan, for instance, notes that the contemporary American adult population "is emphatically private in its concerns.... Only a bare majority of possible voters go to the polls in the United States, even in presidential elections. Barely 10 percent of citizens can name their local congressman.... Their concerns are domestic, private, and familial."[36] Whether education itself plays a causal role in this retreat into domesticity is not clear (though popular candidates for blame do include boring curricula, bad teaching, and the alienating effects of compulsory schooling). But this much is evident: even if education does encourage civic participation in U.S. adolescents, this encouragement often lacks sufficient staying power to motivate their future adult selves.

Finally, and above all, Enlightenment intellectuals also viewed education as a means toward enlightenment itself. Education was valued especially because it was believed to be the best means for developing people's ability to make use of their own understanding without direction from others, and to instill in them habits of public, critical examination and debate, thereby ushering in what Kant called "the genuine age of *criticism*, to which everything must submit" (*Pure Reason* A xi n.). But is there any solid evidence that two centuries of explosive growth in education have intellectually transformed human beings in this manner? Again, for reasons indicated earlier, empirical data on this question are virtually nonexistent, but the general lack of inquiry into the matter itself inclines one toward a negative answer. In opposition to the concept of an enlightened public sphere, contemporary intellectuals often trot out the familiar (if not always consistent) objections that there simply is no neutral space where participants can form judgments as autonomous reasoners, shedding their particular social and political identities and memberships, and that there are no objective and universal standards by means of which doctrines can be impartially assessed.[37] But what has caused more severe damage to the idea of the public sphere is the double blow of the retreat into domesticity as well as the pronounced turn toward vocationalism in higher education. In both cases, the result is often simply a lack of interest and developed capacity for public debate. To this extent, Kant's remark in 1784 that he and his contemporaries did not yet live in an enlightened age, and that in order for this to occur "a good deal more is required for people on the whole to be in the position . . . of using their own understanding confidently and well . . . without another's guidance" (*Enlightenment* 8: 40) remains true today. Similarly, Condorcet's hope for a future "condition in which everyone will have the knowledge necessary to conduct himself in the ordinary affairs of life, according to the light of his own reason, to preserve his mind free from prejudice"[38] is still unrealized.

However, even though the Enlightenment educational goals of intellectual, civic, and moral transformation are not widely endorsed at present, I believe that an informed assessment of these goals should not conclude with a call for their dismissal. Their current lack of popularity does not, in my view, indicate that they are incompatible with human nature (in part because the historical record on these topics is not static; for instance, in the not too distant past, Americans experienced much higher civic participation rates).[39] Here the situation differs in at least one basic respect from our earlier assessment of Enlightenment religious ideals, and the resultant salvaging operation thus takes a different turn. In the latter case, the goal of a single world faith has persistently been resisted by most people since the Enlightenment, and we did appeal to this fact in arguing for dismissal of this goal. But we also showed that commitment to this goal itself has no necessary connection to the achievement of other important Enlightenment religious goals such as the lessening of religious violence, greater toleration of religious differences, and a stronger commitment to the common morality thesis. In the case of religion, human propensities as revealed over the course of time, when combined with a simple analysis of the extent to which commitment to a goal is necessary in pursuit of other important goals, together led to a rejection of the Enlightenment unity thesis in religion. But in the sphere of education, neither of these conditions holds. The evidence regarding human propensities is weaker (again, civic participation rates have been much higher in the recent past), and no informed observer would consider arguing that commitment to the goal of an enlightened public sphere is unnecessary for improving civic life. So the proper conclusion here is not rejection of but rather endorsement of and renewed commitment to the ideal. Those who believe in the importance of Enlightenment educational ideals need to work harder to convince the rest of us that education should be more than a Brotstudium.

....

In sum, the Enlightenment's biggest successes in the area of education lie in the increased accessibility of education at all levels to (nearly) all people that we find at present, and in the related widespread growth of literacy.[40] On the other hand, Enlightenment intellectuals' stress on education as a vehicle of intellectual, civic, and moral transformation has been de-emphasized in the contemporary world, to the detriment of the latter. Although certain aspects of Enlightenment intellectuals' faith in the transformative power of education to shape intellectual and moral character do not always survive scrutiny (for instance, their tendency to think that education necessarily improves moral character is clearly false), their assumption that compatible internal, attitudinal changes need to accompany external, societal changes if the latter are to be freely adopted and made efficacious seems to me to be clearly correct. This leads to an awkward conclusion: however numerous the external signs of a global civil society may be at present, most people still do not morally endorse it. To this extent, education—from an Enlightenment perspective—has failed.

8

....

Economics

E conomics is another one of our core areas of investigation where, at first glance, Enlightenment hopes for the future appear to have been largely realized. In recent years more and more governments have relaxed controls on trade and expressed support for market economies, and the currently much-invoked (and much-contested) concept of *globalization* is often held to be another clear link to Enlightenment economic goals. But here as elsewhere, first impressions can be deceiving. Let us start with some observations on globalization.

Globalization

The Supreme Being forged the bonds of commerce in
order to incline the peoples of the earth to keep peace
with each other and to love each other.

—François Véron de Forbonnais,
"Commerce," s.v. *Encyclopédie* (1753)

The term "globalization" is used in different ways by different writers. As one participant in the debate unhelpfully concludes, after trotting out a lengthy list of characteristics thought to be associated with globalization, it is "a rubric for varied phenomena."[1] The phenomena referred to by the rubric also tend to vary from discipline to discipline. Another participant observes, "In social science there are as many conceptualizations of global-ization as there are disciplines.... Each social science claims globalization, privileges its disciplinary angle, and treats its debates as authoritative without awareness or acknowledgement of their partial status."[2] At bottom, as the suffix "-ization" indicates, globalization refers to *a process* rather than to something static: "the process of creating something 'global.' "[3] But while everyone agrees that the process of globalization is taking place now and that it is intensifying, there is less consensus on when it began, in part (again) because different authors are referring to different processes. In the following discussion I canvass the major competing definitions of globalization, noting where Enlightenment hopes for a future world brought together through commerce and trade do or do not fit with these contemporary definitions.

The most widely discussed dimension of globalization is *economic*, and here writers are referring to the process "by which the whole world becomes a single market" and in which "goods and services, capital, and labor are traded on a worldwide basis, and information and the results of research flow readily between countries."[4] Commentary on economic globalization—the recent outbreak of books and articles on the topic notwithstanding—is not new. Some of the most vivid descriptions of the process are still to be found in Marx and Engels's *Manifesto of the Communist Party* (1848). Under capitalism, they note, commerce and industry have acquired "an impetus never before known," one that has "given a cosmo-politan character to production and consumption in every country," one where old, locally based industries are dislodged by new ones "whose products are consumed not only at home, but in every quarter of the globe."[5]

Economic globalization, the process of creating a global economy and of people being brought into closer economic association, is an inherent feature of modern capitalism, and as such was already well under way in the late eighteenth century. As we have seen, Enlightenment intellectuals were well aware of the growth of capitalism, discussed it extensively in their writings, and—though extremely critical of certain phenomena often asso-ciated with it, such as colonization, empire building, and the slave trade, and though insisting that it must always be constrained by principles of justice—on the whole endorsed it. Assigning a precise starting date to economic globalization is probably futile, in part because the process is very uneven and does not affect all parts of the world at the same time or to the same degree. But one popular candidate among economic historians is the European voyages of discovery in the late fifteenth and early sixteenth centuries. According to Ronald Findlay and Kevin H. O'Rourke, "The 'globalization' of the world economy in the sense of the linking of markets in the Old and New Worlds that had hitherto been separated . . . begins in this period . . . the European Voyages of Discovery across the Atlantic and around the Cape of Good Hope to the eastern seas, shortly followed by the crossing of the Pacific and the circumnavigation of the globe."[6]

A second dimension of globalization is *sociological*, in which case it refers to the process by which social groups are increasingly influenced and shaped by distant factors. Anthony Giddens is often associated with this particular perspective. In *The Consequences of Modernity* he writes, "Globalisation can . . . be defined as the intensification of worldwide social relations which link distant localities in such a way that local happenings are shaped by events many miles away and vice versa."[7] Along with this rather abstract notion of time-space compression found in sociological discussions of globalization goes an "intensification of consciousness of the world as a whole" within people's minds, an increased awareness that the traditional constraints of geography on social arrangements are receding.[8]

Extensive theorizing about when sociological globalization begins dates only from the early 1990s, but an awareness and endorsement of the basic phenomenon did exist in the Enlightenment. For instance, when Paine praises international trade as "a pacific system, operating to cordialize mankind," a system that will eventually act to a "universal extent,"[9] he is, among other things (more on this below), referring to a process of increased time-space compression and interconnectedness among different social groups. Similarly, when Kant envisions the *Handelsgeist* helping eventually to promote a community of the nations of the earth where "a violation of *Recht* on *one* place of the earth is felt in *all*" (*Peace* 8: 360), he too—in part—is also referring to a process of growing social connectivity between people.

A third aspect of globalization is *cultural*, and here the term refers to processes by which different cultures become integrated. However, the dominant descriptions of cultural globalization at present are not ones that see a blending together of formerly distinct cultures, but rather ones that bemoan a cultural imperialism in which one culture imposes—through the forces of mass media—its tentacles around the globe. Benjamin Barber's

depressing description of the global influence of transnational corporations—
"one McWorld tied together by communications, information, entertainment, and commerce"[10]—is perhaps the most well-known version of this
type of cultural globalization. At the same time, more optimistic perspectives
on cultural globalization that stress hybridization and creolization rather than
cultural imperialism—processes "marked by an organization of diversity
rather than by a replication of uniformity"[11]—have also been developed
recently.

In asking where Enlightenment intellectuals stood with regard to
cultural globalization, one needs to tread lightly, in part because of these
conflicting conceptions of cultural globalization, but also because of the
tremendous elasticity of the term "culture." As Gavin Kitching notes,
" 'culture' in its most general usage can embrace just about *anything and
everything* that human beings do—everything from their most private beliefs
and practices (sexuality/religion) to their most public forms of behavior
(occupational structures, sports activities, ways of shopping)."[12]

Very briefly, there are certain respects in which Enlightenment intellectuals advocated cultural globalization, and other respects in which they
did not. They did endorse the conscious formation of global political, legal,
religious, and moral cultures that would enable all peoples of the earth to
address human rights concerns by means of a shared conceptual vocabulary of transnational norms. And they hoped that international cultural
development, spurred by the growth of commerce, would itself contribute
to world peace. As Kant remarks in *Perpetual Peace*, "As culture grows and
human beings gradually move towards greater agreement over their principles, they lead to mutual understanding and peace" (8: 367). But convergence on basic principles of human rights and on norms of war and peace
by no means necessitates the creation of an imperialistic world culture.
Indeed, regional variations in political, legal, religious, and moral cultures
that stem from distinct historical traditions are to be encouraged as long as
they do not conflict with minimal transnational norms. And in the many
other areas of human culture that do not contribute to the formation of
these norms—food, clothing, sports, music, and so forth—Enlightenment
intellectuals certainly did not advocate cultural globalization. Kant, for
instance, in *Perpetual Peace*, speaks strongly against the *Zusammenschmelzung*
(melting together) of different nationalities: peoples "are not to be fused into
a single state"; "*nature wills* it otherwise" (8: 354, 367). As Thomas
McCarthy notes in his essay "On Reconciling Cosmopolitan Unity and
National Diversity," "Kant was indeed a cosmopolitan thinker, but he was
also concerned to reconcile his universalistic aspirations with the diversity

of national cultures, of which he had a wider knowledge than most of his contemporaries. Kant did, after all, lecture on anthropology and geography at Königsberg University for more than thirty years; he was, in fact, the first to do so."[13] In sum, Enlightenment intellectuals advocated a minimalist cultural globalization in the sense that they sought to construct a shared global culture of human rights and a commitment to peace. But their conception of cultural global unity was also conceived as one that would be compatible with national diversity and local traditions.

Finally, a fourth central component within current globalization debates, prominent in international relations and political science writings, concerns *political* globalization. To what extent is a global politics coming into being? Two major signs of increased political globalization discussed in this body of literature include the emergence and growth of intergovernmental organizations (IGOs) and international nongovernmental organizations (INGOs). Prominent examples of the former include, at the global level, the United Nations and the World Trade Organization, and at the regional level the European Union. Well-known examples of the latter include Amnesty International and Greenpeace. Impressed by the growth of both IGOs and INGOs[14] and the increasing difficulties that autonomous states face in coping with the transnational effects of economic globalization, global warming, and environmental degradation, some political observers claim that "the modern nation state itself—that artifact of the eighteenth and nineteenth centuries—has begun to crumble."[15] Others caution that reports of the death of the nation-state have been greatly exaggerated, but concede that the sheer dominance of this particular type of political arrangement, an arrangement that also now exhibits considerable uniformity around the world, is itself a sign of political globalization.[16]

If we ask where Enlightenment intellectuals stood regarding political globalization, the answer is clear. They hoped that the future would bring increased political globalization, and, as we saw earlier ("Peace through Federation" in chapter 5), the very idea of what are now called IGOs begins in the Enlightenment. At the same time, the intergovernmental organizations that they did envision were often only regional and Eurocentric rather than global, and even the exceptions (such as Crucé's and Kant's proposed federations) focused exclusively on the problem of establishing a peaceful order between states. Broader issues of international distributive justice and environmental stewardship were not part of Enlightenment global politics. Also, most Enlightenment theorizing about global politics was premised on the assumption that the nation-state—albeit one with reduced powers of sovereignty—would continue to be the dominant political unit.

But what about INGOs—international nongovernmental organizations composed of individuals from different countries who band together to promote social and political change? Do we find any evidence of this portent of political globalization in the Enlightenment? I believe that its ancestry tracks directly back to the Enlightenment ideal of the "Republic of Letters," an informal network of contacts and correspondence among intellectuals from different countries, described by an anonymous participant as follows: "In the midst of all the governments that decide the fate of men; in the bosom of so many states, the majority of them despotic . . . there exists a certain realm which holds sway only over the mind . . . that we honour with the name Republic, because it preserves a measure of independence, and because it is almost its essence to be free. It is the realm of talent and thought."[17] While the Republic of Letters was always more of a conceptual space than an actual one (it did not have a list of dues-paying members), a number of concrete institutions did grow out of it: "academies, book fairs, clubs, salons, societies, libraries, gazettes, newspapers, and periodicals," all of which "were designed to facilitate the circulation of information and the pursuit of knowledge."[18] These associated institutions also embodied the group's ideals of tolerance, cosmopolitanism, intellectual independence, and impartiality, ideals that contemporary INGOs continue to espouse.

This brief survey of different conceptions of globalization, though by no means exhaustive, does enable us to see some of the ways in which Enlightenment intellectuals themselves participated in a debate that now dominates social science discussion. But missing from present-day social science discussions of globalization is the central dimension of Enlightenment concern: *moral* globalization. Enlightenment intellectuals viewed these four aspects of globalization—economic, social, cultural, and political— merely as favorable conditions for moral globalization, which for them was by far the most important dimension of globalization. The expansion of free trade, the spread of republican government, the increase in cross-cultural contact, the growth of international law—these and other related (exterior) institutional developments in modern human life were expected to eventually effect an (interior) attitudinal transformation. The kind of "complex connectivity"[19] that Enlightenment authors hoped to see arise from the multiple globalizing tendencies of modernity was a distinctly *moral* connectivity, one that would interconnect people morally so that "a violation of *Recht* on *one* place of the earth is felt in *all*."

However, at present, there are no clear signs that moral globalization is occurring. While the small chorus of contemporary authors concerned with global justice is defending one or another version of the cosmopolitan ethical commitments that Enlightenment intellectuals hoped would take root as a result of institutional development,[20] the basic attitudinal changes in people's hearts and minds that were expected to follow modernity's institutional developments are not readily detectable on any wide-scale basis. Commerce has not served "to cordialize mankind"; it has not inclined the peoples of the earth "to keep peace with each other and to love each other." This unpleasant fact should lead us to reexamine the Enlightenment's assumption that external institutional change would help produce interior attitudinal change. Two centuries of increased trade and commerce have still not produced the hoped-for results. The Enlightenment thesis regarding humanity's eventual moralization and the means by which it would be achieved, it seems safe to say, lacks empirical support. And the evident lack of moralization in the contemporary world itself contributes to the further, darker result that Enlightenment ideals in general lack strong support at present. A misjudgment about the means toward Enlightenment is itself now in danger of imploding into a rejection of the ends of Enlightenment.

But to return to a somewhat more modest point: any and all attempts to establish an easy linkage between the Enlightenment and contemporary globalization must be rejected. Contemporary globalization is decidedly not the Enlightenment's "troubling fulfillment,"[21] but rather a misappropriation of its ideals, a hijacking of its hopes.

Poverty within and between Nations

Not favored spots alone, but the whole Earth.

—Wordsworth, *The Prelude*, X.701

Poverty between Nations

Easier to observe and measure than internal changes in people's moral beliefs is a rise or fall in their standard of living. As I noted earlier, Condorcet's first hope for the future condition of the human race was "the abolition of inequality between nations." While many of his contemporaries were less sanguine regarding the chances of ever completely eliminating inequality between nations, most of them certainly believed that inequality would and should at least decrease substantially as trade and commerce between nations increased. Smith himself helped substantially to change general attitudes toward the poor when he stressed that "it is but equity... that they who feed, cloath, and lodge the whole body of the people, should have such a share of the produce of their own labour as to be themselves tolerably well fed, cloathed and lodged" (*WN* I.viii.36).[22] But has inequality between nations in fact decreased over the past two centuries? Surprisingly, the answer is an emphatic *no*.

The historical and international statistics on poverty are truly terrifying. For instance, according to economic historian David Landes, at present "the difference in income per head between the richest industrial nation, say Switzerland, and poorest nonindustrial country, Mozambique, is about 400 to 1. Two hundred and fifty years ago, this gap between richest and poorest was perhaps 5 to 1, and the difference between Europe and, say, East or South Asia (China or India) was around 1.5 or 2 to 1."[23] Although other economic historians do not report such huge differences in wealth between nations during either the Enlightenment or at present (a reason, here as elsewhere, not to overobjectify the numbers), there is nevertheless a wide consensus that "the world economy has become far more unequal over the last two centuries."[24] Paul Bairoch, for instance, estimates that the gap between rich and poor nations during the Enlightenment was even smaller than Landes suggests: "The differences in the international levels of income were very limited before the strong upheaval introduced by the industrial revolution. The gap between the least developed or poorest country and the richest was probably in the range of only 1.0 to 1.6. If we refer to broader economic entities, such as Western Europe or China, the gap was even more limited, of the order of 1.0 to 1.3 or less."[25] Angus Maddison, while citing past intercountry income spreads that are closer to Landes's estimates, does not see the present gap as being quite so extreme. According to his data, "In 1820 the intercountry income spread was probably about 4:1; in 1913 it was 10:1; in 1950 it was 26:1; in 1973 it was 36:1, and in 1989 it was 39:1."[26] Similarly, Stanley L. Engerman and Kenneth L. Sokoloff, in a table listing "gross domestic product per capita in selected new world economies, 1700–1989," cite an intercountry income spread of approximately 2:1 in 1800 and close to 6:1 in 1989.[27] But again, though scholars' numerical estimates concerning intercountry income spread vary somewhat, the general picture is sadly clear: rather than declining, inequality between nations has in fact grown substantially over the past two centuries.

Part of the explanation for the substantial growth in intercountry inequality is that there are many more sovereign states at present than there were two hundred years ago, and some of the younger states are not doing well at all. In 1800, there were only fifty-something sovereign nation-states; today there are close to two hundred. And most of the poorest countries at present have attained independence fairly recently. As Jeffrey Sachs notes, "The overwhelming share of the world's extreme poor, 93 percent in 2001, live in three regions: East Asia, South Asia, and sub-Saharan Africa. Since 1981, the numbers of extreme poor have risen in sub-Saharan Africa, but have fallen in East Asia and South Asia."[28] The post–World War II anticolonial revolution has indeed put "the world in pieces," and some of the resultant economic pieces are horrifying.[29] Sovereign states generally have their own trade policies, their own currencies, their own laws regarding business contracts and labor regulations, and so forth. While consensus on the overall consequences of this recent huge increase in the number of sovereign states is not forthcoming (due in part to irresolvable differences of opinion concerning the importance of national sovereignty and the right to self-determination vis-à-vis economic growth), given the growing disparity in income between the richest and poorest nations, it is no secret that the economic effects of the proliferation of sovereignty have been disastrous. From a purely economic perspective, dividing the world into two hundred distinct economies is extremely inefficient.[30] However, this is not to say that a functioning global economy and nationalism are flatly incompatible. To assume that the forces of economic globalization must necessarily lead to the demise of the nation-state is both to beg the question in favor of a world state and to ignore present-day political realities.[31] The nation-state is not about to disappear any time soon.

One may be tempted to see a partial fulfillment of Enlightenment economic hopes in figures that indicate a decrease in intercountry income spread over the past two hundred years for those countries belonging to "the West European capitalist core and its offshoots" (the offshoots are Australia, Canada, and the United States). According to Maddison, for instance, we do find a gradual convergence within this group, "from an income spread of 2.3:1 in 1820 to 1.5:1 in 1989."[32] But the problem here is that this decrease in inequality applies only to countries within one elite group—a group that already "had a clear lead" over other countries at the end of the eighteenth century, and one that has increased its lead substantially since then.[33] The gradual spreading of economic progress over all nations of the earth that Kant, Condorcet, Smith, and many other Enlightenment intellectuals predicted would occur has clearly not happened. Not only has economic progress not spread outward to other countries, it has in fact contracted inward, making those nations that were richer two centuries ago exponentially richer today.

World Poverty

*Men are like plants: they never grow well unless they
are well cultivated. Among people living in poverty, the
human race loses and even degenerates.*

—Montesquieu, *The Persian Letters* (1721)

Although the belief that poverty is preventable was born in the Enlightenment,[34] Enlightenment efforts to eradicate poverty clearly did not succeed, and
neither have subsequent ones. Each year at present some 18 million people
"die prematurely from poverty-related causes. This is one-third of all human
deaths—50,000 every day, including 34,000 children under age five."[35] If we
multiply this annual death-from-poverty figure by only fifteen years, when
the cold war ended and politicians began talking about a new world order
replacing the old one of containment and détente, we arrive at an even more
horrifying figure: "This 15-year death toll of 270 million is considerably larger
than the 200-million death toll from all the wars, civil wars, genocides and
other government repression of the entire 20th century combined."[36]

However, while the total number of people living in extreme poverty
at present is staggeringly high—approximately 1.1 billion in 2001[37]—the
proportion of the world's population living in extreme poverty has fallen
substantially since the Enlightenment. The world population in 1800 was
only about 900 million; by 2001 it had exploded to 6.1 billion. Today
approximately 1 out of 6 human beings lives in extreme poverty; in 1800
the figure was closer to 5 out of 6. For instance, according to the authors of
a study entitled "Inequality among World Citizens: 1820–1992," in 1820
84 percent of the world's inhabitants lived in a state of extreme poverty,
compared to 24 percent in 1992.[38] The latter figure has shrunk further
since the early 1990s, to about 16.6 percent, primarily because of strong
economic improvement in the regions of East Asia and China.

For some, these figures are "causes for qualified optimism. From being
universal, extreme poverty has become, if not rare, the affliction of less than
a quarter of a vastly increased human population."[39] Others argue that the
deaths of innocent people do not become "morally less troubling the more
world population increases. What matters morally is the *number* of people in
extreme poverty."[40] In terms of absolute numbers, there clearly are substantially more extremely poor people on our planet at present than there
were two hundred years ago—by about 50 percent. Either way, the

Enlightenment's belief that poverty can and should be ended has not yet been translated into an effective plan of action, and this is another of its hopes for the future of humanity that has yet to be realized.

From Civic Culture to Consumer Culture

Somewhere between the lofty but hard-to-measure goal of an internal attitudinal transformation triggered by the spread of commerce and the clear-cut hypothesis that inequality and poverty would be strongly reduced by lowering trade barriers and deregulating markets lay the Enlightenment hope that the new commercial society would in turn give rise to a new active and engaged public sphere. The commercial spirit itself would help cultivate conversation and sociability, out of which would come a new mode of public discourse in which civic-minded (and newly educated) individuals would openly debate issues of public concern. Key developments within the rise of capitalism that were believed to contribute to the birth of the public sphere include "the growth of reading and writing publics, the rise of novels, newspapers and political journalism," and "the proliferation of public spaces where people socialized or sought entertainment—coffeehouses, pleasure gardens, public theaters."[41] Most crucial of all to this process of individuals coming together to argue and discuss public issues was the use of shared norms of reason: "The medium of this political confrontation was peculiar and without historical precedent: people's public use of their reason."[42]

Contemporary scholars tend to associate this famous thesis concerning the new significance of public debate in political life during the late Enlightenment with Jürgen Habermas's pioneering first book, *Strukturwandel der Öffentlichkeit: Untersuchungen zur einen Kategorie der bürgerlichen Gesellshaft* (1962), first translated into English in 1989 under the title *The Structural Transformation of the Public Sphere: An Inquiry into a Category of Bourgeois Society*.[43] But the type of public sphere or public (*Öffentlichkeit*) that Habermas analyzes in this work is also described in great detail by Kant and other Enlightenment authors. Indeed, as Habermas himself explicitly acknowledges at the beginning of a fifteen-page analysis of Kant's position on this topic, "The idea of the bourgeois public sphere attained its theoretically fully developed form with Kant's elaboration of the principle of publicity" (102).

Kant discusses the principle of publicity in a number of different texts (Habermas's examination of Kant's position includes multiple citations

from nine different works), but the most famous—and most accessible—
version is to be found in his short essay *An Answer to the Question: What Is
Enlightenment?* (1784), when he discusses "the public use of reason": "By the
public use of one's own reason I understand that use which someone makes
of it *as a scholar* before the entire public of the *world of readers*" (8: 37). As
Habermas notes (and as Kant's own subsequent examples illustrate), Kant
is not referring here only to professional scholars, but to "anyone who
understood how to use his reason in public" (105). Also, Kant demarcates
the boundaries of the public sphere before which people are to make use
of their reason extremely broadly: as he remarks at one point, "the public
in the strict sense, that is, the world" (8: 38). But in order for the public use
of reason to effectively function as a vehicle of critique and enlightenment
in political matters (or any other matter brought before the public), reason
must be free and uncensored. This linking of freedom and the public is
what Habermas calls Kant's "postulate of publicity as a principle" (106),
and it is also presented in *What Is Enlightenment?*: "The *public* use of reason
must always be free, and it alone can bring about enlightenment among
human beings" (8: 37).

But the second half of Habermas's study deals with the "structural
transformation" of the Enlightenment public sphere in the nineteenth and
twentieth centuries, and here the story becomes decidedly less upbeat. The
active, engaged sense of a public developed in the Enlightenment, he
asserts, "was replaced by the pseudo-public or sham-private world of
culture consumption" (160), a world in which "rational-critical debate
had a tendency to be replaced by consumption" (161), where "the public
is split apart into minorities of specialists who put their reason to use
nonpublicly and the great mass of consumers whose receptiveness is public
but uncritical" (175). Consumption on this view is passive, private, and
uncritical: consumers are literally brainwashed by the forces of mass media
and advertising to buy goods that they do not need or even truly want (and
often cannot afford) and to acquiesce to the status quo.

Habermas's pessimism concerning twentieth-century consumer society
is strongly reminiscent of Horkheimer and Adorno's earlier critique of "the
culture industry" in the *Dialectic of Enlightenment*. They too saw the mass
culture engineered by capitalism as fostering passive conformity and assent.
In a mass society where culture infects everything with sameness, consumers are tricked by the advertising industry not only to purchase goods they
do not need but also to compulsively imitate cultural images and messages
"which, at the same time, they recognize as false."[44] But the locus classicus
of this attitude toward consumerism is Marx's discussion of commodity

fetishism in *Capital* (1867), a process whereby ordinary commodities that are in reality products of human labor acquire a "mystical character" and are "changed into something transcendent,"[45] and thus perceived falsely as forces endowed with intrinsic powers beyond human making.

Criticisms of Habermas's interpretation of the public sphere are legion. He has been accused of ignoring the presence of a thriving consumer culture in eighteenth-century Enlightenment Europe, of being blind to the multiple civic and political dimensions of consumerism itself, of over-idealizing the Enlightenment public sphere, particularly with regard to its alleged inclusiveness and universality, of presupposing a false dichotomy between private and public spheres, and more. Additionally, the Marxist critique of consumption in mass society (from which Habermas borrows) as passive and apolitical itself suffers from a self-referential incoherence: for how is it that critical theorists, themselves members of contemporary society, are able to resist the seductive forces of the culture industry? One social historian, after surveying a number of recent works on the topic, concludes,

> With regard to consumption, it is perhaps better to disregard Habermas's liberal public sphere and think in terms more of competing publics founded on various ideological schemas. Certainly when we look at women's role in consumer politics, notions of a public/private division are contradicted in so many circumstances that one questions entirely the value of the separate spheres analysis.... What is not needed are the increasingly futile debates as to whether consumerism is a good or a bad thing.[46]

We need not assess these different critiques here; indeed, for the sake of argument let us assume that they are all true. For the criticism we wish to make is a more fundamental one that nearly all parties in the debate will readily accept: the kind of public that Enlightenment theorists envisioned growing out of commercial society—an engaged, critical civic culture open to all, in which participants communicate as equals, using shared norms of reason—does not exist at present. And to the extent that a public possessing these characteristics was one of the main expected fruits of new economic developments during the Enlightenment, the harvest in this area has been barren.

In sum, first impressions to the contrary, Enlightenment hopes for the future in the area of economics have not been realized. Economic globalization has not yet contributed to any noticeable moral globalization, and the latter was held to be the former's primary reason for existing. Nor has the liberalization of trade and commerce eliminated poverty. Indeed, inequality between and within nations has increased drastically over the past two hundred years, and many in the affluent West have backtracked to a pre-Enlightenment acceptance of the view that the poor will always be with us, and that they deserve kindness and compassion rather than justice. Regardless of how much shoppers may wish to celebrate consumerism as a source of creativity and empowerment, there is no evidence that this activity produces active participants in an engaged civic culture. The means advocated for the achievement of Enlightenment economic ends have not been proven to be effective, and—partly as a result of the former—public support for the ends themselves is now distressingly weak.

9

....

Politics

Proliferation of Sovereign States

Nationalism was the first ideal examined in my earlier chapter on politics in the Enlightenment. What has happened in this area of political thought since the Enlightenment? The basic picture concerning nationalism from the Enlightenment to the present is one of explosive growth, particularly during the second half of the twentieth century. At the end of the eighteenth century, many areas outside of Europe were colonies under the control of European states such as Spain, Portugal, France, and England.[1] In eighteenth-century Europe, many principalities were still parts of larger kingdoms and not yet sovereign states. But over the past two centuries, the Enlightenment nationalist conviction that each people has the right to self-government has been acted on with repeated frequency by subsequent generations.

The Americas present the most startling change with respect to nationalism. In 1800, the United States was the sole sovereign nation in this part of the world. Canada, Mexico, and countries in Central America, the Caribbean region, South America—two hundred years ago, all of the lands in these areas were colonies of either Britain, Spain, France, Portugal, or the Netherlands. The vast majority of countries in the Americas achieved independence in the nineteenth century.

In Africa, European colonists were slower to move. By the end of the eighteenth century, several parts of Africa's perimeter were already under Spanish, Portuguese, British, or Dutch control, but few Europeans had yet even stepped foot in the interior region. (As Kant remarked in his *Lectures on Physical Geography* [1802], "The interior of Africa is as unknown to us as the regions of the moon"; 9: 229.)[2] Partly as a result, it is virtually impossible to determine accurately the number of sovereign states that existed in Africa at this time. We can, however, at least note how late eighteenth-century European and American geographers described this "unknown" continent. Jedidiah Morse (1761–1826), for instance, in *The American Geography* (1796), lists twenty African "nations"; William Guthrie (1708–70), in *A New System of Modern Geography* (first American ed., 1794) lists sixteen "principal nations" (along with fifteen "noteworthy islands"); and the anonymously published *Geography for Youth* (fourth ed., London, 1790) reports that "Africa is divided into 15 principal parts" and also has seven "principal islands."[3] Unfortunately, many of the African states that did exist at this time were not able to maintain sovereignty for long. By the end of the nineteenth century, every part of Africa except Liberia (independence declared in 1847) and Ethiopia had become either a colony or a protectorate of some European state. Most of the currently recognized sovereign African states did not achieve independence until the 1960s.

Asia, site of some of the world's oldest civilizations and most extensive empires, was also coming under increasing European control during the eighteenth century. However, in comparison with Africa and the Americas, Asian states were better able to hold their own against outside colonizing forces. Here too, although an accurate tally of the number of sovereign states existing in Asia at this time is very hard to come by, we can at least note how Western geographers of the time described the situation: Morse lists six Asian "nations" and fourteen islands; Guthrie, seven nations and fourteen islands; the anonymous author of *Geography for Youth*, six "parts" of Asia and sixteen "principal Asiatic islands."[4]

In eighteenth-century Europe (as elsewhere), absolute monarchy was still the dominant form of government, and the effects of Enlightenment nationalist impulses were only just beginning to be felt. While the late eighteenth-century geographers cited earlier were much better acquainted with Europe than with other continents, the situation with respect to European governance was also very volatile, and hence even here no clear consensus existed among them concerning the number of sovereign states. Enlightenment geographers also lacked even a settled vocabulary for describing the political divisions of Europe. Morse, for instance, lists seventeen "principal states" in Europe, elsewhere describing three empires, twelve kingdoms, and eleven republics; Guthrie, in his "grand division" of Europe, lists sixteen kingdoms; and according to *Geography for Youth* there were twenty-six "principal sovereignties" in Europe.[5]

Although it is not possible to offer a precise answer to the question "How many sovereign states existed in 1800?" these data suggest a rough estimate lying somewhere in the fifties. However, accurate figures for the period 1900 to the present are readily available, and here the data clearly do point to a proliferation of sovereign states. According to one influential study, "In 1900, there were 55 sovereign states, 80 in 1950, and today there are 192."[6]

At the same time, contrary to what is often assumed, life does not necessarily improve for people once they become citizens of a sovereign state rather than subjects in a colony, empire, or protectorate. The explosive growth of sovereign states since the Enlightenment (again, particularly in the second half of the twentieth century) has also led to heightened concern about the phenomenon of "failed states," nations that have achieved not only political sovereignty, but also less desirable results such as flagrant human rights abuses against their own citizens, economic collapse, civil war, crumbling state infrastructures, and domestic chaos. As one author notes, "It was fashionable for a period...to speak of 'democratic transitions,' as though the final destination were a given. In reality, some countries will make it, some will remain stuck in failed and weak governance, some will become wards of the international system, some will descend into chaotic warlord struggles, and others will revert to authoritarianism."[7]

Given both the legacy of colonialism (many postcolonial states were not well prepared for self-governance) and the depressing fact that many of the newer states are extremely poor, resource-deprived, and geographically disadvantaged, it should come as no surprise that numerous states at present are at risk of failure.[8] At the same time, the phenomenon of state failure is hardly new. When judged by the cold criteria of failure and success, states are not terribly different from individuals: some have flourished, a great many have muddled along, and some have failed. Within each category there exists a wide range of performance possibilities, and movement between the categories is also a distinct option. There are often second chances in life for both persons and states, but permanent collapse is always a distinct possibility. Although there is no political or psychological formula that enables us to predict accurately what percentage of states or individuals will fail, experience shows that examples of both types of failure (temporary and permanent) will always be with us. What makes the phenomenon of state failure *seem* new stems from a combination of short-term memory and simple arithmetic: states have always failed, but at present there are more sovereign nations than ever, increasing the pool of potential failures.

In the end, how should one evaluate the explosion in self-governance that has transpired over the past two centuries? Is it a good thing or a bad thing? Numerically speaking, the increase is nearly fourfold. However, as the specter of state failure continues to haunt some while the Enlightenment dream of world federation energizes and frustrates others, this may be one clear case where bigger isn't better. Certainly different parties will reach strongly divergent conclusions about the growth of sovereignty since the Enlightenment, depending on what criteria they use in making their evaluations. Some observers will side with Herder and Fichte (and, to a lesser extent, Rousseau), who were prescient in emphasizing the fundamental importance of cultural, linguistic, and ethnic factors in shaping human identity. For better or worse, many peoples' sense of self, particularly those who are members of new states, continues to be bound up with "primordial sentiments": "the gross actualities of blood, race, language, locality, religion, and tradition."[9] As a result, there remains a "call to difference" within modernity (though it is certainly not a new call), and answering this call is "a matter of dignity, in which one's self-worth is engaged."[10] At the same time, Herder and Fichte's separatist paranoia against the *Vermischung* of different peoples was also a harbinger of the dark side of post-Enlightenment nationalism, a side that continues to wreak havoc in human life.

Is there a way to acknowledge the importance of achieving and sustaining cultural identity without necessarily yoking it to statehood? One reason for doing so is the simple but painful fact that some peoples and nationalities do not have enough economic heft to become viable nations.[11] Many of the younger sovereign states are not exactly thriving, and some are candidates for outright state failure. From the standpoint of economic efficiency, the post-Enlightenment proliferation of states has been a disaster. A second reason for detaching cultural identity from statehood is that as the number of sovereign states increases, so too does the difficulty of achieving effective international cooperation. That "the continual splitting up of old nations, ex-colonies, and ex-federations" makes an effective world federation "less likely with every passing year"[12] is not quite a necessary truth, for there is always the remote possibility that the growing brood of nations will come to further agreement on the need for an effective international rule of law. But it may be a political truth.

One middle option that was ignored by both the ethnic/cultural nationalists of the Enlightenment (who maintained that there should be one state for each people) and the civic/political nationalists (who downplayed primordial attachments and uncritically accepted Crèvecoeur's prediction that individuals of all nations who became U.S. citizens would be happily "melted into a new race of men") is what one commentator calls a "sub- and inter-statist conception of self-determination." This middle option acknowledges the significance of cultural nationalism, but detaches it from state sovereignty. The right to self-determination is now interpreted "as a right within the state; never as a right to independent statehood." But it is also interpreted as a right that applies to *all* peoples, not just to ethnic majorities: "Self-determination is not a right of majority nations within states *vis-à-vis* national minorities, but rather a right to which each national group in the world is entitled."[13] If a way could be found to make this middle option politically feasible, a double benefit would ensue: the insights of ethnic/cultural nationalism concerning human identity formation would be retained while the multiple damages caused by separatist nationalism and state proliferation would be lessened.

Regardless of one's views on identity formation, in the final analysis the post-Enlightenment proliferation of states cannot be viewed as a victory for Enlightenment political thinking for the simple reason that many states at present do not behave in the way that Enlightenment nationalists thought sovereign states should and would behave. The nationalistic fervor that exploded after the Enlightenment was not Enlightenment nationalism. Enlightenment nationalists of all persuasions (ethnic/cultural as well as civic/political) assumed that nations that realized their right to self-determination would recognize that all nations possess this same right. They thought their liberal nationalism would bring an end to colonialism and empire building. Similarly, as concerns domestic policy, Enlightenment nationalists of all stripes assumed that the rights of minorities would be protected by the new nation-states; this also has not proved to be the case. Finally, Enlightenment liberal nationalism was held to be completely consistent with cosmopolitanism, but much post-Enlightenment nationalism has been decidedly noncosmopolitan.

The ideal of nationalism as envisioned by Enlightenment intellectuals was thus intended as a kind of domestic and foreign policy panacea, a force that would serve to promote peace abroad as well as dignity and respect for all citizens within the boundaries of each state. But the subsequent reality of nationalism has turned out quite differently. Here as elsewhere, a degenerate form of Enlightenment ideals has taken the place of the original. A post-Enlightenment phenomenon that shares a name with an Enlightenment ideal and may look similar to it on the surface is in reality something very different.

Democratization

As discussed earlier, a second central political ideal espoused by Enlightenment intellectuals was republicanism, by which they meant a form of government marked by competitive elections for political representatives; the separation of executive, legislative, and judicial powers; and the rule of law. For better or worse, the term "republicanism" is seldom used by laypeople at present to describe contemporary political regimes possessing these characteristics and has been largely replaced by "democracy." Enlightenment authors, adhering more closely to etymology than contemporary writers have done, tended to strongly differentiate republicanism from democracy. Indeed, the term "democracy" was not used a great deal in the eighteenth century, and when it was used it often carried a derogatory sense quite different from its contemporary universally laudatory connotation.[14] Not until after World War I (when Woodrow Wilson pledged to "make the world safe for democracy") did "democracy" come to be "a term of approval in practically every context."[15] Kant, for instance, in *Perpetual Peace*, derides democracy as "a *despotism* because it establishes an executive power in which all decide for and, if need be, against one (who thus does not agree)" (8: 352). Similarly, Madison in *Federalist Paper* No. 10 complains that democracies "have ever been spectacles of turbulence and contention; have ever been found incompatible with personal security or the rights of property; and have in general been as short in their lives as they have been violent in their deaths."[16] In both cases (and this is characteristic of Enlightenment usage of the term "democracy"), the authors are referring to the classical model of direct, participatory democracy: "rule by the people," *dēmokratia*. But modern nation-states tend to be much larger and more populous than ancient city-states, and these two facts were repeatedly appealed to in making the case that the classic model of democracy would not work well in a modern setting. In practice (if not always in academic discussion), the weaker model of indirect, representative government gradually came to replace that of direct democracy, eventually even appropriating the very name "democracy" itself. Over the years, the dominant meaning of "democracy" has shifted from "government by the people" to "government approved by the people."[17] This minimalist conception of democracy—"electoral democracy"[18]—has virtually replaced the original maximalist conception of *dēmokratia*. As one author notes,

> If the term "democracy" is restricted to political systems in which all citizens participate in day-to-day policy making, then there are no democracies among the nations of the world. It is doubtful if a unit as large as a nation can work as a pure democracy. The relevant national experiences today are found in political systems where representative leaders are chosen through competitive elections. The competitive electoral context, with several political parties organizing the alternatives that face the voters, is the identifying property of the contemporary democratic process. To study political performance in democratic systems among today's nations means to study political performance in those nations characterized by competitive elections in which most citizens are eligible to participate.[19]

However, both classical, direct citizen-participation democracies as well as their modern, electoral descendents often lack further features that were particularly important to Enlightenment republicans such as separation of powers, rule of law, and protection of minority rights. These integral features of Enlightenment republicanism tend today (keeping in mind that not all writers employ the same terminology) to be grouped under the label "liberal democracy." Liberal democracy (roughly speaking) = electoral democracy + separation of powers + rule of law + protection of basic liberties of speech, assembly, religion, and property; and liberal democracy (roughly speaking) = Enlightenment republicanism. Alternatively put, minimalist electoral democracy without any constitutional safeguards = "illiberal democracy," a disturbing phenomenon marked by human rights abuses and civil strife that has risen sharply in recent decades.[20] Indeed, Edward Mansfield and Jack Snyder, in *Electing to Fight: Why Emerging Democracies Go to War*, argue that minimalist electoral democracies that lack the rule of law and a free press are also particularly prone to war: "When these institutions are absent or weak, politicians have incentives to resort to violent nationalist appeals, tarring their opponents as enemies of the nation in order to prevail in electoral competition."[21]

Summing up: just as Adams, Jefferson, Paine, and Madison all complained about the vagueness of the term "republicanism," so today there remains a "lack of consensus on the meaning of *democracy*."[22] The two meanings of the term that have achieved the most discussion in recent years are illiberal or "electoral democracy" and "liberal democracy." The latter term, again, is essentially what Enlightenment authors meant by "republicanism." However, at bottom contemporary authors who warn us of the dangers of illiberal democracy seem to be merely echoing and reinforcing the importance of the earlier Enlightenment distinction between democracy and republicanism. All parties agree that we need more of the latter.

Keeping these terminological shifts and disagreements in mind, let us now ask: How has democracy fared since the Enlightenment? To what extent has the number of democratic states grown since the Enlightenment? Insofar as democracy has grown, to what extent does its growth allow us to say that, at least in this particular area of human life, Enlightenment ideals have been realized—that the political world they wanted is the one we now have?

In 1750, "no democratic institutions at the national level existed in the Western world."[23] By the late eighteenth century, there were only three partial or restricted democracies (the United States, the French Republic, and Switzerland), and if one drops the qualifiers "partial or restricted" the number quickly drops back to zero.[24] The number of democratic states definitely expands after this point, but not as rapidly as one might think. (As was also the case with the statistics regarding the proliferation of national sovereignty, the growth in democracy was very slow at first, accelerating most rapidly in the last quarter of the twentieth century.) Also, unlike the post-Enlightenment growth in nationalism, post-Enlightenment democratization has occurred in waves, each of which "was followed by a reverse wave in which some but not all of the countries that had previously made the transition to democracy reverted to nondemocratic rule."[25] According to one study, "There were only about 9 democracies among the 48 nations in 1902, 22 democracies among the 64 independent nations in 1920, 21 democracies among the 65 nations in 1929–30, 29 democracies among the 121 nations in 1960."[26] Freedom House, author of the most influential study, offers the following fuller picture:

> In 1900, there were no states which could be judged as electoral democracies by the standard of universal suffrage for competitive multiparty elections. The U.S., Britain, and a handful of other countries

possessed the most democratic systems, but their denial of voting rights to women, and in the case of the U.S. to black Americans, meant that they were countries with restricted democratic practices. The states with restricted democratic practices were 25 in number and accounted for just 12.4 percent of the world population.... At mid-century, there were 22 democracies accounting for 31 percent of the world population and a further 21 states with restricted democratic practices, accounting for 11.9 percent of the globe's population. By the close of our century liberal and electoral democracies clearly predominate.... Electoral democracies now represent 120 of the 192 existing countries and constitute 62.5 percent of the world's population. At the same time liberal democracies—i.e. countries Freedom House regards as free and respectful of basic human rights and the rule of law—are 85 in number and represent 38 percent of the global population.[27]

These data do clearly support the claim that democratic sovereignty within states—both in its electoral and liberal variants—has grown enormously since the Enlightenment. While electoral and liberal democracies are certainly not the only kinds of democracies, and while some critics maintain that neither of them is the most desirable kind of democracy (see also below), the sheer numerical growth in this area is extremely impressive. From 0 to 120 electoral democracies in two hundred years, and from 0 to 85 liberal democracies within the same time frame—of all the Enlightenment hopes for the future examined in part I of this study, democracy has achieved the highest degree of realization in the post-Enlightenment world. Although no existing republic or liberal democracy (again, contemporary liberal democracy comes closest to Enlightenment republicanism) is perfect, this particular Enlightenment ideal, unlike several others, has not devolved into a degenerate form. Over the years liberal democracy, though certainly not immune to criticism, has, so to speak, stayed true to form.[28]

Above all, Enlightenment authors defended republicanism/liberal democracy because they believed it would help promote positive changes in human attitudes and behavior. The establishment and spread of republican regimes would eventually contribute to moralization: as more countries established liberal democratic institutions, more people would in turn become morally better. The American Benjamin Rush, for instance, predicted confidently in 1786 that "our republican forms of government will in time beget republican opinions and manners. All will end well."[29] Similarly, Kant viewed republican regimes as one of a number of key institutions that would enable human beings to take "a great step toward morality" (*Peace* 8: 375 n.) by reducing violence among citizens, encouraging respect for the rule of law, and, most important of all, eventually bringing an end to war, or at least to war between fellow republican regimes. As we saw earlier, Paine, Smith, and many other Enlightenment authors shared the conviction that republics were more inherently peace-loving than nonrepublics. Briefly, Kant's argument in support of this conviction is that a republican regime is one where "the consent of the citizens of a state is required in order to decide whether there shall be war or not" (*Peace* 8: 350). Taxpaying citizens are the ones who ultimately pay for wars, and they will be understandably cautious in declaring war. On the other hand, in a nonrepublican regime a narrow ruling class that does not serve at the pleasure of the people can readily declare war with little personal risk and without consulting the citizenry. Because the citizens in a republic must directly bear the burdens and costs of wars and because this fact will enter into their own deliberations about whether to declare war (and also because nonrepublican rulers can shelter themselves from the horrors of war in ways that a whole nation cannot), republics will be less inclined to war than nonrepublics.

A number of contemporary political scientists have written about the "cultural conditions for democracy,"[30] yet there is virtually no work at present that tries to test the Enlightenment hypothesis that liberal democracy contributes to a morally better culture. The former body of literature concerns alleged cultural *preconditions for* stable democracy; the latter Enlightenment hypothesis is about cultural and moral *outcomes of* democracy. The contemporary reticence to examine the Enlightenment moralization hypothesis stems from a variety of factors, including both conceptual difficulties in coming to agreement on what exactly "morally better" means as well as practical difficulties in determining when internal attitudinal change really has occurred. The one clear exception to this generalization concerns the "democratic peace" thesis, which is fairly easy to test empirically. A substantial body of literature exists on this topic, most of which does support the Enlightenment claim that republican regimes are more peaceful—at least toward their republican neighbors. As Michael Doyle notes, "Liberal states do exercise peaceful restraint, and a separate peace exists among them. . . . And as the number of Liberal states increases, it announces the possibility of global peace this side of the grave or world conquest." But he then adds, "Peaceful restraint seems to work only in Liberals' relations with other Liberals. Liberal States have fought numerous wars with non-Liberal states."[31]

The biggest concern regarding the recent nearly global trend toward democratization is whether it will achieve "consolidation" or suffer a reversal. Samuel Huntington and others have emphasized that the first two waves of democratization were followed by reverse waves. They have also pressed Hume's question: Will the future be conformable to the past? While theorists living in secure democracies are busy at present offering advice to new democracies on how to best achieve consolidation, there are no guarantees that consolidation will be achieved, much less that the current trend toward democratization will expand further in the future.

Liberal democracy is also not without its critics. On the left, the two most persistent criticisms involve calls for more direct citizen participation in decision making (in effect, a return to the model of classical democracy) and concerns about whether the formal, legal quality promised by constitutional republics can be truly meaningful in the face of the glaring social and economic inequalities tolerated by free market systems (a rebuke whose ancestry lies in Marxist critiques of "bourgeois democracy").[32] Enlightenment intellectuals hoped that the future would bring less inequality between and within nations, and to the extent that both types of inequality are still amply present the means that they advocated in pursuit of these goals need to be reexamined and revised. But stronger forms of democracy, if they are to be adopted, need to be built on top of rather than (as has been tried in the past) in place of secure liberal foundations. A free press and legal protection of civil liberties are essential features of republicanism and liberal democracy that should not be sacrificed under any circumstances. For once they are forfeited, we have replaced the original Enlightenment political ideal with a distortion.

Thus even if the liberal republic "has lost a good deal of its radical cachet" since the Enlightenment, it remains the case that this particular form of polity should remain "the point of reference for movements committed to social change and for those interested in the protection of civil liberties."[33] While the recent strong growth of liberal democracy can only be applauded from an Enlightenment perspective, we need also to remind ourselves of the sobering fact that at present well over half of the world's population does not live in republican regimes. We still have a very long way to go before Jefferson's vision of a world in which republican government has spread "to some parts sooner, to others later, but finally to all" becomes a reality. It is certainly not yet the case that "all eyes are opened, or opening, to the rights of man."[34]

10

International Relations

League of Nations, United Nations, Warring Nations

The two most significant institutional offspring of the Enlightenment ideal of peace through federation are the League of Nations, established after World War I, and the United Nations, founded after World War II. The first institution lived a very short and troubled life, and even today there remains a lack of consensus regarding what (if any) lessons subsequent generations have learned from its existence. The League arose quickly out of the devastation of World War I—the most destructive war humanity had (yet) faced, but also a powerful stimulus for forcing people to think concretely about ways to prevent future wars. U.S. President Woodrow Wilson played a key role in the League's formation, but his own rigidity and self-righteousness were also ultimately factors in his country's refusal to join the League: "He saw compromise as tantamount to humiliation."[1] In an address before Congress on January 8, 1918, Wilson laid out his vision of "the programme of the world's peace,...our programme,...the only possible programme." He summarized the plan in fourteen points, the last one of which reads: "A general association of nations must be formed under specific covenants for the purpose of affording mutual guarantees of political independence and territorial integrity to great and small states alike."[2] Wilson also subsequently chaired the committee established to write a draft of the covenant for the future League of Nations, and succeeded in making the covenant itself part of the Versailles Peace Treaty; nations that ratified the treaty thus also obligated themselves to observe the terms of the covenant.[3]

Consisting of twenty-six articles, the covenant lays out the League's aims, the rights and responsibilities of its members, and the rules by which it is to conduct its business. Articles 1 through 7 concerned membership and organization, providing both for an Assembly composed of representatives of all members of the League, and a Council composed of "Representatives of the Principal Allied and Associated Powers, together with Representatives of four other Members of the League" (Article 4.1).[4]

Articles 8 and 9 dealt with armaments reduction. Members were obligated both to reduce their "national armaments to the lowest point consistent with national safety and the enforcement by common action of international obligations" (8.1) and "to interchange full and frank information as to the scale of their armaments, their military, naval, and air programmes and the condition of such of their industries as are adaptable to warlike purposes" (8.6). Article 10 required members "to respect and preserve as against external aggression the territorial integrity and existing political independence of all Members of the League"[5] when advised to do so by the Council—in effect, a collective security provision. Articles 11 through 17 provided for the establishment of a "Permanent Court of International Justice" (14), for arbitration and conciliation, and for sanctions against aggressors. Each member state accepted obligations both to submit "any dispute likely to lead to a rupture . . . either to arbitration or to inquiry by the Council" (12.1) and to suspend "all trade or financial relations" with any fellow member who went to war in violation of the covenant (16.1).

The remaining articles dealt with treaties (18 through 21), colonial mandates (22), international cooperation in humanitarian enterprises (23 through 25), and amendments to the covenant (26). Under Article 23, for instance, members were obligated to work together "for the prevention and control of disease" (f); to stop "the traffic in women and children, and the traffic in opium and other dangerous drugs" (c); and "to secure and maintain fair and humane conditions of labour for men, women and children, both in their own countries and in all countries to which their commercial and industrial relations extend" (b).

Whether "the Covenant has some claim to be considered among...[the] highest moments of history"[6] is extremely doubtful, but even skeptics must concede that much good eventually came of it. For the League that came into being as a result, despite its often-repeated litany of failures and short-lived existence, did succeed, for the first time in human history, in putting "into concrete form the dreams and hopes of all those who had worked for peace through the centuries. It...left its legacy in the widespread acceptance of the idea that the nations of the world could and must work together for the collective security of them all."[7] And for a very brief moment, it did seem to many observers that "the Enlightenment liberals had, to all appearances, finally triumphed."[8] In the field of international relations, Enlightenment liberals hoped for a future where, above all, nations would mutually guarantee each other's security by "open covenants of peace" rather than by secret diplomacy and the traditional balance of power. Additionally, they wanted to see "national armaments...reduced to the lowest point consistent with domestic safety," "freedom of navigation upon the seas," and the removal "of all economic barriers and establishment of an equality of trade conditions among all nations consenting to the peace." Finally, the desire to provide "mutual guarantees of political independence and territorial integrity to great and small states alike" also formed a central part of Enlightenment dreams for humanity's future in the area of international relations.[9]

At the same time, several key differences between Enlightenment peace through federation proposals and the League of Nations should be noted. First and foremost, the League had much weaker enforcement mechanisms for promoting and maintaining peace. There was no League military force, no compulsory arbitration, no mandatory disarmament. These were three key ingredients in all of the peace through federation proposals examined earlier. Second (although here the comparison is not entirely fair, since none of the Enlightenment proposals ever made the difficult move from theory into practice), the League was highly politicized from the very start. Germany, the loser in the war, had no voice in the planning process. Britain, France, and the United States were often at cross-purposes and tried to bend the covenant to suit their own perceived national interests. Just as Leibniz, Rousseau, and others criticized Sully's *Grand Design* for placing French political interests above the cause of international peace, so the League was often seen more as the outcome of conflicting attempts to solve various political problems rather than as a serious plan for peace. Third, although the League officially echoed Crucé's and Kant's proposals in being a worldwide federation, in reality it continued the (Western) Eurocentrism that tainted the Enlightenment federation projects of Saint-Pierre, Sully, and Penn. Many of the most important details were hammered out by representatives of the Big Four (Britain, France, Italy, the United States) in private meetings. "By their offhand treatment of the non-European world," MacMillan notes, the peacemakers of 1919 "stirred up resentments for which the West is still paying today. They took pains over the borders in Europe, even if they did not draw them to everyone's satisfaction, but in Africa they carried on the old practice of handing out territory to suit the imperialist powers. In the Middle East, they threw together peoples, in Iraq most notably, who have still not managed to cohere into a civil society."[10]

In sum, the League of Nations was by no means a simple instatement of Enlightenment peace through federation proposals. There were fundamental differences between the two—differences that, from the standpoint of international peace, greatly weakened both the integrity and effectiveness of the 1919 League.

But comparisons with Enlightenment federation proposals aside, why was the League so unsuccessful? Two reasons stand out. First, several of the world's most powerful nations were not initially members. Because the covenant was drafted by the victorious powers, Germany was kept out until September 1926—and by October 1933, Hitler had already given notice that Germany intended to withdraw. The USSR was also excluded until September 1934—and by December 1939, it was declared to be no longer a member by Council resolution. Stranger still, the United States, despite (and to some extent because of) President Wilson's central role in creating the League, was never a member. After an acrimonious debate, the U.S. Senate refused to ratify the Treaty of Versailles, of which the League covenant had been made a part.

The causes behind the U.S. refusal to join the League were complex and multiple: personal animosity (Senator Henry Cabot Lodge, a leading opponent of the League, detested Wilson, and the feeling was mutual), party politics (Lodge was a Republican; Wilson, a Democrat), stubbornness (Wilson would not accept any Senate amendments to the covenant), and isolationist sentiment were all certainly contributing factors.[11] But the dominant and most disturbing cause was national sovereignty. Americans (or at least their elected senators) viewed Article 10 of the covenant—with its requirement that member states, upon recommendation of the Council, collectively act "to respect and preserve as against external aggression the territorial integrity and existing political independence of all Members of the League"—as a violation of the declaration of war clause in the U.S. Constitution. As Senator Lodge put it, in one of his many speeches on the topic, "Under the Constitution of the United States the Congress alone has the power to declare war. . . . No American soldiers or sailors must be sent to fight in other lands at the bidding of a league of nations. American lives must not be sacrificed except by the will and command of the American people acting through their constitutional representatives in Congress."[12] But as Wilson correctly noted, "Article 10 seems . . . to constitute the very backbone of the whole Covenant. Without it the League would be hardly more than an influential debating society."[13] Any international federation of states that aims at peace will remain ineffective unless and until its members first agree to give up the traditional, unrestricted right to wage war in pursuit of state policies and then commit themselves to taking collective action against outbreaks of aggression.

At any rate, the absence of Germany, the USSR, and the United States from the opening meeting of the League's Assembly in 1920 greatly reduced its significance. As an editorial in the *Manchester Guardian* rightly remarked, "The League, as it exists today, is a fragment, and a fragment which, unless enlarged and reinforced, cannot permanently fulfill its mission. What sort of League is that from which three of the greatest and most populous nations of the world are left out? It is a beginning, but it cannot be an end."[14]

The second and more obvious reason behind the League's lack of success is that it displayed an increasing lack of will and effectiveness in maintaining peace during the 1930s. Members failed to take sufficient action when Japan invaded Manchuria in 1931, and again when Italy attacked Ethiopia in 1935. And, most catastrophic of all, the League did not stand up to Hitler. "The dynamic leaders of the interwar years— Mussolini, Hitler, the Japanese militarists—sneered at the League and ultimately turned their backs on it. Its chief supporters—Britain, France and the smaller democracies—were lukewarm and flaccid."[15] As Robert Cecil remarked in a speech at the final session of the League Assembly, "Why, then, did it fail? . . . it failed solely because the Member states did not genuinely accept the obligation to use and support its provisions."[16] Faced with increasing outbreaks of war arising in different sectors of the world, the League (although it did not officially disband until 1946) essentially collapsed in 1939.

Ultimately, behind the U.S. refusal to join the League, the failure of member states to strongly support its provisions, and the ridicule it received from more "dynamic leaders" lay the brute fact that the Enlightenment ideal of a federation of states aiming at peace was not yet acceptable to a sufficient number of people. Powerful states were not yet willing to give up their right to declare war in order to join a federal union.

The successor institution to the League of Nations is the United Nations, established immediately after World War II. This time around, the United States was heavily involved not only in the planning process (President Franklin Roosevelt coined the term "United Nations" in 1942; important preliminary negotiations took place in 1944 in Dumbarton Oaks, Washington, DC; and the UN Charter was signed in San Francisco on June 26, 1945) but was also a strongly supportive founding member.[17] The USSR was also a founding member of the UN, and while Japan and Germany did not join until later (1956 and 1973, respectively), one clear reason for the longer life (if not greater success) of the UN in comparison with the League is that a larger number of powerful states were active participants from the start.

The aims and structure of this second twentieth-century international organization are laid out in the charter of the United Nations, a document that both echoes and departs from a number of themes in the earlier covenant of the League of Nations. Consisting of a preamble and nineteen chapters divided into 111 articles, the charter opens by advancing four broad goals: (1) "to save succeeding generations from the scourge of war, which twice in our lifetime has brought untold sorrow to mankind"; (2) "to reaffirm faith in human rights";[18] (3) "to establish conditions under which ... respect for ... international law can be maintained"; and (4) "to promote social progress and better standards of life in larger freedom."[19] As a means of advancing these goals, the charter makes provisions for six principal organs: "a General Assembly, a Security Council, an Economic and Social Council, a Trusteeship Council, an International Court of Justice, and a Secretariat" (Art. 7.1). Comments on select aspects of these structures follow.

The General Assembly consists "of all the Members of the United Nations" (9.1), each member having one vote (18). At its founding in 1945, the UN had fifty-one member states. Since then its membership has expanded nearly fourfold (2006: 192 members), a growth caused primarily by decolonization and the breaking up of older states. Essentially the legislative branch of the UN, the Assembly has extremely broad powers of discussion and recommendation (it "may discuss any questions on any matters within the scope of the present Charter" and "make recommendations ... on any such questions or matters" [10]), and it also has the power to "consider and approve the budget of the Organization" (17.1), as well as to determine the assessments of member countries (17.2). However, it does not have the power to take action on matters of international security. This power is reserved for the Security Council.

Responsibility for determining whether "any threat to the peace, breach of the peace, or act of aggression" has occurred lies with the Security Council (39), as does responsibility for deciding what, if any, action is to be taken (40–49). The Council consists of five permanent members (China, France, Russian Federation, United Kingdom, United States) and ten nonpermanent members elected by the General Assembly for two-year terms (Art. 23, as revised in 1965).[20] In addition to the Council's strong executive decision-making authority on all security matters, a further controversial feature is that nine affirmative votes are needed on all substantive matters, "including the concurring votes of the permanent members" (27.2). In other words, unanimity on the part of the five "great powers" is required on all substantial matters, which in turn means that each of the five permanent members possesses a veto power. If any one of the five permanent members is opposed to a nonprocedural resolution, the resolution fails. According to many historians, the problem of the great-power veto caused "the most serious, as well as the most dramatic, controversy" at the original San Francisco Conference in 1945, a controversy that "can hardly be characterized as negotiation. In the end, in order to get it through the Conference, the great powers had to state quite baldly that unless . . . [the great-power veto] was accepted, there would be no world organization."[21]

The Security Council is clearly the most powerful of the six UN principal organs, and over the years its composition, procedures, and powers have been the subject of continual criticism.[22] Nearly everyone (except of course for the five permanent members, who covet their current status) agrees that changes are in order. The present Security Council is a reflection of post–World War II political and economic realities, and some of these realities have shifted dramatically in the subsequent years. Its present composition is indisputably out of date, a fact that even UN officials recognize, but which they have not yet been able to change. For instance, in November 2003 Secretary-General Kofi Annan called on a sixteen-member panel of experts to study ways of reforming the UN; the panel's report was released in December 2004. The panel made over one hundred recommendations, and the ones that understandably attracted the most attention concerned Security Council reform. Described as "the most sweeping changes in its history,"[23] the main recommendation on this topic called for expanding Security Council membership from its present fifteen members to twenty-four members. But panel members themselves were unable to agree on further specifics in this area (how would the new members be selected?), and so they suggested two options. Option 1 would add six new permanent members (the likely candidates are Brazil, Germany, India, Japan, Egypt, and either Nigeria or South Africa) as well as three new nonpermanent members. Option 2 would create a new tier of eight semipermanent members elected for renewable four-year terms and one additional nonpermanent member.

However, neither option touches the controversial great-power veto. Under both proposals, the right to cast vetoes would continue to be limited to the five original permanent members. Hard political facts undoubtedly lie behind this timidity. As noted earlier, it has been documented that the major powers would never have joined the UN in the first place without the guarantee of a veto right, and it seems clear that they would at least threaten to desert it if and when this right is rescinded. Also, as a practical matter, amending the veto system will prove extremely difficult. Article 108 of the UN charter stipulates that all charter amendments must be adopted by "a vote of two thirds of the members of the General Assembly and ratified in accordance with their respective constitutional processes by two thirds of the members of the United Nations, including all the permanent members of the Security Council." It is very difficult to envision any (let alone all five) of the current permanent Security Council members voting in favor of an amendment to rescind their veto rights.

At present the prospects for any of these recommendations concerning Security Council reform appear dim. Though it is to be hoped that one or another version of them will eventually be approved, the apparent untouchability of the great-power veto serves as yet another reminder of the distance between Enlightenment hopes and contemporary realities. The veto right enables those few states who possess it not only to reject the majority will of the nations of the world, but also to maintain their traditional shields of sovereignty. It makes some states much more equal than others. The basic principle of the moral and legal equality of all states—a principle advocated by all of the Enlightenment proposals examined earlier—has yet to be realized by the United Nations.

Returning to our overview of the six principal organs of the UN, the Economic and Social Council consists of "fifty-four Members of the United Nations elected by the General Assembly" (Art. 61, as revised in 1973; originally, membership was set at eighteen). Its functions and powers are limited to making or initiating "studies and reports with respect to international economic, social, cultural, educational, health, and related matters" and to making "recommendations with respect to any such matters to the General Assembly" (62). The Trusteeship Council, the fourth principal UN organ, deals with the administration and supervision of trust territories (territories that are not self-governing) and replaces the earlier mandate system of the League of Nations. The Trusteeship Council suspended operation in November 1994, with the independence of Palau, the last remaining UN trust territory. This particular UN organ would seem to be a likely candidate for abolition, though some have argued that in the future it should be used to "help failed states recover their independence and sovereignty."[24]

The International Court of Justice is "the principal judicial organ of the United Nations" (92) and supersedes the Permanent Court of International Justice established by the League of Nations. Like its predecessor, the International Court is empowered to hear only a very limited range of cases. Disputes must be submitted voluntarily by states as opposed to individuals,[25] and because there is no independent enforcement body for international law, the Court also relies on voluntary compliance. Its decisions are in effect advisory opinions only. Delegates at the 1945 San Francisco Conference heatedly debated the issue of whether the Court should have the power of compulsory jurisdiction, but here too (compare the debate over veto rights in the Security Council), the great powers strenuously opposed the idea. The proposal for compulsory jurisdiction "encountered powerful opposition; both the Soviet Union and the United States made it clear that they could not accept the Statute if such a clause were included."[26]

Finally, the Secretariat, the sixth principal organ of the UN, is headed by the secretary-general, who is "the chief administrative officer" of the UN (97). The UN secretary-general is granted more power than his predecessor in the League, for the secretary-general "may bring to the attention of the Security Council any matter which in his opinion may threaten the maintenance of international peace and security" (99). The right conferred to the secretary-general under Article 99 is "a quite special right which goes beyond any power previously accorded to the head of an international organization," one that requires "the exercise of the highest qualities of political judgment, tact, and integrity."[27]

The UN has survived (if not exactly thrived) for more than fifty years, even though its strongest successes have been "less in the field of peace between the major powers than in other areas."[28] In spite of the many legitimate criticisms that have been leveled at it over the years, the nations of the earth have at least reached a stage where they agree that it is

important for them to sit and listen to each other, and that they can and
must work together for the collective security of all. However, the gaps
between Enlightenment hopes concerning international federations and
contemporary realities remain numerous and large. First, as concerns
voting rights for members of such federations, all of the Enlightenment
peace through federation proposals examined earlier advocated a simple
"one state, one vote" principle—all states were viewed as moral and legal
equals. None of the earlier proposals argued that certain more powerful
states should be granted veto rights over the proposals of less powerful
member states. While the historical record indicates that "there would
be no world organization" without the great-power veto, the present
UN—even a modestly reformed, future UN with an expanded Security
Council—is still very far from being the democratic world organization of
states envisaged by Enlightenment intellectuals. The UN does not view all
members as equals, but grants special voting privileges to a small group of
wealthy and powerful states. Second, the nations of the world still have not
come at all close to endorsing any sort of compulsory arbitration system for
resolving their differences. Nor has the idea of an effective international
military force, one sufficiently strong to enable the UN Security Council to
carry out its decisions and to serve as a standing deterrent to wars between
states, received any substantial support. Fourth, no serious movement
toward disarmament has occurred. These were all common elements in
Enlightenment peace through federation proposals.[29]

But the single most disturbing development in the area of international relations since the founding of the UN has been humanity's increased
acceptance of war as a normal mode of life. By all accounts, the UN's
success in achieving its stated primary goal of saving "succeeding generations from the scourge of war" is poor. In the fifty-plus years since its
founding, there have been substantially more wars fought than in the fifty
years prior to its founding.[30] It is not clear that people presently even
believe war should still be regarded as a scourge. Far from moving toward
the future envisioned by Saint-Pierre and many other Enlightenment intellectuals—a condition of "perpetual peace" where states "have renounced
and renounce forever . . . resort to arms" in order to settle their disputes—we
have increasingly embraced Clausewitz's counterview that "war is simply a
continuation of political intercourse, with the addition of other means."[31]
Within the sphere of international relations, contemporary humanity's
strongest rejection of Enlightenment hopes lies in its continual resort to
and endorsement of war. To praise the UN for having created an "international civil society," and to compare its achievements with "a sort of second

Enlightenment movement,"[32] is thus to grossly overstate matters. To the extent that we have a functioning international civil society at present, the UN itself is not primarily responsible for bringing it into being and sustaining it. And the analogy to the Enlightenment is much too overdrawn. What Enlightenment intellectuals wanted in an international federation was above all an institution that would greatly reduce, and ideally end, the outbreak of war. This is precisely what we do not have.

The Moral Pressure of Human Rights

The most significant development in international law since the Enlightenment has been the human rights movement, a movement that signals a basic shift in focus from states or nations to individual human beings. But to the extent "that pronouncements of human rights are quintessentially ethical articulations, and . . . are *not*, in particular, putative legal claims,"[33] they share with their natural and international law antecedents a normative character that sits uneasily with positive law. All of them continue to fall prey to Hobbes's verdict that they "are not properly laws," since there is no lawgiver in the international arena. However, as we shall see, this does not mean that they are without effect.

Issuing out of the terrors of World War II, the imperative to promote and encourage "respect for human rights" is stressed at the beginning of the UN Charter (Article 1.3; see also preamble). The new focus on human rights received a special emphasis in U.S. President Harry S. Truman's address to the closing session of the founding conference of the UN, when he stated, "We have good reason to expect the framing of an international bill of rights . . . that . . . will be as much a part of international life as our own Bill of Rights is a part of our Constitution."[34] But the goal of an "international bill of rights" has proved elusive; indeed, if by "bill" one means a formal legal document that ensures sufficient guarantees for the rights in question, the term is a misnomer. Today, more than half a century after Truman's speech, "the international capacity to enforce the requirements of human rights law on states is at best embryonic."[35] From the beginning, the familiar objection of national sovereignty has repeatedly been used as a roadblock to implementing human rights. States (particularly powerful states) do not want other states telling them what to do.

The first major setback to instantiating the bill came when the commission (chaired by Eleanor Roosevelt)[36] charged with drafting it decided, in response to political and ideological differences that were creating an impasse, "to divide it into three parts: a Declaration, a Covenant, and machinery for implementation."[37] Work on part I, the declaration, understandably went quickly, for it was intended merely as a statement of general principles rather than a document containing explicit legal obligations. The result was the Universal Declaration of Human Rights, approved unanimously (with eight abstentions) by the UN General Assembly on December 10, 1948, and today still "arguably the single most important international instrument ever negotiated."[38]

Consisting of a preamble and thirty articles, the Universal Declaration is much shorter than either the League of Nations Covenant or the UN Charter. It opens with the assertions that "all human beings are born free and equal in dignity and rights" (Art. 1), and that "everyone is entitled to all of the rights...set forth in this Declaration, without distinction of any kind, such as race, colour, sex, language, religion, political or other opinion, national or social origin, property, birth or other status" (2).[39] The rights set forth in the declaration are extensive and include a variety of different types of rights. The basic types may be summarized as follows:[40]

1. Personal rights such as "the right to life, liberty and security of person" (3); privacy (12); freedom of movement (13.1); the right to own property (17.1); and the right to freedom of thought, conscience, and religion (18).

2. Procedural rights associated with the rule of law such as equal recognition before the law and equal protection of the law (7); "effective remedy" for violation of legal rights (8); presumption of innocence (11.1); and prohibition of arbitrary arrest (9).

3. Political rights such as "the right to freedom of opinion and expression" (19); "freedom of peaceful assembly and association" (20); the right to take part in the government of one's country (21.1); and the right to "periodic and genuine elections which shall be by universal and equal suffrage" (21.3).

4. Economic and social rights such as "the right to social security" (22); "free choice of employment" and "protection against unemployment" (23.1); "just and favourable remuneration" (23.3); the right to "reasonable limitation of working hours and periodic holidays with pay" (24); rights to "food, clothing, housing and medical care and necessary social services" (25); and "the right to education" (26.1).[41]

The 1948 declaration was intended as a broad statement of principles, not as a legally binding document. Included in it was both the proclamation that "human rights should be protected by the rule of law" and the aspiration that "every individual and every organ of society... shall strive by teaching and education to promote respect for these rights" (preamble), but there was nothing specific that actually had the force of law. The next step in communicating the international bill—a step that would last nearly twenty years—was to bring the declaration closer to implementation by means of a covenant that would contain explicit legal obligations when ratified by member states. Here a second major setback occurred. In 1951 the original draft covenant was split in two, due to the drafters' own sense that "the difficulties which may flow from embodying in one covenant two different kinds of rights" could not be overcome.[42] In its place two separate covenants were proposed: one dealing with political and civil rights, a second with social, economic, and cultural rights. Both covenants were eventually concluded in 1966 and entered into force in 1976 (though many UN member states have still not ratified either one).

And what became of the third part of the international bill, "machinery for implementation"? The story here is still not over, but its narrative path is even murkier. Article 40 of the International Covenant on Civil and Political Rights requires states "to submit reports on the measures they have adopted which give effect to the rights recognized herein and on progress made in the enjoyment of those rights."[43] These reports are then submitted to the secretary-general, who in turn transmits them "for consideration" to the Human Rights Committee (whose members "shall be persons of high moral character and recognized competence in the field of human rights"; 40.2, 28.2). Under Article 41, states ratifying the Civil and Political Covenant also have the option of recognizing "the competence of the Committee to receive and consider communications" from other states regarding alleged rights violations that have also opted to accept this procedure. Even here, though, the committee's task is simply to promote an amicable solution; it is not empowered to render a binding verdict. Something a bit closer to (but still distant from) the latter is found in the (First) Optional Protocol to the Covenant on Civil and Political Rights. States adhering to it recognize the committee's authority to hear "communications from individuals claiming to be victims of violations of any of the rights set forth in the Covenant." After hearing such communications, the protocol then directs the committee to "forward its views to the State Party concerned and to the individual" (5.4). But what happens after the committee's views are forwarded to the relevant parties? The protocol says only that "the Committee shall include in its annual report . . . a summary of its activities" (6).

A similar vagueness infects the International Covenant on Economic, Social, and Cultural Rights. States ratifying it agree "to undertake to submit . . . reports on the measures which they have adopted and the progress made in achieving the observance of the rights recognized herein" (16). These reports are eventually to be transmitted to the Human Rights Commission (as of 2006, the Human Rights Council) "for study and general recommendation" (19)—but nothing more.

In short, the machinery for implementation of the International Bill of Rights does not work well. At the same time, many of these design flaws are intentional, for their presence enabled states prideful of their domestic sovereignty to still get on board. As Farer and Gaer note, "These weak and for the most part optional instruments of compliance mollified the opposition of those numerous governments hostile to external assessment of their domestic behaviour."[44] Additionally, many of the norms articulated in the two covenants allow for exceptions, but this too eases the pressure of compliance placed on states. The Civil and Political Covenant, for instance, allows states to suspend certain rights "in time of public emergency which threatens the life of the nation . . . to the extent strictly required by the exigencies of the situation" (4). (However, the covenant also insists that the rights to life, to freedom from torture and slavery, and to freedom of thought, conscience, and religion may at no time be abrogated; §§6, 7, 8, 18.) Similarly, the same covenant also allows that the right to freedom of expression may "be subject to certain restrictions . . . as are provided by law and are necessary . . . for the protection of national security or of public order (*ordre public*), or of public health or morals" (19).

In the International Covenant on Economic, Social, and Cultural Rights, the wiggle room is even larger, in part because (as critics never tire of pointing out) in many countries at present it is simply not feasible to instantly realize such rights for all citizens, due to a lack of requisite social institutions.[45] Each state ratifying this second covenant is obligated merely "to take steps . . . to the maximum of its available resources, with a view to achieving progressively the full realization of the rights recognized in the present Covenant by all appropriate means" (2). However, what these means are is never specified. Variants of this softer language of progressive realization (a favorite formula is "undertake to ensure") occur in many of the covenant's subsequent articles (see §§3, 8, 11, 12, 14, 15, 16). Also, while the Civil and Political Covenant frequently employs phrases such as "everyone shall have the right to . . . " (see, for instance, §§16, 18, 19, 22) or "no one shall be . . . " (§§7, 8, 11, 15), the Social, Economic, and Cultural Covenant normally says only that "States Parties recognize the right of everyone to . . . " (e.g., §§7, 9, 11, 12, 13, 15). The latter language is clearly weaker, for it shifts the responsibility of implementation over to states, but contains no sanctions for noncompliance.

In sum, the International Bill of Rights is certainly not an instrument of law that provides a reliable mechanism for the enforcement of rights. Despite the proliferation of human rights declarations and covenants over the years (I have discussed only a few of them), human beings at present do not possess a "bill" of such rights in any strict legal sense. But we should not infer from this that human rights talk is meaningless or ineffective, or side with Bentham when he proclaims that "rights are, then, the fruits of law, and of law alone. There are no rights without law—no rights contrary to the law—no rights anterior to the law. . . . There are no other than legal rights;—no natural rights—no rights of man, anterior or superior to those created by the laws."[46]

On the contrary, even though many legitimate human rights claims are still not legally enforceable at present, they are able to function on their own as ethical demands on institutional orders and governments, demands that are often surprisingly effective in promoting needed social, political, and legislative reforms. In recent years, human rights have begun to assume a distinctive role in international life, "the role of a moral touchstone—a standard of assessment and criticism for domestic institutions, a standard of aspiration for their reform, and increasingly a standard of evaluation for the policies and practices of international economic and political organizations."[47] Implementing human rights through new laws is certainly one way to proceed, but, as Amartya Sen points out, there are many ways of pursuing human rights, not all of which involve legislation. For instance, in addition to the legislative route there is the recognition route, which happens when a society formally acknowledges (without juridical enforcement) the legitimacy of certain human rights claims. Additionally, there is the agitation route, which involves putting social pressure on government agencies to ensure compliance with international human rights ordinances, again without the luxury of legal sanctions.[48] To put it in more Kantian terms, human rights discourse is itself part of the necessary vocabulary for "the public use of one's reason," where each person is regarded as a member "of the society of citizens of the world" and by means of which all participants try to further humanity's progress toward enlightenment (*Enlightenment* 8: 37).

Global Jurisdiction versus National Sovereignty

International tribunals and courts are another institutional development advocated by Enlightenment intellectuals that has achieved limited success in recent times. Many Enlightenment authors advocated a world court before which states would bring their disagreements in order to prevent the outbreak of war. For instance, in several of the peace through federation proposals examined earlier (Crucé, Penn, Saint-Pierre), all member states were required to enter into binding arbitration to resolve disagreements, and states that were not parties to the dispute were required to function collectively as a third-party arbitration panel whose responsibility was to resolve the dispute. Some of the Enlightenment peace through law writings examined earlier also contained similar proposals. Rachel, for instance, advocated the founding of a "College of Fecials," wherein "controversies which have arisen between States should be cognized and argued and decided, in such sort that nothing save necessity would open the way to war, it being undertaken only against those who have declined to obey a judgment rendered, or who in other ways have shown contumacy towards the authority and decrees of this College."[49]

The most obvious difference between Enlightenment proposals in this area and their contemporary offspring is that Enlightenment "world courts" were intended solely to prevent or at least greatly minimize the outbreak of war, whereas contemporary tribunals and courts are generally juridical responses to the catastrophes of war—for instance, prosecution of crimes against humanity committed during war. (From an Enlightenment perspective, the more recent international tribunals and courts are thus yet another sign of contemporary humanity's tolerance for war.) A second difference is that Enlightenment international courts were designed to hear only disputes between states, whereas the contemporary international tribunals and courts that are the focus of this section are specifically empowered to prosecute individuals (including state officials and military personnel).[50] Nevertheless, both share the core features of a court that is international in composition and character and that possesses strong prosecutorial powers of compulsory jurisdiction. The international tribunals and courts that are of concern here also represent an important vehicle for the implementation and legal enforcement of at least some basic human rights. The prosecutions, convictions, and punishments with which they are concerned stand in stark contrast to the programmatic and aspirational tones that are traditionally associated with human rights discourse.

Article 6 of the Charter of the International Military Tribunal set up by the Allied powers (United States, USSR, Britain, France) to try Nazi war criminals at Nuremberg gave the tribunal jurisdiction over three kinds of crimes: crimes against peace (essentially, participating in a war of aggression), war crimes (murder, ill treatment, and deportation of either civilians or prisoners of war), and crimes against humanity ("namely, murder, extermination, enslavement, deportation, and other inhumane acts committed against any civilian population, before or during the war, or persecution on political, racial or religious grounds").[51] The third category, as Steiner and Alston note, "represented an important innovation. There were few precedents for the use of the phrase 'crimes against humanity' as part of a description of international law, and its content was correspondingly indeterminate."[52] However, the phrase "crimes against humanity," though not used by Enlightenment authors as part of a description of international law, is one with which they would have felt at home, and it owes at least part of its ancestry to the centrality of natural rights in Enlightenment political theory. In fact, Kant at one point even uses the phrase "crimes...perpetrated against humanity itself" (*Verbrechen...an der Menschheit selbst ausgeübt*) to describe rape and certain other crimes (*Morals* 6: 363).

Any of these three acts—crimes against peace, war crimes, crimes against humanity—the authors of the Nuremberg charter emphasized, are crimes "whether or not in violation of the domestic law of the country where perpetrated" (Art. 6). Additionally, individuals committing such acts were to be held legally responsible regardless of their official government positions (Art. 7) and regardless of whether they were acting on orders of their government or military superiors (Art. 8).

Twenty-two defendants were tried at the Nuremberg tribunal. Of these, nineteen were convicted (most of the convictions were for war crimes and crimes against humanity),[53] and twelve were sentenced to death. The tribunal was not without its critics. The most popular criticism was that it was an example of "victor's justice." The Allies had won the war, and they essentially controlled every aspect of the proceedings: writing the charter, deciding which crimes to prosecute and which individuals to bring to trial, choosing the judges and prosecutors, and also interpreting the crimes described in the charter in such a way that they applied to their opponents but not to themselves (the horrendous bombings of Dresden, Tokyo, Hiroshima, and Nagasaki notwithstanding). A second criticism was that the tribunal was an example of ex post facto law: declaring an act to be illegal that was actually legal when it was committed.

These criticisms are not without merit. However, as Ian Brownie notes,

> Whatever the state of law in 1945, Article 6 of the Nuremberg Charter has since come to represent general international law. The Agreement to which the Charter was annexed was signed by the United States, United Kingdom, France, and USSR, and nineteen other states subsequently adhered to it. In a resolution adopted unanimously on 11 December 1946, the General Assembly affirmed "the principles of international law recognized by the Charter of the Nuremberg Tribunal and the judgment of the Tribunal."[54]

More generally, the Nuremberg tribunal helped to create a needed momentum: it showed that international law can be effective in prosecuting the most horrendous crimes, "that it can deal with great matters and that legal process may be relied upon to deal appropriately with the most grievous offenses by human beings against other human beings."[55]

The definitions of international war crimes in the Nuremberg charter were later expanded and reworked in the International Criminal Tribunals for the former Yugoslavia (1993) and Rwanda (1994). Article 5 of the Statute for the Yugoslavia Tribunal, for instance, divides crimes against humanity into nine distinct categories, one of which is rape ("when committed in armed conflict, whether international or internal in character, and directed against any civilian population").[56] This time around, the charge of victor's justice was absent. The trial of Slobodan Milosevic, former president of Yugoslavia, came about because the very government that he once led sent him to court. The Milosevic trial "is not justice exacted by the occupying force against the leaders of a nation that has been forced into unconditional surrender."[57]

However, to claim that post–World War II international war crimes tribunals constitute "the enforcement revolution in human rights"[58] is a bit of an overstatement. For of course only a very tiny fraction of the internationally recognized human rights are being enforced by such tribunals. (No government officials are about to be punished anytime soon for failing to provide their citizens with "periodic holidays with pay.") Also, enforcement of those human rights that do fall under the purview of the tribunals' charters and statutes is highly selective and limited—not all offenders are brought to justice. Still, the activities of these tribunals are at least convincing markers of an emerging human rights "minimalism." At least sometimes, we are willing to take firm legal steps "to stop torture, beatings, killings, rape, and assault and to improve, as best we can, the security of ordinary people."[59] Some human rights have happily moved beyond the category of moral aspirations and into that of (occasionally) enforceable legal claims.

The main problem with the international tribunals is that they are temporary phenomena, specially set up to respond to specific catastrophes committed in particular conflicts. To make the prosecution of crimes against humanity a stable feature of international law, a permanent international criminal court is needed. This is not a new issue. In 1948, the UN General Assembly instructed the International Law Commission (ILC) to study the possibility of establishing an international criminal court. For many years during the cold war era no action was taken. Writing in 1980, one historian concluded that "this vein of possible progress" had dried up: "Nothing came of the ILC's 1951 proposals for a 'draft code of offences against the peace and security of the world' and for an international criminal court; nor has anything concrete, as a matter of fact, been done about them since."[60] But in 1998 a UN-sponsored diplomatic conference was held in Rome, the outcome of which was the overwhelming adoption (by a vote of 120 to 7, with 21 abstentions) of a statute for the establishment of a permanent International Criminal Court (ICC) with limited jurisdiction over the crime of genocide, crimes against humanity, war crimes, and the crime of aggression.[61] The Rome Statute came into force after sixty states ratified it, which occurred in July 2002. As of July 2006, one hundred states have ratified the statute, and the ICC is now a functioning institution, with all senior officials (judges, prosecutor, and registrar) in place.[62]

As the first permanent juridical institution with jurisdiction over individuals who commit the most egregious violations of human rights, the establishment of the ICC is another clear sign of progress in minimal human rights enforcement. However, from the start the United States has been strongly opposed to the court. At the 1998 Rome Conference, the United States was one of only seven states to vote against the statute (the other no votes came from Iraq, Iran, Libya, Algeria, Sudan, and China). President Clinton, in one of his final acts of office at the end of December 2000, signed the treaty but did not attempt to have it ratified by the Senate, where fierce opposition to its terms was expected. In May 2002 the Bush administration sent a letter to UN Secretary-General Kofi Annan stating, "The United States does not intend to become a party to the treaty"[63]—in effect, "unsigning" the Rome Statute. In addition, beginning in 2002 the U.S. government undertook several strategies for shielding U.S. soldiers and government officials from prosecution by the ICC, including national legislation (the American Servicemembers Protection Act, the Nethercutt Amendment), sponsorship of UN Security Council Resolution 1422 (which provided U.S. members of peacekeeping operations with immunity from ICC prosecution), and the signing of bilateral immunity agreements with numerous individual states who were told that their U.S. military and economic aid would be withdrawn if they did not sign.

Present U.S. opposition to the ICC is eerily reminiscent of its earlier opposition to the League of Nations. In both instances, the central objection is that the institution in question violates the principle of national sovereignty. In the case of the League of Nations, the U.S. Congress insisted that no American soldier could be "sent into battle except by the constituted authorities of his own country."[64] In the case of the ICC, U.S. opposition is based primarily on the premise that only U.S. courts should be allowed to try U.S. citizens. And the sovereignty issue certainly did not temporarily fade with the founding of the UN. As we saw earlier, the United States and other powerful states agreed to join the UN only on the condition that they be given great-power vetoes, a device that allows them to put a stop to any and all Security Council proposals that are perceived to impinge on their national sovereignty.

However, insofar as no state has been granted a veto to shield its citizens from potential prosecution by the ICC, this new court is, in a sense, a stronger international institution than the UN. For the ICC is empowered to pursue cases against individuals who commit crimes in countries that have ratified the treaty, even if the individuals' own countries have not ratified it. Thus at present, a U.S. soldier or politician who commits crimes against humanity in, for example, Brazil could be prosecuted by the ICC— if U.S. national courts themselves refused to take action. (The ICC is designed merely to be "complementary to national criminal jurisdictions" [preamble, Rome Statute]; it has jurisdiction only in cases where the relevant national authorities are unwilling or unable to carry out their own investigations.) And the remote possibility that American citizens who violate international criminal law could find themselves before the ICC is, again, the main reason for U.S. opposition to the Court.

Without the participation and support of the world's most powerful nation, the ICC's goal of global jurisdiction over the most egregious violations of human rights is in jeopardy. It is also one more indication that in the ongoing "tug of war between the claims of humanity and those of sovereignty,"[65] the claims of sovereignty are still often winning. The traditional principle of national sovereignty has both an internal and an external face: internally, it concerns a state's alleged right to complete judicial autonomy in dealing with its own citizens; externally, a state's alleged right to go to war. Unless and until both of these aspects of national sovereignty are moderated by an effective international governance system committed to the rule of law, Enlightenment hopes for the future in the sphere of international relations will not come to pass. Despite all the present chatter about humanity's globalization-induced "complex connectivity," the nations of the earth have still not reached a stage where "a violation of *Recht* on *one* place of the earth is felt in *all.*"

....

At bottom, the present situation with regard to Enlightenment ideals in the sphere of international relations is very similar to that of education. In both cases, it appears at first glance as though subsequent generations have indeed realized a good many Enlightenment hopes. And indeed, in a superficial sense, we have. However, the reality underneath the surface is quite different. We now have a variety of minimally functional but by no means robust international institutions and an abundance of global rules, and they are both contributing to the creation of a global civil society. But we don't have peace.

Conclusion

*We talk a lot about Enlightenment and desire more
light. But, my God, what is the use of light if people
either have no eyes or intentionally shut those they have?*

—Georg Christoph Lichtenberg,
The Waste Books (1796–99)

History Test

One straightforward way of assessing Enlightenment ideals pursued in the
present study involves looking at how human beings after the Enlightenment have responded to these ideals. Crudely put: Which ideals have been
resisted or rejected, which embraced but still not realized, and which
realized? A key assumption of this strategy is that human experience, as
revealed through history, should itself be used to evaluate ideals. Using
history in this manner offers us a way to deliberate about at least some of
our ends (namely, those ends to which others before us have also subscribed), a way that seems epistemologically modest and noncontentious.
This strategy of using history as a testing ground for ideals is itself borrowed
from Enlightenment intellectuals, for many of them held that the primary
value of history lies in what it tells us about human nature. We should study
history to learn about human nature; once we understand human nature
we are better able to see what people can and cannot do. Hume, for

instance, in his *Enquiry Concerning Human Understanding* (1748), states that history's chief use

> is only to discover the constant and universal principles of human nature, by shewing men in all varieties of circumstances and situations, and furnishing us with materials, from which we may form our observations, and become acquainted with the regular springs of human action and behaviour. These records of wars, intrigues, factions, and revolutions, are so many collections of experiments, by which the politician or moral philosopher fixes the principles of his science; in the same manner as the physician or natural philosopher becomes acquainted with the nature of plants, minerals, and other external objects by the experiments which he forms concerning them.[1]

Included within the philosophical historian's "collections of experiments" can and should be human beings' attempts to realize ideals: Which attempts were successful, and which ones were not? For which ones is the verdict still out? Bolingbroke, in his *Letters on the Study and Use of History* (1735), offers a similar appreciation of history's potential for evaluating ideals when he remarks, "By knowing the things that have been, we become better able to judge of the things that are."[2] Once we construe the "things" that have been and are more expansively to include ideals and human beings' attempts to realize them, we can then use history itself to assess these efforts.

In his preface to *Anthropology from a Pragmatic Point of View* (1798), Kant also points to "world history" as one of the primary "aids" (*Hilfsmittel*) in the study of anthropology (7: 121).[3] The empirical science of anthropology, which for Kant is "not a description of human beings, but of human nature" (*Friedländer* 25: 471), needs to familiarize itself with a wide range of human activity in different times and places in order to arrive at a defensible account of human nature. Indeed, when he stresses the importance of world history for anthropology in the preamble to the *Friedländer* anthropology lectures (1775–76), Kant specifically links his own project to Hume's earlier historical investigations:

> Nature has its phenomena, but human beings also have their phenomena. No one has yet written a world history, which was at once a history of humanity, but only of the state of affairs and of the change

in the kingdoms, which as a part is indeed major, but considered in the whole, is a trifle. All histories of wars amount to the same thing, in that they contain nothing more than the descriptions of battles. But whether a battle has been more or less won makes no difference in the whole. This is why more attention should be given to humanity. In his *History of England*, Hume provided a proof of this. To observe human beings and their conduct, to bring their phenomena under rules, is the purpose of anthropology. (25: 472)

Part of paying attention to humanity includes, or at least should include, paying attention to how previous generations of human beings have coped with ideals. This in essence is what I earlier called the *principle of psychological and historical realism*. On this view, data regarding human nature, as disclosed through history, should themselves be used to assess ideals. However, one complication (of which Hume and Kant were both well aware) is that using history in this manner involves a "peculiar disadvantage, which is not found in natural [science], that in collecting its experiments, it cannot make them purposively, with premeditation, and after such a manner as to satisfy itself concerning every particular difficulty which may arise."[4] In other words, controlled and repeatable experiments are not feasible here; as a result, the tests conducted by philosophical historians are never entirely fair or completely objective. As regards ideals, for instance, human beings seldom if ever implement them in the original form advocated by their authors, but nearly always in some compromised, less-than-pure form. This complication of compromised implementation also needs to be factored into any final assessment.

However, there is at least one fundamental respect in which my own use of history does diverge strongly from Enlightenment assumptions about history. As is well known, Enlightenment authors approached the study of history with a robust teleological assumption of progress. Kant, for instance, in his *Idea for a Universal History with a Cosmopolitan Intent* (1784), starts from the assumption that he can locate "an *aim of nature* in this nonsensical course of things human," and believes he can trace humanity's "steps from crudity [*Rohigkeit*] toward culture" (8: 18, 21). Turgot, in his lecture "On the Successive Advances of the Human Mind" (1750), speaks for many Enlightenment intellectuals when he pronounces confidently that the study of world history reveals how "manners are gradually softened, the human mind takes enlightenment, separate nations draw nearer to each other, commerce and policy connect at last all parts of the globe, and the total mass of the human race, by the alternations of calm and agitation, of good conditions and of bad, marches always, although slowly, towards still higher perfection."[5]

At the same time, Enlightenment thinking about progress is not as naïve as it is often taken to be. Kant, for instance, clearly recognized that human beings are not irrevocably fated or causally determined to achieve progress. Whether human beings will actually reach a stage of development where they are all "cosmopolitically united" (*Anthropology* 7: 333) depends on what they choose to do. As we saw in our earlier examination of Kant's philosophy of history and its relation to his views about peace through federation, he explicitly rejects any and all confident claims of linear progress: "No one can guarantee that now, this very moment, with regard to the physical disposition of our species, the epoch of its decline would not be liable to occur" (*Conflict* 7: 83). Similarly, Voltaire's famous characterization of history as "little else than a long succession of useless cruelties . . . a collection of crimes, follies, and misfortunes"[6] also serves as a needed correction to popular misconceptions regarding alleged Enlightenment credulity about progress.

Nevertheless, most Enlightenment writers did believe that the line of progress across the centuries was clear, and that it would remain clear in the future. However, this assumption has not been feasible for some time, and the present study rejects it. In many respects, post-Enlightenment history has simply not gone in the direction that Enlightenment intellectuals predicted and hoped it would go. Nietzsche was right, at least on this point: "Looking at nature as if it were proof of the goodness and care of a god; interpreting history in honour of some divine reason, as a continual testimony of a moral world order and ultimate moral purposes . . . that is *over* now; that has conscience *against* it."[7]

Two centuries is a fairly long stretch of time for human beings, and I believe that this time frame constitutes a reasonably just yardstick by means of which to measure their success or failure in realizing ideals. Philosophers may object to the coarseness of such a strategy, protesting that the truth or falsehood of a belief bears no necessary connection to the degree of popular support associated with it. Also, as noted earlier, historical tests of ideals are never entirely fair, in part because the ideals in question are seldom implemented in the original form advocated by their authors, but rather in a diluted (and sometimes distorted) form. Both objections are noted, but I believe that the intended line of questioning is nevertheless appropriate. History does give ideals their day in court (albeit one where the tribunal of reason is seldom entirely impartial), and while the peculiar disadvantages of the study of human nature must always be kept in view, at some point we are entitled, indeed compelled, to judge which ideals have succeeded and which have failed, which need to be revised in the light of experience and practice and which rejected, which are compatible with and tolerated by the particular characteristics of human beings and which are not.

Keeping these remarks in mind, let us now draw together our earlier assessments of the current status of Enlightenment ideals within each of the five fields of investigation, applying the former to the latter.

Religion

Of the five areas examined in this study, religion has fared the worst since the Enlightenment. Enlightenment intellectuals looked forward to a religious future in which sectarian differences would no longer be a source of enmity and hatred, one where their descendants would eventually come to believe that "there is only *one* [true] *religion*; but there can be many different kinds of *faith*," and that "the moral improvement of human beings constitutes the true end of all religion of reason" (Kant, *Religion* 6: 107, 112). But the increasingly popular fundamentalist and evangelical turns in religion have taken humanity down a very different road. Enlightenment ideals about what shape and direction religion should take have been firmly rejected by subsequent generations. Two core features of Enlightenment religiosity—the unity thesis (all historical faiths are manifestations of one universal religion) and the morality thesis (religion's proper purpose is moral rather than theological)—have been firmly and steadily resisted by subsequent generations. While I have argued that we today still have much to learn from the spirit of Enlightenment natural religion, at this point prudence suggests that several Enlightenment religious ideals need to be modified in light of historical experience. The deistic fantasy of a universal religion is not about to be realized anytime soon.

Education

Education, in comparison with religion, is an area in which many Enlightenment hopes for the future seem to have been fulfilled. Most human beings now live in a schooled world, and the battle against illiteracy has been largely won. But once we move beneath the rosy surface, true achievement of Enlightenment educational ideals is much more difficult to detect. The widespread growth and accessibility of education at all levels that the peoples of the world have enjoyed since the Enlightenment has not led to intellectual and civic transformation, much less to moral transformation. Increasingly, education at all levels is being reduced to a *Brotstudium*—something valued for its economic utility, but not for its transformative possibilities.

But does historical experience conclusively show that these latter ideals simply don't fit with human nature? In the case of education (unlike that of religion), I think the answer is no. Other hypotheses (in particular, the conjecture that the ideals in question have yet to be pursued seriously) remain to be tested. However, one simple but hard lesson here is that it is much harder to change human attitudes than Enlightenment theorists realized. Institutional change does not necessarily lead to attitudinal change. Although most Enlightenment intellectuals did not view the relationship between external institutional development and internal attitudinal change as one of simple causal connection, they did all share the belief that the cultural and institutional reforms examined in this study would prove to be extremely favorable conditions for attitudinal change. At present there is insufficient evidence to support this assumption—many of the institutions are here, but the attitudes are not. A related misassumption is the belief that institutions affect all individuals in the same manner. This is clearly false. For some people, education is an intellectually and morally transformative experience; for many others it is a ticket to a remunerative career; for some it somehow manages to be both; and for still others, it is none of the above.

The explanation for the error of assuming that institutional change would lead to attitudinal change is not (as is frequently alleged) that Enlightenment intellectuals were unaware of the depths of human depravity. Kant, for instance, wrote at length on the radical evil in human nature and criticized his contemporaries both for assuming that the human will was uncorrupted and for their failure to take action against "the *malice* (of the human heart), which secretly undermines the disposition with self-corrupting principles" (*Religion* 6: 57). Similarly, Voltaire was no stranger to the pervasiveness of evil: "Confess it freely—evil stalks the land / Its secret principle unknown to us."[8] Rather, the problem is simply that many Enlightenment intellectuals overestimated the plasticity of human nature.

At the same time, to jump to the other pole of this debate and claim that people are not affected by the world they live in is even more implausible. Kant, in his more metaphysical moments, makes this mistake, asserting that human beings as free moral agents can affect nature, but that nature and the external environment in general cannot affect free moral agency. In his *Critique of Pure Reason*, for instance, he declares that human beings in their capacity as moral agents follow "a rule and order that is entirely other from the natural order" (A 550/B 578).[9] People *are* affected by the institutional, cultural, and natural environments they live in, but they are not all affected in the same way and to the same degree, nor are they affected as readily and as easily as Enlightenment reformers thought. To this extent, the more metaphysical Kant was right: there remains a gap between nature and morality, between outer and inner; changes in human beings' external environments do not necessarily bring about changes in their internal attitudes. And so we are left in a gray middle region: the natural and cultural environments in which human beings live have *some* impact on their moral attitudes and characters, but attempting to bring about changes in the latter by modulating the former is no easy matter. Moralization is not necessarily the straightforward causal result of institutional development.

Economics

Economics is another area where, at least on the surface, many Enlightenment hopes seem to have been realized in the contemporary world. Over the past two hundred years, the new commercial society championed by Enlightenment intellectuals has flourished, the number of market economies has grown enormously, and trade and contact between countries have increased by massive proportions. But here too it is clear that achieving desired institutional reforms does not always lead to the desired attitudinal changes. Economic globalization has not led to moral globalization, and the latter is what Enlightenment intellectuals were primarily advocating when they looked to a future in which nations would be drawn nearer to each other through commerce.

Also, in economics as elsewhere, several of the hoped-for effects—effects that were themselves used to justify the proposed institutional and policy changes—are still not visible. The economic means advocated by Enlightenment intellectuals have not led to their predicted outcomes. The most obvious example is that freedom of trade has not led to the elimination—or even the reduction—of poverty. On the contrary, inequality between nations, far from diminishing since the Enlightenment, has in fact grown by astronomical proportions. And while the percentage of the world's population living in poverty at present is less now than it was two hundred years ago, in absolute numbers world poverty has increased over the past two centuries rather than decreased. Additionally, the "Free-Trade principle" has yet to "act on the moral world as the principle of gravitation in the universe,—drawing men together, thrusting aside the antagonism of race, and creed, and language, and uniting us in the bonds of eternal peace."[10] Montesquieu and many Enlightenment intellectuals to the contrary, peace is not necessarily "the natural effect of trade." Finally, the explosion of commerce has not led to the creation of an active and engaged public sphere, but merely to something closer to Habermas's "sham private world of culture consumption."

Looking at Enlightenment economic ideals through the lens of history provides us with the clearest case of a situation in which many of the ideals and policies were strongly embraced by subsequent generations, but in which the predicted results simply did not follow. In other words, what the history test shows in this particular instance is not that Enlightenment ideals should be rejected because they do not square with human nature, but that the economic means advocated by Enlightenment intellectuals for achieving certain goals (peace, a strong civic culture, and the elimination of poverty) have proven to be ineffective. If these goals are still desired, different means now need to be employed.

It is important to note that this intermittent uncoupling of, or lack of instrumental efficacy between, means and ends is nowhere near as severe as certain critics of the Enlightenment maintain. No reasonable survey of post-Enlightenment history can support the outlandish claims of Horkheimer and Adorno that the Enlightenment resulted in totalitarianism or ushered in "the administered world." As Roy Porter notes, this is "historical baloney; after all, the Nazis loathed the *philosophes*."[11] Also, this particular problem area is not as severe as the one of institutional change and moralization. Means can and should be revised and reformulated in the light of practice. The means advocated by Enlightenment intellectuals were never intended as eternal verities standing outside of history, but were put forward in a spirit of experimentation. They are always subject to correction. As Hume remarked, the human being, unlike other animals, "traces causes and effects to a great length and intricacy; extracts general principles from particular appearances; improves upon his discoveries; corrects his mistakes; and makes his very errors profitable."[12]

Politics

From a simple quantitative perspective, the two Enlightenment political ideals examined in part I—nationalism and republicanism—have both fared extremely well since the Enlightenment. In the case of nationalism, the number of sovereign states has essentially quadrupled over the past two centuries. But here as elsewhere, numbers tell only a small part of the story. The nationalistic fervor that exploded after the Enlightenment was often simply not an Enlightenment nationalism. In neither their foreign nor their domestic policies do most nations at present embody Herder's vision of "fatherlands lying peacefully beside each other and supporting each other as families."[13] Here as elsewhere, a familiar but disturbing pattern emerges: a degenerate form of Enlightenment ideals has taken the place of the original.

Additionally, the inherent tension between the goals of nationalism and of global governance becomes increasingly harder to balance as the number of sovereign states multiplies. Enlightenment intellectuals held this tension in check by advocating reduced powers of sovereignty (the right both to wage war and to judge human rights violations were to be transferred over to the international level), but many contemporary states continue to resist this solution. Contemporary nations' insistence on absolute sovereignty, when combined with their recent extremely high birth rate, amounts to a double blow against the Enlightenment ideal of an effective world federation.

As regards republicanism, the strong growth of democracy in today's world surely counts as one of the few uncontestable bright spots in any audit of the fate of Enlightenment ideals. In the course of two centuries, humanity has moved from 0 to 120 electoral democracies, which means that at present, slightly over three-fifths of all sovereign states are electoral democracies. Of all the ideals examined in this study, democracy has received the highest level of realization in the post-Enlightenment world. At the same time, it cannot be overstressed that electoral democracies are only distant relatives of Enlightenment republicanism. Contemporary liberal democracies, with their multiple commitments not only to competitive and periodic elections but also to the rule of law, separation of powers, and protection of civil liberties, are much closer relatives. But at present, well over half of the world's population does not live in liberal democracies. And while the claim that "democracy is the best form of government" enjoys overwhelming support at present, its current popularity should not blind us to the fact that neither electoral nor liberal democracies have brought forward several of the key results that Enlightenment intellectuals believed republicanism would bring. Democracies have only occasionally reduced inequalities between citizens, and they have certainly not produced morally better individuals.

In sum, when we look at the legacy of Enlightenment political ideals over the past two centuries, we see a very high level of endorsement by subsequent generations, but also frequent misreadings of the content of these ideals (especially in the case of nationalism), as well as further indications of the failure of institutional change to lead to moralization.

International Relations

Finally, in the area of international relations, Enlightenment hopes for the future have met with mixed success. As regards the Enlightenment goal of peace through federation, we now have the United Nations, a worldwide organization that is in fact much more extensive, both in its membership and its mission, than many of the predecessor proposals put forward by Enlightenment intellectuals. But the UN's track record in achieving and maintaining world peace is extremely poor (it is hardly a project of "*perpetual* peace"), and its internal structure pays much more allegiance to existing political power relations among nation-states than Enlightenment authors would have tolerated. At the same time, contemporary humanity's increased willingness to embrace war as a normal and legitimate mode of action constitutes its single strongest rejection of Enlightenment hopes in all five of the areas examined. Each time a new war of aggression ignites, a still extant barbarism breaks through our civilized veneer.[14] We have not yet even begun to "learn to regard war as the most dreadful of all scourges, the most terrible of crimes."[15]

As concerns the Enlightenment pursuit of peace through law, there are signs of hope in the post–World War II human rights movement as well as in the recent establishment of the International Criminal Court. Both developments indicate an increased desire on the part of the peoples of the world to employ international norms in evaluating human behavior. However, human rights at present still function primarily as moral touchstones rather than legal norms backed by effective enforcement mechanisms, albeit touchstones that are increasingly invoked by growing numbers of both governmental and nongovernmental agencies as well as individuals throughout the world. The U.S. opposition to the recent effort to establish a permanent international criminal court is only one of many illustrations of the continuing stalemate between the principles of national sovereignty and global jurisdiction. At bottom, many states are not yet willing to heed international norms in either their foreign or domestic policies.

....

On my reading, the only Enlightenment ideals that unambiguously fail the history test are in the area of religion. Both the unity thesis and the morality thesis have been steadily and firmly rejected by subsequent generations, and I think that by now it is safe to infer that these particular ideals do not fit well with human nature. (However, as I argued in chapter 6, adopting these ideals is not in itself necessary for the successful pursuit of the most fundamental Enlightenment religious ideals. The most one can say by way of criticism here is that Enlightenment intellectuals occasionally misidentified what is actually needed in the area of religion.) Additionally, examining the post-Enlightenment history of Enlightenment ideals reveals that human beings have sometimes pursued distorted versions of Enlightenment ideals (for instance, as regards nationalism and education) and that Enlightenment means have not always led to Enlightenment ends. The clearest examples of the latter lie in the field of economics. But there is also the much broader and more fundamental problem of the Enlightenment moralization thesis. The widespread Enlightenment assumption that external institutional change would lead to desired internal attitudinal change still lacks sufficient empirical support. And (again) the lack of success in achieving moralization has itself contributed to an extensive reversal (or at least to a plateau) with respect to all of the remaining Enlightenment ideals. The strong momentum that existed among earlier generations for realizing these ideals is now absent. At present, insufficient numbers of people care about them.

Nevertheless, many Enlightenment hopes cannot be reasonably ruled out of court by any history test. What remains to be said about them?

Hope after Horror

A caliph once when his last hour drew nigh,
Prayed in such terms as these to the most high:
"Being supreme, whose greatness knows no bound,
I bring thee all that can't in Thee be found;
Defects and sorrows, ignorance and woe."
Hope he omitted, man's sole bliss below.

—Voltaire, *The Lisbon Earthquake*

Within the Christian tradition, hope is viewed as one of the three theological virtues, virtues that, according to Aquinas, "have God as their object, inasmuch as by them we are rightly ordered to God;... are infused in us by God alone; and... are made known to us only by divine revelation in Sacred Scripture."[16] On this reading, hope is not a natural virtue like courage or justice, but rather a gift from God that requires divine assistance for its development. It is primarily because of these strong theological connotations that hope is not a topic of central concern in classical and modern moral philosophy. Indeed, until Kant posed the question "What may I hope?" arguing that it was one of three or (in later formulations) four fundamental questions that philosophy was obligated to address,[17] philosophers, as opposed to theologians, had little to say about hope.

However, hope did not exactly flourish as a philosophical topic after Kant, due in part to the very success of numerous eighteenth- and nineteenth-century robust philosophies of progress to which Kant himself was still attached, albeit insecurely. For if progress is inevitable, why worry about hope? We can be certain that things will continue to improve. But as Gabriel Marcel notes, "The truth is that there can strictly speaking be no hope except when the temptation to despair exists."[18] Hope is the overcoming of the temptation to despair—the two must therefore exist together. Additional damage to hope occurred in the late nineteenth century, when nihilism began to replace progress in certain influential philosophies of history. Thus Nietzsche, in the preface to *The Will to Power*, announces, "What I relate is the history of the next two centuries. I describe what is coming, what can no longer come differently: *the advent of nihilism*. This history can be related even now; for necessity itself is at work here. . . . For some time now, our whole European culture has been moving as toward a catastrophe."[19]

Nevertheless, it was neither philosophical nor literary prophecies that extinguished hope for the greatest numbers of people in the twentieth century, but rather a deluge of gruesome, undeniable facts. The twentieth century set new records for horror. Tzvetan Todorov, for instance, opens his discussion of what went wrong in the twentieth century, with the following well-known litany:

> The Great War of 1914–18 left eight and a half million dead on the battlefield, maimed another six million, and slaughtered a further ten million civilians. In the same period, Turkey caused the deaths of over one and a half million Armenians; Soviet Russia, which came into being in 1917, killed five million in the course of political repression, and another six million in the artificial famine of 1932–33. The Second World War brought about the deaths of at least thirty-five million people in Europe alone (twenty-five million of them in the Soviet Union), including the annihilation of at least six million

who were Jewish, or Romany, or mentally retarded. Allied bombing of civilian targets in Germany and Japan caused several hundred thousand further deaths. To which we must add the bloody conflicts between the European powers and their colonial populations: the French in Madagascar, Indochina, and Algeria; the British in Kenya, Malaya, Cyprus; and so on.

Such are the dates and crude statistics of the major killing fields of the twentieth century. If the eighteenth century is commonly known as the "Age of Enlightenment," should we not therefore call the twentieth century the "Age of Darkness"?[20]

While the outpouring of pessimism and despair engendered by these and still other events has also helped to contribute to the reemergence of substantial philosophies of hope by, among others, Gabriel Marcel and Ernst Bloch, it is difficult to disagree with Richard Rorty's observation that at present human beings suffer from "a loss of hope," a loss caused at least in part by "an inability to construct a plausible narrative of progress."[21]

It seems necessary to agree with the platitude that some degree of hope is necessary in human life, for without it, how could we work efficaciously to achieve what we believe is attainable? Somewhere between shallow optimism, naïve certainty, and wishful thinking on the one side, and cynicism, resignation, and nihilism on the other, lies a fundamentally necessary appetite that enables us to move ahead and to make reasonable efforts to achieve at least some of what we aim at. If we were completely without hope, we would be static—destitute of goals and unable to move under our own direction. As Nietzsche notes, "*Duration* 'in vain,' without end or aim, is the most *paralyzing* idea."[22] Kant, in his *Anthropology*, makes a similar point: "overwhelming sadness (which is alleviated by no hope)" is an affect "that threatens life" (7: 254). But given that human beings need *some* hope, how much hope is reasonable with respect to Enlightenment ideals at present? In what ways can these hopes be grounded?

I start from the assumptions that any justifiable hope after horror needs to be a more sober and chastened hope, a hope that does not want to get fooled again, a hope that has tried to free itself from illusion, a vigilant hope. Taking some cues from Kant (as I have throughout this study), let me now conclude by sketching the main ways that he sought to ground Enlightenment hopes for the future, and then offering some observations regarding the extent (if any) to which these hope strategies can still be employed fruitfully.

Possibility

The most straightforward work that philosophy can do on behalf of hope is to employ a *possibility argument*. We cannot legitimately hope for impossible things. If reason and evidence can show that what is aimed at is at least within the realm of the possible, then it is not irrational to hope for its realization. Indeed, as hope boosters of all persuasions never tire of reminding those who give in to despair, once rationally legitimated hope comes into play the odds of achieving one's goals become greater. Hope energizes us to work toward the realization of our goals.

Kant employs a version of the possibility argument in part III of his *Theory and Practice* essay (1793), in his reply to Mendelssohn's rejection of speculation about moral progress. As long as reason cannot prove the impossibility of these hopes for a better future, he says in effect, and as long as we continue to believe that we ought to work on them (I discuss this "ought" below), we should continue to strive for their realization:

> It does not matter how many doubts may be raised against my hopes from history, which, if they were proved, could move me to desist from a task so apparently futile; as long as these doubts cannot be made quite certain I cannot exchange the duty (as something *liquidum*) for the rule of prudence not to attempt the impracticable (as something *illiquidum*, since it is merely hypothetical); and however uncertain I may always be and remain as to whether something better is to be hoped for the human race, this cannot infringe upon the maxim, and hence upon its presupposition, necessary for practical purposes, that it is feasible [*tunlich*]. (8: 309)[23]

I believe that this basic strategy for grounding Enlightenment hopes is still applicable; indeed, my own principle of psychological and historical realism is itself another form of the possibility argument. There are of course many different types of possibility (logical, conceptual, physical, etc.). The kind of possibility made use of here is *human possibility*: Is the ideal humanly feasible? However, this notion of human possibility is not rigid, for human nature itself includes the passions of hope as well as despair, and the more the former rather than the latter attaches itself to goals that are not groundless fantasies, the greater the likelihood that these goals will be realized. Applying the principle of psychological and historical realism was intended to show that achieving some Enlightenment ideals is not humanly possible, in the sense that they do not fit with human nature as revealed in history. Some ideals fail the history test, but many others do not. So an effective employment of the possibility argument can also indicate which goals remain feasible.

At the same time, hopes that survive the possibility argument do not get a free ride, for the argument shows us only that they are possible. But what most people really want to know is not just whether realizing their hopes is possible (only irrational people pursue impossible goals), but whether realization is likely or probable and whether any concrete evidence exists to support probability. What additional philosophical strategies can be employed to give hope a more secure footing?

Signs

A second Kantian strategy for grounding Enlightenment hopes involves looking for indications in history and nature that our moral efforts are not in vain and that the world around us is not hostile to them.[24] Kant's most famous example of a historical clue of this sort is the French Revolution, an event, he declares, that is to be viewed as "a *historical sign* (*signum rememorativum, demonstrativum, prognostikon*) demonstrating the tendency of the human race in its entirety" (*Conflict* 7: 84)—the tendency, that is, "to be the *cause* of its own advance toward the better" (7: 84) through the spreading of republican values and increased respect for human rights. What nourishes humanity's hopes here is not the actual outcome of this or any other revolution (as Kant concedes, it "may succeed or miscarry"; 77: 85),[25] but rather the basic attitude of enlightened individuals around the globe toward the event, an attitude marked by "a universal yet disinterested sympathy" (7: 85). We find this attitude, he adds, "in the hearts of all spectators (who are not engaged in the game themselves)." It is "a wishful *participation* that borders closely on enthusiasm, the very expression of which is fraught with danger," and because the attitude is both universal and unselfish it "therefore can have no other cause than a moral disposition in the human race" (7: 85).

Kant's belief that international public support for the French Revolution would contribute to the gradual spreading of Enlightenment values and an eventual realization of its hopes was shared by many of his contemporaries, as was his conviction that public reaction to the revolution was itself a concrete sign of moral progress. The poet Hölderlin, for instance, wrote to his brother in 1790, just after the start of the revolution, "We live in a period of time in which everything is working toward better days. These seeds of

Enlightenment, these mute desires and aspirations of individuals for the cultural development of the human race, will spread and grow strong and bear glorious fruit."[26] Paine declared in *The Rights of Man* (1791–92) that from "the revolutions of America and France, and the symptoms that have appeared in other countries, it is evident that the opinion of the world is changed with respect to systems of government."[27]

As regards signs of progress in nature, for Kant there are a multitude of them, since nature itself is to be studied as a teleological system and viewed as if it were the work of a wise artist who does nothing in vain and who arranges all individual events into a meaningful whole. Humanity, as part of nature, is to be viewed as an organism whose innate capacities develop very slowly through history. In his *Lectures on Pedagogy*, for instance, he states, "Many germs lie within humanity, and now it is our business to develop the natural dispositions proportionally and to unfold humanity from its germs and to make it happen that the human being reaches his destiny" (9: 445). In the process of witnessing and helping these germs to develop and bear fruit over time, we also acquire hope that "in the end that which nature has as its highest aim will finally come about—a universal *cosmopolitan condition*, as the womb in which all predispositions of the human species will be developed" (*Universal History* 8: 28).

To his credit, Kant repeatedly warns that these teleological reflections on nature and history are to be regarded merely as "a heuristic principle for inquiry" (*Judgment* 5: 411). The idea of purposiveness is merely a regulative principle that helps orient human understanding, not a constitutive principle that determines the objective reality of events or contributes directly to knowledge of them (5: 404; cf. *Pure Reason* A 179–81/B 221–23; A 644/B 672). Indeed, if we were to overobjectify these clues and construe them as guarantees of progress, we would undermine our own moral freedom and responsibility, as well as remove the background of uncertainty that is essential to hope. We would simply acquiesce to the allegedly objective natural purposes and historical tendencies within and around us, rather than work actively to realize our ideals. This strong cautionary note regarding purposiveness is yet another indication that Kant's perspective on progress is much less dogmatic than that of most other modern philosophies of history. On Hegel's view, for instance, "World history is the progress of the consciousness of freedom—a progress whose necessity [*Notwendigkeit*] it is our business to comprehend."[28] No warnings here about the danger of confusing constitutive with regulative principles. But again, there is no need to wrestle with hope when confronted by a progress that is necessary, and any "freedom" associated with such necessity would (as Kant remarks elsewhere) "at bottom be nothing better than the freedom of a turnspit, which, when once it is wound up, also accomplishes its movements of itself" (*Practical Reason* 5: 97).

When these clues are read in the appropriate cautious spirit recommended by Kant, they seem to amount to a stronger version of the possibility argument. For now we are pointing to concrete developments that suggest that the eventual realization of our goals is not just humanly possible in a bare, abstract sense, but that it is also connected to detectable features in human nature and history. However, any and all such signs, correctly interpreted, still amount only to inspirational hints that something may happen—not that it will or must. At any rate, hope after horror needs to be particularly wary of purported signs of progress, simply because in the past these signs have often been misread. Rather than fall into complacency, it is better to remain vigilant.

Duty

As one would expect, appeals to duty also play a strong role in Kant's efforts to ground Enlightenment hopes for the future. Human beings should seek to realize Enlightenment aspirations not as optional projects that they may simply choose to endorse or reject, not as supererogatory acts of charity or generosity that confer special merit on their benefactors, but as part of the comprehensive duty to promote the highest good. The highest good—defined tersely in the second *Critique* as "happiness distributed in exact proportion to morality" (5: 110)—refers to an ideal world in which all moral agents receive happiness in accordance with their virtue. But it is also to be understood as "the unconditioned totality of the object of pure practical reason" (5: 108): the systemic union of all of practical reason's ends.[29] When the highest good is articulated in this more comprehensive sense, it becomes an ideal that unites all of our efforts to construct a moral world. Seeking peace, reducing poverty, promoting respect for human rights: these along with still other Enlightenment ideals all compose different aspects of the highest good.

The promotion of the highest good, Kant holds, "is an *a priori* necessary object of our will and inseparably bound up with the moral law" (5: 114). However, how and why the duty to seek the highest good follows from the moral law remains a matter of controversy. Kant does not explicitly refer to the highest good in any of his formulations of the categorical imperative, and some scholars have concluded that this alleged duty simply "does not exist."[30] But a promising hypothesis for grounding the highest good in the moral law is the kingdom of ends formula of the categorical imperative. For like the highest good, the kingdom of ends also represents a totality: in the *Groundwork* Kant describes it as "the *allness* [*Allheit*] or totality of the system" of ends (4: 436), a system composed of rational beings as ends in themselves, the particular ends that they set for themselves (their own desires for happiness), as well as their end of promoting the happiness of others (cf. 4: 433). The kingdom of ends thus refers to an ideal moral community in which all moral agents both respect each others' dignity and help one another to realize their legitimate ends. Understood in this way, it does appear that the highest good is "the condition that would obtain if the kingdom of ends were established."[31]

At any rate, however one ultimately judges the success of his effort, it is clear that Kant sought to ground Enlightenment reform efforts in our duty to promote the highest good. As he states in the third *Critique*, "We are determined *a priori* by reason to promote with all of our powers the best for the world [*das Weltbeste*], which consists in the combination of the greatest good for rational beings in the world with the highest condition of the good for them, i.e., the combination of universal happiness with the most lawful morality" (5: 453). As we saw earlier, in his reply to Mendelssohn in *Theory and Practice* Kant also integrates this duty strategy of justifying hope with the possibility strategy. We have a duty to pursue these ends, and unless and until reason can prove their impossibility, duty holds the upper hand over prudential concerns about attempting the impracticable. As he puts it, "I rest my case on my innate duty . . . (the possibility of this must, accordingly, also be assumed)" (8: 309). In effect, this is yet another application of the "ought implies can" principle. It does not make sense to say that we ought to do what is impossible, but once reason declares that we have a duty the obligation continues to hold unless and until we can show that what duty demands is impossible.

The job of demonstrating morality's demands remains a central task of moral philosophy, and clearly if we are genuinely motivated by the belief that justice requires us to strive to reduce poverty, promote peace, and establish a more effective international justice system, we will pursue these goals with more energy and commitment than we would if we thought they were merely optional projects. My principle of continued need and importance is itself a relative of Kant's duty strategy. In both cases, a rationale is provided to show people that they ought to pursue certain ends, and in both cases the relevant "ought" is a strong one that cannot be easily dismissed. Those Enlightenment goals that pass the history test (which, again, is a form of the possibility strategy) are still subject to the principle of continued need and importance, and none of these latter goals appears to be refuted by it. However, the conviction of duty (and/or the belief that the goals one is pursuing are necessary and important for human flourishing and a decent life), in and of itself, does not necessarily ground hope. Believing that one has a duty to pursue an immensely difficult goal such as world peace, or believing that the promotion of such a goal is immensely important, does not on its own give one reason to hope that the goal will be realized, particularly if one also senses that insufficient numbers of other people share the belief. The two beliefs together (viz., I know that I ought to pursue this goal, and I know that most people feel likewise), if acted on, might provide grounds for hope. But this is not our present situation. Today there is insufficient evidence to support the second belief. So the duty strategy on its own cannot ground hope.[32]

Moral Faith

Finally, Kant's most ambitious strategy for grounding Enlightenment hopes is by way of his famous argument for moral faith. As we saw in the previous section, we have a duty to seek the highest good along with all of the ancillary ends that come under it. But in order for this duty to make sense, we must also assume the conditions for the possibility of the highest good. As he states in the second *Critique*, "We *ought* to strive to promote the highest good (which must therefore be possible)" (5: 125). Here again Kant is appealing to a version of "ought implies can." However, the sense of possibility being invoked now is a stronger one than he employed earlier in the possibility strategy. There "possibility" was used in a minimalist sense: if reason and evidence cannot show that achieving our goals is impossible, then our doubts about achieving them cannot be made certain and we may still legitimately hope to realize our goals. It is also a stronger form of possibility than one finds in the signs strategy. For the signs were by no means guarantees: they were merely indications that our efforts seem to be connected with visible tendencies in human nature and history. But now possibility is meant in a stronger sense. We need assurance that the realization of our goals is not impossible, yes—however, we need to also assume that the world is not hostile to our efforts, that our own evil propensities will not thwart them, that there is indeed some likelihood that our efforts will succeed. Without this stronger sense of possibility we would fall into despair and give up the moral struggle. But we ourselves are unable to meet the moral demand to realize the highest good; it lies beyond our finite capacities. Realizing the highest good is possible only on the assumption that there is a God who will assist us. Thus Kant's moral argument for God's existence: "It is morally necessary to assume the existence of God" (*Practical Reason* 5: 125). Or, as he states in *Religion*, "Since by himself the human being cannot realize the idea of the highest good . . . he finds himself driven to believe in the cooperation or the management of a moral ruler of the world, through which alone this end is possible" (6: 139; cf. 5).[33]

Unlike the traditional arguments for God's existence, Kant's moral argument does not claim to offer objective proof that God actually exists. Quite the contrary. We are talking now only about a subjective necessity on the part of human beings who want their moral deliberations to be consistent, a point he insists on in each of the three *Critiques* (A 829/B 857; 5: 125–26, 450–51). But in arguing that human beings need to invoke God's assistance in order to meet morality's demands, he is definitely trying to provide a philosophical argument in defense of hope construed as a theological virtue. Ultimately, for Kant as for Aquinas, it is faith in divine grace and providence that is our strongest source of hope. At the same time, the moral faith strategy also remains a type of possibility argument. It by no means offers a guarantee that our hopes will be realized. On the contrary, each person "must so conduct himself as if everything depended on him, and only on this condition may he hope that a higher wisdom will grant the completion of his well-intentioned effort" (*Religion* 6: 101). Or, as Benjamin Franklin put it, "God helps them that help themselves."[34]

But is this kind of hope still available after the horrors of the past and present centuries? Contemporary intellectuals have frequently asserted, for instance, that "whatever was left of religious faith before Auschwitz could not survive it."[35] Is the theological virtue of hope still an option? Our earlier look at contemporary religion in chapter 6 would seem to provide a quick answer in the affirmative: religion has persisted in modernity; horror has not stopped it. At the same time, our analysis also showed that while religious faith flourishes in the contemporary world, most present-day religious believers are employing the theological virtue of hope not to seek assurance that humanity's efforts to realize Enlightenment ideals will eventually succeed, but rather for other purposes. Since the Enlightenment, the basic object of religious hope has shifted from cosmopolitan moral community to personal salvation. Enlightenment intellectuals invoked God precisely to ground their hopes for humanity's better future. The Kantian argument that faith in God is needed in order to make the duty to promote the highest good practicable is itself yet another illustration of what we called the morality thesis—the view that religion's proper purpose is moral rather than theological.

At bottom, philosophy's worthier attempts to ground hope all amount to different types of possibility arguments. This is entirely appropriate, for the logic of hope demands that it keep its distance from both certitude as well as cynicism. These strategies for grounding hope are still available to us at present, despite the many severe challenges thrown at them by recent horrors. Human beings need goals, and they also need hope in order to make sustained efforts toward their goals. Without goals and the hope that sustains them, we fall into resignation, an affect that eventually threatens to destroy life itself. If the response at this point is "Very well then, but why *these* ideals?" I can only respond that they still seem to me to be the best and most appropriate ones. The burden thus falls on those who reject Enlightenment ideals to show the superiority of their hopes and to convince the rest of us that they indeed have a better idea.

But given that Enlightenment intellectuals were wrong in some of their assumptions about how to achieve these ideals, are Enlightenment texts still the best source for these ideals? At the risk of appearing irreparably nostalgic, let me answer with a qualified yes. These texts do remain our best starting point for serious reflection on improving the human condition by peaceful and open means. Should they be our sole resource or the end point of our investigations? Of course not, for they contain errors that we can correct, and many new problems face us today that Enlightenment intellectuals did not anticipate. But what existed for a brief period during the Enlightenment was an enviable level of international consensus on, and commitment to, making a moral world—a new force in history that has yet to be matched. It was this spirit that Cassirer invoked when he said that we today must "find a way to release again those original forces which brought forth and molded" the Enlightenment.[36] Whether humanity will ever succeed in releasing again these forces remains to be seen. But if we give up trying, we are lost.

Notes

Introduction

1. Cassirer, *The Philosophy of the Enlightenment*, viii. See also J. K. Wright, "'A Bright Clear Mirror.'"

2. Bergk, "Does Enlightenment Cause Revolutions?" 231. (Karl Marx, in his eleventh Thesis on Feuerbach, criticized philosophers for having only "interpreted" the world. The point, he asserted, "is to change it.") Particularly after the start of the French Revolution in 1789, the issue of the relationship between enlightenment and revolution was on many people's minds. Not all Enlightenment intellectuals endorsed Bergk's position. Johann Heinrich Tieftrunk, for instance, concluded his 1794 essay "On the Influence of Enlightenment on Revolutions" by remarking that true enlightenment is "far removed from promoting violent revolutions" (224). For discussion, see Schmidt, "Introduction," 11–15. For analysis of conservative French reaction to the Enlightenment, see McMahon, *Enemies of the Enlightenment*.

3. Karl Popper, in his classic discussion, deems piecemeal social engineering "to be methodologically sound" and "a reasonable method of improving the lot of man," insofar as it recognizes that "every generation of men, and therefore also the

living, have a claim," and does not necessarily employ "a blueprint of society as a whole." Utopian engineering, by contrast, always employs a blueprint of society as a whole and "demands a strong centralized rule of a few . . . which therefore is likely to lead to a dictatorship" (*The Open Society and Its Enemies*, 1: 158, 159). More recently (and with slightly different terminology), James C. Scott has asserted that "utopian aspirations per se are not dangerous," but that the utopian vision goes wrong "when it is held by ruling elites with no commitment to democracy or civil rights and who are therefore likely to use unbridled state power for its achievement" (*Seeing Like a State*, 89). When the utopian vision goes wrong in the manner described, it results in what Scott calls "authoritarian social engineering" (194). See also Friedrich A. Hayek, *The Road to Serfdom* (Chicago: University of Chicago Press, 1944), 125.

4. James Scott, for instance, claims both that "industrial-strength social engineering was born" in the Enlightenment, and that "an Enlightenment belief in the self-improvement of man became, by degrees, a belief in the perfectibility of the social order" (*Seeing Like a State*, 91, 92–93). He seems to be unaware of Popper's earlier claim that Plato is the grandfather of utopian social engineering. However, Scott's real animus is against authoritarian "high modernists" of the nineteenth and twentieth centuries—not a single Enlightenment intellectual even appears in his "Hall of Fame of high-modernist figures" (88).

5. For a response to these and other accusations, see Robert Darnton, "The Case for Enlightenment: George Washington's False Teeth," in *George Washington's False Teeth*, 12–19.

6. Horkheimer and Adorno, *Dialectic of Enlightenment*, 4, xi. Jean Améry, after citing these and several other remarks from *Dialectic*, offers the following response: "Every one of them contains resistance against logic, irrational rage against the technical-industrial world, the wholly false conception that the historical Enlightenment was nothing but the instrument of a brutal bourgeoisie that was securing its dominion" ("Enlightenment as Philosophia Perennis," in *Radical Humanism*, 9). See also Daniel Gordon's introduction to his edited anthology, *Postmodernism and the Enlightenment*, 1–6.

7. Foucault, *Discipline and Punish*, 30. Foucault's attitude toward the Enlightenment fluctuated over the years. One of his first publications was a French translation of Kant's *Anthropology from a Pragmatic Point of View* (*Anthropologie du point de vue pragmatique*) (Paris: J. Vrin, 1964), and in late works such as "What Is Enlightenment?" he announced that he would like his own work to be understood as a part of the "critical ontology of ourselves" that Kant's work initiated (32–50, at 47, 50). For discussion, see Norris, "What Is Enlightenment?" 159–96.

8. MacIntyre, *After Virtue*, 51. For discussion, see Wokler, "Projecting the Enlightenment."

9. Cassirer, *The Philosophy of the Enlightenment*, xi–xii.

10. Here too my view is similar to Cassirer's. Kant's "own systematic edifice," he writes, "overshadows the Enlightenment even while it represents its final glorification" (*The Philosophy of the Enlightenment*, 274). For further discussion, see my *Kant's Impure Ethics*; "The Second Part of Morals"; and "Applying Kant's Ethics."

11. For discussion, see Louden, *Morality and Moral Theory*. See also Clarke and Simpson, *Anti-Theory in Ethics and Moral Conservatism*; Crisp and Slote, *Virtue Ethics*.

12. B. Williams, *Truth and Truthfulness*, 39. For discussion of Williams's criticisms of moral philosophy, see Louden, "The Critique of the Morality System."

13. Cf. Habermas, "Kant's Idea of Perpetual Peace."

14. *Encyclopedia of the Enlightenment*, s.v. "Aufklärung," by Fania Oz-Salzberger, 1: 97. For representative writings from the German Enlightenment, see Bahr, *Was ist Aufklärung?*; Ciafardone, *Die Philosophie der deutschen Aufklärung*.

15. Pocock, *Barbarism and Religion*, 1: 7; Schmidt, "Inventing the Enlightenment," 442. See also Porter and Teach, *The Enlightenment in National Context*.

16. Israel, *Radical Enlightenment*, v. Although the most radical recent splinterings of the Enlightenment have been geographical, milder conceptual splinterings are also possible. For examples of the latter, see Gary Gutting's trichotomy of "philosophical," "humanistic," and "radical" Enlightenments in *Pragmatic Liberalism*, 75–79, 118–24; and Ian Hunter's dichotomy of "civil" and "metaphysical" Enlightenments in *Rival Enlightenments*.

17. Darnton, *George Washington's False Teeth*, 11.

18. See Dupré, *The Enlightenment and the Intellectual Foundations of Modern Culture*.

19. Foucault, "What Is Enlightenment?" 43, 42; Plato, *Apology* 38a. Cf. Hilary Putnam, who remarks in "The Three Enlightenments" that "the earlier Platonic enlightenment" shares with "the seventeenth- and eighteenth-century enlightenment, the Enlightenment with a capital 'E' . . . the same aspiration to reflective transcendence, the same willingness to criticize conventional beliefs and institutions, and to propose radical reforms" (*Ethics without Ontology*, 94).

Chapter I: Religion

1. Juergensmeyer, *Terror in the Mind of God*, 225; cf. 242–43. Juergensmeyer leans heavily on McMahon's *Enemies of the Enlightenment* for his interpretation of the Enlightenment (see *Terror in the Mind of God*, xvi, 224–25, 239, 269 n. 37, 272 n. 19, 274 n. 45). In his own text, McMahon summarizes Enlightenment thought (or rather, conservative French reaction to French Enlightenment thought) as follows: "At the most fundamental level, [Enlightenment] *philosophie* was accused of subverting the foundations of the Catholic religion, leading necessarily to the wholesale destruction of the faith" (*Enemies of the Enlightenment*, 32). Juergensmeyer's error is to mistake this French Counter-Enlightenment portrayal of the French Enlightenment for the Enlightenment itself.

2. Gray, *Enlightenment's Wake*, 145; cf. 31, 146.

3. Gay, *The Enlightenment*, 1: 373. In Gay's case, it is also worth asking whether his own personal antireligious attitude may have influenced his reading of the Enlightenment. In his memoir of the years he spent as a boy in Nazi Berlin, he writes, "My parents made me into a village atheist, and, with a few psychological refinements, I have remained one. . . . My upbringing was not simply irreligious; it was antireligious. My father was a true son of the Enlightenment" (*My German Question*, 48, 50).

4. Israel, *Radical Enlightenment*, 79. For Israel, as one reviewer notes, "all roads in the Enlightenment lead to and from Spinoza" (Nadler, "Review Article," 290).

5. Himmelfarb, *The Roads to Modernity*, 18, 38. Himmelfarb's two main goals are to make the Enlightenment "more British" and to make the British Enlightenment more inclusive (6). The present study, while not denying regional differences in Enlightenment thinking, stresses the unity of Enlightenment thought with regard to moral ideals and the means of realizing them. In the present chapter, I intend to deflate the myth of the antireligious Enlightenment—for all Enlightenments, including the French.

6. In arguing that the Enlightenment was fundamentally religious rather than antireligious, I do not disagree with Robert Merrihew Adams's observation that Enlightenment religiosity is different in kind from contemporary religiosity—so different "as often to seem invisible" ("Reading the Silences," 282). Even here, though, I do dissent from at least part of Adams's own characterization of Enlightenment religiosity—namely, his claim that it was "both rationalistic and individualistic in ways that many, perhaps most, students of religion today have come to believe, on both theological and anthropological grounds, that authentic religion cannot be" (282). The claim that Enlightenment religiosity was rationalistic is obviously true, but the claim that it was individualistic is open to argument. Kant, for instance, while urging readers to have the courage to use their own reason in matters of religion (*Enlightenment* 8: 35), also held that human beings must seek moral community through membership and participation in religious institutions. As he writes in *Religion within the Boundaries of Mere Reason*, "The dominion or the good principle is not otherwise attainable, as far as human beings can work toward it, than through the setting up and diffusion of a society in accordance with, and for the sake of, the laws of virtue—a society which reason makes it a task and a duty of the entire human race to establish in its full scope" (6: 94). For discussion, see Louden, "The Church as Moral Community," in *Kant's Impure Ethics*, 124–32.

7. However, the real Mendelssohn was a bit more conservative than Nathan. In a letter to Swiss theologian Johann Casper Lavater written in December 1769, Mendelssohn writes, "All of our rabbis teach unanimously that the written and oral laws in which our *revealed* religion consists are only binding for our own nation" (*Gesammelte Schriften Jubiläumsausgabe*, 7: 10). The character of Nathan in Lessing's play does not accept revealed religion, whereas Mendelssohn does. I thank Niko Strobach for conversation on this point.

8. Quotations are from Act III, scene vii of Lessing, *Nathan der Weise*. For discussion, see Allison, *Lessing and the Enlightenment*, 139–47; Yasukata, *Lessing's Philosophy of Religion*, 72–89; Gurewitsch, "An 18th-Century Plea for Tolerance Resounds Today."

9. Allison, *Lessing and the Enlightenment*, 145. Lessing's writings also contain less allegorical and more direct expressions of the unity thesis. For instance, near the beginning of *Die Erziehung des Menschengeschlechts* (1780), he writes, "The first human being was furnished at once with a concept of the one God... [but] as soon as human reason, left to itself, began to elaborate it, it broke up the one immeasurable into many measureables" (*Die Erziehung des Menschengeschlechts und andere Schriften*, §6,

p. 8). In *Das Testament Johannis* (1777) he compresses John's theology into the simple maxim "Little children, love one another. . . . This alone, if it is done, is enough, is sufficient and adequate" (40–41). For further discussion, see Henry Chadwick's introduction to Lessing, *Lessing's Theological Writings*.

10. Pierre Bayle, *Philosophical Commentary on the Words of Jesus Christ* (1687–88), in Kramnick, *The Portable Enlightenment Reader*, 79.

11. Quotations are from Herbert, *De Veritate* (1624), in Gay, *Deism*, 32 (hereafter cited in the body of the text). For general discussion, see Byrne, "The Distant God of Deism," in *Religion and the Enlightenment*, 99–123; Beiser, *The Sovereignty of Reason*; and the essays in Lund, *The Margins of Orthodoxy*.

12. Paine, *The Age of Reason*, in *The Thomas Paine Reader*, 400 (hereafter cited in the body of the text).

13. Voltaire, in Kramnick, *The Portable Enlightenment Reader*, 132.

14. Voltaire, "Religion," in Kramnick, *The Portable Enlightenment Reader*, 119.

15. Rousseau, *The Social Contract*, trans. Cranston, IV.8 (p. 185); *Emile, or, On Education*, 308; cf. 311–12.

16. For Voltaire's response to d'Holbach, see Kramnick, *The Portable Enlightenment Reader*, 131–32. The citation from d'Holbach's *Common Sense* is also in *The Portable Enlightenment Reader*, 141.

17. Hyland, Gomez, and Greensides, *The Enlightenment*, 87. See also Adams, "Reading the Silences," 282.

18. Hume, *Dialogues Concerning Natural Religion*, part XII, 227. For further discussion of Hume's attenuated deism, see Gaskin, *Hume's Philosophy of Religion*, 219–23. See also Himmelfarb's discussion of Hume's skeptical stance toward religion, where she argues that he "had enough religion to support the church establishment, in part as a corrective to zealotry, but also because the belief in God and immortality had a salutary effect on people's lives" (*The Roads to Modernity*, 40).

19. Benjamin Franklin, "Something of My Religion . . . ," in Kramnick, *The Portable Enlightenment Reader*, 166–67. Franklin's list of fundamental principles of all sound religion overlaps considerably with Herbert's five Common Notions. For instance, Herbert's third Notion, as we saw earlier, holds that "the most important part of religious practice" concerns the connection between moral virtue and religious piety.

20. Paine, *The Age of Reason*, in *The Thomas Paine Reader*, 400. Friedrich Schleiermacher, in *On Religion: Speeches to Its Cultural Despisers* (1799), was one of the first to protest against the Enlightenment effort to moralize religion. In his view, religion "must be set off" from morality, "renounces herewith all claims to whatever belongs to" morals, and "is opposed to" ethics "in everything that makes up its essence and in everything that characterizes its effects" (19, 22, 22–23). For discussion of Schleiermacher's ethical theory, see the introduction in Schleiermacher, *Lectures on Philosophical Ethics*.

21. I have prepared a new English translation of this text, which is included in Kant, *Anthropology, History, and Education*.

22. For further discussion of prayer as a means to moral ends, see Palmquist, "Kant's Critical Hermeneutic of Prayer." Palmquist overstates matters when he

calls Kant "a man of prayer" (598), but he is correct in noting that on Kant's view legitimate prayer must serve "a higher moral end" (590).

23. Joseph Priestley, *Letters to Dr. Horsley* (1783), in Kramnick, *The Portable Enlightenment Reader*, 156.

24. Thomas Jefferson to Dr. Benjamin Rush, April 21, 1803, in Kramnick, *The Portable Enlightenment Reader*, 163, 165. In arguing his case that the moral doctrines of Jesus "were more pure and perfect than those of the most correct of the [ancient] philosophers," Jefferson chastises the latter for being "short and defective" in "developing our duties to others" and for failing to inculcate "peace, charity, and love to our fellow men, or . . . the whole family of mankind" (165, 164). See also Jefferson's famous edited version of the Gospels, reprinted in Jefferson, *The Jefferson Bible*.

25. Rousseau, *Emile*, 311–12; see also *The Social Contract* IV.8 (p. 185).

26. Lessing's ring parable, in its concluding claim that religious believers everywhere must prove the authenticity of their faith through "gentleness and heartfelt agreeableness, with benevolence," is yet another example of the morality thesis.

27. Hume, *Dialogues Concerning Natural Religion*, part XII, 220.

28. Outram, *The Enlightenment* (2005), 113. Similarly, Robert Wokler, in defending the "Enlightenment Project" against the bizarre claim of Horkheimer, Adorno, Bauman, and others that it was responsible "for the virtual extermination of European Jewry, planned and executed in the most methodical manner," writes, "If a spirit of tolerance was not at the heart of that Project, then it was nothing" ("Multiculturalism and Ethnic Cleansing in the Enlightenment," 77, 79).

29. Locke, *A Letter Concerning Toleration* (1689), 52 (hereafter cited in the body of the text). Locke actually wrote *three* different letters on toleration, and was working on a fourth when he died in 1704. But his first *Letter* of 1689 remains his most influential statement on the matter. For a contrast between moderate Lockean and radical Spinozistic theories of toleration, see Israel's discussion in *Radical Enlightenment*, "Spinoza, Locke, and the Enlightenment Struggle for Toleration," 265–70.

30. "ABSOLUTE LIBERTY . . . IS THE THING THAT WE STAND IN NEED OF" (Locke, "To the Reader," in *A Letter Concerning Toleration*, 12). (Locke's text was originally composed in Latin and printed in Holland.) Locke's theory of toleration is perhaps most famously associated with the so-called doctrine of the separation of church and state. In the First Amendment to the Constitution of the United States (1791), for instance, we read, "Congress shall make no law respecting an establishment of religion, or prohibiting the free exercise thereof." And near the beginning of his *Letter*, Locke writes, "I esteem it above all things necessary to distinguish exactly the business of civil government from that of religion, and to settle the just bounds that lie between the one and the other" (17). However, one should not infer from Locke's remark—as many people unfortunately do—that he sought to devalue the importance of religion in human life. Quite the contrary. In his view, the "principal and chief care of everyone ought to be of his own soul first" (49). However, "the care of souls cannot belong to the civil magistrate" (18).

31. Bayle, *Philosophical Commentary on the Words of Jesus Christ, "Compel Them to Come In,"* in Kramnick, *The Portable Enlightenment Reader,* 79 (hereafter cited in the body of the text).

32. Voltaire, "Toleration," in *Philosophical Dictionary* (1764), 387, 393–94. Perez Zagorin, in *How the Idea of Religious Toleration Came to the West,* describes Voltaire as standing "at the forefront of the Enlightenment movement for religious toleration" (294).

33. Voltaire, "Toleration," 392. See also the entry "Sect," 374–76. (The claim that there are no sects of mathematicians is arguable, but I shall not pursue that issue here.) Peter Gay, at the conclusion of a section entitled "Toleration: A Pragmatic Campaign" in volume 2 (*The Science of Freedom*) of *The Enlightenment: An Interpretation,* glosses Enlightenment theories of toleration (including his favorite, Voltaire's) by repeating a formula that first appeared in volume 1: "Relativism, Eclecticism, and toleration are so intimately related that they cannot be strictly separated even in thought. Relativism is a way of looking at the world, the recognition that no single set of convictions has absolute validity; Eclecticism is the philosophical method consequent on relativism—since no system has the whole truth, and most systems have some truth, discriminating selection among systems is the only valid procedure. Toleration, finally, is the political counterpart of this world view and this method: it is a policy for a large and varied society" (400 n. 3; cf. 1: 163). However, none of the Enlightenment theories of religious toleration presently under consideration rests on an assumption of relativism. Also, Gay's own position is inconsistent, for once relativism is assumed, there is no way to defend the procedure of "discriminating selection." On what basis are the selections to be justified?

34. Voltaire, *Treatise on Toleration* (1763), 89. However, Voltaire's claim that all human beings are children of one father does not square well with his well-known commitment to polygenesis. Elsewhere he states, "None but the blind can doubt that the whites, the negroes, the Albinoes, the Hottentots, the Laplanders, the Chinese, the Americans, are races entirely different" ("Of the Different Races of Men," 5).

35. Stephen Eric Brenner, *Reclaiming the Enlightenment: Toward a Politics of Radical Engagement* (New York: Columbia University Press, 2004), 141. While I share Brenner's conviction that "Enlightenment thinking remains the best foundation for any genuinely progressive politics not simply in the West but in those states that suffered most at its hands" (159), I believe he errs in equating the Enlightenment with secularism. As I have argued throughout this chapter, it is simply not the case that "most philosophes considered religious faith nothing more than superstition" (166).

36. Hume, "Of Superstition and Enthusiasm," in *Essays Moral, Political, and Literary,* 79.

37. *Encyclopedia of Religion,* s.v. "Enlightenment," by Allen W. Wood, 5: 113. As Wood also notes, Locke, in his *Essay Concerning Human Understanding,* connects faith to reason in a similar manner when he writes, "He that believes, without having any reason for believing, may be in love with his own fancies; but neither seeks

truth as he ought, nor pays the obedience due to his Maker, who would have him use those discerning faculties he has given him, to keep him out of mistake and error" (IV.17.24). Unfortunately, in Locke's theory of religious toleration as presented in the first *Letter*, this moral and religious obligation to seek truth is overridden by "public safety" strictures against atheists and Catholics.

38. Penelhum, "Hume's Criticisms of Natural Theology," 22. Similarly, Susan Neiman describes natural religion as "the Enlightenment's best hope.... Natural religion was meant to do away with the misery caused by revealed religion, serving as a force for unity instead of division" (*Evil in Modern Thought*, 149).

Chapter 2: Education

1. Gay, *The Enlightenment*, 2: 499. Carl L. Becker puts the same point in more sarcastic dress when he asserts that the fourth "essential article of the religion of the Enlightenment" is that "the first and essential condition of the good life on earth is the freeing of men's minds from the bonds of ignorance and superstition" (*The Heavenly City*, 102–3). For discussion and data concerning increased literacy rates in Enlightenment Europe, see Munck, *The Enlightenment*, 46–59; and *Encyclopedia of the Enlightenment*, s.v. "Literacy," by R. A. Houston, 2: 413–18. The broad historical trend, Munck notes, "is not in dispute: literacy, by whatever standards it is measured, increased significantly almost everywhere for both men and women during the eighteenth century" (48).

2. Locke, *An Essay Concerning Human Understanding* II.i.2; *Some Thoughts Concerning Education*, § 1, in *Some Thoughts Concerning Education and Of the Conduct of the Understanding*. Similarly, in § 32 of *Some Thoughts Concerning Education*, he states, "The difference to be found in the manners and abilities of men is owing more to their *education* than to anything else."

3. "I imagine the minds of children as easily turned this or that way, as water itself" (Locke, *Some Thoughts Concerning Education*, § 2). In his conclusion, Locke emphasizes that his remarks on education were "designed for a gentleman's son who, then being very little, I considered only as white paper or wax to be molded and fashioned as one pleases" (§ 216).

4. Aristotle, for instance, writes in his *Politics*, "Since there is a single end for the city as a whole, it is evident that education must necessarily be one and the same for all, and that the superintendence of it should be common and not on a private basis" (VIII.1.1337a21–24). However, his argument is meant to apply only to citizens within the polis—not to women, noncitizens, and slaves within the polis, and not to anyone outside of it. In Enlightenment writing on education we find for the first time multiple assertions of the position that *all* people should be educated. For discussion, see Curren, *Aristotle on the Necessity of Public Education*.

5. Jefferson, *A Bill for the More General Diffusion of Knowledge*, in *Writings*, 365. Similarly, in his letter of April 24, 1816, to P. S. Dupont de Nemours, Jefferson proclaims that "the diffusion of knowledge among the people" is the

chief instrument by which human progress is to be effected (*Writings*, 1388). And in his letter to George Wythe of August 13, 1786, he states, "I think by far the most important bill in our whole code is that for the diffusion of knowledge among the people.... Preach, my dear Sir, a crusade against ignorance: establish & improve the law for educating the common people" (*Writings*, 859). For discussion, see Brann, "Jeffersonian Ambivalences." For other important Enlightenment statements regarding education in the United States, see Rudolph, *Essays on Education in the Early Republic*; Vassar, *Social History of American Education*, vol. 1.

    6. Condorcet, *The Nature and Purpose of Public Instruction*, in *Selected Writings*, 111, 134. Coeducation was also an innovative feature of Jefferson's bill defending free public elementary education: "At these schools all the free children, male and female, ... shall be intitled to receive tuition gratis, for the term of three years" (*Writings*, 367). See also Benjamin Rush's important 1787 essay, "Thoughts upon Female Education, Accommodated to the Present State of Society, Manners, and Government in the United States of America," reprinted in Rudolph, *Essays on Education in the Early Republic*, 27–40. By "free children" Jefferson does mean to exclude slaves; he regarded blacks as "inferior to the whites in the endowments both of body and mind" (*Notes on the State of Virginia*; in *Writings*, 270). However, in Condorcet's case we do find a position that stops at neither gender nor race, one that is truly universal: "Either no individual of the human species has any true rights, or all have the same. And he who votes against the rights of another, of whatever religion, color, or sex, has thereby abjured his own" (*On the Admission of Women to the Rights of Citizenship*, in *Selected Writings*, 98).

    7. Condorcet, *Report on the General Organization of Public Instruction*, in La Fontainerie, *French Liberalism and Education*, 323. Turgot was also a strong supporter of equality of educational opportunity. In his brief *Memorial on Education*, he urges the formation of "a new system of education—which ... would serve to train, in all classes of society, virtuous and useful men—just in spirit and pure in heart, zealous citizens" (in La Fontainerie, *French Liberalism and Education*, 180). Unfortunately, Condorcet's plan for national education, presented to the French National Assembly at a time when the revolution was entering a much more radical and turbulent phase, was not well received. For discussion, see Palmer, *The Improvement of Humanity*, esp. 124–39.

    8. Condorcet, *Report on the General Organization of Public Instruction*, 326.

    9. Gay, "Locke on the Education of Paupers," 190. As Jennifer J. Popiel notes, Locke's focus on education within the home by private tutors (continued by Rousseau, at least in *Emile*), also does not link the improvement of society with the creation of organized forms of schooling ("Education," *Encyclopedia of the Enlightenment*, 1: 382–83).

    10. Louis-René de Caradeuc de La Chalotais, *Essay on National Education*, in La Fontainerie, *French Liberalism and Education*, 59–60. Voltaire himself endorsed this passage, writing to La Chalotais, "I thank you for forbidding labourers to study. I, who cultivate the earth, ask you for workmen, and not for tonsured clerics. Above all, send me some *Ignorantin* Brothers to drive my ploughs or to yoke them" (as cited by La Fontainerie in his introduction, 39). See also Palmer, *The Improvement of*

Humanity, 57, 237; Baker, *Condorcet*, 289; Chisick, *The Limits of Reform*, esp. 89–90. On the related issue of the popularization of the Enlightenment, see *Encyclopedia of the Enlightenment*, s.v. "Popularization," by Chisick, 3: 329–334; Gay, "A Faith for the Canaille," in *The Enlightenment*, 2: 517–28.

11. Rousseau, *On the Social Contract, Discourse on the Origin of Inequality, Discourse on Political Economy*, 177, 178.

12. Rousseau, *Emile, or, On Education*, 363, 386. For another early statement on coeducational public education, see Amable-Louis-Rose de Lafitte du Courteil's 1797 essay, *Proposal to Demonstrate the Necessity of a National Institution in the United States of America, for the Education of Children of Both Sexes* (etc.), reprinted in Rudolph, *Essays on Education in the Early Republic*, 225–70.

13. Mary Wollstonecraft, *A Vindication of the Rights of Woman*, in *The Vindications*, 136, 129–30.

14. Ibid., 167, 185.

15. Diderot is a good representative here. On his view, there are two kinds of knowledge: primary and secondary. "Primary knowledge," he holds, "is necessary to all," but different professions require different amounts of it: "the laborer needs less than the factory worker, the factory worker needs less than the shopkeeper, the shopkeeper less than the soldier, the soldier less than the magistrate or the ecclesiastic, and these latter less than the statesman" (*Plan for a Russian University*; in La Fontainerie, *French Liberalism and Education*, 217–18). In the case of La Chalotais, there is also the question of whether his opposition to teaching the working class to read and write is consistent with his own commitment to basic Enlightenment values. Regarding the latter, he writes, in his *Essay*, "Knowledge is necessary to man. . . . Ignorance is good for nothing, and it is harmful to everything" (41). "The most enlightened people (all other things being equal, or even not entirely so) will always have the advantage over those that are less so" (42). "Enlightenment leads ordinarily to truth; darkness and ignorance lead to vice" (p. 142). Cf. Chisick, *The Limits of Reform*, 91–92.

16. La Fontainerie, "Introduction" to La Chalotais, *Essay on National Education*, in *French Liberalism and Education*, 37, 53. According to Palmer, "The phrase 'national education' was popularized by the *Essai d'éducation nationale* of Caradeuc de La Chalotais" (*The Improvement of Humanity*, 53; cf. 57, 237).

17. Rousseau, *Considerations on the Government of Poland*, in *Rousseau on International Relations*, 172.

18. Adam Smith, *An Inquiry into the Nature and Causes of the Wealth of Nations*, V.i.f.54. For discussion, see Rothschild, "Condorcet and Adam Smith," 209–26. For a twentieth-century analogue, see Milton Friedman's advocacy of educational vouchers in *Capitalism and Freedom*, 89.

19. Diderot, *Observations sur le Nakaz*, in *Political Writings*, 141. A more morally compelling version of the argument against state monopolies on education was made later by John Stuart Mill. In *On Liberty* (1859), he argues that children have a universal right to education, and that a correlative "duty of enforcing universal education" falls on the state. However, on Mill's view the state's duty of enforcing universal education does not translate into universal state education:

> That the whole or any large part of the education of the people should be in
> State hands, I go as far as anyone in deprecating. All that has been said of the
> importance of individuality of character, and diversity in opinions and
> modes of conduct, involves, as of the same unspeakable importance, diversity
> of education. A general State education is a mere contrivance for molding
> people to be exactly like one another....An education established and
> controlled by the State should only exist, if it exist at all, as one among
> many competing experiments. (104–5)

For discussion, see Amy M. Schmitter, Nathan Tarcov, and Wendy Donner, "Enlightenment Liberalism," in *A Companion to the Philosophy of Education*, ed. Randall Curren (Malden, MA: Blackwell, 2003), esp. 89–90.

20. For a recent appreciation, see Munzel, "Kant on Moral Education."

21. Similarly, at the conclusion of his *Collins* moral philosophy lectures, he asserts, "Not a single ruler has ever contributed anything to the perfection of humanity, to inner happiness, or the worth of mankind; they have merely looked always to the prosperity of their domains, which for them is the primary concern" (27: 471).

22. Jefferson, "Plan for Elementary Schools" (September 1817), in *Thomas Jefferson on Democracy*, 90. But perhaps Jefferson would concur with Mill's later proposal for resolving the tension between the duty of universal education and the right of parental free choice: "public examinations, extending to all children and beginning at an early age," is the best instrument "to make the universal acquisition and...retention of a certain minimum of general knowledge virtually compulsory" (*On Liberty*, 105).

23. Lessing, *Die Erziehung des Menschengeschlects* (1777), § 82, in *Die Erziehung des Menschengeschlechts und andere Schriften*, 28.

24. Quotations are from Condorcet, *The Nature and Purpose of Public Instruction* (1791), in *Selected Writings*.

25. Jefferson, *Notes on the State of Virginia* (1787), *Query XIV*, in *Writings*, 273. In later stages of education, when the student's judgment is sufficiently matured for religious inquiries, Jefferson counsels skepticism and free inquiry. In a letter of August 10, 1787, to his nephew Peter Carr, advising him on his education, Jefferson writes, in a Kantian vein, "Fix reason firmly in her seat, and call to her tribunal every fact, every opinion. Question with boldness even the existence of a god; because, if there be one, he must more approve of the homage of reason, than that of blindfolded fear" (*Writings*, 902; cf. Kant, *Critique of Pure Reason* A xi).

26. Jefferson, *A Bill for the More General Diffusion of Knowledge*, in *Writings*, 367; cf. 272, 459. Adam Smith also stresses the three Rs: "The most essential parts of education,...to read, write, and account, can be acquired at so early a period of life, that the greater part even of those who are to be bred to the lowest occupations, have time to acquire them before they can be employed in those occupations. For a very small expence the publick can facilitate, can encourage, and can even impose upon the whole body of the people, the necessity of acquiring these most essential part of education" (*The Wealth of Nations*, V.i.f.54).

27. Jefferson, *Report of the Commissioners for the University of Virginia*, in *Writings*, 459. Jefferson's plan for the University of Virginia was his most successful educational

innovation. It was the first nonsectarian and publicly funded university established in the United States. See also the section on "Enlightened Universities," below.

28. Condorcet, *Sketch for a Historical Picture of the Progress of the Human Mind*, in *Selected Writings*, 265. Condorcet also held that greater equality of education would lead to greater economic equality among citizens: "With greater equality of education there will be greater equality in industry and so in wealth" (266). Condorcet's *Sketch* was written shortly before his death in prison under the hands of the Jacobins.

29. Jefferson, *A Bill for the More General Diffusion of Knowledge*, in *Writings*, 365. A virtually identical phrase occurs in *Notes on the State of Virginia*; see *Writings*, 274.

30. "It is universally acknowledged, that there is a great uniformity among the actions of men, in all nations and ages, and that human nature remains still the same, in its principles and operations. The same motives always produce the same actions: The same events follow from the same causes.... Mankind are so much the same, in all times and places, that history informs us of nothing new or strange in this particular" (Hume, "Of Liberty and Necessity," in *An Essay Concerning Human Understanding* [1748], 55).

31. Jefferson to Peter Carr, August 10, 1787, in *Writings*, 901.

32. Beiser, "Romanticism," 135, 137. Similarly, James A. Leith, in his survey of eighteenth-century writings on education, remarks, "Utility appears repeatedly in proposed reforms in various countries" ("Introduction," 16).

33. D'Alembert, "School," in *The Encyclopedia: Selections*, ed. Stephen J. Gendzier (New York: Harper Torchbooks, 1967), 224–25.

34. Ibid., 225.

35. Diderot, *Plan of a University for the Russian Government*, in La Fontainerie, *French Liberalism and Education*, 246–47.

36. Ibid., 243–44.

37. Gay, *The Enlightenment*, 2: 510. It should also be noted that *Bildung* (a broad term variously translated as "formation," "self-realization," "culture," "education"), which Beiser regards as the lead concept in romantic philosophy of education ("Romanticism," 132–34), is also central to many German Enlightenment writers on education, particularly Kant. Edward Franklin Buchner, for instance, notes that *Bildung* "is very generally used by Kant, and is, perhaps, next to 'morality,' the most important item in his conception of education" (in Kant, *The Educational Theory of Immanuel Kant*, 101 n. 2). See also Thomas E. Willey, "Kant and the German Theory of Education." Willey correctly points to Kant as the founder of "a rich, nuanced and essentially anti-utilitarian educational philosophy contained in the term *Bildung*" (543).

38. La Chalotais, *Essay on National Education*, in La Fontainerie, *French Liberalism and Education*, 51; cf. 143–44, 147, 151, 154–55. See also Chisick, *The Limits of Reform*, 91.

39. Locke, *Some Thoughts Concerning Education*, §§ 135, 136; cf. §§ 157, 158. See also Schmitter et al., "Enlightenment Liberalism," 82–83.

40. Rousseau, *The Social Contract*, IV.8; 185 in Cranston's edition. For discussion, see Gourevitch, "The Religious Thought."

41. Rousseau, *Emile*, 311–12.

42. Since Condorcet allows that facts (but again: only facts) about the constitution of one's country form a legitimate part of public instruction, why should not the same hold for the political, moral, and religious heritage of one's country? If the latter are approached descriptively rather than prescriptively, they too would meet Condorcet's strictures.

43. For recent discussions, see Herman, "Training to Autonomy"; Munzel, "Kant, Hegel, and the Rise of Pedagogical Science."

44. Kant explores the different formulas of the categorical imperative in the *Groundwork of the Metaphysics of Morals* (4: 421–37).

45. Jefferson reserves several of the subjects in Kant's list (those outside of the three Rs) for post–primary school education. Surprisingly, he was a strong supporter of the teaching of Greek and Latin at the secondary (or what he called "grammar") school level. In *Query XIV* he writes, "The learning Greek and Latin, I am told, is going into disuse in Europe. I know not what their manners and occupations may call for: but it would be very ill-judged in us to follow their example in this instance" (*Writings*, 273). Condorcet, on the other hand, held that teaching the traditional classical curriculum was irrelevant to modern life and even dangerous, insofar as it substituted eloquence for reason. See Baker, *Condorcet*, 297–98.

46. Kant discusses religious education toward the end of his section on "Practical Education" in the *Lectures on Pedagogy*; see 9: 493–96. His final advice to teachers on the subject of religious education is to stress to students that "in spite of the diversity of religions there is nevertheless unity of religion everywhere" (9: 496).

47. There is a very brief discussion of patriotism in the *Vigilantius* lectures (27: 673–74), and of patriotic versus paternalistic governments in *Theory and Practice* (8: 291). For a defense of Kant's "modest patriotism" with reference to the latter text, see H. Williams, *Kant's Political Philosophy*, 131–32, 275.

48. Niedermeier, "Campe als Direktor des Dessauer Philanthropins," 46. Campe succeeded Basedow as director of the Institute in 1776, though he left after one year. For discussion, see chapter 15 of Quick, *Essays on Educational Reformers*. For a selection of Basedow's writings, see *Ausgewählte pädagogsiche Schriften*.

49. This is a lecture transcription from Kant's 1775–76 anthropology course. An English translation of *Friedländer*, prepared by G. Felicitas Munzel, will appear in Kant, *Lectures on Anthropology*.

50. Kant, *Essays Regarding the Philanthropinum*, 2: 448, 451. My translations of these two essays are included in Kant, *Anthropology, History, and Education*.

51. On this last point Basedow owes a debt to Locke. Locke views Latin "as absolutely necessary to a gentleman," but does not endorse "the ordinary way of learning it in a grammar school." Rather, he suggests that teachers "trouble the child with no *grammar* at all, but to have *Latin*, as English has been, without the perplexity of rules, talked into him" (*Some Thoughts Concerning Education*, §164).

52. As cited by Niedermeier, "Campe als Dirketor des Dessauer Philanthropins," 46 n.7.

53. See Kant's famous definition of enlightenment in *An Answer to the Question: What Is Enlightenment?* 8: 35. For discussion of the seventeenth-century background

to Kant's conception of enlightenment as something that requires the public exercise of reason, see Losonsky, *Enlightenment and Action*.

54. Munck, *The Enlightenment*, 57. See also Ulrich Im Hof's discussion of "Education, Schools and Popular Enlightenment" in *The Enlightenment*, esp. 206–7. For an overview of universities during the Enlightenment, see *Encyclopedia of the Enlightenment*, s.v. "Universities," by Laurence Brockliss, 4: 204–12.

55. McClelland, *State, Society, and University*, 28. See also Melton, *Absolutism*, 116; Munck, *The Enlightenment*, 57 n. 8.

56. Smith, *The Wealth of Nations*, V.i.f, 32, 19, 8, 35. At Oxford, for instance, Smith claimed that "the greater part of the publick professors have ... given up altogether even the pretence of teaching" (V.i.f.8).

57. The other eight were William and Mary, Yale, New Jersey (later renamed Princeton University), King's (later Columbia University), Philadelphia (later University of Pennsylvania), Rhode Island (later Brown University), Queen's (later Rutgers University), and Dartmouth. For discussion, see Rudolph, *The American College and University*, 3–22. The oldest universities in the New World are Mexico University and the University of San Marcos in Lima, Peru, both founded in 1551.

58. Rudolph notes that in 1779, when Jefferson was governor of Virginia as well as a member of William and Mary's board of visitors, "he called for the abolition of the professorships of divinity and of oriental languages. The college, said Jefferson, must free men from superstition, not inoculate them with it" (*The American College and University*, 41). Cf. *Query XV* in *Notes on the State of Virginia* (1781), in *Writings*, 276–77. Many American colleges and universities founded prior to the University of Virginia were of course influenced to a greater or lesser degree by Enlightenment thinking, but not in their original charters. For instance, Rudolph notes that new professorships

> of economics, natural history, and French revealed in 1792 that Columbia had been bitten by the Enlightenment. At Union [College] a few years later French, American history, and constitutional government broke into the old course of study. At the University of North Carolina plans were projected in 1795 for a course to consist of a professorship of chemistry, agriculture, and the mechanic arts, a professorship of belles-lettres, and a professorship of languages, including that most neglected and perhaps most useful of all languages, English. (41–42)

59. Jefferson, *Writings*, 372, 272. See also Brann, "Jeffersonian Ambivalences," 274; Mondale and Patton, *School*, 23.

60. Bergk, "Ueber die Einschränkung der Freiheit zu studieren durch den Staat," 7. The article is dated April 25, 1800. Later in the essay Bergk declares, "Money and class [*Geld und Stand*] are the most inappropriate and ignoble conditions that the state can choose for conferring permission to study" (10). For discussion, see La Vopa, *Grace, Talent, and Merit*, 48–50, 393. I would like to thank Niko Strobach for obtaining a photocopy of Bergk's essay for me. As La Vopa notes at the beginning of his study, many of the principal figures in the German Enlightenment themselves came "from the plebian depths" (2). A partial list

includes the philosophers Christian Wolff, Immanuel Kant, and Johann Gottlieb Fichte (who, like Bergk, also argued that university education should be open to all), as well as the classicists Johann Joachim Winckelmann and Christian Gottlob Heyne. Bergk, who also published under the pseudonym "Fr. Ch. Starke," edited several versions of Kant's popular anthropology lectures, including the famous *Menschenkunde* transcription (1831). I have prepared an English translation of parts of this text, forthcoming in Kant, *Lectures on Anthropology*.

61. Jefferson, "Report of the Commissioners for the University of Virginia," in *Writings*, 459–60.

62. Jefferson, "From the Minutes of the Board of Visitors, University of Virginia, 1822–25," in *Writings*, 479.

63. Ibid., 479–80. As Brann notes, the last document in the list later became "a founding document of the states' rights faction" ("Jeffersonian Ambivalences," 278).

64. Jefferson to George Tickner, July 16, 1823, as cited by Brann, "Jeffersonian Ambivalences," 277. Similarly, Rudolph writes, "One of the most liberating regulations in the history of American higher education . . . was the one adopted by the University of Virginia board of visitors in 1824: 'Every student shall be free to attend the schools of his choice, and no other than he chooses.' At the University of Virginia every student was a free agent" (*The American College and University*, 126).

65. Jefferson to Priestley, January 18, 1800, in *Writings*, 1070, 1071.

66. Jefferson, *Report of the Commissioners*, 462–64. Under chemistry Jefferson also included agriculture, a discipline about which he was particularly passionate. Earlier he had written that agriculture "is the first in utility, and ought to be the first in respect. . . . It is a science of the very first order. . . . In every College and University, a professorship of agriculture, and the class of its students, might be honored as the first. Young men, closing their academical education with this, as the crown of the sciences . . . , instead of crowding the other classes, would return to the farms of their fathers" (letter to David Williams, 1803, in *Thomas Jefferson on Democracy*, 89).

67. Jefferson, *Report of the Commissioners*, 467.

68. Jefferson to Thomas Cooper, November 2, 1822, in *Writings*, 1463–65. Even in his earlier recommendation not to establish a professorship of divinity (n. 67), it is important to note that Jefferson aimed only to exclude sectarian religion from the curriculum—not those aspects of religion that are "common to all sects." The professor of ethics was expected to discuss with students the nature and existence of God, to explore the relationship between morality and religion, and so forth.

69. McClelland, *State, Society, and University*, 2, 22. See also Turner, "University Reformers," 2: 495–532; Brockliss, "Curricula," 2: 568. Much valuable information about the rise of the modern research university in Enlightenment Germany is also available in W. Clark, *Academic Charisma*. However, Clark's focus on the "material practices of academics" and their connection to "the transformation of academic charisma" (6) is quite different from my present concerns about Enlightenment ideals in higher education.

70. Turner, "University Reformers," 501. See also König, "Der Kampf gegen die Universitäten seit 1760," in *Vom Wesen der Deutschen Universität*, 22–27. One

prominent critic cited by Turner is Johann Heinrich Campe (1746–1818), who served briefly as director of the Phlanthropinum after Basedow's resignation in 1776. In his *Allgemeine Revision des gesammten Schul- und Erziehungswesen* (Vienna, 1792), Campe asks, "And who should educate them [the students]? Certainly not the professors. Who could require that of them? They have not studied the theory of education" (148; as cited by Turner on 502). See also McClelland, *State, Society, and University*, 78–79.

71. Paulsen, *German Education*, 117. See also Randall Collins's discussion of "The German University Revolution" in *The Sociology of Philosophies*, esp. 638–60.

72. Wolff's remarks were made in a lecture entitled *Oratio de Sinarum philosophia practica* (Discourse on the Practical Philosophy of the Chinese), first delivered at Halle in 1721. For discussion, see Louden, " 'What Does Heaven Say?' "

73. McClelland, *State, Society, and University*, 39. See also Hammerstein, "Epilogue," 2: 629. For a detailed historical study of Göttingen University, see Selle, *Die Georg-August-Universität*.

74. Kant, in his *Conflict of the Faculties*, writes,

> The philosophy faculty consists of two departments: a department of *historical cognition* (including history, geography, philology and the humanities, along with all the empirical knowledge contained in the natural sciences), and a department of *pure rational cognition* (pure mathematics and pure philosophy, the metaphysics of nature and of morals). And it also studies the relation of these two divisions of learning to each other. It therefore extends to all parts of human cognition (including, from a historical viewpoint, the teachings of the higher faculties). (7: 28)

Kant tried to raise the status of the philosophy faculty in a more intellectually direct manner, arguing that its function is "to discover the truth for the benefit of all" the faculties, and that "*truth* (the essential and first condition of learning in general) is the main thing, whereas the *utility* the higher faculties promise the government is of secondary importance" (7: 28). This last citation also provides additional support for our earlier argument against the claim that Enlightenment educational reforms were dominated by concerns of utility.

75. McClelland, *State, Society, and University*, 38. See also Turner, "Reformers and Scholarship in Germany," 504; Paulsen, *German Education*, 121.

76. Münchhausen, "Nachträgliches Votum," in Emil F. Roessler, *Die Gründung der Universität Göttingen: Entwürfe, Berichte, und Briefe der Zeitgenossen* (Göttingen, 1855); as cited by McClelland, 43.

77. Turner, "Reformers and Scholarship in Germany," 520. See also McClelland, *State, Society, and University*, 40–41. The Berlin Academy of Sciences, founded by Leibniz in 1700, was not a teaching institution.

78. Bruford, *Germany in the Eighteenth Century*, 244. See also McClelland, *State, Society, and University*, 60; Paulsen, *German Education*, 121–22; Mann, "The Past as Future?"; Grafton, "Polyhistor into *Philolog*."

79. Paulsen, *German Education*, 188. See also W. Clark, "The Seminars," in *Academic Charisma*, 158–79.

80. Humboldt, *The Limits of State Action*, 10 (translation altered slightly). John Stuart Mill would later use this passage as the epigraph for *On Liberty*. For discussion

of Humboldt's political and educational theory, see Sorkin, "Wilhelm von Humboldt." See also *Encyclopedia of the Enlightenment*, s.v. "Humboldt, Wilhelm von," by Gerald N. Izenberg, 2: 232–33.

81. La Vopa, *Grace, Talent, and Merit*, 265. See also Beiser, "A Romantic Education." In addition to his contributions to the founding of the University of Berlin, Humboldt was also responsible for two fundamental reforms in German secondary education. First, he introduced the *Staatsexamen*, mandatory state certification by comprehensive examination of Gymnasium instructors according to discipline. This assured that only university-educated candidates would be able to teach at the secondary level, and also required candidates to demonstrate proficiency in the discipline that they would teach. Second, "he universalized and brought under state control the final examination upon completion of the curriculum of the *Gymnasium*, the *Abitur*. Further, he enhanced its importance by granting anyone who successfully completed this examination the unequivocal right to enter and study at any university in Prussia" (Fallon, *The German University*, 18).

82. Paulsen, *German Education*, 184. Paulsen (1846–1908) was himself a professor of philosophy at Berlin. See also W. Clark, "Romantic Ideologies and the University of Berlin," in *Academic Charisma*, 442–46.

83. Humboldt, "On the Relative Merits of Higher Institutions of Learning," in *Humanist without Portfolio*, 132, 135. Similarly, in his earlier work, *The Limits of State Action*, Humboldt stresses that "freedom is required for the development of human powers" (10, translation altered slightly).

84. Humboldt, "On the Relative Merits," 132–33 (translation altered slightly). For the original German text of Humboldt's essay (*Über die innere und äussere Organisation der höheren wissenschaftlichten Anstalten in Berlin*), see vol. 10 of his *Gesammelte Schriften*, 250–60. In *The Limits of State Action*, Humboldt argued that *Bildung* requires both freedom and social intercourse—"the voluntary interchange of one's individuality with that of others" (Sorkin, "Wilhelm von Humboldt," 58–59). In his later writings on education, the teacher–student relationship is conceptualized in terms of the social intercourse condition for *Bildung*.

85. Schleiermacher, *Occasional Thoughts on Universities*. For discussion, see Fallon, *The German University*, chap. 4.

86. Fichte, *Addresses to the German Nation*, 166; cf. 12–13; "Deduzierter Plan einer zu Berlin zu errichtenden höhern Lehranstalt, die in gehöriger Verbindung mit einer Akademie der Wissenschaften stehe," reprinted in Anrich, *Die Idee der deutschen Universität*, 191–92, cf. 139.

87. German texts of the Berlin writings of Humboldt, Schleiermacher, Fichte, Schelling, and Steffens are available in Anrich, *Die Idee der deutschen Universität*. For discussion, see König, *Vom Wesen der deutschen Universität*, esp. 76–97, 133–43, 154–66, 181–89; McClelland, *State, Society, and University*, 105–40; and Fallon, *The German University*, chaps. 2–4.

88. See Rudolph, *The American College and University*, 99–100, 118, 120, 233–34, 268–72, 283–84, 335; Fallon, *The German University*, 1–3, 51–52; W. Clark, *Academic Charisma*, 462–64. Johns Hopkins University (incorporated in 1867,

opened in 1876) is the most frequently cited example of an American graduate university founded on the German model.

Chapter 3: Economics

1. Adam Smith, *The Wealth of Nations*, I.ii.1 (hereafter cited in the body of the text, and abbreviated as *WN*).

2. Pocock, *Barbarism and Religion*, 2: 169. See also Montesquieu's discussion, "How Commerce broke through the Barbarism of Europe," in *The Spirit of the Laws* (1748), trans. Thomas Nugent (New York: Hafner, 1949), I.xxi.20.

3. Consider Smith's vivid description of the dehumanization caused by "the progress of the division of labour":

> The employment of the far greater part of those who live by labour, that is, of the great body of the people, comes to be confined to a few very simple operations, frequently to one or two. . . . The man whose whole life is spent in performing a few simple operations, of which the effects too are, perhaps, always the same, or very nearly the same, has no occasion to exert his understanding, or to exercise his invention in finding out expedients for removing difficulties which never occur. He naturally loses, therefore, the habit of such exertion, and generally becomes as stupid and ignorant as it is possible for a human creature to become. The torpor of his mind renders him, not only incapable of relishing or bearing a part in any rational conversation, but of conceiving any generous, noble, or tender sentiment, and consequently of forming any just judgment concerning many even of the ordinary duties of private life. Of the great and extensive interests of his country he is altogether incapable of judging. . . . His dexterity at his own particular trade seems, in this manner, to be acquired at the expense of his intellectual, social, and martial virtues. (*WN* V.i.f.50)

Smith's argument for the necessity of universal education in modern society derives in large part from these observations, and several commentators have suggested that Marx's own theory of alienation owes a serious debt to them. For discussion, see Griswold, *Adam Smith*, 292–95, 299–301.

4. Voltaire, *Letters Concerning the English Nation*, in Gay, *The Enlightenment*, 155. See also the selections from Voltaire in H. C. Clark, *Commerce, Culture, and Liberty*, 265–81.

5. Montesquieu, *The Spirit of the Laws*, I.xx.7.

6. Diderot, "Extracts from the *Histoire des Deux Indes*," in *Political Writings*, 189. Although Abbé Raynal was the credited author of the *Histoire*, Diderot himself wrote many of the most notable passages. Mason and Wokler have collected what they believe are Diderot's contributions in their anthology, noting that because of the collaborative nature of the work "we cannot always be sure that the printed version reflects his exact words . . . [but] there are good reasons for supposing that all the passages given here are accurate reflections of Diderot's thought" (166). See also H. C. Clark's excerpts from the second edition of the *Histoire* in *Commerce,*

Culture, and Liberty, 610–23, esp. 615. For discussion, see Muthu, "Diderot and the Evils of Empire: The *Histoire des deux Indes*," in *Enlightenment against Empire*, 72–121.

7. In *The Wealth of Nations* Smith writes, "Commerce and manufactures gradually introduced order and good government, and with them, the liberty of individuals, among the inhabitants of the country, who had before lived almost in a continual state of war with their neighbours, and of servile dependency upon their superiors.... Mr. Hume is the only writer who, so far as I know, has hitherto taken notice of it" (III.iv.4).

8. Hume, "Of Refinement in the Arts," in *Essays Moral, Political, and Literary*, 270 (hereafter cited in the body of the text, and abbreviated as *RA*).

9. Similarly, in "Of Commerce" Hume defends the following maxim: "The greatness of a state, and the happiness of its subjects, how independent soever they may be supposed in some respects, are commonly allowed to be inseparable with regard to commerce; and as private men receive greater security, in the possession of their trade and riches, from the power of the public, so the public becomes powerful in proportion to the opulence and extensive commerce of private men" (*Essays*, 255).

10. Ibid., 265. Similarly, William Hazeland, in *A View of the Manner in Which Trade and Civil Liberty Support Each Other* (1756), argues that trade promotes liberty (as well as equality) by emancipating "the meaner people from their subjection to the land-owners" (in H. C. Clark, *Commerce, Culture, and Liberty*, 409).

11. Hume, "Of the Jealousy of Trade," in *Essays*, 328. For general discussion, see Istvan Hont's important collection of essays, *Jealousy of Trade*.

12. See also Plato, *Republic* 555 c–d; Aristotle, *Politics* 1256b30–1258a18; Matthew 6:25–34, 10:9–10; Luke 6:20–21, 12:22–31, 18:18–27. For discussion, see *Encyclopedia of the Enlightenment*, s.v. "Luxury," by Helena Rosenblatt, 2: 440–45; Eugene Rotwein, "Editor's Introduction," in Hume, *Writings on Economics*, xci–civ; Berry, "Adam Smith and the Virtues of Commerce"; Griswold, *Adam Smith*, 16–17, 265–66.

13. Hume, "Of Refinement in the Arts," in *Essays*, 269. Other important Enlightenment texts on luxury include Jean-François Melon, *A Political Essay upon Commerce* (1734), and Voltaire's poems "The Worldling" (1736) and "The Man of the World" (1738), reprinted in H. C. Clark, *Commerce, Culture, and Liberty*, 254–75.

14. Hume, "Of Refinement in the Arts," in *Essays*, 269. In calling innocent luxury a virtue, Hume is also challenging Mandeville's position that vices can be beneficial to society. Here his own commitment to a utilitarian conception of virtue and vice becomes apparent. As he remarks at the end of the essay, "Indeed it seems upon any system of morality, little less than a contradiction in terms, to talk of a vice, which is in general beneficial to society" (280).

15. And for which he seems to have paid a price. Emma Rothschild, in commenting on the "exiguous" and "disobliging" obituaries of Smith, cites from one that asserts, "Dr Smith's system of political economy is not essentially different from that of Count Verri, Dean Tucker, and Mr Hume" (*Economic Sentiments*, 52).

16. For discussion, see Werhane, *Adam Smith*, 168–73. Strictly speaking, Smith holds that the division of labor itself gives rise to industrialization. But both factors are treated as causal agents that contribute to the growth of commercial society.

17. Fleischacker, *A Third Concept of Liberty*, 172.

18. Fleischacker, in "Values behind the Market," cites this passage (along with many others) as evidence of Smith's influence on Kant's economic views, claiming that it is "unlikely" that Kant came up with the idea of a free trade doctrine "on his own" (385). I see no compelling reason to assume that Kant derived this doctrine from Smith. For Kant, the defense of free trade stems from his larger thesis concerning our innate "unsociable sociability." See also the section on "International Trade," below.

19. See also Fleischacker, "Values behind the Market," 393; *A Third Concept of Liberty*, 215–40.

20. Kant's main contention here is that the *Handelsgeist* "cannot coexist with war" (8: 368)—free trade serves to secure peace between nations. I discuss this claim in chapter 5 (see also section on "International Trade," below).

21. See also *Idea for a Universal History* (8: 21). Predictably, Fleischacker also points to each of these points as constituting further evidence of a Kant–Smith connection ("Values behind the Market," 385, 389). Again, I am inclined to say simply that Smith and Kant agree with each other here, rather than assert that Kant "borrowed" these ideas from Smith. The idea that human history progresses through successive stages goes back at least as far as Vico. See, e.g., Kramnick, *The Portable Enlightenment Reader*, 351; Pittock, "Historiography," 259–60.

22. Cf. *Conjectural Beginning of Human History* (8: 119). Similarly, Hume, in "The Sceptic," writes, "It is certain, that a serious attention to the sciences and liberal arts softens and humanizes the temper, and cherishes those fine emotions, in which true virtue and honour consists. It rarely, very rarely happens, that a man of taste and learning is not, at least, an honest man, whatever frailties may attend him" (*Essays*, 170; cf. Kant, *Menschenkunde*, 25: 1172).

23. What laws to "furnish guidance" to luxury is Kant proposing here? He goes on to assert that "the flabby kind of luxury must be restricted" (*muß eingeschränkt seyn*), and includes under this heading "effeminacy of dress in men, delicacy in eating, and coddling of every kind" (27: 397).

24. Gay, *The Enlightenment*, 2: 367.

25. Griswold, for instance, remarks that "Smith does not explicitly connect morality with 'autonomy'—not a word he uses—or with the notion of a freely legislating 'will'—a word he rarely uses" (*Adam Smith*, 115).

26. Gay, *The Enlightenment*, 2: 367.

27. Fleischacker, *A Third Concept of Liberty*, 185. Cf. "Values behind the Market," 387.

28. I have recently prepared a new translation of this text; see Kant, *Anthropology from a Pragmatic Point of View*.

29. Adam Smith, *The Theory of Moral Sentiments*, II.ii.3.4, II.ii.3.3 (hereafter cited in the body of the text, and abbreviated as *TMS*). For a detailed examination of Smith's treatment of justice, see Fleischacker, *On Adam Smith's "Wealth of Nations,"* part IV. Fleischacker argues both that the popular libertarian reading of Smith's account of justice "is a mistake" (145), and that Smith in fact "helped bring about the peculiarly modern view of distributive justice: the view according to which it is a duty, and not just an act of grace, for the state to alleviate or abolish poverty" (226).

30. Adam Smith, *Lectures on Jurisprudence, Report of 1762–63*, i.1, i.14 (this set of lectures is usually referred to as *LJ(A)*). Smith borrows the language of "perfect" rights from Hutcheson and Pufendorf. These *Lectures* are the closest approximation we have to Smith's long-planned but unfinished "account of the general principles of law and government" (*TMS* VII.iv.37).

31. For further discussion, see Kaufman, *Welfare in the Kantian State*, esp. 4–35; Rosen, "Justice and Social Welfare," in *Kant's Theory of Justice*, 173–208. For related discussion on Smith to which I am indebted, see Viner, "Adam Smith and Laissez Faire," in *The Long View and the Short*, esp. 236–41; and Werhane, *Adam Smith*, 165–66.

32. See *Dictionary of the History of Ideas*, s.v. "Enlightenment," by Hellmut O. Pappe, 2: 90b. According to Norman Hampson, "British overseas trade increased by about one-half" during the period 1715–40, and French foreign trade "more than doubled" between 1715 and 1755 (*The Enlightenment*, 47). Similarly, E. J. Hobsbawm claims that "international trade had more than doubled in value between 1720 and 1780" (*The Age of Capital*, 50).

33. Hume, "Of the Jealousy of Trade," in *Essays*, 327–28.

34. Ibid., 331.

35. In Hume's case, each country's inherent economic strengths ultimately stem from the harmonious order of nature: "Nature, by giving a diversity of geniuses, climates, and soils, to different nations, has secured their mutual intercourse and commerce, as long as they remain industrious and civilized" (ibid., 329).

36. Hume, "Of the Balance of Trade," in *Essays*, 324. Cf. Rotwein's introduction to Hume, *Writings on Economics*, lxxvi.

37. Cf. Viner, "Adam Smith and Laissez Faire," in *The Long View and the Short*, 242. As noted earlier, Smith's defense of the British Navigation Act is an additional example of protectionist thinking.

38. François Quesnay, *General Rules for the Economic Government of an Agricultural Kingdom* (1758), in Kramnick, *The Portable Enlightenment Reader*, 501. Smith rejected Quesnay's position that agriculture is "the sole source of the revenue and wealth of every country" (*WN* IV.ix.2), as well as his tendency to stigmatize "merchants, artificers, and manufacturers" as "the unproductive class" (*WN* IV.ix.15).

39. Franklin, *Introduction to a Plan for Benefiting the New Zealanders* (1771), in *Silence Dogood*, 666–67; Franklin, letter to Robert R. Livingston of July 22, 1783, in *Autobiography*, 325. In a letter to Hume of September 27, 1760, Franklin writes, "I have lately read with great Pleasure, as I do everything of yours, the excellent essay on the *Jealousy of Commerce* [*sic*]: I think it cannot but have a good Effect in promoting a certain Interest too little thought of by selfish Man, and scarce ever mention'd, so that we hardly have a Name for it; I mean the *Interest of Humanity*, or common Good of Mankind" (*Autobiography*, 37).

40. Jefferson, *Writings*, 443. In a later letter to a friend who was seeking advice on what to read, Jefferson writes, "If your views of political inquiry go further, to the subjects of money & commerce, Smith's Wealth of Nations is the best book to be read" (Jefferson to John Norvell, June 14, 1807, in *Writings*, 1176). See also Fleischacker, "Adam Smith's Reception."

41. Paine, *The Rights of Man*, in *The Thomas Paine Reader*, 309.

42. Bentham also includes economic factors in his litany of arguments against colonialism: "You will, I say, give up your colonies...because you get nothing by governing them, because you cannot keep them, because the expense of trying to keep them would be ruinous" (*Emancipate Your Colonies!* [1793], in *The Works of Jeremy Bentham*, 4: 417). See also Bentham, *Colonies, Commerce, and Constitutional Law*, esp. 21–22. For general discussion, see Muthu, *Enlightenment against Empire*.

43. Condorcet, "The Future Progress of the Human Mind," from *Sketch for a Historical Picture of the Human Mind* (1793), in Kramnick, *The Portable Enlightenment Reader*, 28. Bentham also appealed to moral considerations: "Give up your colonies—because you have no right to govern them, because they had rather not be governed by you, because it is against their interest to be governed by you" (*Emancipate Your Colonies!*, in *Works*, 4: 417).

44. Nicholas Barbon, *A Discourse of Trade*, in H. C. Clark, *Commerce, Culture, and Liberty*, 81. For a critique of the commerce–peace connection, see Hirschman, "Money-Making and Commerce as Innocent and *Doux*," in *The Passions and the Interests*, 56–63, esp. 62, where he notes, "The persistent use of the term *le doux commerce* [gentle commerce] strikes us as a strange aberration for an age when the slave trade was at its peak and when trade in general was still a hazardous, adventurous, and often violent business." Again, though, Enlightenment intellectuals were by no means unaware of the darker, disruptive side of commerce. And most of them were strongly opposed to the slave trade.

Chapter 4: Politics

1. Glover, "Nations, Identity, and Conflict," 28–29; Darnton, *George Washington's False Teeth*, 19; cf. 77, 86.

2. Gray, *Enlightenment's Wake*, 13; cf. 5, 16.

3. In the American *Declaration of Independence* (1776) we are told, "Governments are instituted among Men, deriving their just powers from the consent of the governed...[and] whenever any Form of Government becomes destructive of these ends, it is the right of the People to alter or abolish it, and to institute a new Government." Similarly, the French *Declaration of the Rights of Man and Citizen* (1789) states, "The source of all sovereignty resides essentially in the nation, no individual may exercise authority not emanating expressly therefrom." Enlightenment political events that helped stir nationalist sentiment include the American and French Revolutions, as well as the sale of Corsica by the Genoese to the French (1768) and the First Partition of Poland by Prussia, Russia, and Austria (1775).

4. Bell, *The Cult of the Nation*, 6. Similarly, E. J. Hobsbawm claims that "the modern sense of the word ["nation"] is no older than the eighteenth century, give or take the odd predecessor" (*Nations and Nationalism*, 3). See also Munck, "Nation, Homeland, and Patriotic Identity," in *The Enlightenment*, 199–203; Hont, *Jealousy of*

Trade, 137–38; Kohn, *Nationalism*, 29–30. For a critique of the view that "nations and nationalism are the product of 'modernization' and the conditions of modernity," see Anthony D. Smith, *The Antiquity of Nations*, esp. 14.

5. Plattner, "Rousseau and the Origins of Nationalism," 194. (I am indebted to this essay on several points in the following discussion.) See also Greenfeld, "The Philosophical Basis of the French Idea of the Nation: Rousseau's *Social Contract*," in *Nationalism*, 172–77; Cobban, "Rousseau and the Nation State," in *Rousseau and the Modern State*, 99–125.

6. Rousseau, *On the Social Contract, Discourse on the Origin of Inequality, Discourse on Political Economy*, 168. Future references are cited in the body of the text and are to this edition. See also *The Social Contract*, bk. II, chap. 1.

7. Rousseau and Herder, *On the Origin of Language*, 5. This essay remained unpublished during Rousseau's lifetime, and was probably written during 1753–54. For discussion, see Hendel, *Jean-Jacques Rousseau*, 1: 66–71, 2: 332.

8. In his discussion of the legislator in *The Social Contract*, for instance, Rousseau declares:

> He who dares to undertake the establishment of a people should feel that he is, so to speak, in a position to change human nature, to transform each individual (who by himself is a perfect and solitary whole), into a part of a larger whole from which this individual receives, in a sense, his life and his being; to alter man's constitution in order to strengthen it; to substitute a partial and moral existence for the physical and independent existence we have all received from nature. (39)

9. Rousseau, *Constitutional Project for Corsica*, in *Rousseau on International Relations*, 150. (The *Corsica* and *Poland* essays are reprinted in this volume. Future references to both are cited in the body of the text.)

10. Stanley Hoffman and David Fidler, "Introduction" to Rousseau, *Rousseau on International Relations*, lx, lvi; cf. Plattner, "Rousseau and the Origins of Nationalism," 188–89. Recall also Rousseau's dedication to the Republic of Geneva in the *Second Discourse*, in which he praises the land of his birth for being "a society of a size limited by the extent of human faculties, that is to say, limited by the possibility of being well-governed" (106).

11. Margalit, "The Moral Psychology of Nationalism," 77. See also Beiner, "The Ethnic/Civic Question," in *Theorizing Nationalism*, 12–14, along with the essays by Bernard Yack, Kai Nielsen, and Will Kymlicka in the same volume; and Chaim Gans's discussion of cultural and statist nationalism in *The Limits of Nationalism*, 7–17.

12. But an even worse mistake is to de-nationalize Herder's concern for culture and language, as Michael Forster does in the introduction to his anthology of Herder's works: "Herder is often classified as a 'nationalist' or (even worse) a 'German nationalist,' but this is deeply misleading and unjust" (*Philosophical Writings*, xxxi–xxxii). For a corrective, see Beiser, "The Myth of the Apolitical German," in *Enlightenment, Revolution, and Romanticism*, 7–10.

13. Berlin, *Vico and Herder*, 157, 181, 182–83.

14. Herder, *Philosophical Writings*, 413.

15. *Routledge Encyclopedia of Philosophy*, s.v. "Nation and Nationalism," by David Miller, 6: 659.

16. Herder, *Dissertation on the Reciprocal Influence of Government and the Sciences* (1780), in *J. G. Herder on Social and Political Culture*, 229. As Barnard notes in his monograph on Herder's political thought, for Herder man is "of necessity a political creature" (*Herder's Social and Political Thought*, 55).

17. Herder is frequently lauded for his rejection of the concept of race; see, e.g., Hyland et al., *The Enlightenment*, 6–7; Bernasconi and Lott, *The Idea of Race*, ix, 23; Zammito, *Kant, Herder*, 345. Earlier, in *Ideas for a Philosophy*, he does state that while some authors "have thought fit to employ the term *races* [*Rassen*] for four or five divisions…I see no reason for employing this term" (in D. Williams, *The Enlightenment*, 204; cf. *Letters for the Advancement of Humanity*, in *Philosophical Writings*, 393–94). However, regardless of whether opposition to "wild mixing" is based on nationalist or racialist sentiment, this segregationism is morally unjustifiable.

18. Herder, in D. Williams, *The Enlightenment*, 210. (Williams's extracts from Herder's *Ideas* are taken from Herder, *Herder on Social and Political Culture*). Cf. Barnard, *Herder's Social and Political Thought*, 58.

19. Barnard, *Herder's Social and Political Thought*, 59. Cf. Ergang, *Herder*, 243.

20. Herder, *Ideas for a Philosophy*, in D. Williams, *The Enlightenment*, 204.

21. Herder, *Letters for the Advancement of Humanity*, as cited by Berlin, *Vico and Herder*, 159.

22. Herder, *Yet Another Philosophy of History* (1774), in *J. G. Herder on Social and Political Culture*, 186.

23. Herder, *J. G. Herder on Social and Political Culture*, 216, 209; cf. 206. See also Rousseau's warning that local customs "are daily being bastardized by the general European tendency to adopt the tastes and manners of the French" (*Poland*, 170).

24. Herder, *J. G. Herder on Social and Political Culture*, 310.

25. Barnard, *Herder's Social and Political Thought*, 86; Berlin, *Vico and Herder*, 181.

26. For discussion of authoritarian versus liberal forms of nationalism, see *Routledge Encyclopedia of Philosophy*, s.v. "Nation and Nationalism," by Miller, 6: 657–62. See also Gans, "Liberal and Non-liberal Nationalisms," in *The Limits of Nationalism*, 17–22. However, Gans incorrectly labels Herder as a proponent of romantic (nonliberal) cultural liberalism (22), rather than as a defender of the liberal cultural nationalism that Gans himself advocates.

27. Herder, *Yet Another Philosophy of History*, in *J. G. Herder on Social and Political Culture*, 205. Forster's insistence that Herder's "fundamental position in international politics is a committed cosmopolitanism" ("Introduction" to Herder, *Philosophical Writings*, xxxii) is a stretch. For Herder, nations are fundamental sources of identity, have intrinsic value, and are proper objects of unconditional loyalty. Cosmopolitans reject each of these claims. For discussion, see C. Jones, *Global Justice*, 206–7, 15–16.

28. In Herder, *On World History*, 270.

29. Herder, in *On World History*, 106. For discussion, see Barnard, "From Nationalism to Internationalism: *Humanität*," in *Herder's Social and Political Thought*, 88–108.

30. Herder, *On World History*, 271.

31. Ergang, *Herder and the Foundations of German Nationalism*, 99.

32. Herder, *Letters for the Advancement of Humanity*, in *Philosophical Writings*, 394, 395, 396.

33. Barnard, *Herder's Social and Political Thought*, 108.

34. Herder, *Letters for the Advancement of Humanity*, in *Philosophical Writings*, 379. Herder's claim that "fatherlands" do not fight each other should also be compared to Kant's thesis, discussed in the next chapter, that republics do not engage in war with one another.

35. Fichte, *The Vocation of Man*, 107. Anthony J. La Vopa, in *Fichte*, acknowledges that Fichte "*did* become a founder of at least one 'ism.' With the *Addresses to the German Nation* he made himself one of the icons of modern German nationalism" (11). But he finds no evidence of nationalist sentiment in Fichte's early writings: "As late as 1799, however, I find no indications that he was moving toward that answer. Fichte's nationalism was the product of a later phase of his intellectual career" (11–12).

36. Fichte, *Early Philosophical Writings*, 153–54, 156.

37. As cited by Hans Kohn in "The Paradox of Fichte's Nationalism," 321. See also Engelbrecht, *Johann Gottlieb Fichte*, 150–51.

38. Fichte, *Die Grundzüge des gegenwärtigen Zeitalters*, 219–20 (end of 14th Lecture). Cf. Meinecke, *Cosmopolitanism and the National State*, 73; Kohn, "The Paradox of Fichte's Nationalism," 325; Engelbrecht, *Johann Gottlieb Fichte*, 91.

39. As cited by Engelbrecht, *Fichte*, 96–97, 98; and by Kelly, *Idealism, Politics and History*, 259. Fichte's (or at least the *early* Fichte's) cosmopolitan commitment is part of what makes him a voice of the Enlightenment. Cf. La Vopa: "Fichte's vision was, arguably, the ultimate articulation of a normative idea at the core of the Enlightenment's self-understanding and vision of a more rational social order" (*Fichte*, 14).

40. Fichte, *Addresses to the German Nation*, 227–28 (hereafter cited in the body of the text by page number. I have altered a few of the translations).

41. For a critique of Fichte's "fantasy of language purity," see Martyn, "Borrowed Fatherland." Martyn argues that Fichte's own examples of "true German" are in fact instances of "loan translations," that is, words that seem to be made of domestic linguistic elements, but that are actually coined as literal part-for-part translations of foreign words. See, e.g., Fichte's proposal to use "Menschenfreundlichkeit" in place of "Humanität," the latter of which is derived from Latin (*Addresses*, 55–57; it is also worth noting here that Herder preferred "Humanität," though he was well aware of its foreign sources). According to Martyn, *Menschenfreundlichkeit* itself is coined from the Greek *philanthropos*. See also Elie Kedourie's discussion of Fichte on the relation of language to nation in *Nationalism*, 64–68.

42. Kelly, introduction to Fichte, *Addresses*, xxxii. See also Kelly, *Idealism, Politics, and History*, 265–66.

43. Aristotle, *Metaphysics*, IV.4 1006a4–5.

44. Cf. Thomas J. Schlereth: "For all their talk of the necessity of the civilization of the 'world-city,' few Enlightenment cosmopolites denied the existence of

separate nations or encouraged the extinction of nationalities" (*The Cosmopolitan Ideal*, 106). See also Wokler, "The Enlightenment, the Nation-state and the Primal Patricide of Modernity," esp. 162, 167.

45. Vincent, *Nationalism and Particularity*, 198. See also Kant's remarks concerning "dutiful global and local patriotism" in the *Vigilantius* ethics lectures: "both are proper to the cosmopolite" (27: 674). One alleged exception is Voltaire, who questions the value of national affiliation when he notes, "It is sad that in order to be a good patriot one is very often then enemy of the rest of mankind" ("*Patrie*," in *Philosophical Dictionary*, reprinted in D. Williams, *The Enlightenment*, 180). But even he seems ultimately to be striving for a way to reconcile love of country with love of humanity: "The man who would want his homeland never to be larger, or smaller, or richer or poorer would be a citizen of the world" (180).

46. Hume, "Of National Characters," in *Essays*, 198, 204. Cf. Schlereth, *The Cosmopolitan Ideal in Enlightenment Thought*, 104.

47. Schlereth, *The Cosmopolitan Ideal*, 104; Hume; "Of the Origin of Government," in *Essays*, 37.

48. Cf. Kenneth Baynes: "Kant seems to reject the idea of a world state or world republic precisely because it would have to acquire the same powers of sovereignty that he believes rightly belong only to the nation state as an independent moral-legal person" ("Communitarian and Cosmopolitan Challenges," 221). See also Vincent, *Nationalism and Particularity*, 26–27.

49. For helpful discussion on this point, see H. Williams, *Kant's Political Philosophy*, esp. 170, 182.

50. However, the fact that a people have not formed a civil state does not give other peoples who have formed such states the right to take possession of the former's land without their consent. Such settlement, regardless of the colonizers' good intentions, "may not take place by force but only by contract, and indeed by a contract that does not take advantage of the ignorance of those inhabitants with respect to ceding their lands" (6: 353). See also H. Williams's discussion of what he calls Kant's "test of independence" for nations in *Kant's Political Philosophy*, 250–51. Ultimately, as he notes, it is very difficult to apply Kant's test for determining which peoples or nations constitute sovereign states with much precision or objectivity in the real world. One result is that "Kant leaves undecided how we are to ascertain whether a state properly belongs to the international community or not" (251).

51. Vincent, *Nationalism and Particularity*, 95. See also my discussion of "Peoples" in *Kant's Impure Ethics*, 87–93.

52. Allen Wood thus misstates matters when he remarks that Kant regards national differences "as matters of *character*—that is, as the results of free agency" (*Kant's Ethical Thought*, 206). As Kant explains earlier in his *Anthropology*, he "uses the word *character* in two senses": physical and moral (7: 285). The language of "innate" and "unchangeable" indicates that national character falls under physical character rather than moral. Aspects of character that are "the results of free agency" fall under moral character.

53. Roger Scruton, "The First Person Plural," in Beiner, *Theorizing Nationalism*, 281.

54. J. Hector St. John Crèvecoeur, *Letters from an American Farmer* (London: Davies and Davis, 1782), reprinted in Snyder, *The Dynamics of Nationalism*, 258–59 (from Letter III). The author's real name was Michel Guillaume Saint-Jean de Crèvecœur (1735–1813). He lived in North America from 1759 to 1780 and from 1783 to 1790. For related readings, see chapter 12 ("American Nationalism") of Snyder's anthology; and Brooks Gruver, *American Nationalism*. For discussion, see Kohn, *The Idea of Nationalism*, esp. 263–328, and *American Nationalism*. See also chapter 5 ("In Pursuit of the Ideal Nation: The Unfolding of Nationality in America") in Greenfeld, *Nationalism*.

55. Jefferson, *The Writings of Thomas Jefferson*, ed. Lipscomb and Bergh, 10: 325, as cited by Kohn, *The Idea of Nationalism*, 290. At the same time, Jefferson's own states'-rights position often placed him at odds with the stronger nationalism of the Federalists, and the Constitution itself represents a compromise between these two groups. As Greenfeld points out, "The word 'nation' was never once mentioned in the text; the Constitution was of 'these United States.' " This was one of several instances in which "a clever use of language allowed the avoidance of dealing with problematic issues" (*Nationalism*, 431, 559 n. 69).

56. Paine, *The American Crisis*, 16 (1783), in *The Writings of Thomas Paine*, 1: 374–75. Cf. Greenfeld, *Nationalism*, 425–26; Savelle, "Nationalism and Other Loyalties."

57. Franklin, *On a Proposed Act to Prevent Emigration*, in *Silence Dogood*, 703. Cf. Schlereth, *The Cosmopolitan Ideal*, 105.

58. Jefferson, *A Summary View of the Rights of British America*, in *Writings*, 105–6. Cf. Kohn, *The Idea of Nationalism*, 275–76; Schlereth, *The Cosmopolitan Ideal*, 105.

59. Paine, *Letter to the Abbé Raynal*, in *The Thomas Paine Reader*, 166. Cf. Schlereth, *The Cosmopolitan Ideal*, 106.

60. Beiner, "Introduction: Nationalism's Challenge to Political Philosophy," in *Theorizing Nationalism*, 1.

61. Paine, *Common Sense* (1776), in *The Thomas Paine Reader*, 65, 80. Cf. 93.

62. Franklin to Samuel Cooper, May 1, 1777, in *The Writings of Benjamin Franklin*, 7: 56; Jefferson to Priestley, June 19, 1802, in *The Writings of Thomas Jefferson*, ed. Lipscomb and Bergh, 10: 324. Cf. Schlereth, *The Cosmopolitan Ideal*, 106–7; Kohn, *American Nationalism*, 144.

63. Jefferson, *The Writings of Thomas Jefferson*, ed. Washington, 7: 496. Cf. Kohn, *The Idea of Nationalism*, 280.

64. According to Dorinda Outram, "The central failure of the Enlightenment was in the way it dealt with difference . . . within the framework of a universal humanity" (*The Enlightenment* [1995], 79).

65. The "republicanism-liberalism" literature is extensive. Alan Gibson surveys much of it in "Ancients, Moderns and Americans." Other relevant studies are Appleby, *Liberalism and Republicanism*; Kramnick, *Republicanism and Bourgeois Radicalism*; Zuckert, *The Natural Rights Republic*. In my view, attempts such as Gordon S. Wood's to summarize "the essence of republicanism" during and after the American Revolution as consisting simply in "the sacrifice of individual interests to the greater good of the whole," while capturing the core of what is traditionally

meant by "classical republicanism," do not fit well with most American or European Enlightenment discussions of republicanism (*The Creation of the American Republic*, 53).

66. Cicero, *Republic*, I, 25; Plato, *Republic*, 466 a.

67. *Routledge Encyclopedia of Philosophy*, s.v. "Republicanism," by Russell L. Hanson, 281. For additional discussion, see Wootton, "Introduction: The Republican Tradition: From Commonwealth to Common Sense," in *Republicanism, Liberty, and Commercial Society*, 1–41. The literature on "classical vs. modern" republicanism is also extensive. See, e.g., Pocock, *The Machiavellian Moment*; Fontana, *The Invention of the Modern Republic*; Gelderen and Skinner, *Republicanism*.

68. Montesquieu, *The Spirit of the Laws*, I.viii.16.

69. Rousseau, *Considerations on the Government of Poland*, in *Rousseau on International Relations*, 174–75. In the *Social Contract*, Rousseau also proclaims that "every legitimate government is republican," although here his definition of "republic" makes no reference to size: "I . . . call every state ruled by laws a republic, regardless of the form its administration may take. For only then does the public interest govern, and only then is the 'public thing' [*res publica*] something real" (II.6, 38).

70. Paine, *The Rights of Man, Part II*, in *Political Writings*, 167–68. G. S. Wood, in citing Paine's remark that a republic "is not any *particular form* of government," adds, "Republicanism meant more for Americans than simply the elimination of a king and the institution of an elective system. It added a moral dimension, a utopian depth, to the political separation from England—a depth that involved the very character of their society" (*The Creation of the American Republic*, 47).

71. Paine, *The Rights of Man, Part II*, 168. Jefferson also complains of the vagueness of the term "republic" and then proceeds to identify representative government as its core: "It must be acknowledged that that the term *republic* is of very vague application in every language. Witness the self-styled republics of Holland, Switzerland, Genoa, Venice, Poland. . . . Governments are more or less republican as they have more or less of the element of popular election and control in their composition" (Jefferson to John Taylor, May 28, 1816, in *Writings*, 1392, 1395).

72. Paine, *The Rights of Man, Part II*, 168, 169, 167, 170.

73. Paine, *The Rights of Man, Part I*, 79. Cf. Hanson, "Republicanism," 281.

74. Rossiter, *The Federalist Papers*, No. 14, 100, 104. Similarly, Jefferson, in his letter to François D'Ivernois of February 6, 1795, writes, "I suspect that the doctrine, that small States alone are fitted to be republics, will be exploded by experience, with some other brilliant fallacies accredited by Montesquieu & other political writers" (*Writings*, 1024). Hume had earlier challenged common opinion in arguing that a republic could actually function better in a large territory: "Though it is more difficult to form a republican government in an extensive country than in a city; there is more facility, when once it is formed, of preserving it steady and uniform, without tumult and faction. . . . In a large government, which is modelled with masterly skill, there is compass and room enough to refine the democracy" ("Idea of a Perfect Commonwealth," in *Essays*, 527–28). Did Madison "seize on David Hume's radical suggestion?" Cf. G. S. Wood, *Creation of the American Republic*, 504–5.

75. *The Federalist Papers*, No. 39, 241.

76. *The Federalist Papers*, No. 10, 81.

77. Ibid., 82. Cf. Arendt, *On Revolution*, 229.

78. *The Federalist Papers*, No. 10, 78.

79. Ibid., 79.

80. Ibid., 80.

81. Paine also believed that republics were the best hope for peace: "Why are not republics plunged into war, but because the nature of their government does not admit of an interest distinct from that of the nation" (*The Rights of Man, Part I*, in *Political Writings*, 142). For related discussion, see chapter 5, "International Relations."

82. See also Friedrich Schlegel, "Essay on the Concept of Republicanism occasioned by the Kantian Tract 'Perpetual Peace' " (1796), in Beiser, *The Early Political Writings*, 95–112. In opposition to Kant, Schlegel argues that republicanism is "necessarily democratic" (102). But like other romantics, he values ancient republics over modern ones: "The political culture of the modern state is in a state of infancy compared to the ancient" (103); as a result he fails to consider extended republics, separation of powers, minority rights, and so forth.

83. Separation of powers and protection of minority rights are also important aspects of Madisonian republicanism, even though Madison does not explicitly refer to them in his earlier-cited definitions of "republic." In *Federalist* No. 51, for instance, he makes his case "for that separate and distinct exercise of the different powers of government...essential to the preservation of liberty" (321). This arrangement is necessary, he adds, for government "to control itself" (322). For discussion, see Rahe, *Republics Ancient and Modern*, 599–614. H. Williams also notes several similarities between Kant's and Madison's views about republics, adding that "the newly-instituted American system of government must surely have caught Kant's eye when writing, for it was both representative and firmly based on the separation of powers" (*Kant's Political Philosophy*, 176; cf. 188–89, nn. 31 and 35). William A. Galston, on the other hand, in "What Is Living and What Is Dead in Kant's Practical Philosophy?" bemoans the fact that Kant and Madison both reject "the civic republic tradition," opting instead for a modern " 'invisible hand' theory of republican politics, in which institutional contrivances make good what James Madison called the defect of better motives" (218–19).

Chapter 5: International Relations

1. Balch, *Émeric Crucé*, 24. See also Johnson, *The Quest for Peace*, 177–78; Hinsley, *Power and the Pursuit of Peace*, 20–22; D. Hunter, *World Citizenship and Government*, 65–70. For a note on the original Cyneas, see Montaigne, *The Complete Essays*, 196.

2. Balch, *Émeric Crucé*, 35–36; Hinsley, *Power and the Pursuit of Peace*, 20.

3. Hinsley, *Power and the Pursuit of Peace*, 23. Not until the appearance of Kant's *Toward Perpetual Peace* in 1795 do we find a federation proposal that is both as international in scope and as directly concerned with peace as Crucé's. But Kant, like most of his contemporaries (with the important exception of Leibniz), was unaware of Crucé's work.

4. Crucé, *The New Cyneas*, 94. See also Souleyman, *The Vision of World Peace*, 10.

5. Crucé, *The New Cyneas*, 84–86. Cf. D. Hunter, *World Citizenship and Government*, 69.

6. Hinsley, *Power and the Pursuit of Peace*, 23.

7. Sully, *Sully's Grand Design of Henry IV*, 17. (Future references are to the Garland edition, and are cited in the body of the text.) See also Ogg's introduction, 9; Hinsley, *Power and the Pursuit of Peace*, 24–25.

8. Leibniz, "Observations on the Abbé's *Project for Perpetual Peace*" (1715), in *Political Writings*, 179. See also Hinsley, *Power and the Pursuit of Peace*, 25. Rousseau also suspected that Sully's *Grand Design* was prompted "by the secret hope of humbling a formidable enemy," an impulse "which it could hardly have drawn from the incentive of the common good" (*Judgment on Perpetual Peace*, in S. E. Cooper, *Peace Projects of the Eighteenth Century*, 117–19).

9. Penn, *An Essay towards the Present and Future Peace of Europe*, in S. E. Cooper, *Peace Projects of the Seventeenth Century*, 6. (Future references are to this edition, and are cited in the body of the text). At the end of the *Essay* Penn explicitly acknowledges his debt to Sully and Henry IV: "I have very Little to answer for in all this Affair; because, if it succeed, I have so Little to deserve: For this *Great King's Example tells us it is fit to be done*" (21).

10. Hinsley, *Power and the Pursuit of Peace*, 33. But this is not to say that criticism of infidels is totally absent from Penn's account. In Penn's view, one "*manifest Benefit*" of his proposal is that "*the Reputation of Christianity will in some Degree be recovered in the Sight of Infidels*" (14).

11. An English translation of parts of this work appears in D. Williams, *The Enlightenment*, 356–63 (hereafter cited in the body of the text). For discussion, see Perkins, *The Moral and Political Philosophy of the Abbé de Saint-Pierre*.

12. An English translation of this edition was printed in London in 1714 under the title *A Project for Settling an Everlasting Peace in Europe*. Excerpts from this translation are reprinted in C. Brown, Nardin, and Rengger, *International Relations in Political Thought*, 394–98.

13. An English translation of parts of the latter text appears in *Selections from the Second Edition of the Abrege du Projet de Paix Perpetuelle*, trans. H. Hale Bellot, with an introduction by Paul Collinet, Grotius Society Publications, Texts for Students of International Relations. No. 5 (London: Sweet & Maxwell, 1927). It is reprinted under the title *A Shorter Project for Perpetual Peace* in S. E. Cooper, *Peace Projects of the Eighteenth Century*. A complete, contemporary translation of at least one edition of Saint-Pierre's peace project is sorely needed.

14. Banishment "from Europe" (= expulsion from the European Union?) is an alternative strategy proposed for those member states that refuse "to take the path of arbitration to settle their future differences"; *Mémoire pour render la paix perpétuelle en Europe*, 362. In his 1713 text, Saint-Pierre is more blunt about the need for a credible threat of force: any sovereign "who shall refuse a Regulation of the Society, or a Judgement of the Senate, shall be declared an Enemy to the Society, and it shall make War upon him" (in C. Brown et al., *International Relations in Political Thought*, 396).

15. Saint-Pierre, *A Shorter Project for Perpetual Peace*, in S. E. Cooper, *Peace Projects of the Eighteenth Century*, 25 (hereafter cited in the body of the text). Penn stressed this same point in his earlier proposal.

16. Frederick the Great to Voltaire, April 12, 1742, in Voltaire, *Letters of Voltaire and Frederick the Great*, 161.

17. Mastnak, "Abbé de Saint-Pierre," 572. Mastnak's critique (he labels Saint-Pierre's European Union " 'organized might' set free from the idea of right"; 598) should be compared with Perkins's more balanced assessment.

18. Rousseau, *The Confessions*, 437, 421. See also Roosevelt, *Reading Rousseau in the Nuclear Age*, 90–96; Hassner, "Rousseau and the Theory and Practice of International Relations," 204–7.

19. Rousseau, *The Confessions*, 436.

20. Ibid., 437. Rousseau next applied his two-pronged treatment to Saint-Pierre's "Polysynodie" (1719), a political work in which the abbé challenged the powers of the king, a move that in turn contributed to his dismissal from the French Academy. "I finished this work in the same manner as the preceding, both abstract and judgment," Rousseau writes, "but I stopped there, as I did not intend to finish this undertaking, which I ought never to have commenced" (*Confessions*, 437).

21. Rousseau, *The Political Writings*, 1: 360.

22. Rousseau, *Judgment on Perpetual Peace*, in S. E. Cooper, *Peace Projects of the Eighteenth Century*, 129. (Future references are to this edition, and are cited in the body of the text.) Rousseau goes on to speculate that perpetual peace "will come back again as a reasonable project" if and when "another Henry IV and Sully appear." But he also adds that even a charismatic and popular leader like Henry did not and could not succeed in realizing the project: "It could only have been done by violent means which would have staggered humanity" (129).

23. See, e. g., Hinsley, *Power and the Pursuit of Peace*, 52, 54; Hassner, "Rousseau and the Theory and Practice of International Relations," 207, 216; Hoffman, "Rousseau on War and Peace," in *The State of War*, 54.

24. Rousseau, *The State of War* (probably written in the 1750s, but not published until 1896), in *Rousseau on International Relations*, 43.

25. Anthologies dealing with Kant's proposal include Bohman and Lutz-Bachmann, *Perpetual Peace*; Höffe, *Immanuel Kant*. See also A. W. Wood, "Kant's Project for Perpetual Peace"; Kleingeld, "Kant's Theory of Peace."

26. Cf. A. W. Wood, "Kant's Project for Perpetual Peace," 66, 67; Kleingeld, "Kant's Theory of Peace," 483. Similarly, C. Brown et al. note that Kant's theory of international relations is "a source of inspiration and ideas for liberals and radicals, at least some supporters of the states-system, and many of those who seek (however gently) to transcend it" (*International Relations in Political Thought*, 391).

27. For example, in *Perpetual Peace*, where he contrasts "the positive idea *of a world republic*" to "the *negative* surrogate of a *league*" of sovereign nations (8: 357), and at the end of *Theory and Practice*, where he puts his "trust in theory, which proceeds from the principle of right," a principle that supports the establishment of "a universal state of nations" (*ein allgemeiner Völkerstaat*; 8: 313; cf. 311).

28. Doyle, *Ways of War and Peace*, 258. See also his earlier article, "Kant, Liberal Legacies, and Foreign Affairs," part 1, 227.

29. A. W. Wood, "Kant's Project for Perpetual Peace," 62.

30. For a good defense of this interpretation, see Kleingeld, "Kant's Theory of Peace."

31. This particular feature of Kant's project, often dubbed the "democratic peace thesis," has received a great deal of attention in recent social science writing. Michael Doyle's version of the thesis runs as follows: "*Even though liberal states have become involved in numerous wars with nonliberal states, constitutionally secure liberal states have yet to engage in war with one another*" ("Kant, Liberal Legacies, and Foreign Affairs," 213; cf. *Ways of War and Peace*, 264–65).

32. For a fuller survey, see Wynner and Lloyd, *Searchlight on Peace Plans*. In part II of their study, the authors examine thirty-six different peace plans published between 1623 and 1800. Souleyman, in *The Vision of World Peace*, also explores thirty-six different peace projects, all published in France between 1600 and 1800. Of particular note—given his strong disagreements with Kant on foundational matters in ethical theory and philosophical method generally—is Jeremy Bentham's *Plan for an Universal and Perpetual Peace* (written between 1786 and 1789, first published posthumously in 1843). Despite their deep-seated philosophical differences, Bentham and Kant agree on a number of basic points at the more practical level of institutional reform. For discussion, see Conway, "Bentham on War and Peace."

33. Important early articulations are found in both Aristotle ("a natural justice that is common to all, even to those who have no association or covenant with each other"; *Rhetoric*, I.13, 1373b8–9) and Cicero ("There will not be different laws at Rome and Athens, but one eternal and unchangeable law will be valid for all nations and all times" *De Re Publica* III.xxii.33). For discussion, see d'Entrèves, *Natural Law*, 25–26.

34. Cf. Hedley Bull, who notes that "Grotius was clearly intent that his doctrine should have the . . . effect . . . of excluding occasions of war" ("The Grotian Conception of International Society," 55).

35. Grotius, *The Law of War and Peace* (*De Jure Belli ac Pacis Libri Tres*, 1625), II.xxiv.8, 9 (hereafter abbreviated as *JBP* and cited within the body of the text by book, chapter, and section number; passages from the prolegomena are cited by section number).

36. Benedict Kingsbury and Adam Roberts, "Introduction: Grotian Thought in International Relations," in Bull, Kingsbury, and Roberts, *Hugo Grotius and International Relations*, 28 n. 90.

37. Bentham, *An Introduction to the Principles of Morals and Legislation*, 296 n. See also the *Oxford English Dictionary*, s.v. "international"; Janis, "Jeremy Bentham and the Fashioning of 'International Law.' " For a helpful overview, see Walker, *The Oxford Companion to Law*, s.v. "International Law (public)."

38. *The Oxford Classical Dictionary*, s.v. "praetor," by Piero Treves and Eastland Stuart Stavely. See also C. Nussbaum, *A Concise History of the Law of Nations*, 13–14. The Roman *ius gentium*, though traditionally translated as "law of nations," did not

originally refer to laws governing relations among independent states. Rather, it was "a national Roman law—though sometimes borrowed from foreign sources" (C. Nussbaum, *A Concise History*, 14), as well as a private rather than public law, one concerned with relations among individuals rather than states. In modern terms, Roman *ius gentium* corresponds roughly to "private international law."

39. As cited by d'Entrèves, *Natural Law*, 29. Ernest Barker's claim that "Roman jurists were never agreed that there was any distinction between *jus gentium* and *jus naturale*" (translator's introduction to Gierke, *Natural Law and the Theory of Society*, xxxvi) is an overstatement. For d'Entrèves also cites from Ulpian's *Institutes* (early third century A.D.), where he lays out a tripartite division of law that clearly distinguishes *ius gentium* from *ius naturale*: "Private law is threefold; it can be gathered from the precepts of nature, or from those of the nations, or from those of the city" (*Natural Law*, 29). At most we can say that *some* Roman jurists identified the two forms of law. Similarly, Gierke's own assertion that "the common foundation of both *jus naturale* and *jus gentium* in the dictates of natural reason" came to be emphasized more strongly in the Middle Ages oversimplifies matters (*Natural Law and the Theory of Society*, 38).

40. Suárez, *On Laws and God the Lawgiver*, in *Selections from three Works*, II.xvii.1. (Future references are to this edition, and are cited in the body of the text by book, chapter, and section number.) For discussion, see Schneewind, *The Invention of Autonomy*, 58–66; Haakonssen, *Natural Law and Moral Philosophy*, 16–24.

41. Hobbes, *Leviathan* (1651), II.xxvi, 174; II.xxx, 232. Cf. d'Entrèves, *Natural Law*, 122. For discussion, see Bobbio, *Thomas Hobbes and the Natural Law Tradition*. In his earlier work, *De Cive* (1642), Hobbes also asserts that the precepts of natural law and the law of nations "are the same" (*On the Citizen*, XIV.4).

42. As Kingsbury and Roberts note, "By the 1920s it was widely accepted that the foundational structure of modern international law emerged over a long period, doctrinal responsibility being collegiate and owing a great deal to other historical developments" ("Introduction: Grotian Thought in International Relations," 3 n. 5). See also Tuck, "The 'Modern' Theory of Natural Law." 99–119.

43. D'Entrèves, *Natural Law*, 53–54; Schneewind, *The Invention of Autonomy*, 68. C. Nussbaum's blunt claim that Grotius "removes the natural law from theology" in prolegomena §11 overstates matters (*A Concise History of the Law of Nations*, 108).

44. Tuck, *Natural Rights Theories*, 67. See also Haakonssen, *Natural Law and Moral Philosophy*, 27; Kingsbury and Roberts, "Introduction," 31–32. Suárez had earlier offered a similar rights-based notion of natural law when he stated that "this name [*ius*] is properly wont to be bestowed upon a certain moral power which every man has, either over his own property or with respect to that which is due to him" (*De Legibus*, in *Selections*, I.ii.5). So the emphasis on rights within natural law theory does not start with Grotius. Also, Tuck is not the first to detect this shift. Basil Willey notes, "It was the idea of a controlling *Law* of Nature which officially dominated the Middle Ages, rather than that of the liberating *Rights* of Nature;...in passing into the seventeenth and eighteenth centuries, 'Nature' ceases to be mainly a regulating principle, and becomes mainly a liberating principle" (*The Eighteenth Century Background*, 16). Cf. d'Entrèves, *Natural Law*, 61.

45. Schneewind, *The Invention of Autonomy*, 70. Cf. C. Nussbaum, *A Concise History of the Law of Nations*, 102–3.

46. Adam Smith, *The Theory of Moral Sentiments*, VII.iv.37.

47. A new edition of this text, which contains Barbeyrac's extensive commentary, has recently been made available by Liberty Fund. See Grotius, *The Rights of War and Peace*, edited and with an introduction by Richard Tuck. According to Tuck, the 1738 English translation "was in large part the work of John Morrice" (xxxv).

48. Jean Barbeyrac, "Notes on Grotius's *On the Law of War and Peace*," in D. Williams, *The Enlightenment*, 373.

49. Cf. Francis Stephen Ruddy, who notes that "although Grotius maintains *jus gentium* rights do not take priority over the natural law" in time of war, "nonetheless, the slaughter of women and children, unlimited booty, slavery of prisoners of war, and poisoning of water supplies are permitted"—all of which are contrary to natural law (*International Law in the Enlightenment*, 25).

50. C. Nussbaum, *A Concise History of the Law of Nations*, 147. Leonard Krieger claims that the focus of Pufendorf's Heidleberg chair was actually a bit different: "The original offer was a chair in Roman law, but Pufendorf refused it.... Pufendorf requested instead an appointment as professor of politics on the law faculty, but the Elector... then proposed an associate professorship (*Extraordinarius*) of international law and philology in the philosophical faculty. Pufendorf was later to exalt the dignity and novelty of the post by recollecting it erroneously as the first chair of natural and international law" (*The Politics of Discretion*, 19).

51. Pufendorf, *On the Law of Nature and Nations*, II.iii.23. Future references are to this edition (abbreviated as *JNG*) and are cited in the body of the text by book, chapter, and section number. For two different approaches to Pufendorf, see Schneewind, *The Invention of Autonomy*, 118–40; I. Hunter, *Rival Enlightenments*, 148–96.

52. Cf. Hobbes, *Leviathan*, I.xiii, 80. Cf. Hidemi Suganami, "Grotius and International Equality," in Bull et al., *Hugo Grotius and International Relations*, 228.

53. Cf. Grotius, *JBP*, prolegomena § 6. For discussion, see Hochstrasser, "*Socialitas* and the History of Natural Law: Pufendorf's Defence of *De Jure Naturum et Gentium*," in *Natural Law Theories*, 40–71.

54. For related discussion, see Tuck, *The Rights of War and Peace*, 149–50; Schneewind, *The Invention of Autonomy*, 128–29.

55. Rachel, *Dissertations on the Law of Nature and of Nations* (*De Jure Naturae et Gentium Dissertationes*, 1676), II.xciii (hereafter cited in the body of the text).

56. Unlike the later "legal positivists," Rachel and his followers did accept the validity of natural law.

57. Zouche, *An Exposition of Fecial Law*, I.i.1. For discussion of Zouche and Rachel, see C. Nussbaum, *A Concise History of the Law of Nations*, 164–67, 172–74.

58. In citing Pufendorf, Rachel mistakenly refers to *De Jure Naturae et Gentium* "bk. 2, ch. 3, § 22" (II.xc). But the passage he quotes is to be found in § 23.

59. This second argument, though ingenious, comes with a heavy price. For in admitting that the remote cause of the obligation to obey pacts between

sovereigns lies in natural law, Rachel is dangerously close to forfeiting his own commitment to an independent law of nations.

60. Cf. Zouche, *An Exposition of Fecial Law*, I.i.1. Originally, the *fetiales* were priests whose office was to ascertain the lawfulness of Rome's treaties and declarations of war. See *The Oxford Classical Dictionary*, s.v. "Fetiales," by Herbert Jennings Rose.

61. Wolff, *The Law of Nations*, § 3. Future references are to this edition and are cited in the body of the text according to section number. "R" indicates that the text cited occurs in a Remark immediately following the relevant section.

62. For helpful discussions of Wolff's method, see Manfred Kuehn's entry on Wolff in the *Encyclopedia of the Enlightenment*, 4: 263–66; Schneewind, *The Invention of Autonomy*, 431–42; Cavallar, *The Rights of Strangers*, 208–21.

63. In fairness to Wolff's opponents, it should be pointed out that his "scientific method" is not simply a matter of admitting "as true only what is inferred as a necessary consequence from previous conclusions." To make deductive inferences, one needs premises and assumptions. One debatable Wolffian assumption is that "nature herself has established society among all nations and binds them to preserve society" (§ 7). If one rejects his assumption that states are irresistibly drawn to form a civil society among themselves (cf. discussion of Vattel, below), many of Wolff's subsequent conclusions do not follow. For related discussion, see C. Nussbaum, *A Concise History of the Law of Nations*, 152; Tuck, *The Rights of War and Peace*, 187–88.

64. Otfried Nippold, introduction to Wolff, *The Law of Nations*, lii; Tuck, *The Rights of War and Peace*, 187. C. Brown et al. correctly stress the hypothetical nature of Wolff's approach in *International Relations in Political Thought*, 322.

65. Vattel, *The Law of Nations*, 6a–7a (hereafter cited in the body of the text).

66. Cf. Ruddy: "Wolff had created a system of obligations and rights of individuals living in a natural (pre-civil) society. Vattel applied this system to states, *mutatis mutandis*, as if they were individuals living together in a natural, but not a civil, society" (*International Law in the Enlightenment*, 312). For general discussion of Vattel, see C. Nussbaum, *A Concise History of the Law of Nations*, 156–64; Tuck, *The Rights of War and Peace*, 191–96; Hochstrasser, *Natural Law Theories*, 176–83; Cavallar, *The Rights of Strangers*, 306–17.

67. Hochstrasser, *Natural Law Theories*, 182. Cf. Ruddy, *International Law in the Enlightenment*, 281–83.

68. C. Nussbaum, *A Concise History of the Law of Nations*, 162. Cf. Ruddy, *International Law in the Enlightenment*, 284–85.

69. C. Brown et al., *International Relations in Political Thought*, 323. See also Forsyth, "The Tradition of International Law," 34–39.

70. Robert George, editor of *Natural Law Theory: Contemporary Essays*, begins by heralding the "broad revival of interest in natural law theory among mainstream legal, political, and moral philosophers" (v). However, the contributors demonstrate little interest in international law. For instance, the index to the volume contains no entries under either "international law" or "law of nations." Also, they are much more influenced by ancient and medieval natural law than by

Enlightenment natural law. In the index, there are thirty-three entries under "Aquinas" and "Thomism," twenty-six under "Aristotle" and "Aristotelian tradition," but only one each under "Grotius" and "Pufendorf." There are no entries at all under "Rachel," "Wolff," or "Vattel."

71. John Rawls's effort to show how "the law of peoples" (his rendering of *ius gentium*, traditionally translated as "law of nations") may be developed out of basic principles of justice has attracted a great deal of attention in political philosophy. But whether this effort will have much impact on contemporary international law work remains to be seen. He himself warns that his "monograph on the Law of Peoples is neither a treatise nor a textbook on international law"; he chooses the name "peoples" rather than "nations" or "states" to distinguish his own thinking "from that about political states as traditionally conceived, with their powers of sovereignty." See Rawls, *The Law of Peoples*, 3 n.1, 5, 25.

Part II: Now

1. Condorcet, "The Future Progress of the Human Mind," in Kramnick, *The Portable Enlightenment Reader*, 27. Keith Michael Baker, in "On Condorcet's 'Sketch,' " describes this text as "perhaps the most influential formulation of the idea of progress ever written" (56).

2. Ishay, *The History of Human Rights*, 8. Ishay is summarizing rather than endorsing the view of Enlightenment critics here. Her own position is that the legacy of the European Enlightenment "supercedes other influences" for our current understanding of human rights, but that the subsequent socialist tradition also makes important contributions. Her own defense of "a flexible conception of international justice" is "inspired by a radical perspective on Kantian ethics" (7, 11).

3. Cioran, *History and Utopia*, 87. Unlike Condorcet and other Enlightenment philosophes who articulated hopes for better times, Cioran himself predicted a global totalitarian future for humanity: "The scattered human herd will be united under the guardianship of one pitiless shepherd, a kind of planetary monster before whom the nations will prostrate themselves in an alarm bordering on ecstasy" (41). What evidence does he offer in support of this prediction? "The coming tyranny strikes me as so decisively apparent that it seems unworthy to attempt to demonstrate its well-foundedness. . . . No, I am not extravagant, or mistaken" (55).

4. Cobban, *In Search of Humanity*, 224, 225; cf. 227.

5. Ibid., 225, 228, 229.

6. Baker, "On Condorcet's 'Sketch,' " 62.

7. Vogler, *Reasonably Vicious*, 12. Vogler distinguishes several different versions of instrumentalism on 12–13 and goes on to defend a particular view about practical reason which she calls "the *standard picture*," according to which "practical reason is primarily calculative" (22). But this calculative view of practical reason is itself part of what is normally meant by *instrumentalism*.

8. Hume is traditionally read as an arch instrumentalist, in large part because of comments like the following: " 'Tis not contrary to reason to prefer the destruction of the whole world to the scratching of my finger" (*A Treatise of Human Nature*, II.iii.3). What he is usually interpreted as asserting here is that all ends are set by desires, and that reason's job is merely to determine the most efficient means toward the ends that we desire. However, as I show in my conclusion (see "History Test"), following Hume's own views about the chief use of history offers us one way to rationally evaluate certain kinds of ends.

Chapter 6: Religion

1. For a defense of the secularization thesis, see Wilson, "Secularization and Its Discontents," in *Religion in Sociological Perspective*, 148–79. For challenges to the thesis, see the essays in Hammond, *The Sacred in a Secular Age*; Martin, "The Secularization Issue." See also Connolly, *Why I Am Not a Secularist*. However, insofar as Connolly opposes "a religiously centered politics" and is explicitly not "the defender of a specific church" (4), and particularly because he also aspires "to a critical liberalism that both expands and thickens the range of secularism" (10), it would appear that he is after all—the title of his book notwithstanding—a secularist.

2. Huntington, *The Clash of Civilizations*, 95–96. Is Western Europe an exception? See Lilla, "Godless Europe."

3. Swatos, "Introduction" to *A Future for Religion?* xiii.

4. Barrett, Kurian, and Johnson, *World Christian Encyclopedia*, Table 1-1. These data are also available on the Internet at http://www.globalchristianity.org (accessed June 29, 2006).

5. In large part because of their ecumenical orientation and their espousal of liberal and humanistic values, the Baha'is were a central target of persecution by Shi'ite clerics after the Iranian Revolution of 1978–79. Ann Elizabeth Mayer writes, "To destroy Baha'ism and the values it stood for, the regime undertook persecutions, imprisonments, and executions of Baha'is and Baha'i institutions were dismantled. Enormous pressure was exerted on Baha'is to repent of their theological errors and return to the Islamic fold" ("The Fundamentalist Impact," 342).

6. Dewey, *A Common Faith*, 27, 33. Richard Rorty, among others, has recently tried to update this Deweyan faith. At the conclusion of "Anticlericalism and Atheism," he writes:

> My sense of the holy, insofar as I have one, is bound up with the hope that someday, any millennium now, my remote descendants will live in a global civilization in which love is pretty much the only law. In such a society, communication would be domination-free, class and caste would be unknown, hierarchy would be a matter of temporary pragmatic convenience, and power would be entirely at the disposal of the free agreement of a literate and well-educated electorate. (in Rorty and Vattimo, *The Future of Religion*, 40)

7. Wagar, *The City of Man*, 168; cf. 64. Baha'ism is an example of the first tendency, Dewey's common faith of the second. Individual authors advocating a version of the conservative program discussed by Wagar include William Ernest Hocking, Arthur Toynbee, and Charles Morris. Erich Fromm, Julian Huxley, and Erich Kahler are advocates of the radical program.

8. Hick, *An Interpretation of Religion*, 235–36. See also Hick and Knitter, *The Myth of Christian Uniqueness*; *Faith and Philosophy* 14 (1997), which contains several responses to Hick's lead article, "The Epistemological Challenge of Religious Pluralism."

9. Hick, *An Interpretation of Religion*, 240. Henry Rosemont Jr., in *Rationality and Religious Experience*, defends a similar position when he states that "in many basic respects all sacred texts are saying the same things, and contain the same truths we can all come to believe without in any way surrendering our rationality" (11).

10. Griffiths, *Problems of Religious Diversity*, 59, xv; cf. 96, 129. Griffiths's more modest thesis of open inclusivism is much further away from the Enlightenment unity thesis than is Hick's pluralistic hypothesis. Griffiths rejects the Kantian strategy for appreciating religious diversity (a strategy, as we saw earlier, that is endorsed by many Enlightenment religious reformers) on the grounds that it amounts "to telling religious people that they misunderstand their religion" (43). Griffiths treats religion "in phenomenal terms, which is to say in terms of how forms of life of a certain sort seem to those who inhabit them" (43)—ultimately, a version of the familiar "If it seems right to them, it is right." Hick, on the other hand, endorses Kant's strategy (or at least a position that is "a highly generalized version of Kant's complex theory") in *An Interpretation of Religion*, 240–46.

11. Ogden, *Is There Only One True Religion*, 44; cf. 29. Ogden is thus employing a version of Hume's criterion of meaningfulness against religious exclusivism ("Does it contain any experimental reasoning concerning matter of fact and existence?"), albeit in a way that later logical positivists would reject, since they regarded all theological claims as *Unsinn*.

12. James, *The Varieties of Religious Experience*, 31–32 (author's italics deleted); Otto, *The Idea of the Holy* (1917). See also Eliade, *The Sacred and the Profane*.

13. Data taken from *World Christian Encyclopedia*, Table 1-5. For discussion, see Goodstein, "More Religion."

14. In 1920, Curtis Lee Laws, at a meeting of the Northern Baptist Convention, first coined the term, defining the "fundamentalist" as one who is willing "to do battle royal for the Fundamentals" of the faith (Marsden, *Fundamentalism*, 159). See also Armstrong, *The Battle for God*, 174; Ammerman, "North American Protestant Fundamentalism," 2. Bernard Lewis warns that recent Islamic radical and militant movements are "loosely and inaccurately designated as 'fundamentalist'" (*What Went Wrong?* 106). However, as he himself notes, they all "share the objective of undoing secularizing reforms of the last century, abolishing the imported codes of law and social customs that came with them, and returning to the Holy Law of Islam and an Islamic political order" (106), so they do fit Armstrong's model of a "militant form of piety whose objective is to drag God and religion from the sidelines, to which they have been relegated in modern secular culture, and bring

them back to center stage. These 'fundamentalists,' as they are called, are convinced that they are fighting for the survival of their faith in a world that is inherently hostile to religion. They are conducting a war against secular modernity" (*The Battle for God*, vii). See also Hick's "Epilogue," where he refers all too briefly to "a wide resurgence of the 'us against them' attitude in the forms of both religious fundamentalism and political nationalism," a "retrenching into intensified allegiance to one's own group," and an opposition to "a world-wide or species-wide loyalty" (*An Interpretation of Religion*, 377).

15. Lilla, "Church Meets State." Fundamentalists tend to be more critical of modernity and secularism than do evangelicals; the latter "engage the culture and share their faith," while the former "are more prone to create separatist enclaves" (Goodstein, "More Religion," 4). However, from the perspective of Enlightenment religiosity, the similarities between these two groups outweigh their differences. All evangelicals and fundamentalists make strongly exclusivist claims that pit one faith against another.

16. Huntington, *The Clash of Civilizations*, 64.

17. Johann Georg Hamann, letter to Christian Jacob Kraus of December 18, 1784, in Schmidt, *What Is Enlightenment?* 147; *Metacritique on the Purism of Reason* (1784), in Schmidt, *What Is Enlightenment?* 155. For discussion, see Berlin, *The Magus of the North*.

18. Jefferson to Benjamin Rush, April 21, 1803, in *Writings*, 1123, 1125.

19. Hick, *An Interpretation of Religion*, 149; cf. 312–13. Wagar, in his discussion of twentieth-century approaches to religious unity, also concludes that moral consensus is much more evident than theological: "If we descend from the mountain peaks of theology to the plateau of ethics, all the formulas for the spiritual unification of man converge in perfect harmony" (*The City of Man*, 171).

20. See, e.g., Wattles, *The Golden Rule*, esp. 182–89; Bok, "Golden Rule." See also Gene Outka and John Reeder Jr., eds., *Prospects for a Common Morality* (Princeton: Princeton University Press, 1993); Richard Madsen and Tracy B. Strong, eds., *The Many and the One: Religious and Secular Perspectives on Ethical Pluralism in the Modern World* (Princeton: Princeton University Press, 2003).

21. President Bush, for instance, in a meeting with Arab leaders at Sharm El-Sheik, Egypt, on June 3, 2003, invoked a version of the common morality thesis when he remarked, "It's the call of all religions—that each person must be free and treated with respect. And it is with that call that I feel passionate about the need to move forward so that the world can be more peaceful, more free and more hopeful" ("Five Arab Leaders"). But events both before and after his speech indicate that too many people continue to give only lip service to such convictions.

22. Cf. John Rawls's discussion of "Toleration and the Common Interest," in *A Theory of Justice*, esp. 214. See also Gordon Schochet's entry on "Toleration" in the *Encyclopedia of the Enlightenment*, 4: 165–70.

23. Strictly speaking, the fallibility of beliefs argument does not necessarily presuppose an underlying truth—*all* of the beliefs could be wrong. But I don't think that most Enlightenment intellectuals interpreted the argument in this manner.

24. Nietzsche, "Those Who 'Improve' Humanity," § 1, in *Twilight of the Idols* (1889), 38. See also Hick's discussion of "The Problem of Conflicting Truth-Claims" in *An Interpretation of Religion*, 362–66; Griffith's chapter on "Religious Diversity and Truth," in *Problems of Religious Diversity*, 21–65. Most religious believers, of course, would resist efforts to apply Nietzsche's dictum to the truth-claims of their own religion. For a defense of the view that Nietzsche did not dismiss the category of truth, see B. Williams, *Truth and Truthfulness*, esp. 16–18.

25. A. W. Wood, *Kant's Ethical Thought*, 319. Describing Kant as "fundamentally a *religious* thinker" whose "highest hopes for human history are pinned on religious values and religious institutions," Wood draws the logical conclusion that "from a Kantian standpoint . . . religion has thus far failed humanity" (318, 319).

26. Novalis, *Christianity or Europe: A Fragment* (1799), in Beiser, *The Early Political Writings*, 70–71.

27. Juergensmeyer, *Terror in the Mind of God*, 243. In his preface to the paperback edition, Juergensmeyer expresses the hope that people will find in religion "a cure for violence instead of a cause" (xii). The recommended "moderation in religion's passion" achievable by a commitment to Enlightenment values that he advocates in his conclusion (243) can contribute to this cure.

28. Schleiermacher, *On Religion*, 109, 110. Traces of this romantic protest against natural theology are still detectable in contemporary literature; see, e.g., Hauerwas, *With the Grain of the Universe*. At the same time, in my view those few contemporary scholars who do defend natural theology are not putting it to its best use. James F. Sennett and Douglas Groothuis, for instance, with no hint of irony, proclaim that "*natural theology is alive and well in contemporary philosophy*" ("Introduction" to *In Defense of Natural Theology*, 15). However, both they and the contributors to their anthology attempt to use natural theology only to defend the claims of their own specific versions of Christianity—not as a way of building bridges between faiths.

29. As a reviewer of Hick's *Interpretation of Religion* notes, "It would be nice to find a way in which all believers could somehow turn out to be both intellectually respectable and also believers in much the same thing. But it seems impossible to attain when it is religious experience rather than natural theology which is the source of intellectual respectability, for that experience is not of 'the Real,' but of Yahweh, or Kali, or Krishna, or Christ" (Grover, review). The same criticism applies to Schleiermacher's attempt to ground religion in "intuition and feeling." For intuition, as he himself notes, "is and always remains something individual, set apart, the immediate perception, nothing more" (*On Religion*, 26; cf. 22).

30. Rawls, *Political Liberalism*, 133–72. For related discussion, see Bielefeldt, " 'Western' versus 'Islamic' Human Rights Conceptions?" 114–17; J. Cohen, "Minimalism about Human Rights."

31. Riem, *On Enlightenment*, 172.

32. I exclude here the Aztec religion, which did endorse human sacrifice.

33. See Cheah and Robbins, *Cosmopolitics*. There is a burgeoning academic literature on cosmopolitanism at present. However, the role of religion in fostering

cosmopolitan attitudes and beliefs is conspicuously absent from most of these discussions.

Chapter 7: Education

1. Mitchell, *International Historical Statistics*, 704.

2. Data available at http://www.unicef.org (accessed July 3, 2006). For discussion, see Sengupta, "African Girls' Route to School."

3. Condorcet, "The Future Progress of the Human Mind," in Kramnick, *The Portable Enlightenment Reader*, 27.

4. Brockliss, "Humboldt's Rift."

5. Greene, *The Revolutionary Generation*, 123. See also Rudolph, *The American College and University*, 21–22.

6. Eells, *Baccalaureate Degrees Conferred*, 20–21. See also Eells, "Early Baccalaureate Degrees," in *Degrees in Higher Education*, 83–86. Assuming that "by 1760, the population of the colonies was about 1,600,000" (S. Cohen, *Education in the United States*, 1: xvi), Greene's claim that only 1 out of every 1,000 American colonists attended college is a bit low.

7. Houston, *Literacy in Early Modern Europe*, 84. As noted in chapter 2, university enrollment declined significantly in Germany during the eighteenth century.

8. Houston, *Literacy in Early Modern Europe*, 84.

9. Ryan, *Liberal Anxieties*, 145; Sherman, Honegger, and McGivern, *Comparative Indicators of Education*, 19.

10. Sherman et al., *Comparative Indicators of Education*, 19.

11. M. Nussbaum, *Cultivating Humanity*, 294.

12. "International Comparisons of Education," in *Digest of Education Statistics, 2001*, Table 411. Available at http://necs.ed.gov (accessed July 3, 2006).

13. Keane, *Global Civil Society?* 129.

14. Rudolph, *The American College and University*, 311. The movement for separate women's colleges in the United States also began in the 1830s. According to Rudolph, "The first experiment in women's collegiate education was the Georgia Female College at Macon, chartered in 1836" (311).

15. *NCES Digest of Education Statistics Tables and Figures*, Table 248, "Earned degrees conferred by degree-granting institutions, by level of degree and sex of student: 1869–70 to 2009–10." Available at http://nccs.gov.ed (accessed July 3, 2006).

16. Bradshaw and Wallace, *Global Inequalities*, 22 (authors' data taken from World Bank, *World Development Report 1995*).

17. *NCES Digest of Education Statistics Tables and Figures*, Table 327, "Current-fund revenue of degree-granting institutions, by source: 1980–81 to 1995–96." Available at http://nces.ed.gov (accessed July 3, 2006).

18. Houston, *Literacy in Early Modern Europe*, 49.

19. Ibid., 49, 50.

20. Greene, *The Prerevolutionary Generation*, 117; cf. 289. See also Butts and Cremin, *A History of Education*, 100–104. Tocqueville, in *Democracy in America* (1835),

cites extensively from the *Code of 1650*, "a compilation of the earliest laws and orders of the General Court of Connecticut," in support of his claim that "it is the provisions for public education which, from the very first, throw into clearest relief the originality of American civilization." The *Code*, he notes, contains provisions "establishing schools in all townships and obliging the inhabitants, under penalty of heavy fines, to maintain them" (41 n. 18, 45). However, both the actual extent of public schooling in prerevolutionary America and the degree to which its educational policy represented an advance over Western Europe's are significantly less than Tocqueville claims.

21. Reprinted in S. Cohen, *Education in the United States*, 1: 394. The religious incentive behind colonial New England education schemes stands in stark contrast to Enlightenment calls for a more secular education that would combat superstition.

22. Cremin, *Traditions of American Education*, 28. However, Cremin also maintains that "literacy rates in the colonies on the eve of the Revolution were only slightly below those in England" (32–33). Again, there is no necessary connection between school attendance and literacy.

23. U.S. Bureau of the Census, *Historical Statistics*, "High School Graduates, by Sex: 1870 to 1970," 379. Although the first publicly supported U.S. secondary school was founded in 1635 (Boston Latin School), private academies were the dominant form of secondary school in the United States until the Civil War, and there were not very many of them. The first was founded in 1750 by Benjamin Franklin in Philadelphia. According to the original *Advertisement*, students admitted to the Philadelphia Academy were to be taught "the Latin, Greek, English, French, and German Languages, together with History, Geography, Chronology, Logic, and Rhetoric; also Writing, Arithmetic, Merchants Accounts, Geometry, Algebra, Surveying, Gauging, Navigation, Astronomy, Drawing in Perspective, and other mathematical Sciences; with natural and mechanical Philosophy, &c.... at the Rate of Four Pounds per annum, and Twenty Shillings entrance" (reprinted in S. Cohen, *Education in the United States*, 1: 510).

24. Tyack and Cuban, *Tinkering toward Utopia*, 21; Sherman et al., *Comparative Indicators of Education*, 19. See also U.S. Bureau of the Census, *Historical Statistics of the United States*, 369.

25. *Education at a Glance: OECD Indicators*, 2001 ed., Table A2.2a. Available at http://www.oecd.org (accessed July 3, 2006). G-8 (Group of eight) is the grouping of eight of the world's leading industrialized nations: France, Germany, Italy, Japan, the United Kingdom, the United States, Canada, and Russia (the European Union also participates). The hallmark of the G-8 is an annual economic and political summit of the heads of government with international officials.

26. Newman, *The Idea of a University*, 134. Liberal knowledge, Newman continues, is "a gentleman's knowledge," and thus "we contrast a liberal education with a commercial education or a professional" (137, 133). Famous as Newman's definition of liberal education is, it is also an extreme one that does not find many supporters at present. For most contemporary supporters of liberal education do not view education strictly as an end in itself. Martha Nussbaum, for instance, in

explicating and endorsing Seneca's classical position, writes, "The only kind of education that really deserves the name *liberalis*, or, as we might literally render it, 'freelike,' is one that makes pupils free, able to take charge of their own thought and to conduct a critical examination of their society's norms and traditions" (*Cultivating Humanity*, 30; cf. 293). Her conception of liberal education is much closer to Enlightenment views about education.

27. Keane, *Global Civil Society?* 129.

28. Locke, *Some Thoughts Concerning Education*, § 1.

29. As George Dennis O'Brien notes, "The fact of the matter is that higher education has no necessary connection to political acumen or moral sense" (*All the Essential Half-Truths*, 154). Similarly, Ryan, in *Liberal Anxieties*, observes, "We are all too ready to suppose that a person who has been 'properly' educated will be full of all the virtues. But ... goodness and cleverness do not always go together" (26).

30. Basedow, as cited by Niedermeier in "Campe als Dirketor des Dessauer Philanthropin," in *Visionäre Lebensklugheit*, 46 n. 7.

31. See M. Nussbaum, *Cultivating Humanity*, for a defense as well as an informal survey of some of these curricula.

32. Jefferson, *Notes on the State of Virginia*, in *Writings*, 274.

33. Rousseau, *Discourse on Political Economy*, in *On the Social Contract*, 178.

34. Rousseau, *Considerations on the Government of Poland*, in *Rousseau on International Relations*, 172.

35. International Association for the Evaluation of Educational Achievement, *Citizenship and Education in Twenty-Eight Countries: Civic Knowledge and Engagement at Age Fourteen*, 2001. Figures taken from Table 6.3, 124. Available at: http://www.wam.umd.edu/~jtpurta/ (accessed July 3, 2006).

36. Ryan, *Liberal Anxieties*, 61–62. Tocqueville, in discussing public spirit in the United States, writes, "Sometimes there comes a time in the life of nations when old customs are changed, mores destroyed, beliefs shaken, and the prestige of memories has vanished, but when nonetheless enlightenment has remained incomplete." In such cases, men "retreat into a narrow and unenlightened egoism. Such men escape from prejudices without recognizing the rule of reason" (*Democracy in America*, 236).

37. The second claim seems self-referentially incoherent, for it defends a universal and objective standard while denying that such a thing exists. As John Searle remarks, "One can't make sense out of presenting a thesis, or having a belief, or defending a view without presupposing certain standards of rationality" ("Is There a Crisis," 544). For general discussion of the concept of an enlightened public sphere, see Calhoun, *Habermas and the Public Sphere*.

38. Condorcet, *Sketch for a Historical Picture of the Progress of the Human Mind* (tenth stage), in Kramnick, *The Portable Enlightenment Reader*, 27.

39. Robert D. Putnam charts in detail changes in America's civic involvement in *Bowling Alone*. "American history carefully examined," he notes, "is a story of ups and downs in civic engagement, *not just downs*—a story of collapse *and* of renewal" (25). During the first two-thirds of the twentieth century, Americans experienced "ever deeper involvement in the life of their communities" (27), but

in the last third they suffered a precipitous decline. The major causes for the decline, Putnam argues, are work-related pressures of time and money, suburbanization and commuting, television and electronic entertainment, and generational change (283). For a more upbeat assessment that argues that we are currently experiencing civic renewal, see Gastil and Levine, *The Deliberative Democracy Handbook*.

40. Cf. Werner Schneiders, who, in surveying "the failure [*Scheitern*] of the Enlightenment," points to one notable exception: "In the field of education and culture, the Enlightenment has accelerated the general process of modernization through the struggle against illiteracy" (*Das Zeitalter der Aufklärung*, 130).

Chapter 8: Economics

1. Mittelman, *Globalization*, 2. Mittelman adds that the rubric also "interrelates multiple levels of analysis: economics, politics, culture and ideology" (2). But this is also unhelpful, for different authors choose different levels of analysis to employ in their discussions, and there is no consensus on how to interrelate the various levels.

2. Pieterse, *Globalization and Culture*, 60, 15. Pieterse offers a helpful survey of competing definitions of globalization on 14–21.

3. Kitching, *Seeking Social Justice*, 12.

4. Black, *A Dictionary of Economics*, s.v. "globalization." See also Bhagwati, *In Defense of Globalization*, 3–4; Stiglitz, *Globalization and Its Discontents*, 9–10; World Bank, *Globalization, Growth, and Poverty*, 3–4; Wolf, *Why Globalization Works*, esp. 13–16.

5. Marx and Engels, *Manifesto of the Communist Party* (1848), 8, 10–11, 11 (translation altered slightly).

6. Ronald Findlay and Kevin H. O'Rourke, "Commodity Market Integration, 1500–2000," in Bordo, Taylor, and Williamson, *Globalization in Historical Perspective*, 16. (I have reversed the authors' sentence order in the quoted passage.) See also Felicity A. Nussbaum's remarks concerning the debate regarding where and when globalization began in the introduction to her anthology, *The Global Eighteenth Century*, 1–18, esp. 3. It is true that some ancient cultures engaged in extensive long-distance cross-cultural trade. Richard Tuck, for instance, notes that "the Romans were constantly engaged in trade and warfare with exotic peoples beyond the empire's borders—extending even to the Chinese" ("The Making and Unmaking of Boundaries," 143). But such phenomena do not refer to a "version of globalization" (Buchanan and Moore, "Introduction," 3), for they do not indicate the creation of a global economy. For an opposing view that holds that globalization is a "deep historical process," one that begins long before "the journeys of modernity," see Pieterse, *Globalization and Culture*, 24–27.

7. Giddens, *The Consequences of Modernity*, 64. See also Bauman, *Globalization*, esp. 59–60.

8. Robertson, *Global Theory*, 8. See also Waters, *Globalization*, 3.

9. Paine, *The Rights of Man, Part II*, in *Political Writings*, 196.

10. Barber, *Jihad vs. McWorld*, 4, cf. 97. See also Featherstone, *Global Culture*; Tomlinson, *Globalization and Culture*; Lechner and Boli, *World Culture*.

11. Hannerz, "Cosmopolitans and Locals," 237. See also Pieterse *Globaliza-tion and Culture*, 47, 80, 83; Lechner and Boli, *World Culture*, 52–56.

12. Kitching, *Seeking Social Justice*, 120. See also Pieterse's discussion of differ-ent concepts of culture in *Globalization and Culture*, 47, 78–81, 116–17. In the present discussion I adopt his open-ended definition of culture as "behavior and beliefs that are learned and shared: learned so it is not 'instinctual' and shared so it is not individual" (46).

13. McCarthy, "On Reconciling Cosmopolitan Unity and National Diversi-ty," 205. See also McCarthy's recommended alterations in Kantian cosmopolitan-ism on 215–16.

14. According to Lechner and Boli, the number of IGOs expanded from 37 in 1909 to 2,545 in 2000, while the number of INGOs exploded from 374 to 25,269 during this same time period (*World Culture*, Table 5.2, 130). Cf. Hobsbawm, *Nations and Nationalism*, 181.

15. Ohmae, *The End of the Nation State*, 214. See parts V and VI of Lechner and Boli, *The Globalization Reader*, for additional texts on political globalization.

16. Lechner and Boli, *The Globalization Reader*, 211–12. Additional skepticism concerning the death of the nation-state can be gleaned from Wagar's discussion of mid-twentieth-century proposals for world government. In the late 1940s, he notes, "the world government movement fathered about seventy organized groups around the world which enrolled hundreds of thousands of members. Nearly one quarter of the members of American Congress and the British Parliament gave continuing support for years to resolutions favoring, in principle, a world federal government . . . the chorus grew until it seemed, for a brief descriptive moment, irresistible" (*The City of Man*, 221). Overoptimism concerning the alleged inevitabil-ity of global governance is not a new phenomenon.

17. Anon., *Histoire de la République des Lettres en France* (Paris, 1780), 5–6, quoted in Daston, "The Ideal and Reality," 367–68.

18. *Encyclopedia of the Enlightenment*, s.v. "Republic of Letters," by Ruth Whelan, 3: 437. See also Darnton, *George Washington's False Teeth*, 19, 80, 86.

19. Tomlinson regards complex connectivity as "an empirical condition of the modern world" and defines globalization in terms of it: "Globalization refers to the rapidly developing and ever-densening network of interconnections and interdepen-dences that characterize modern social life" (*Globalization and Culture*, 1–2). See also Ulrich Beck's discussion of "cosmopolitan empathy" in *The Cosmopolitan Vision*, 5–8.

20. See, e.g., Pogge, *Global Justice*; De Greiff and Cronin, *Global Justice and Transnational Politics*. Economist Jeffrey Sachs's call for an "enlightened globaliza-tion" is also relevant here. We need "a globalization that addresses the needs of the poorest of the poor; the global environment, and the spread of democracy. It is the kind of globalization championed by the Enlightenment—a globalization of democracies, multilateralism, science and technology, and a global economic system designed to meet human needs. We could call this an Enlightened Globali-zation" (*The End of Poverty*, 358).

21. F. Nussbaum, "Introduction" to *The Global Eighteenth Century*, 3. At the same time, other writers make the opposite mistake of drawing no connection at all

between contemporary globalization and Enlightenment views of the future. Thomas L. Friedman, for instance, in defining globalization as "this new system" with "its own unique logic, rules, pressures and incentives," completely overlooks contemporary globalization's historical antecedents and influences (*The Lexus and the Olive Tree*, 6–7). The same mistake is made by John Keane, when he claims that the present-day project of "global civil society" constitutes "a new world-view, radically different from any that has existed before" (*Global Civil Society?* 1).

22. For discussion, see Fleischacker, "Smith's Contribution to the Politics of Poverty," in *On Adam Smith's "Wealth of Nations,"* 205–8.

23. Landes, *The Wealth and Poverty of Nations*, xx.

24. Peter H. Lindert and Jeffrey G. Williamson, "Does Globalization Make the World More Unequal?" in Bordo et al., *Globalization in Historical Perspective*, 227. See also World Bank, *Globalization, Growth, and Poverty*, 26–27.

25. Paul Bairoch, "The Main Trends in National Economic Disparities Since the Industrial Revolution," in Bairoch and Levy-Leboyer, *Disparities in Economic Development*, 3. Landes says that he is "relying, with some modifications, on bold estimates by Paul Bairoch" (*The Wealth and Poverty of Nations*, 533 n. 3; see n. 23 above). But Bairoch's own estimates are not as bold as Landes's. Another scholar claims that "the rich–poor country income differential" has risen "from 3:1 in 1800, to 10:1 in 1900, to 60:1 in 2000" and is "still rising exponentially" (Jacobsen, "Poverty and War").

26. Maddison, "Explaining the Economic Performance of Nations," 23. Maddison's figures apply to a sample of forty-three countries, and neither Switzerland nor Mozambique is included in his list.

27. Engerman and Sokoloff, "Factor Endowments," 270. Cf. Landes, *The Wealth and Poverty of Nations*, 292. Engerman and Sokoloff's sample consists of eight countries in South, Central, and North America. See also Coatsworth, "Notes on the Comparative Economic History of Latin America and the United States," 10–30.

28. Sachs, *The End of Poverty*, 21. Cf. Lant Pritchett, "Comment," in Bordo et al., *Globalization in Historical Perspective*, 274. Another reason for the present gulf between rich and poor countries is that before 1800 all regions were relatively poor and there simply was little if any economic growth, and since then the growth has been very uneven, with most of it going to the richest countries. As Sachs notes, before 1800, "there had been virtually no sustained economic growth in the world" (27), and "today's richest regions have experienced by far the greatest economic progress" (29) over the past two centuries.

29. Geertz, "The World in Pieces: Culture and Politics at the End of the Century," in *Available Light*, 218, 235. Richard Rorty views the recent proliferation of nation-states even more darkly: "Achieving a liberal utopia on a global scale would require the establishment of a world federation, exercising a global monopoly of force. . . . The continual splitting up of old nation states, ex-colonies and ex-federations makes a world government less likely with every passing year" (*Philosophy and Social Hope*, 274).

30. Cf. Wolf: "Why should one stop at 200 pieces? Why not break the world economy up into 10,000 countries, 600,000 tribes or 6 billion self-sufficient human

beings?... The logical destination of a movement dedicated to self-sufficiency must be the atomization of humanity" (*Why Globalization Works*, 3–4; cf. 194–99).

31. John Agnew predicts the nation-state's demise in "Global Hegemony versus National Economy: The United States in the New World Economy," in Demko and Wood, *Reordering the World*, 279. For a defense of the moral significance of collective self-governance, see Macedo, "What Self-Governing Peoples Owe to One Another." See also Paul Kael's discussion of the right of self-determination in *European Conquest*, esp. 11–12, 126–36.

32. Maddison, "Explaining the Economic Performance of Nations," 23. Cf. Landes, *The Wealth and Poverty of Nations*, 58–59.

33. Maddison, "Explaining the Economic Performance of Nations," 23. See also Paul Bairoch's table of "historical trends in economic growth, 1800–1990," in *Economics and World History*, 7. In this table, the annual growth rates of the volume of GNP per capita for developed countries are always higher than they are for third world countries.

34. See *Encyclopedia of Enlightenment*, s.v. "Poverty," by Kathyrn Norberg, 3: 347–52, esp. 352; G. S. Jones, *An End to Poverty?* esp. 224; Ringen, "Band of Hope."

35. Pogge, *World Poverty and Human Rights*, 2; cf. 97.

36. Pogge, "Real World Justice," 31.

37. Sachs, *The End of Poverty*, 20. The World Bank has defined "extreme poverty" as an income of $1 per day, measured at purchasing power parity.

38. Bourguignon and Morrisson, "Inequality among World Citizens," Table 1, 731–32. See also Wolf, *Why Globalization Works*, 157–66.

39. Wolf, *Why Globalization Works*, 158.

40. Pogge, "Real World Justice," 32. Cf. Huston Smith, who notes that the Enlightenment's hope of eliminating poverty "must face the fact that more people are hungry today than ever before" (*Why Religion Matters*, 152).

41. Melton, *The Rise of the Public*, 13; cf. 5.

42. Habermas, *The Structural Transformation of the Public Sphere*, 27. (Future references to this work are cited in the body of the text by page number.)

43. In his translator's note to the English translation, Thomas Burger discusses several terms that present problems to the translator. One such term is *bürgerlich*, "an adjective related to the noun *Bürger*, which may be translated as 'bourgeois' or 'citizen.' *Bürgerlich* possesses both connotations" (xv). I believe that both connotations need to be kept in mind in discussing the Enlightenment public sphere.

44. Horkheimer and Adorno, *Dialectic of Enlightenment*, 94, 136. Herbert Marcuse presents a similar critique of consumer society in *One Dimensional Man*.

45. Marx, *Capital*, 1: 71.

46. Hilton, "Review Article," 665.

Chapter 9: Politics

1. Colonialism intensified throughout the nineteenth and early twentieth centuries, and the earlier Enlightenment arguments condemning it seem to have had little if any effect. Edward Said writes:

In 1800 Western powers claimed 55 per cent but actually held approximately 35 per cent of the earth's surface, and by 1878 the proportion was 67 per cent, a rate increase of 83,000 square miles per year. By 1914, the annual rate had risen to an astonishing 240,000 square miles, and Europe held a grand total of roughly 85 per cent of the earth as colonies, protectorates, dependencies, dominions and commonwealths. No other associated set of colonies in history was as large, none so totally dominated, none so unequal in power to the Western metropolis. (*Culture and Imperialism*, 8)

2. Similarly, Jedidiah Morse remarks in *The American Geography*, that "there are scarcely any two nations, or indeed any two of the learned, that agree in the modern division of Africa; and for this very reason, that scarcely any traveller has penetrated into the heart of the country; and consequently we must acknowledge our ignorance of the bounds and even the names of several of the inland nations, which may still be reckoned among the unknown and undiscovered parts of the world" (2: 599). See also Gutherie, *A New System of Modern Geography*, 2: 150–51. I would like to thank Joseph Wood and George Carhart for bringing these materials to my attention.

3. Morse, *The American Geography*, 2: 600; Gutherie, *A New System of Modern Geography*, 2: 151; Anon., *Geography for Youth*, 197.

4. Morse, *The American Geography*, 2: 458; Gutherie, *A New System of American Geography*, 2: 37; Anon., *Geography for Youth*, 153.

5. Morse, *The American Geography*, 2: 3, 2; Gutherie, *A New System of American Geography*, 1: 77; Anon., *Geography for Youth*, 27.

6. Freedom House, *Democracy's Century: A Survey of Global Political Change in the 20th Century*, 3, press release, December 7, 1999. Formerly available at http://www.freedomhouse.org/reports/century.html (accessed September 20, 2003). In 2006 there were 192 member states in the United Nations. Data available at http://www.un.org/Overview/unmember.html (accessed July 12, 2006). States that are not members include Switzerland, Myanmar (formerly Burma) and Taiwan. Other nonmembers are the West Bank, Gaza Strip, and the Vatican City. See also Central Intelligence Agency, *The World Fact Book*.

7. C. A. Crocker, "Engaging Failed States," 35. See also Langford, "Things Fall Apart."

8. See Rotberg, "Failed States," 131.

9. Geertz, "Primordial and Civic Ties," 31, 30.

10. Taylor, "Nationalism and Modernity," 44, 45. Taylor's views on this matter have, I believe, been strongly influenced by his own Herderian sympathies. See, e.g., his brief discussion of Herder's notion of national culture in *Sources of the Self*: "Each people has . . . a right and a duty to realize its own way and not to have an alien one imposed on it" (415, cf. 376). See also his essay, "The Importance of Herder," in *Philosophical Arguments*, 79–99.

11. Hobsbawm argues that during the rise of nationalism up to 1870 a simple "threshold principle" was adhered to: "Self-determination for nations applied only to what were considered to be viable nations: culturally, and certainly economically" (*Nations and Nationalism*, 32). After 1880, this threshold principle was abandoned:

"Henceforth, *any* body of people considering themselves a 'nation' claimed the right to self-determination which, in the last analysis, meant the right to a separate sovereign independent state for their territory" (102). I am not convinced that Herder, Fichte, or Rousseau paid sufficient attention to the economic side of the threshold principle. If this is true, then abandonment of (or rather inattention to, which in this case leads to the same result) the principle was present from the beginning of Enlightenment theorizing about nationalism.

12. Rorty, *Philosophy and Social Hope*, 274.

13. Gans, *The Limits of Nationalism*, 4. Gans's position owes some debts to Will Kymlicka's work on rights for minority cultures. See, e.g., *Liberalism, Community, and Culture*, 206–19, and *Multicultural Citizenship*.

14. As David Wootton notes in the preface to his edited anthology, *Divine Right and Democracy*, "Democracy is now seen as so evidently admirable that there is scarcely a country in the world which does not claim either to be a democracy or to have the intention of becoming one" (10). Richard Bellamy makes a similar observation: "Most regimes today regard themselves as either democratic or as moving towards the establishment of democracy. This universal praise of democracy has produced considerable confusions in the use of the concept, since large differences clearly exist between these self-styled democratic political systems" (introduction to Bobbio, *The Future of Democracy*, 1). For a good historical discussion of the different meanings of "democracy," see *Dictionary of the History of Ideas*, s.v. "Democracy," by Stephen R. Graubard, 1: 652–67. For a more recent investigation, see Dunn, *Democracy: A History*.

15. Benn and Peters, "The Meaning of 'Democracy,' " in *The Principles of Political Thought*, 393. One question that Dunn sets out to answer in his *Democracy* is the following: "Why should it be the case that, for the first time in the history of our still conspicuously multi-lingual species, there is for the present a single world-wide name for the legitimate basis of political authority?" (15).

16. Madison, *Federalist Paper* No. 10; in Rossiter, *The Federalist Papers*, 81.

17. Schumpeter, *Capitalism, Socialism and Democracy*, 246. "Approved by" should be understood weakly: the phrase means only that officeholders have won their positions in a competitive election; not that citizens actually like them or approve of all of their decisions. As Schumpeter writes later, "The democratic method is that institutional arrangement for arriving at political decisions in which individuals acquire power to decide by means of a competitive struggle for the people's vote" (269).

18. See Diamond, *Developing Democracy*, 8–10; Huntington, *The Third Wave*, 9.

19. Powell, *Contemporary Democracies*, 3.

20. See Zakaria, "Illiberal Democracy," esp. 22.

21. Mansfield and Snyder, *Electing to Fight*, 2.

22. Diamond, *Developing Democracy*, 7. See also Huntington, *The Third Wave*, 5–13; Held, *Democracy and the Global Order*, 3–16. In his discussion, Diamond refers to a 1997 study that identifies "more than 550 subtypes of democracy" (7).

23. Huntington, *The Third Wave*, 13. See also Potter, Goldblatt, Kiloh, and Lewis, *Democratization*, 46.

24. Doyle, *Ways of War and Peace*, Table 8.1, "The Liberal Community (by date 'Liberal')," 261. Doyle is interested in tracking the growth of what he calls "Liberal regimes," but what he means by this term is essentially synonymous with liberal democracy or Enlightenment republicanism. He also notes some "domestic variations" within the three late eighteenth-century liberal regimes: Switzerland was liberal only in certain cantons; the United States "was liberal only north of the Mason-Dixon line until 1865, when it became Liberal throughout" (264 n. 4). Temporal fluctuations should also be noted; for example, France did not remain democratic for long. Also, none of these states practiced universal suffrage during this time period (hence "partial or restricted").

25. Huntington, *The Third Wave*, 15–16. For discussion, see 13–26.

26. Powell, *Contemporary Democracies*, 238 n. 3. See also Rustow, *A World of Nations*, Table 5, "Contemporary Democratic Systems," 290 (Dankwart lists thirty-one contemporary democratic systems); Doyle, "The Liberal Community," in *Ways of War and Peace*, 262–64 (Doyle lists sixty-eight liberal regimes for the period 1945–90). The numbers vary in part because different authors employ different conceptions of "democracy" in their analyses.

27. Freedom House, *Democracy's Century*, 2–3. See also Freedom House's annual *Freedom in the World* ranking, which attempts to assess not only the political systems of each country, but also their performance with respect to human rights, economic freedom, and the rule of law. In 2006, they judged eighty-nine countries to be "free," representing 46 percent of the world's population. Data available at http://www.freedomhouse.org (accessed July 12, 2006).

28. Skeptic Norberto Bobbio itemizes democracy's "broken promises" as follows: "the survival of invisible power, the persistence of oligarchies, the suppression of mediating bodies, the renewed vigour in the representation of particular interests, the break-down of participation, the failure to educate citizens (or to educate them properly)." But he then adds that some of these promises "could not objectively be kept and were thus illusions from the outset, others were not so much promises as misplaced hopes, still others as it turned out came up against unforeseen obstacles. In none of these circumstances is it appropriate to speak of the 'degeneration' of democracy" (*The Future of Democracy*, 19).

29. As cited by G. S. Wood in *The Creation of the American Republic*, 426.

30. Diamond, *Developing Democracy*, 171; cf. 65–74. See also Huntington, *The Third Wave*, 298–311, particularly his discussion and defense of "the Western culture thesis," the restrictive version of which holds that "only Western culture provides a suitable base for the development of democratic institutions and democracy" (298).

31. Doyle, *Ways of War and Peace*, 265, 265–68; cf. 300. See also Table 8.2, "International Wars Listed Chronologically," 266–67. For discussion, see Brown, Lynn-Jones, and Miller, *Debating the Democratic Peace*. John R. Oneal and Bruce M. Russett even claim to be able to give some quantitative precision to the democratic peace thesis: "An autocracy and a democracy are not simply as prone to conflict as two autocratic regimes; they are substantially more inclined to violence.... The likelihood of a dispute between two autocracies, all else being

equal, is .071; it is .137 for an autocracy and a democracy. The strength of the democratic peace is indicated by the relatively low probability of a dispute, .054, between two democracies" ("The Classical Liberals Were Right," 288). Jack S. Levy summarizes the debate as follows: "The evidence is conclusive that democratic states have been involved, proportionately, in as many wars as non-democratic states. There is one aspect of the military behavior of democratic states, however, that is clearly distinguished from that of non-democratic states: liberal or democratic states do not fight each other" ("Domestic Politics and War," 87). See also Rawls's discussion of "Democratic Peace Seen in History," in *The Law of Peoples*, 51–54; Huntington, *The Third Wave*, 29 n. 22.

32. See, e.g., Pateman, *The Problem of Political Obligation*; Macpherson, *The Life and Times of Liberal Democracy*. For discussion, see Held, *Models of Democracy*, 263–73. See also Bruce Ackerman and James S. Fishkin's more recent defense of "deliberative democracy" in *Deliberation Day*.

33. Bronner, *Reclaiming the Enlightenment*, 59.

34. Jefferson to Roger C. Weightman, June 24, 1826, in *Writings*, 1517.

Chapter 10: International Relations

1. Steel, "The Missionary," 27.

2. Quoted in Lodge, *The Senate and the League of Nations*, 88, 90; see also MacMillan, *Paris 1919*, 496; J. M. Cooper, *Breaking the Heart of the World*, 24. Lodge, a Republican and chairman of the Senate Foreign Relations Committee, was Wilson's chief opponent in the subsequent debate over U.S. involvement in the League, and his opposition forces eventually proved victorious. He prefaces his reprinting of Wilson's address by remarking that it "reveals so completely Mr. Wilson's steady adherence to his policy of bringing about a peace which should be due to him and in which he should play the part of the mediator and maker of world peace by him arranged" (84). Their disagreements were both political and personal; as MacMillan notes, "The two men had been antagonists for years" (152).

3. G. Scott, *The Rise and Fall of the League of Nations*, 15; MacMillan, *Paris 1919*, 276, 489; Hinsley, *Power and the Pursuit of Peace*, 310–11.

4. At first, Great Britain, France, Italy, and Japan were the only representatives in the first group. The full text of the covenant, which was adopted on April 28, 1919, is reprinted as Appendix I in Henig, *The League of Nations*, 179–89. (Quotations are taken from this source.) See also Walters, *A History of the League of Nations*, 40–63; Hinsley, *Power and the Pursuit of Peace*, 309–22.

5. According to Lodge, Article 10 "did more than all other provisions put together to defeat the treaty" in the U.S. Senate (*The Senate and the League of Nations*, 184; cf. MacMillan, *Paris 1919*, 489–90, 492). As interpreted by Lodge and other senators, Article 10 would have required the United States "to interfere in controversies between nations" and to employ its military forces for such purposes. Each requirement, they held, involved an infringement on congressional powers.

In essence, Lodge and the other senators who voted against the Peace Treaty invoked a state sovereignty argument against Article 10. J. M. Cooper, in *Breaking the Heart of the World*, also regards Article 10 as the "most important and ... most controversial feature" of the entire Covenant (10), and discusses it at length throughout his book.

6. Walters, *A History of the League of Nations*, 42. (Walters writes as a former deputy secretary-general of the League.)

7. MacMillan, *Paris 1919*, 84. J. M. Cooper, who focuses on the U.S. Senate fight over—and eventual rejection of—the League, concludes his analysis by claiming that "for all his flaws and missteps, Wilson was right. He should have won the League fight. His defeat did break the heart of the world" (*Breaking the Heart of the World*, 433; see also 9). But good also sometimes comes from heartbreak.

8. Howard, *The Invention of Peace*, 61. Howard credits Kant with "the invention of peace": "If anyone could be said to have invented peace as more than a mere pious inspiration, it was Kant" (31).

9. Quotations are taken from Wilson's first, fourth, second, third, and fourteenth points. See MacMillan, *Paris 1919*, 495–96; Lodge, *The Senate and the League of Nations*, 88–90.

10. MacMillan, *Paris 1919*, 493.

11. Instrumental in the U.S. refusal to sign the treaty was a small band of sixteen senators known as the "irreconcilables," who were opposed to the League under any form. For discussion, see Stone, *The Irreconcilables*. They drew their inspiration in part from Thomas Jefferson's advice to form "entangling alliances with none" ("First Inaugural Address," March 4, 1801, in *Writings*, 494) as well as from the following statement in the 1823 Monroe Doctrine: "In the wars of the European powers in matters relating to themselves we have never taken any part, nor does it comport with our policy to do so." See also MacMillan, *Paris 1919*, 9, 95–97, 488; J. M. Cooper, *Breaking the Heart of the World*, 126–239; Lodge, *The Senate and the League of Nations*, 137, 163, 175, 186, 202–5. However, Lodge himself was by no means an isolationist; indeed, in a June 1915 commencement address at Union College he even put forward the radical idea of a "united nations determined to ... prevent war" (*The Senate and the League of Nations*, 130).

12. Lodge, *The Senate and the League of Nations*, 183; cf. 173, 176. See also MacMillan, *Paris 1919*, 489, 490–92; J. M. Cooper, *Breaking the Heart of the World*, 59, 134–36, 311–12, 347–48, 419. Article I, Section 8 of the U.S. Constitution reads, "The Congress shall have the Power ... To declare War."

13. Lodge, *The Senate and the League of Nations*, 302; cf. 184. See also MacMillan, *Paris 1919*, 492; Cooper, *Breaking the Heart of the World*, 155.

14. As cited by G. Scott, *The Rise and Fall of the League of Nations*, 73. See also Howard's discussion in *The Invention of Peace*, 62–67.

15. MacMillan, *Paris 1919*, 83; see also J. M. Cooper, *Breaking the Heart of the World*, 402–3, 405.

16. Speech made by Robert Cecil at the final session of the League Assembly, April 9, 1946, reprinted in Henig, *The League of Nations*, 166. See also G. Scott, *The Rise and Fall of the League of Nations*, 399–405. Hinsley is much more skeptical in his

assessment: "The League could not have worked.... It failed for the deeper reason that its basic conception is impracticable at any time" (*Power and the Pursuit of Peace*, 335, 321). For additional assessments, see Kelsen, "The Experiences of the League of Nations," in *Peace through Law*, 49–55; Luard, "The Lessons of the League," in *A History of the United Nations*, 1: 3–16.

17. In comparing the relevant actions of the U.S. Senate Committee on Foreign Relations in 1945 and 1919, Ruth B. Russell writes, "Its approval this time was unqualified, and was given by a vote of 20 to 1" (*A History of the United Nations Charter*, 941). As noted earlier (n. 11), Lodge did invoke the term "united nations" in his 1915 commencement address at Union College. But it is not clear that Roosevelt was aware of Lodge's earlier usage. See J. M. Cooper, *Breaking the Heart of the World*, 408–9, 409 n. 60.

18. There was no mention of human rights in the League of Nations Covenant, and this is one area where the United Nations represents a clear advance over its predecessor. The UN's stress on the importance of human rights becomes even more pronounced in the Universal Declaration of Human Rights, passed by the UN General Assembly on December 10, 1948. See also "The Moral Pressure of Human Rights," below.

19. The charter is reprinted as an appendix in Goodrich, Hambro, and Simons, *Charter of the United Nations*, as well as in Roberts and Kingsbury, *United Nations, Divided World*. Quotations (cited by article number) are taken from the latter source. Extensive and up-to-date information about the UN is also available at http://www.un.org (accessed July 19, 2006).

20. The Republic of China (Taiwan) was a member until 1971; since then the People's Republic of China has represented China. After the breakup of the USSR in 1989, the Russian Federation retained a permanent seat. In the original charter, Security Council membership was set at eleven, six of which were nonpermanent members.

21. Russell, *A History of the United Nations Charter*, 713. See also Goodrich et al.'s commentary on Article 27 in *Charter of the United Nations*, 215–31; Roberts and Kingsbury, "Introduction: The UN's Role in International Society Since 1945," in *United Nations, Divided World*, 41.

22. Roberts and Kingsbury, "Introduction" to *United Nations, Divided World*, 39. See also 377–78, 441–45.

23. Hoge, "U.N. Report Urges Big Changes." All factual data concerning the panel's report are taken from this article.

24. Kennedy, *The Parliament of Man*, 263. As Kennedy notes, Article 76 of the charter states that the purpose of the Trusteeship Council is "to promote the political, economic, social, and educational advancement" of the lands in question. But as he also points out, reviving the Council is "politically impossible": it hints of "covert Western colonialism and patronizing" (263).

25. "Only states may be parties before the Court" (Article 34.1, *Statute of the International Court of Justice*). The *Statute* is reprinted as an Appendix in Goodrich et al., *Charter of the United Nations*. In 2002, the International Criminal Court came into existence. Unlike the International Court of Justice, the International Criminal

Court is empowered to prosecute certain crimes committed by individuals. For discussion, see "Global Jurisdiction and National Sovereignty," below.

26. Goodrich et al., *Charter of the United Nations*, 547. See also Russell, *A History of the United Nations*, 877–78, 886–88.

27. *Report of the Preparatory Commission*, 87, as cited by Goodrich et al., *Charter of the United Nations*, 589.

28. Roberts and Kingsbury, "Introduction" to *United Nations, Divided World*, 19. Cf. Kennedy, *The Parliament of Man*, 285.

29. Detailed proposals for revising the UN along Enlightenment lines have been made, but they have received very little popular or political support. For example, in 1958 Grenville Clark and Louis B. Sohn published *World Peace through World Law*, an elaborate set of plans designed "to carry out complete and universal disarmament and to strengthen the United Nations through the establishment of such legislative, executive and judicial institutions as are necessary to maintain world order" (xv). Chief among their proposals were the following: (1) "complete disarmament, under effective controls, of each and every nation" (xv); (2) elimination of all national military forces, to be replaced by the "United Nations Peace Force" (xxix); (3) a popularly elected and much stronger General Assembly, with each nation's voting strength to be determined by its population, and with full power to enact all laws necessary for the maintenance of world peace (xix–xxii); (4) abolition of the UN Security Council, to be replaced by an expanded Executive Council in which the four largest nations would enjoy permanent membership but no right of a "crippling veto" (xii, xxii–xxiii); (5) a reorganized International Court of Justice with compulsory jurisdiction, along with a new "World Equity Tribunal," charged with handling disputes between nations "which cannot be satisfactorily settled on the basis of applicable legal principles" (xxxiii); and (6) establishment of a "World Development Authority" whose function would be "to assist in the economic and social development of the underdeveloped areas of the world, primarily through grants-in-aid and interest-free loans" (xxxvi). In the second edition (1960), Clark optimistically predicted that by 1965–67 "a comprehensive plan for total and universal disarmament and for the necessary world institutions to make, interpret and enforce world law in the field of war prevention will have been officially formulated and will have been submitted to all nations for approval" (xliii), but in the author's note added to the third edition he confessed, "The peoples have been more apathetic, the governments more timid and fortune less kind than I had hoped" (liv). As Frederick the Great noted regarding Saint-Pierre's proposal, "The thing is most practicable; for its success all that is lacking is the consent of Europe and a few similar trifles."

30. See, e.g., Doyle's table of "International Wars Listed Chronologically" in *Ways of War and Peace*, 266–67.

31. Clausewitz, *On War* (1832), 605; cf. 87.

32. Kennedy, *The Parliament of Man*, 288. See also 45, 236–39.

33. Sen, "Elements of a Theory of Human Rights," 321. See also Sen's *Development as Freedom*, 229.

34. As cited by Tom J. Farer and Felice Gaer, "The UN and Human Rights;" in Roberts and Kingsbury, *United Nations, Divided World*, 247. See also Peter Meyer, "The International Bill: A Brief History," in P. Williams, *The International Bill of Rights*, xxiv.

35. Beitz, "Human Rights as a Common Concern," 269.

36. The Human Rights Commission was abolished by the UN General Assembly in 2006 and replaced by the Human Rights Council. The Commission had been the subject of criticism for many years, primarily because countries with poor human rights records were themselves often members of it and used their membership to shield themselves from sanctions. The good news is that the UN, despite its slow-moving and bloated bureaucracy, is occasionally able to reform itself. The bad news is that the United States is often one of the main impediments to needed change. The only countries voting against the resolution were Israel, the Marshall Islands, Palau, and the United States. See T. Wright, "Annan Cautions Rights Council to Avoid Rifts."

37. Meyer, "The International Bill: A Brief History," xxx. Cf. Farer and Gaer, "The UN and Human Rights," 248–49.

38. Sands, *Lawless World*, 11. The abstentions came primarily, but not exclusively, from the Soviet bloc: South Africa, the Soviet Union, Ukraine, Byelorussia, Czechoslovakia, Poland, Yugoslavia, and Saudi Arabia. Here, too, the issue of national sovereignty exerted its influence. The Soviet UN delegate, trying unsuccessfully to postpone a vote on the declaration, complained to the Assembly that "a number of articles completely ignore the sovereign rights of democratic governments. . . . The question of national sovereignty is a matter of greatest importance" (as cited by Farer and Gaer, "The UN and Human Rights," 248; Meyer, "The International Bill: A Brief History," xxx–xxxi).

39. The *Universal Declaration* is reprinted in Hayden, *The Philosophy of Human Rights*, 353–58. Quotations, cited by Article section, are taken from this source. See also the extensive set of human rights documents in Brownlie and Goodwin-Gill, eds., *Basic Documents on Human Rights*.

40. See Meyer, "The International Bill," xxvi, xxix–xxx; Beitz, "Human Rights as a Common Concern," 271; and Ishay, *The History of Human Rights*, 3–4, 222–23. There is not complete consensus regarding these categories of rights, but as Beitz notes, "It is less important to agree about categories than to appreciate the scope and detail of the enumerated rights" (271). One category in Beitz's own list that I have not included here is "rights of communities." At least in the 1948 declaration, this type of right seems to be absent. As Farer and Gaer note, "The UN Declaration seemingly adheres to the view that minorities as collective entities have no rights independent of the individuals comprising them" ("The UN and Human Rights," 293). Subsequent debate over implementing the declaration produced a simpler typology: civil and political rights (categories 1–3, above) versus social and economic rights (category 4). This dichotomy of rights continues to generate a great deal of debate. For a classic discussion, see Cranston, "Human Rights, Real and Supposed."

41. A possible fifth category of rights emerges in Article 28: "Everyone is entitled to a social and international order in which the rights and freedoms set forth in this

Declaration can be fully realized." Ishay, following René Cassin, describes § 28 metaphorically as part of "the roof of the portico" (*The History of Human Rights*, 3, 223); Thomas Pogge argues that it "does not add a further right to the list" of human rights, but rather says "something about what a human right is," namely, a claim "on the institutional order" in which one lives ("Human Rights and Responsibilities," 164). In my view, § 28 does add a further right that does not fit into any of the above categories: the right to have one's human rights implemented and enforced.

42. As cited by Meyer, "The International Bill," xxxii–xxxiii. See also Farer and Gaer, "The UN and Human Rights," 250.

43. Both covenants (along with the protocols to the Covenant on Civil and Political Rights) are reprinted in the annex to Steiner and Alston, *International Human Rights in Context*. Quotations, cited by Article section number, are taken from this source.

44. Farer and Gaer, "The UN and Human Rights," 251.

45. Cranston, for instance, points out that "at present it is utterly impossible, and will be for a long time yet, to provide 'holidays with pay' for everybody in the world" ("Human Rights," 170). See also Sen's response to this "feasibility critique" in "Elements of a Theory of Human Rights," 347–48.

46. Bentham, *Pannomial Fragments*, in *A Bentham Reader*, 257. See also Sen, "Elements of a Theory of Human Rights," esp. 316–18.

47. Beitz, "Human Rights as a Common Concern," 269.

48. Sen, "Elements of a Theory of Human Rights," 343–44.

49. Samuel Rachel, *Dissertations on the Law of Nature and of Nations*, II.cxix.

50. As noted earlier, only states may be parties before the International Court of Justice, an organ of the UN. But because this particular court lacks the power of compulsory jurisdiction and renders only advisory opinions on disputes that are voluntarily submitted to it, it offers only a very weak analogy to Enlightenment world court proposals.

51. The relevant portions of the charter are reprinted in Steiner and Alston, *International Human Rights in Context*, 113–14. Quotations are taken from this source. See also Peter Singer's discussion, "The Development of International Criminal Law," in *One World*, 112–20.

52. Steiner and Alston, *International Human Rights in Context*, 115. See also B. S. Brown, "The Statute of the ICC," 70; L. May, *Crimes against Humanity*, 207; cf. 6, 8. May defends a Hobbes-inspired "moral minimalist position in international law where the limit of tolerance and sovereignty is reached when the security of a State's subjects is jeopardized" (12).

53. As L. May notes, " 'Crimes against peace' have never fared well in international law, since it has been so hard to figure out what counts as an *aggressive* as opposed to a *defensive* war" (*Crimes against Humanity*, 6). The crime of aggression is listed within the new International Criminal Court's jurisdiction, but the Court will be able to prosecute people for this crime "only after the parties to the statute have agreed on a definition" of "aggression" (Sands, *Lawless World*, 57; see also B. S. Brown, "The Statute of the ICC," 67).

54. Brownlie, *Principles of Public International Law*, 562.

55. Neier, *War Crimes*, 18. See also Singer, *One World*, 113, 118.

56. Reprinted in Steiner and Alston, *International Human Rights in Context*, 1152. (The remaining eight categories are "murder, extermination, enslavement, deportation, imprisonment, torture, persecutions on political, racial and religious grounds, and other inhumane acts.")

57. Singer, *One World*, 118.

58. Ignatieff, *Human Rights as Politics and Idolatry*, 12.

59. Ibid., 173; see also 95. (Ignatieff's remarks about "the enforcement revolution" and "minimalism" do not seem entirely consistent.)

60. Best, *Humanity in Warfare*, 291. See also Neier, *War Crimes*, 254; Sands, *Lawless World*, 53.

61. Again, the Court will be able to exercise jurisdiction over the crime of aggression only after the parties to the statute have agreed on how to define the crime. See Article 5.2 of the *Rome Statute of the International Criminal Court*, reprinted in Sands, *Lawless World*, 278.

62. Information on the Court (including the text of the *Rome Statute*) is available at http://www.iccnow.org (accessed July 18, 2006). See also Steiner and Alston, *International Human Rights in Context*, 1192–98; Singer, *One World*, 118–120; Neier, "Epilogue: Toward a Permanent International Criminal Court," in *War Crimes*, 252–60; Sands, "A New international Court," in *Lawless World*, 46–68.

63. U.S. Department of State, "International Criminal Court." See also Sands, *Lawless World*, 48–49.

64. Lodge, *The Senate and the League of Nations*, 404; cf. 290–91. Insofar as the United States has been raising sovereignty-based objections to international organizations at least since 1917, Sands's thesis that "with the election of George W. Bush in November 2000," the United States began "a war on [international] law" is false (*Lawless World*, xii). U.S. opposition to global rules does not begin with Bush. And the opposition comes not only from the United States; recall, for example, the USSR's frequent sovereignty-based vetoes of UN Security Council resolutions. All powerful countries, when they are able to do so, will try to play the sovereignty card.

65. Weschler, "Exceptional Cases in Rome," 98. See also Roth, "The Court the U.S. Doesn't Want," 1198, and "The Case for Universal Jurisdiction"; Kissinger, "The Pitfalls of Universal Jurisdiction." However, recently there may be signs that U.S. opposition to the ICC is diminishing slightly. In March 2005, the United States agreed to allow (by not exercising its veto right on UN Security Council Resolution 1593) the situation in Darfur to be referred to the ICC prosecutor. Perhaps, as Elizabeth Rubin notes, "the Bush Administration is reluctantly coming to terms with the usefulness, if not the necessity, of the ICC" ("If Not Peace," 74; see also Sands, *Lawless World*, 248–49).

Conclusion

1. Hume, *Enquiries Concerning Human Understanding*, 65. William B. Todd, in his foreword to Hume's *History of England*, argues that Hume viewed history as a

"corollary discipline" to philosophy (xi), one that allows us to document the "science of man." For a representative sampling of Enlightenment attitudes toward history, see the selections under "Progress and History" in Kramnick, *The Portable Enlightenment Reader*, 351–95.

2. Henry St. John Bolingbroke, *Letters on the Study and Use of History* (1735), in Kramnick, *The Portable Enlightenment Reader*, 358.

3. Kant stresses the importance of history for anthropology in many versions of his anthropology lectures. See, e.g., *Pillau* (25: 734), *Menschenkunde* (25: 857–58), and *Mrongovius* (25: 1212–13).

4. Hume, *A Treatise Concerning Human Nature*, xviii–xix. Kant also comments on these and other differences between the human and natural sciences in his anthropology writings. See *Anthropology* (7: 121), *Mrongovius* (25: 1212), *Busolt* (25: 1437). For discussion, see Louden, *Kant's Impure Ethics*, 66–68.

5. Anne-Robert-Jacques Turgot, "On the Successive Advances of the Human Mind," in Kramnick, *The Portable Enlightenment Reader*, 362. See also the readings in chapter 7 ("Progress") of L. G. Crocker, *The Age of Enlightenment*, 287–320.

6. Voltaire, *Essay on the Manners and Spirits of Nations* (1754), in Kramnick, *The Portable Enlightenment Reader*, 371. David Spadafora, in his entry on "Progress" in the *Encyclopedia of Enlightenment*, goes as far as to say that "there is no longer consensus on the centrality of progress to the Enlightenment" (3: 367). Similarly, Susan Neiman writes, "By 1794, at the very latest, any remaining faith in the inevitability of progress was under fire in practice, through the Terror, and in theory, through Kant's powerful argument that progress was at best an ideal. Humankind's capacity to hope was all that was left to bear witness at the end of the eighteenth century. It is hard to view this as inevitable, or even particularly robust" (*Evil in Modern Thought*, 258).

7. Nietzsche, *The Gay Science*, § 357. Cf. Löwith, *Meaning in History*, v. Kant, despite his best efforts, was not able to break away from Enlightenment assumptions of progress. After acknowledging that humanity's decline may begin at any moment, he goes on to argue that the proposition "the human race has always been in progress toward the better and will continue to be so henceforth" is "not just a well-meaning and a commendable proposition in a practical respect," but rather one that is "valid for the most rigorous theory" (*Conflict of the Faculties* 7: 88–89).

8. Voltaire, *Poem on the Lisbon Disaster* (1756), in Hyland et al., *The Enlightenment*, 80. For additional Enlightenment views concerning evil, see the readings in chapter 2 ("The Problem of Evil") of L. G. Crocker, *The Age of Enlightenment*, 72–96; "The Rise of Theodicy," in Larrimore, *The Problem of Evil*, 147–233.

9. For discussion, see "Nature and Freedom" in Louden, *Kant's Impure Ethics*, 16–19; and Patrick Frierson's account of Kant's "asymmetry requirement" in *Freedom and Anthropology*, 13–30.

10. Cobden, *Speeches on Questions of Public Policy*, 144.

11. Porter, *The Creation of the Modern World*, 486 n. 15. See also Robert Wokler, who notes that "any suggestion to the effect that the philosophy of the Enlightenment somehow culminated in the ideology of Joseph Goebbels or was executed

with the clinical precision of Adolf Eichmann must be false" ("Multiculturalism and Ethnic Cleansing," 69–70).

12. Hume, "Of the Dignity or Meanness of Human Nature," in *Essays*, 82.

13. Herder, *Letters for the Advancement of Humanity*, in Forster, *Philosophical Writings*, 379.

14. Kant put it well in his 1781–82 *Menschenkunde* lectures: "The relationship of states toward one another is the relationship of savages; for as the latter stand under no lawgiver, and are free from all constraint between each other, so this also holds for the former, because each state cares only for its own welfare, without having to give an account to another. However, this clearly reveals a still extant barbarism" (25: 1200).

15. Condorcet, *Sketch for a Historical Picture of the Human Mind* (1793; *Tenth Stage: The Future Progress of the Human Mind*), in *Selected Writings*, 275. On the same page, Condorcet criticizes compatriot Saint-Pierre's European Union proposal in the following prediction: "Organizations more intelligently conceived than those of eternal peace, which have filled the leisure and consoled the hearts of certain philosophers, will hasten the brotherhood of nations, and wars between countries will rank with assignations as freakish atrocities, humiliating and vile in the eyes of nature and staining with indelible opprobrium the country or the age whose annals record them." What "more intelligently conceived" federation did Condorcet have in mind?

16. Thomas Aquinas, *Summa Theologica* I–II.62.1; see also *Corinthians* 13:13.

17. Three questions are posed in the *Critique of Pure Reason* (A 805/B 833) and in the *Menschenkunde* lectures (25: 1198): What can I know? What should I do? What may I hope? A fourth question (What is the human being?), to which the first three all relate, is added later in *The Jäsche Logic* (9: 25), letter to Stäudlin of May 4, 1793 (11: 429), and *Metaphysik Pölitz* (28: 533–34).

18. Marcel, *Homo Viator*, 36. For general discussion, see Philip Stratton-Lake's entry on "Hope" in the *Routledge Encyclopedia of Philosophy*.

19. Nietzsche, *The Will to Power*, § 2. For discussion, see Simon May's four-stage typology of Nietzschean nihilism in *Nietzsche's Ethics*, 155–58. May summarizes stage 4 as a "loss of faith in morality's highest values" (157), but this seems too weak. Nietzsche writes, "This is the most extreme form of nihilism: the nothing (the 'meaningless'), eternally!" (*Will to Power*, § 55). What he is describing is not just the absence of moral value, but the absence of *all* value and meaning: "It now seems as if there were no meaning at all in existence [*gar keinen Sinn im Dasein*], as if everything were in vain" (§ 55). But of course there is also a philosophy of hope in Nietzsche. The coming catastrophe of nihilism is not the last stage of history, but something people must work through in order to reach new values. Eventually, "a countermovement finds expression . . . a movement that in some future will take the place of this perfect nihilism" (preface, § 4).

20. Todorov, *Hope and Memory*, 5.

21. Rorty, *Philosophy and Social Hope*, 232. Similarly, Studs Terkel begins his *Hope Dies Last* with the following observation: "As we enter the new millennium, hope appears to be an American attribute that has vanished for many, no matter what their class or condition in life. The official world has never been more

arrogantly imposed. Passivity, in the face of such a bold, unabashed show of power from above, appears to be the order of the day" (xv). Marcel's main work on hope is *Homo Viator*. For Bloch, see his gargantuan epic, *The Principle of Hope*. Given the centrality of hope in both Kant's and Marcel's work, Bloch's claim that the theme of hope was "as unexplored as the Antarctic" (6) in philosophy before the appearance of his own book is an exaggeration. The most extensive scholarly account of philosophies of hope with which I am familiar is Schumacher, *A Philosophy of Hope: Josef Pieper and the Contemporary Debate on Hope*. As the subtitle indicates, it is primarily an account of the German Catholic philosopher Josef Pieper's work on hope. But Schumacher succeeds well in setting Pieper's view of hope "into dialogue with other contemporary understandings" (3; cf. 5), as well as in analyzing and evaluating these other philosophies of hope.

22. Nietzsche, *The Will to Power*, § 55.

23. Rawls also invokes a version of the possibility argument at the end of *The Law of Peoples* when he states, "The idea of realistic utopia reconciles us to our social world by showing us that a reasonably just constitutional democracy existing as a member of a reasonably just Society of Peoples is *possible*. It establishes that such a world can exist somewhere at some time, but not that it must be, or will be" (127).

24. For a more detailed discussion of these topics to which I am indebted, see Bielefeldt, "Traces of Purposiveness in Nature and History," in *Symbolic Representation*, 117–50.

25. *The Conflict of the Faculties* was first published in 1798, but the passages I have cited from it were probably written in 1795—after the French Reign of Terror (1793–94). Jefferson too remained firm in his support of the French Revolution, declaring in a letter to Elbridge Gerry of January 26, 1799, "I was a sincere well-wisher to the success of the French Revolution, and still wish it may end in the establishment of a free & well-ordered republic" (*Writings*, 1057).

26. Hölderlin, *Werke*, 4: 133.

27. Paine, *The Rights of Man*, in *The Thomas Paine Reader*, 259.

28. Hegel, *Vorlesungen über die Philosophie der Weltgeschichte*, 63. For similar Kantian criticisms of Hegel, see Bielefeldt, *Symbolic Representation*, 127–28.

29. For Bloch, the highest good also symbolizes a totalizing or bringing together of our hopes: "Every hope implies the highest good, bliss let loose such as there has not yet been before" (*The Principle of Hope*, 108). But he rejects the transcendent, other-worldly connotations of Kant's highest good: "Kant ... presented the venerable idea of the highest good and put it in the place where for the sailor the Pole Star stands" (1321). In its place Bloch substitutes a completely immanent, this-worldly highest good: "That which is meant by the highest good, formerly called God, then the kingdom of God, and which is finally the realm of freedom, constitutes not only the purpose-ideal of human history but also the metaphysical latency problem of nature" (1324; cf. 1196).

30. L. W. Beck, *A Commentary on Kant's Critique of Practical Reason*, 244. Earlier versions of Beck's argument were made by Hermann Cohen and Arthur Schopenhauer, among others. For discussion and references, see Louden, "Making the World Moral: The Highest Good," in *Kant's Impure Ethics*, 161–64, esp. n. 43.

31. Guyer, "From a Practical Point of View: Kant's Conception of a Postulate of Pure Practical Reason," in *Kant on Freedom, Law, and Happiness*, 340. For other attempts to link the highest good with the kingdom of ends, see Bielefeldt, *Symbolic Representation*, 78–81, along with his references at n. 33. However, as Frederick Beiser correctly points out in a recent discussion, one problem with this proposal is that "the highest good involves a principle of *distributive justice* not even implicit within the kingdom of ends" ("Moral Faith and the Highest Good," 605).

32. For Kant, of course, all genuine moral duties are categorical and universally binding. As he remarks in the preface to the *Groundwork*, "Everyone must admit that a law, if it is to hold morally, . . . must carry with it absolute necessity; that, for example, the command 'thou shalt not lie' does not hold only for human beings, as if other rational beings did not have to heed it, and so with all other moral laws properly so called" (4: 389). But the gaps between this philosophical conviction and actual practice remain huge. Also, the sheer size and makeup of the highest good as a totality of all ends of pure practical reason create additional problems. So many different (and difficult) projects come under its umbrella, regarding which individuals need to use their own discretion and judgment in deciding which particular ones to commit themselves to, that it is inevitable that insufficient numbers of people will be working for the realization of some (if not all) of them.

33. Beiser's "Moral Faith and the Highest Good" is the best recent discussion of this argument with which I am familiar. See esp. 604–7. To a large extent, he is arguing against contemporary Anglophone philosophers who defend "a completely *secular* and *immanent* conception of the highest good, according to which it is simply a goal of human striving that need not involve the beliefs in the existence of God and immortality" (589). As we saw earlier, Marxist readings of Kant's highest good such as Bloch's also defend a secular and immanent conception. For an approach that puts even more weight on the religious dimension, see Hare, *The Moral Gap*.

34. Franklin, *Poor Richard's Almanack, 1736*, in *Autobiography, Poor Richard, and Later Writings*, 461.

35. Neiman, *Evil in Modern Thought*, 239. See also her references in n. 1. Emmanuel Levinas, for instance, in "Useless Suffering," writes: "The disproportion between suffering and every theodicy was shown at Auschwitz with a glaring, obvious clarity. Its possibility puts into question the multi-millennial traditional faith. Did not the word of Nietzsche on the death of God take on, in the extermination camps, the signification of a quasi-empirical fact?" (377).

36. Cassirer, *The Philosophy of the Enlightenment*, xi–xii.

Bibliography

Ackerman, Bruce, and James S. Fishkin. *Deliberation Day*. New Haven: Yale University Press, 2004.

Adams, John. *Correspondence between John Adams and Mercy Warren*. Edited by Charles F. Adams. Collections of the Massachusetts Historical Society, 1878; reprint ed., New York: Arno Press, 1972.

Adams, Robert Merrihew. "Reading the Silences, Questioning the Terms: A Response to the Focus on Eighteenth-Century Ethics." *Journal of Religious Ethics* 28 (2000): 281–84.

Addison, Joseph. "The Royal Exchange." In *The Portable Enlightenment Reader*, ed. Isaac Kramnick, 480–83. New York: Penguin, 1995.

Allison, Henry E. *Lessing and the Enlightenment: His Philosophy of Religion*. Ann Arbor: University of Michigan Press, 1966.

Améry, Jean. *Radical Humanism: Selected Essays*. Edited and translated by Sidney Rosenfield and Stella P. Rosenfield. Bloomington: Indiana University Press, 1984.

Ammerman, Nancy T. "North American Protestant Fundamentalism." In *Fundamentalisms Observed*, ed. Martin E. Marty and R. Scott Appleby, 1–65. Chicago: University of Chicago Press, 1991.

Anon. *Geography for Youth, or, A Plain and Easy Introduction to the Science of Geography for the Use of Young Gentlemen and Ladies: Containing an Accurate description of the Several Parts of the Known World.* 4th ed. London: W. Lowndes, 1790.

Anrich, Ernst, ed. *Die Idee der deutschen Universität: Die fünf Grundschriften aus der Zeit ihrer Neubegründung durch klassischen Idealismus und romantischen Realismus.* Darmstadt: Wissenschaftliche Buchgesellschaft, 1956.

Appleby, Joyce. *Liberalism and Republicanism in the Historical Imagination.* Berkeley: University of California Press, 1982.

Arendt, Hannah. *On Revolution.* New York: Viking, 1963.

Armstrong, Karen. *The Battle for God: A History of Fundamentalism.* New York: Ballantine Books, 2001.

Bahr, Ehrhard, ed. *Was ist Aufklärung? Thesen und Definitionen.* Stuttgart: Reclam, 1974.

Bairoch, Paul. *Economics and World History: Myths and Paradoxes.* Chicago: University of Chicago Press, 1993.

Bairoch, Paul, and Maurice Levy-Leboyer, eds. *Disparities in Economic Development Since the Industrial Revolution.* New York: St. Martin's, 1981.

Baker, Keith Michael. *Condorcet: From Natural Philosophy to Social Mathematics.* Chicago: University of Chicago Press, 1975.

——. "On Condorcet's 'Sketch.' " *Daedalus* 133 (2004): 56–64.

Balch, Thomas Willing. *Émeric Crucé.* Philadelphia: Allen, Lane & Scott, 1900.

Barber, Benjamin R. *Jihad vs. McWorld: How Globalism and Tribalism Are Reshaping the World.* New York: Ballantine Books, 1995.

Barnard, F. M. *Herder's Social and Political Thought.* Oxford: Clarendon Press, 1965.

Barrett, David B., George T. Kurian, and Todd M. Johnson, eds. *World Christian Encyclopedia.* 2nd ed. New York: Oxford University Press, 2001.

Basedow, Johann Bernhard. *Ausgewählte pädagogische Schriften.* Edited by Albert Reble. Paderborn: Schöningh, 1965.

Bauman, Zygmunt. *Globalization: The Human Consequences.* New York: Columbia University Press, 1998.

Baynes, Kenneth. "Communitarian and Cosmopolitan Challenges to Kant's Concept of World Peace." In *Perpetual Peace: Essays on Kant's Cosmopolitan Ideal,* ed. James Bohman and Matthias Lutz-Bachmann, 219–34. Cambridge, MA: MIT Press, 1997.

Beck, Lewis White. *A Commentary on Kant's Critique of Practical Reason.* Chicago: University of Chicago Press, 1960.

Beck, Ulrich. *The Cosmopolitan Vision.* Translated by Ciarin Cronin. Malden, MA: Polity Press, 2006.

Becker, Carl L. *The Heavenly City of the Eighteenth-Century Philosophers.* New Haven: Yale University Press, 1932.

Beiner, Ronald, ed., *Theorizing Nationalism.* Albany: State University of New York Press, 1999.

Beiser, Frederick C., ed. *The Early Political Writings of the German Romantics.* New York: Cambridge University Press, 1996.

———. *Enlightenment, Revolution, and Romanticism: The Genesis of German Political Thought, 1790–1800.* Cambridge, MA: Harvard University Press, 1992.

———. "Moral Faith and the Highest Good." In *The Cambridge Companion to Kant and Modern Philosophy,* ed. Paul Guyer, 588–629. New York: Cambridge University Press, 2006.

———. "A Romantic Education: The Concept of *Bildung* in Early German Romanticism." In *Philosophers on Education,* ed. Amélie Oksenberg Rorty, 284–99. New York: Routledge, 1998.

———. "Romanticism." In *A Companion to the Philosophy of Education,* ed. Randall Curren, 130–42. Malden, MA: Blackwell, 2003.

———. *The Sovereignty of Reason: The Defense of Rationality in the Early English Enlightenment.* Princeton: Princeton University Press, 1996.

Beitz, Charles R. "Human Rights as a Common Concern." *American Political Science Review* 95 (2001): 269–82.

Bell, David A. *The Cult of the Nation in France: Inventing Nationalism, 1680–1800.* Cambridge, MA: Harvard University Press, 2001.

Benn, S. I., and R. S. Peters. *The Principles of Political Thought.* New York: Free Press, 1965.

Bentham, Jeremy. *A Bentham Reader.* Edited by Mary Peter Mack. New York: Pegasus, 1969.

———. *Colonies, Commerce, and Constitutional Law.* Edited by Philip Schofeld. Oxford: Clarendon Press, 1995.

———. *An Introduction to the Principles of Morals and Legislation.* Edited by J. H. Burns and H. L. A. Hart. Oxford: Clarendon Press, 1996.

———. *A Plan for an Universal and Perpetual Peace.* Introduction by C. John Colombos. London: Peace Book Company, 1939.

———. *The Works of Jeremy Bentham.* Edited by John Bowring. New York: Russell & Russell, 1962.

Bergk, Johann Adam. "Does Enlightenment Cause Revolutions?" In *What Is Enlightenment? Eighteenth-Century Answers and Twentieth-Century Questions,* ed. James Schmidt, 225–31. Berkeley: University of California Press, 1996.

———. "Ueber die Einschränkung der Freiheit zu studieren durch den Staat." *Monatsschrift für Deutsche; Zur Veredlung der Kenntnisse, zur Bildung des Geschmacks, und zu froher Unterhaltung* 1 (1801): 3–16.

Berlin, Isaiah. *The Magus of the North: J. G. Hamann and the Origins of Modern Irrationalism.* London: John Murray, 1993.

———. *Vico and Herder: Two Studies in the History of Ideas.* New York: Viking, 1976.

Bernasconi, Robert, and Tommy L. Lott, eds. *The Idea of Race.* Indianapolis: Hackett, 2000.

Berry, Christopher J. "Adam Smith and the Virtues of Commerce." In *Virtue: Nomos XXXIV,* ed. John W. Chapman and William A. Galston, 69–88. New York: New York University Press, 1992.

Best, Geoffrey. *Humanity in Warfare.* New York: Columbia University Press, 1980.

Bhagwati, Jagdish N. *In Defense of Globalization*. New York: Oxford University Press, 2004.

Bielefeldt, Heiner. *Symbolic Representation in Kant's Practical Philosophy*. Cambridge, UK: Cambridge University Press, 2003.

———. "'Western' versus 'Islamic' Human Rights Conceptions? A Critique of Cultural Essentialism in the Discussion of Human Rights." *Political Theory* 28 (2000): 90–121.

Black, John. *A Dictionary of Economics*. 2nd ed. New York: Oxford University Press, 2002.

Bloch, Ernst. *The Principle of Hope*. 3 vols. Translated by Neville Plaice, Stephen Plaice, and Paul Knight. Cambridge, MA: MIT Press, 1986.

Bobbio, Norberto. *The Future of Democracy: A Defence of the Rules of the Game*. Introduction by Richard Bellamy. Translated by Roger Griffin. Minneapolis: University of Minnesota Press, 1987.

———. *Thomas Hobbes and the Natural Law Tradition*. Translated by Daniela Gobetti. Chicago: University of Chicago Press, 1993.

Bohman, James, and Matthias Lutz-Bachmann, eds. *Perpetual Peace: Essays on Kant's Cosmopolitan Ideal*. Cambridge, MA: MIT Press, 1995.

Bok, Sisela. "Golden Rule." In *Oxford Companion to Philosophy*, ed. Ted Honderich, 321–22. New York: Oxford University Press, 1995.

Bordo, Michael D., Alan M. Taylor, and Jeffrey G. Williamson, eds. *Globalization in Historical Perspective*. Chicago: University of Chicago Press, 2003.

Boswell, James. *The Life of Samuel Johnson*. Abridged, with an introduction by Bergen Evans. New York: The Modern Library, 1952.

Bourguignon, François, and Christian Morrisson. "Inequality among World Citizens." *American Economic Review* 92 (2002): 727–44.

Bradshaw, York W., and Michael Wallace. *Global Inequalities*. Thousand Oaks, CA: Pine Forge Press, 1996.

Brann, Eva T. H. "Jeffersonian Ambivalences." In *Philosophers on Education: New Historical Perspectives*, ed. Amélie Oksenberg Rorty, 273–83. New York: Routledge, 1998.

Brockliss, Laurence. "Curricula." In *A History of the University in Europe*. General Editor, Walter Rüegg. Vol. 2, *Universities in Modern Europe (1500–1800)*, ed. Hilde de Ridder-Symoens, 565–620. New York: Cambridge University Press, 1996.

———. "Humboldt's Rift: What Was—and Is—a University For?" *TLS* 5332 (June 10, 2005): 3.

Bronner, Stephen Eric. *Reclaiming the Enlightenment: Toward a Politics of Radical Engagement*. New York: Columbia University Press, 2004.

Brooks Gruver, Rebecca. *American Nationalism 1783–1830: A Self-Portrait*. New York: G. P. Putnam's Sons, 1970.

Brown, Bartram S. "The Statute of the ICC: Past, Present, and Future." In *The United States and the International Criminal Court*, ed. Sarah B. Sewall and Carl Kaysen, 61–84. Lanham, MD: Rowman & Littlefield, 2000.

Brown, Chris, Terry Nardin, and Nicholas Renegger, eds. *International Relations in Political Thought: Texts from the Ancient Greeks to the First World War.* New York: Cambridge University Press, 2002.

Brown, Michael E., Sean M. Lynn-Jones, and Steven E. Miller, eds. *Debating the Democratic Peace.* Cambridge, MA: MIT Press, 1996.

Brownlie, Ian. *Principles of Public International Law.* 4th ed. New York: Oxford University Press, 1990.

Brownlie, Ian, and Guy S. Goodwin-Gill, eds. *Basic Documents on Human Rights.* 4th ed. New York: Oxford University Press, 2002.

Bruford, W. H. *Germany in the Eighteenth Century: The Social Background of the Literary Revival.* New York: Cambridge University Press, 1965.

Buchanan, Allen, and Margaret Moore, eds. *States, Nations, and Borders: The Ethics of Making Boundaries.* New York: Cambridge University Press, 2003.

Bull, Hedley. "The Grotian Conception of International Society." In *Diplomatic Investigations: Essays in the Theory of International Politics,* ed. Herbert Butterfield and Martin Wight, 51–73. Cambridge, MA: Harvard University Press, 1966.

Bull, Hedley, Benedict Kingsbury, and Adam Roberts, eds. *Hugo Grotius and International Relations.* Oxford: Clarendon Press, 1990.

Butts, R. Freeman, and Lawrence A. Cremin. *A History of Education in American Culture.* New York: Rinehart and Winston, 1953.

Byrne, James M. *Religion and the Enlightenment: From Descartes to Kant.* Louisville, KY: Westminster John Knox Press, 1997.

Calhoun, Craig, ed. *Habermas and the Public Sphere.* Cambridge, MA: MIT Press, 1992.

Cassirer, Ernst. *The Philosophy of the Enlightenment.* Translated by Fritz C. A. Koelln and James P. Pettegrove. Princeton: Princeton University Press, 1951.

Cavallar, Georg. *The Rights of Strangers: Theories of International Hospitality, the Global Community, and Political Justice Since Vitoria.* Aldershot, UK: Ashgate, 2002.

Central Intelligence Agency. *The World Fact Book 2002.* Washington, DC: Office of Public Affairs, 2002.

Cheah, Pheng, and Bruce Robbins, eds. *Cosmopolitics: Thinking and Feeling beyond the Nation.* Minneapolis: University of Minnesota Press, 1998.

Chisick, Harvey. *The Limits of Reform: Attitudes toward the Enlightenment of the Lower Classes in Eighteenth-Century France.* Princeton: Princeton University Press, 1981.

Ciafardone, Raffaele, ed. *Die Philosophie der deutschen Aufklärung: Texte und Darstellung.* Translated by Norbert Hinske and Rainer Specht. Stuttgart: Reclam, 1990.

Cioran, E. M. *History and Utopia.* Translated by Richard Howard. Chicago: University of Chicago Press, 1998.

Clark, Grenville, and Louis B. Sohn. *World Peace through World Law: Two Alternative Plans.* 3rd ed. Cambridge, MA: Harvard University Press, 1966.

Clark, Henry C., ed. *Commerce, Culture, and Liberty: Readings on Capitalism before Adam Smith.* Indianapolis: Liberty Fund, 2003.

Clark, William. *Academic Charisma and the Origins of the Research University.* Chicago: University of Chicago Press, 2006.

Clarke, Stanley G., and Evan Simpson, eds. *Anti-Theory in Ethics and Moral Conservatism*. Albany: State University of New York Press, 1989.

Clausewitz, Carl von. *On War*. Edited and translated by Michael Howard and Peter Paret. Princeton: Princeton University Press, 1976.

Coatsworth, John H. "Notes on the Comparative Economic History of Latin America and the United States." In *Development and Underdevelopment in America: Contrasts of Economic Growth in North America and Latin America in Historical Perspective*, ed. Walker L. Bernecker and Hans Werner Tobler, 10–30. Berlin: Walter de Gruyter, 1993.

Cobban, Alfred. *In Search of Humanity: The Role of the Enlightenment in Modern History*. New York: George Braziller, 1960.

———. *Rousseau and the Modern State*. 2nd ed. Hamden, CT: Archon Books, 1964.

Cobden, Richard. *Speeches on Questions of Public Policy*. Edited by John Bright and James E. Thorold Rogers. London: Macmillan, 1878. Reprinted in *Liberalism: Its Meaning and History*, ed J. Salwyn Schapiro, 144. Princeton: Van Nostrand, 1958.

Cohen, Hermann. "Address to the World Congress for Free Christianity and Religious Progress," July 1913, Paris (unpublished speech, cited in Ernst Cassirer, "Herman Cohen, 1842–1918," *Social Research* 10 [1943]: 219–32).

Cohen, Joshua. "Minimalism about Human Rights: The Most We Can Hope For?" *Ethics@Harvard.edu* (Spring 2003): 2.

Cohen, Sol, ed. *Education in the United States: A Documentary History*. New York: Random House, 1974.

Collins, Randall. *The Sociology of Philosophies: A Global Theory of Intellectual Change*. Cambridge, MA: Harvard University Press, 1998.

Condorcet, Marie Jean Antoine Nicolas Caritat, Marquis de. *The Nature and Purpose of Public Instruction*. In *Selected Writings*, ed. Keith Michael Baker, 105–42. Indianapolis: Bobbs-Merrill, 1976.

———. *Selected Writings*. Edited by Keith Michael Baker. Indianapolis: Bobbs-Merrill, 1976.

Connolly, William E. *Why I Am Not a Secularist*. Minneapolis: University of Minnesota Press, 1999.

Conway, S. "Bentham on War and Peace." In *Bentham: Critical Assessments*, ed. Bhiku Pareku, 3: 966–85. New York: Routledge, 1993.

Cooper, John Milton, Jr.. *Breaking the Heart of the World: Woodrow Wilson and the Fight for the League of Nations*. New York: Cambridge University Press, 2001.

Cooper, Sandi E., ed. *Peace Projects of the Eighteenth Century*. New York: Garland, 1974.

Cranston, Maurice. "Human Rights, Real and Supposed." In *The Philosophy of Human Rights*, ed. Patrick Hayden, 163–73. St. Paul, MN: Paragon Press, 2001.

Cremin, Lawrence A. *Traditions of American Education*. New York: Basic Books, 1977.

Crisp, Roger, and Michael Slote, eds. *Virtue Ethics*. New York: Oxford University Press, 1997.

Crocker, Chester A. "Engaging Failed States." *Foreign Affairs* 82 (2003): 32–45.

Crocker, Lester G., ed. *The Age of Enlightenment*. New York: Harper & Row, 1969.

Crucé, Émeric. *The New Cyneas of Émeric Crucé*. Edited and translated by Thomas Willing Balch. Philadelphia: Allen, Lane & Scott, 1909.

Curren, Randall R. *Aristotle on the Necessity of Public Education*. Lanham, MD: Rowman & Littlefield, 2000.

Darnton, Robert. *George Washington's False Teeth: An Unconventional Guide to the Eighteenth Century*. New York: Norton, 2003.

Daston, L. "The Ideal and Reality of the Republic of Letters in the Enlightenment." *Science in Context* 4 (1991): 367–86.

De Greiff, Pablo, and Ciaran Cronin, eds. *Global Justice and Transnational Politics*. Cambridge, MA: MIT Press, 2002.

Demko, George J., and William B. Wood, eds. *Reordering the World: Geopolitical Perspectives on the 21st Century*. Boulder, CO: Westview Press, 1999.

d'Entrèves, A. P. *Natural Law: An Introduction to Legal Philosophy*. 2nd rev. ed. London: Hutchinson University Library, 1970.

Dewey, John. *A Common Faith*. New Haven: Yale University Press, 1934.

Diamond, Larry. *Developing Democracy: Toward Consolidation*. Baltimore: Johns Hopkins University Press, 1999.

Dictionary of the History of Ideas. Ed. Philip P. Wiener. New York: Charles Scribner's Sons, 1968.

Diderot, Denis. *The Encyclopedia: Selections*. Edited and translated by Stephen J. Gendzier. New York: Harper Torchbooks, 1967.

———. *Political Writings*. Edited by John Hope Mason and Robert Wokler. New York: Cambridge University Press, 1992.

Doyle, Michael. "Kant, Liberal Legacies, and Foreign Affairs." Part 1. *Philosophy and Public Affairs* 12 (1983): 205–54.

———. *Ways of War and Peace: Realism, Liberalism, and Socialism*. New York: Norton, 1997.

Dunn, John. *Democracy: A History*. New York: Atlantic Monthly Press, 2005.

Dupré, Louis. *The Enlightenment and the Intellectual Foundations of Modern Culture*. New Haven: Yale University Press, 2004.

Eells, Walter Crosby. *Baccalaureate Degrees Conferred by American Colleges in the 17th and 18th Centuries*. Washington, DC: U.S. Department of Health, Education, and Welfare, 1958.

———. *Degrees in Higher Education*. Washington, DC: Center for Applied Research in Education, 1963.

Eliade, Mircea. *The Sacred and the Profane*. Translated by W. Trask. New York: Harper & Row, 1961.

Encyclopedia of the Enlightenment. Edited by Alan Charles Kors. New York: Oxford University Press, 2003.

Encyclopedia of Religion. Edited by Mircea Eliade. New York: Macmillan, 1987.

Engelbrecht, H. C. *Johann Gottlieb Fichte: A Study of His Political Writings with Special Reference to His Nationalism*. New York: Columbia University Press, 1933; reprint ed., New York: AMS Press, 1968.

Engerman, Stanley L., and Kenneth L. Sokoloff. "Factor Endowments, Institutions, and Differential Paths of Growth among New World Economies: A View from Economic Historians of the United States." In *How Latin America Fell Behind: Essays on the Economic Histories of Brazil and Mexico, 1800–1914*, ed. Stephen Haber, 260–304. Stanford: Stanford University Press, 1997.

Ergang, Robert Reinhold. *Herder and the Foundations of German Nationalism*. New York: Columbia University Press, 1931; reprint ed., New York: Octagon Books, 1966.

Fallon, Daniel. *The German University: A Heroic Ideal in Conflict with the Modern World*. Boulder: Colorado Associated University Press, 1980.

Featherstone, Mike, ed. *Global Culture: Nationalism, Globalization and Modernity*. Thousand Oaks, CA: Sage, 1990.

Fichte, Johann Gottlieb. *Addresses to the German Nation*. Edited by George Armstrong Kelly. New York: Harper Torchbooks, 1968.

———. *Die Grundzüge des gegenwärtigen Zeitalters*. Edited by Alwin Diemer. Hamburg: Felix Meiner, 1978.

———. *Early Philosophical Writings*. Translated and edited by Daniel Breazeale. Ithaca, NY: Cornell University Press, 1988.

———. *The Vocation of Man*. Edited by Roderick Chisholm. Indianapolis: Bobbs-Merrill, 1956.

"Five Arab Leaders Condemn Terror, Hear Bush Appeal." *Portland Press Herald*, 4 June 2003, 4A.

Fleischacker, Samuel. "Adam Smith's Reception among the American Founders, 1776–1790." *William and Mary Quarterly* 59 (2002): 897–924.

———. *On Adam Smith's "Wealth of Nations": A Philosophical Companion*. Princeton: Princeton University Press, 2004.

———. *A Third Concept of Liberty: Judgment and Freedom in Kant and Adam Smith*. Princeton: Princeton University Press, 1999.

———. "Values behind the Market: Kant's Response to the *Wealth of Nations*." *History of Political Thought* 17 (1996): 379–407.

Fontana, Biancamaria, ed. *The Invention of the Modern Republic*. New York: Cambridge University Press, 1994.

Forsyth, Murray. "The Tradition of International Law." In *Traditions of International Ethics*, ed. Terry Nardin and David R. Mappel, 23–41. New York: Cambridge University Press, 1992.

Foucault, Michel. *Discipline and Punish*. Translated by Alan Sheridan. New York: Vintage Books, 1979.

———. "What Is Enlightenment?" In *The Foucault Reader*, ed. Paul Rabinow, 32–50. New York: Pantheon Books, 1984.

Franklin, Benjamin. *Autobiography, Poor Richard, and Later Writings*. New York: Library of America, 1997.

———. *Silence Dogood, The Busy-Body, and Early Writings*. New York: Library of America, 2002.

———. *The Writings of Benjamin Franklin*. Edited by Albert Henry Smyth. New York: Macmillan, 1907.

Friedman, Milton. *Capitalism and Freedom*. Chicago: University of Chicago Press, 1962.

Friedman, Thomas L. *The Lexus and the Olive Tree: Understanding Globalization*. New York: Anchor Books, 2000.

Frierson, Patrick. *Freedom and Anthropology in Kant's Moral Philosophy*. New York: Cambridge University Press, 2003.

Galston, William A. "What Is Living and What Is Dead in Kant's Practical Philosophy?" In *Kant and Political Philosophy: The Contemporary Legacy*, ed. Ronald Beiner and William James Booth, 207–23. New Haven: Yale University Press, 1993.

Gans, Chaim. *The Limits of Nationalism*. New York: Cambridge University Press, 2003.

Gaskin, J. C. A. *Hume's Philosophy of Religion*. 2nd ed. New York: Macmillan, 1988.

Gastil, John, and Peter Levine, eds. *The Deliberative Democracy Handbook: Strategies for Effective Civic Engagement in the Twenty-First Century*. San Francisco: Jossey-Bass, 2005.

Gay, Peter, ed. *Deism: An Anthology*. Princeton: Van Nostrand, 1968.

———, ed. *The Enlightenment: A Comprehensive Anthology*. New York: Simon & Schuster, 1973.

———. *The Enlightenment: An Interpretation*. 2 vols. New York: Knopf, 1966–69.

———. "Locke on the Education of Paupers." In *Philosophers on Education: New Historical Perspectives*, ed. Amélie Oksenberg Rorty, 190–91. New York: Routledge, 1998.

———. *My German Question: Growing Up in Nazi Berlin*. New Haven: Yale University Press, 1998.

Geertz, Clifford. *Available Light: Anthropological Reflections on Philosophical Topics*. Princeton: Princeton University Press, 2000.

———. "Primordial and Civic Ties." In *Nationalism*, ed. John Hutchinson and Anthony D. Smith, 29–34. New York: Oxford University Press, 1997.

Gelderen, Martin van, and Quentin Skinner, eds. *Republicanism: A Shared European Heritage*. 2 vols. New York: Cambridge University Press, 2002.

George, Robert P., ed. *Natural Law Theory: Contemporary Essays*. Oxford: Clarendon Press, 1992.

Gibson, Alan. "Ancients, Moderns and Americans: The Republican-Liberalism Debate Revisited." *History of Political Thought* 21 (2000): 261–307.

Giddens, Anthony. *The Consequences of Modernity*. Stanford: Stanford University Press, 1990.

Gierke, Otto. *Natural Law and the Theory of Society 1500 to 1800*. Translated by Ernest Barker. New York: Cambridge University Press, 1958.

Glover, Jonathan. "Nations, Identity, and Conflict." In *The Morality of Nationalism*, ed. Robert McKim and Jeff McMahon, 11–30. New York: Oxford University Press, 1997.

Goodrich, Leland M., Edvard Hambro, and Anne Patricia Simons. *Charter of the United Nations: Commentary and Documents*. 3rd rev. ed. New York: Columbia University Press, 1969.

Goodstein, Laurie. "More Religion, but Not the Old-Time Kind." *New York Times*, January 9, 2005, sec. 4, pp. 1, 4.

Gordon, Daniel, ed. *Postmodernism and the Enlightenment: New Perspectives in Eighteenth-Century French Intellectual History.* New York: Routledge, 2001.

Gourevitch, Victor. "The Religious Thought." In *The Cambridge Companion to Rousseau*, ed. Patrick Riley, 193–246. New York: Cambridge University Press, 2001.

Grafton, Anthony. "Polyhistor into *Philolog*: Notes on the Transformation of German Classical Scholarship, 1780–1850." *History of Universities* 3 (1983): 159–92.

Gray, John. *Enlightenment's Wake: Politics and Culture at the Close of the Modern Age.* New York: Routledge, 1995.

Greene, Evarts Boutell. *The Revolutionary Generation 1763–1790.* New York: Macmillan, 1943.

Greenfield, Liah. *Nationalism: Five Roads to Modernity.* Cambridge, MA: Harvard University Press, 1992.

Griffiths, Paul J. *Problems of Religious Diversity.* Malden, MA: Blackwell, 2001.

Griswold, Charles L., Jr. *Adam Smith and the Virtues of Enlightenment.* New York: Cambridge University Press, 1999.

Grotius, Hugo. *The Law of War and Peace.* Translated by Francis W. Kelsey. Oxford: Clarendon Press, 1925; reprint ed., Indianapolis: Bobbs-Merrill, n.d.

———. *The Rights of War and Peace.* 3 vols. Edited and with an Introduction by Richard Tuck. Indianapolis: Liberty Fund, 2005.

Grover, Stephen. Review of *The Interpretation of Religion*, by John Hick. *TLS*, December 22, 1989, p. 1404.

Gurewitsch, Matthew. "An 18th-Century Plea for Tolerance Resounds Today." *New York Times*, October 20, 2002, Arts sec., p. 6.

Gutherie, William. *A New System of Modern Geography, or, A Geographical, Historical, and Commercial Grammar; and Present State of the Several Nations of the World.* 1st American ed. Philadelphia: Matthew Carey, 1794.

Gutting, Gary. *Pragmatic Liberalism and the Critique of Modernity.* New York: Cambridge University Press, 1999.

Guyer, Paul. *Kant on Freedom, Law, and Happiness.* New York: Cambridge University Press, 2000.

Haakonssen, Knud. *Natural Law and Moral Philosophy: From Grotius to the Scottish Enlightenment.* New York: Cambridge University Press, 1996.

Habermas, Jürgen. "Kant's Idea of Perpetual Peace, with the Benefit of Two-Hundred Years' Hindsight." In *Perpetual Peace: Essays on Kant's Cosmopolitan Ideal*, ed. James Bohman and Matthias Lutz-Bachmann, 113–53. Cambridge, MA: MIT Press, 1997.

———. *The Structural Transformation of the Public Sphere: An Inquiry into a Category of Bourgeois Society.* Translated by Thomas Burger. Cambridge, MA: MIT Press, 1989.

Hammerstein, Notker. "Epilogue: The Enlightenment." In *A History of the University in Europe.* General Editor, Walter Rüegg. Vol. 2, *Universities in Early Modern Europe (1500–1800)*, ed. Hilde de Ridder-Symoens, 621–40. New York: Cambridge University Press, 1996.

Hammond, Philip E., ed. *The Sacred in a Secular Age: Toward Revision in the Scientific Study of Religion*. Berkeley: University of California Press, 1985.

Hampson, Norman. *The Enlightenment*. Baltimore: Penguin, 1968.

Hannerz, Ulf. "Cosmopolitans and Locals in World Culture." In *Global Culture: Nationalism, Globalization and Modernity*, ed. Mike Featherstone, 237–51. Thousand Oaks, CA: Sage, 1990.

Hare, John E. *The Moral Gap: Kantian Ethics, Human Limits, and God's Assistance*. Oxford: Clarendon Press, 1996.

Hassner, Pierre. "Rousseau and the Theory and Practice of International Relations." In *The Legacy of Rousseau*, ed. Clifford Orwin and Nathan Tarcov, 200–219. Chicago: University of Chicago Press, 1997.

Hauerwas, Stanley. *With the Grain of the Universe: The Church's Witness and Natural Theology. Being the Gifford Lectures Delivered at the University of St. Andrews in 2001*. Grand Rapids, MI: Brazos Press, 2001.

Hayden, Patrick, ed. *The Philosophy of Human Rights*. St. Paul, MN: Paragon Press, 2001.

Hayek, Friedrich A. *The Road to Serfdom*. Chicago: University of Chicago Press, 1944.

Hegel, Georg Wilhelm Friedrich. *Vorlesungen über die Philosophie der Weltgeschichte: Die Vernunft in der Geschichte*. Edited by Johannes Hoffmeister. Hamburg: Felix Meiner, 1955.

Held, David. *Democracy and the Global Order: From the Modern State to Cosmopolitan Governance*. Stanford: Stanford University Press, 1995.

———. *Models of Democracy*. 2nd ed. Stanford: Stanford University Press, 1996.

Hendel, Charles W. *Jean-Jacques Rousseau: Moralist*. Oxford: Oxford University Press, 1934; reprint ed., New York: Bobbs-Merrill, 1962.

Henig, Ruth, ed. *The League of Nations*. New York: Barnes & Noble, 1973.

Herder, Johann Gottfried. *J. G. Herder on Social and Political Culture*. Translated by F. M. Barnard. New York: Cambridge University Press, 1969.

———. *On World History: An Anthology*. Edited by Hans Adler and Ernest A. Menze. Armonk, NY: M. E. Sharpe, 1997.

———. *Philosophical Writings*. Edited by Michael N. Forster. New York: Cambridge University Press, 2002.

Herman, Barbara. "Training to Autonomy: Kant and the Question of Moral Education." In *Philosophers on Education*, ed. Amélie Oksenberg Rorty, 255–72. New York: Routledge, 1998.

Hick, John. "The Epistemological Challenge of Religious Pluralism." *Faith and Philosophy* 14 (1997): 277–86.

———. *An Interpretation of Religion: Human Responses to the Transcendent*. New Haven: Yale University Press, 1989.

Hick, John, and Paul F. Knitter, eds. *The Myth of Christian Uniqueness: Toward a Pluralistic Theology of Religions*. Maryknoll, NY: Orbis Books, 1987.

Hilton, Matthew. "Review Article: Class, Consumption and the Public Sphere." *Journal of Contemporary History* 35 (2000): 655–66.

Himmelfarb, Gertrude. *The Roads to Modernity: The British, French, and American Enlightenments*. New York: Knopf, 2004.

Hinsley, F. H. *Power and the Pursuit of Peace: Theory and Practice in the History of Relations between States*. London: Cambridge University Press, 1963.

Hirschman, Albert O. *The Passions and the Interests: Political Arguments for Capitalism before Its Triumph*. Princeton: Princeton University Press, 1997.

Hobbes, Thomas. *Leviathan, or, The Matter, Forme and Power of a Commonwealth Ecclesiasticall and Civil*. Edited by Michael Oakeshott. Oxford: Basil Blackwell, 1946.

———. *On the Citizen*. Edited by Richard Tuck and Michael Silverthorne. New York: Cambridge University Press, 1988.

Hobsbawm, E. J. *The Age of Capital 1848–1875*. New York: Scribner's, 1975.

———. *Nations and Nationalism Since 1780: Programme, Myth, Reality*. 2nd ed. New York: Cambridge University Press, 1992.

Hochstrasser, T. J. *Natural Law Theories in the Early Enlightenment*. New York: Cambridge University Press, 2000.

Hocking, William Ernest. *Living Religions and a World Faith*. New York: Macmillan, 1940.

Hof, Ulrich Im. *The Enlightenment*. Translated by William E. Yuill. Cambridge, UK: Blackwell, 1994.

Höffe, Otfried, ed. *Immanuel Kant: Zum ewigen Frieden*. Berlin: Akademi Verlag, 1995.

Hoffman, Stanley. *The State of War: Essays on the Theory and Practice of International Politics*. New York: Praeger, 1965.

Hoge, Warren. "U.N. Report Urges Big Changes: Security Council Would Expand." *New York Times*, December 1, 2004, p. A1.

Hölderlin, Friedrich. *Werke: Geschenkausgabe in vier Bänden*. Edited by Friedrich Beißner and Jochen Schmidt. Frankfurt am Main: Insel Verlag, 1986.

Hont, Istvan. *Jealousy of Trade: International Competition and the Nation-State in Historical Perspective*. Cambridge, MA: Harvard University Press, 2005.

Horkheimer, Max, and Theodor W. Adorno. *Dialectic of Enlightenment: Philosophical Fragments*. Edited by Gunzelin Schmid Noerr. Translated by Edmund Jephcott. Stanford: Stanford University Press, 2002.

Houston, R. A. *Literacy in Early Modern Europe: Culture and Education 1500–1800*. New York: Longman, 1988.

Howard, Michael. *The Invention of Peace: Reflections on War and International Order*. New Haven: Yale University Press, 2000.

Humboldt, Wilhelm von. *Gesammelte Schriften*. Edited by Bruno Gebhardt. Berlin: B. Behr's Verlag, 1903.

———. *Humanist without Portfolio: An Anthology of the Writings of Wilhelm von Humboldt*. Translated by Marianne Cowan. Detroit: Wayne State University Press, 1963.

———. *The Limits of State Action*. Edited by J. W. Burrow. New York: Cambridge University Press, 1969; reprint ed., Indianapolis: Liberty Fund, 1993.

Hume, David. *Dialogues Concerning Natural Religion*. Edited by Norman Kemp Smith. 2nd ed. London: Thomas Nelson & Sons, 1947; reprint ed., Indianapolis: Bobbs-Merrill, 1962.

———. *Enquiries Concerning Human Understanding and Concerning the Principles of Morals*. Edited by L. A. Selby-Bigge and P. H. Nidditch. 3rd rev. ed. Oxford: Clarendon Press, 1975.

——. *An Essay Concerning Human Understanding.* Edited by Eric Steinberg. Indianapolis: Hackett, 1977.

——. *Essays Moral, Political, and Literary.* Edited by Eugene F. Miller. Indianapolis: Liberty Fund, 1985.

——. *The History of England: From the Invasion of Julius Caesar to the Revolution in 1688.* 6 vols. Edited by William B. Todd. Indianapolis: Liberty Fund, 1983.

——. *A Treatise of Human Nature.* Edited by L. A. Selby-Bigge and P. H. Nidditch. 2nd ed. Oxford: Clarendon Press, 1978.

——. *Writings on Economics.* Edited by Eugene Rotwein. Madison: University of Wisconsin Press, 1955.

Hunter, Derek. *World Citizenship and Government: Cosmopolitan Ideas in the History of Western Thought.* New York: Macmillan, 1996.

Hunter, Ian. *Rival Enlightenments: Civil and Metaphysical Philosophy in Early Modern Germany.* New York: Cambridge University Press, 2001.

Huntington, Samuel P. *The Clash of Civilizations and the Remaking of the World Order.* New York: Simon & Schuster, 1996.

——. *The Third Wave: Democratization in the Late Twentieth Century.* Norman: University of Oklahoma Press, 1991.

Hyland, Paul, with Olga Gomez and Francesca Greensides, eds. *The Enlightenment: A Sourcebook and Reader.* New York: Routledge, 2003.

Ignatieff, Michael. *Human Rights as Politics and Idolatry.* Edited and introduced by Amy Gutmann. Princeton: Princeton University Press, 2001.

Ishay, Micheline R. *The History of Human Rights: From Ancient Times to the Globalization Era.* Berkeley: University of California Press, 2004.

Israel, Jonathan I. *Radical Enlightenment: Philosophy and the Making of Modernity 1650–1750.* New York: Oxford University Press, 2001.

Jacobson, C. G. "Poverty and War." *Online Journal of Peace and Conflict Resolution* 3 (2000). http://www.trinstitute.org/ojpcr/.

James, William. *The Varieties of Religious Experience: A Study in Human Nature.* New York: Modern Library, n.d.

Janis, Mark W. "Jeremy Bentham and the Fashioning of 'International Law.'" *American Journal of International Law* 78 (1984): 405–18.

Jefferson, Thomas. *The Jefferson Bible: The Life and Morals of Jesus of Nazareth.* Introduction by Forrest Church. Afterword by Jaroslav Pelikan. Boston: Beacon Press, 1989.

——. *Thomas Jefferson on Democracy.* Edited by Saul K. Padover. New York: D. Appleton-Century-Crofts, 1939.

——. *Writings.* New York: Library of America, 1984.

——. *The Writings of Thomas Jefferson.* Edited by H. A. Washington. New York: H. W. Derby, 1861.

——. *The Writings of Thomas Jefferson,* Edited by Andrew A. Lipscomb and Albert Ellery Bergh. Washington, DC: Thomas Jefferson Memorial Association, 1903–4.

Johnson, James Turner. *The Quest for Peace: Three Moral Traditions in Western Cultural History.* Princeton: Princeton University Press, 1987.

Jones, Charles. *Global Justice: Defending Cosmopolitanism.* New York: Oxford University Press, 1999.

Jones, Gareth Stedman. *An End to Poverty? A Historical Debate.* London: Profile, 2005.

Juergensmeyer, Mark. *Terror in the Mind of God: The Global Rise of Religious Violence.* Berkeley: University of California Press, 2000.

Kael, Paul. *European Conquest and the Rights of Indigenous Peoples: The Moral Backwardness of International Society.* New York: Cambridge University Press, 2003.

Kant, Immanuel. *Anthropologie du point de vue pragmatique.* Translated by Michel Foucault. Paris: J. Vrin, 1964.

———. *Anthropology from a Pragmatic Point of View.* Translated and edited by Robert B. Louden. New York: Cambridge University Press, 2006.

———. *Anthropology, History, and Education.* Edited by Günter Zöller and Robert B. Louden. Cambridge, UK: Cambridge University Press, 2007.

———. *The Cambridge Edition of the Works of Immanuel Kant.* General Editors Paul Guyer and Allen W. Wood. Cambridge, UK: Cambridge University Press, 1992–.

———. *The Educational Theory of Immanuel Kant.* Translated and edited by Edward Franklin Buchner. Philadelphia: J. B. Lippincott, 1904–; reprint ed., New York: AMS Press, 1971.

———. *Kants gesammelte Schriften.* Edited by the Royal Prussian (later German) Academy of Sciences. Berlin: Georg Reimer, later Walter de Gruyter, 1900–.

———. *Lectures on Anthropology.* Edited by Allen W. Wood and Robert B. Louden. New York: Cambridge University Press, forthcoming.

Kaufman, Alexander. *Welfare in the Kantian State.* Oxford: Clarendon Press, 1999.

Keane, John. *Global Civil Society?* New York: Cambridge University Press, 2003.

Kedourie, Elie. *Nationalism.* Rev. ed. New York: Praeger, 1960.

Kelly, George Armstrong. *Idealism, Politics and History: Sources of Hegelian Thought.* New York: Cambridge University Press, 1969.

Kelsen, Hans. *Peace through Law.* Chapel Hill: University of North Carolina Press, 1944; reprint ed., New York: Garland, 1973.

Kennedy, Paul. *The Parliament of Man: The Past, Present, and Future of the United Nations.* New York: Random House, 2006.

Kingsbury, Benedict, and Adam Roberts, "Introduction: Grotian Thought in International Relations." In *Hugo Grotius and International Relations,* ed. Hedley Bull, Benedict Kingsbury, and Adam Roberts, 1–64. Oxford: Clarendon Press, 1990.

Kissinger, Henry. "The Pitfalls of Universal Jurisdiction." *Foreign Affairs* 80 (2001): 86–96.

Kitching, Gavin. *Seeking Social Justice through Globalization: Escaping a Nationalist Perspective.* University Park: Pennsylvania State University Press, 2001.

Kleingeld, Pauline. "Kant's Theory of Peace." In *The Cambridge Companion to Kant and Modern Philosophy,* ed. Paul Guyer, 477–504. New York: Cambridge University Press, 2006.

Kohn, Hans. *American Nationalism: An Interpretive Essay.* New York: Collier Books, 1957.

———. *The Idea of Nationalism.* New York: Macmillan, 1944.

———. *Nationalism: Its Meaning and History.* Princeton: D. Van Nostrand, 1955.

———. "The Paradox of Fichte's Nationalism." *Journal of the History of Ideas* 10 (1949): 319–43.

König, René. *Vom Wesen der Deutschen Universität.* Berlin, 1935; reprint ed., Darmstadt: Wissenschaftliche Buchgesellschaft, 1970.

Kramnick, Isaac, ed. *The Portable Enlightenment Reader.* New York: Penguin, 1995.

———. *Republicanism and Bourgeois Radicalism: Political Ideology in Late Eighteenth-Century England and America.* Ithaca, NY: Cornell University Press, 1990.

Krieger, Leonard. *The Politics of Discretion: Pufendorf and the Acceptance of Natural Law.* Chicago: University of Chicago Press, 1965.

Kymlicka, Will. *Liberalism, Community, and Culture.* Oxford: Clarendon Press, 1989.

———. *Multicultural Citizenship: A Liberal Theory of Minority Rights.* Oxford: Clarendon Press, 1995.

La Fontainerie, François de, ed. *French Liberalism and Education in the Eighteenth Century: The Writings of La Chalotais, Turgot, Diderot, and Condorcet on National Education.* New York: McGraw-Hill, 1932.

Landes, David S. *The Wealth and Poverty of Nations: Why Some Are So Rich and Some So Poor.* New York: Norton, 1999.

Langford, Tonya. "Things Fall Apart: State Failure and the Politics of Intervention." *International Studies Review* 1 (1999): 59–79.

Larrimore, Mark, ed. *The Problem of Evil: A Reader.* Malden, MA: Blackwell, 2001.

La Vopa, Anthony J. *Fichte: The Self and the Calling of Philosophy.* New York: Cambridge University Press, 2001.

———. *Grace, Talent, and Merit: Poor Students, Clerical Careers, and Professional Ideology in Eighteenth-Century Germany.* New York: Cambridge University Press, 1988.

Lechner, Frank J., and John Boli, eds. *The Globalization Reader.* 2nd ed. Malden, MA: Blackwell, 2004.

———. *World Culture: Origins and Consequences.* Malden, MA: Blackwell, 2005.

Leibniz, Gottfried Wilhelm von. *Political Writings.* Edited and translated by Patrick Riley. 2nd ed. New York: Cambridge University Press, 1988.

Leith, James A. "Introduction: Unity and Diversity in Education During the Eighteenth Century." *Studies on Voltaire and the Eighteenth Century* 167 (1997): 13–27.

Lessing, Gotthold Ephraim. *Die Erziehung des Menschengeschlechts und andere Schriften.* Stuttgart: Reclam, 1965.

———. *Lessing's Theological Writings.* Translated by Henry Chadwick. Stanford: Stanford University Press, 1957.

———. *Nathan der Weise.* Stuttgart: Reclam, 1978.

Levinas, Emmanuel. "Useless Suffering." In *The Problem of Evil: A Reader,* ed. Mark Larrimore, 371-80. Malden, MA: Blackwell, 2001.

Levy, Jack S. "Domestic Politics and War." In *The Origin and Prevention of Major Wars*, ed. Robert I. Rotberg and Theodore K. Rabb, 79–100. New York: Cambridge University Press, 1989.

Lewis, Bernard. *What Went Wrong? Western Impact and Middle Eastern Response.* New York: Oxford University Press, 2002.

Lichtenberg, Georg Christoph. *The Waste Books.* Translated and with an introduction by R. J. Hollingdale. New York: New York Review of Books, 2000.

Lilla, Mark. "Church Meets State." *New York Times Book Review*, May 15, 2005, p. 39.

———. "Godless Europe." *New York Times Book Review*, April 2, 2006, pp. 14–15.

Locke, John. *A Letter Concerning Toleration.* Introduction by Patrick Romanell. Indianapolis: Bobbs-Merrill, 1950.

———. *Some Thoughts Concerning Education and Of the Conduct of the Understanding.* Edited by Ruth W. Grant and Nathan Tarcov. Indianapolis: Hackett, 1996.

Lodge, Henry Cabot. *The Senate and the League of Nations.* New York: Charles Scribner's Sons, 1925.

Losonsky, Michael. *Enlightenment and Action from Descartes to Kant: Passionate Thought.* New York: Cambridge University Press, 2001.

Louden, Robert B. "Applying Kant's Ethics: The Role of Anthropology." In *A Companion to Kant*, ed. Graham Bird, 350–64. Oxford: Blackwell, 2006.

———. "The Critique of the Morality System." In *Bernard Williams*, ed. Alan Thomas. Cambridge, UK: Cambridge University Press, 2007.

———. *Kant's Impure Ethics: From Rational Beings to Human Beings.* New York: Oxford University Press, 2000.

———. *Morality and Moral Theory: A Reappraisal and Reaffirmation.* New York: Oxford University Press, 1992.

———. "The Second Part of Morals." In *Essays on Kant's Anthropology*, ed. Brian Jacobs and Patrick Kain, 60–84. New York: Cambridge University Press, 2003.

———. " 'What Does Heaven Say?' Christian Wolff and Western Interpretations of Confucian Ethics." In *Confucius and the Analects: New Essays*, ed. Bryan W. Van Norden, 73–93. New York: Oxford University Press, 2002.

Löwith, Karl. *Meaning in History.* Chicago: University of Chicago Press, 1949.

Luard, Evan. *A History of the United Nations.* New York: St. Martin's, 1982.

Lukes, Steven. *The Curious Enlightenment of Professor Caritat: A Comedy of Ideas.* New York: Verso, 1995.

Lund, Roger D., ed. *The Margins of Orthodoxy: Heterodox Writing and Cultural Response, 1660–1750.* New York: Cambridge University Press, 1995.

Macedo, Stephen. "What Self-Governing Peoples Owe to One Another: Universalism, Diversity, and *The Law of Peoples.*" *Fordham Law Review* 72 (2004): 1721–37.

MacIntyre, Alasdair. *After Virtue: A Study in Moral Theory.* 2nd ed. Notre Dame, IN: University of Notre Dame Press, 1984.

MacMillan, Margaret. *Paris 1919: Six Months That Changed the World.* New York: Random House, 2001.

Macpherson, C. B. *The Life and Times of Liberal Democracy.* New York: Oxford University Press, 1977.

Maddison, Angus. "Explaining the Economic Performance of Nations, 1820–1989." In *Convergence of Productivity: Cross-National Studies and Historical Evidence,* ed. William J. Baumol, Richard R. Nelson, and Edward N. Wolff, 20–61. New York: Oxford University Press, 1994.

Mann, Wolfgang. "The Past as Future? Hellenism, the *Gymnasium,* and *Altertums-wissenschaft.*" In *A Companion to the Philosophy of Education,* ed. Randall Curren, 143–60. Malden, MA: Blackwell, 2003.

Mansfield, Edward D., and Jack Snyder. *Electing to Fight: Why Emerging Democracies Go to War.* Cambridge, MA: MIT Press, 2005.

Marcel, Gabriel. *Homo Viator: Introduction to a Metaphysic of Hope.* Translated by Emma Craufurd. New York: Harper Torchbooks, 1962.

Marcuse, Herbert. *One Dimensional Man: Studies in the Ideology of Advanced Industrial Society.* Boston: Beacon Press, 1964.

Margalit, Avishai. "The Moral Psychology of Nationalism." In *The Morality of Nationalism,* ed. Robert McKim and Jeff McMahan, 74–87. New York: Oxford University Press, 1997.

Marsden, George M. *Fundamentalism and American Culture.* New York: Oxford University Press, 1980.

Martin, David. "The Secularization Issue: Prospect and Retrospect." *British Journal of Sociology* 42 (1991): 465–74.

Martyn, David. "Borrowed Fatherland: Nationalism and Language Purism in Fichte's *Addresses to the German Nation.*" *Germanic Review* 72 (1997): 303–16.

Marx, Karl. *Capital: A Critique of Political Economy.* Edited by Frederick Engels. Translated by Samuel Moore and Edward Aveling. 3rd ed. New York: International Publishers, 1967.

Marx, Karl, and Friedrich Engels. *Manifesto of the Communist Party.* In *Basic Writings on Politics and Philosophy,* ed. Lewis S. Feuer, 1–41. Garden City, NJ: Anchor Books, 1959.

Mastnak, Tomaž. "Abbé de Saint-Pierre: European Union and the Turk." *History of Political Thought* 19 (1998): 570–98.

May, Larry. *Crimes against Humanity: A Normative Account.* New York: Cambridge University Press, 2005.

May, Simon. *Nietzsche's Ethics and His War on "Morality."* Oxford: Clarendon Press, 1999.

Mayer, Ann Elizabeth. "The Fundamentalist Impact on Law, Politics, and the Constitution in Iran." In *Fundamentalisms and the State,* ed. Martin E. Marty and R. Scott Appleby, 115–23. Chicago: University of Chicago Press, 1993. Reprinted in *The Globalization Reader,* ed. Frank J. Lechner and John Boli, 340–47. 2nd ed. Malden, MA: Blackwell, 2004.

McCarthy, Thomas. "On Reconciling Cosmopolitan Unity and National Diversity." In *Alternative Modernities,* ed. Dilip Parameshwar Gaonkar, 197–236. Durham, NC: Duke University Press, 2001.

McClelland, Charles E. *State, Society, and University in Germany, 1700–1914.* New York: Cambridge University Press, 1980.

McMahon, Darrin M. *Enemies of the Enlightenment: The French Counter-Enlightenment and the Making of Modernity.* New York: Oxford University Press, 2001.

Meinecke, Friedrich. *Cosmopolitanism and the National State.* Translated by Robert B. Kimber. Princeton: Princeton University Press, 1970.

Melton, James Van Horn. *Absolutism and the Eighteenth-Century Origins of Compulsory Schooling in Prussian Austria.* New York: Cambridge University Press, 1988.

———. *The Rise of the Public in Enlightenment Europe.* New York: Cambridge University Press, 2001.

Mendelssohn, Moses. *Gesammelte Schriften Jubiläumsausgabe.* Edited by F. Bamberger, I. Elbogen, J. Guttmann, and E. Mittwock. Berlin: Akademie, 1929–38; reprint ed., Stuttgart: Frommann, 1971.

Mill, John Stuart. *On Liberty.* Edited by Elizabeth Rapaport. Indianapolis: Hackett, 1978.

Mitchell, B. R. *International Historical Statistics: The Americas 1750–1988.* 2nd ed. New York: Stockton Press, 1993.

Mittelman, James H., ed. *Globalization: Critical Reflections.* Boulder, CO: Lynne Rienner, 1996.

Mondale, Sarah, and Sarah B. Patton, eds. *School: The Story of American Public Education.* Boston: Beacon Press, 2001.

Montaigne, Michel Eyquem de. *The Complete Essays of Montaigne.* Translated by Donald M. Frame. Stanford: Stanford University Press, 1965.

Montesquieu, Charles-Louis de Secondat. *The Persian Letters.* Edited, translated, and introduced by J. Robert Loy. Cleveland: Meridian Books, 1961.

———. *The Spirit of the Laws.* Translated by Thomas Nugent. New York: Hafner, 1949.

Morse, Jedidiah. *The American Geography, or, A View of the Present State of all the Empires, Kingdoms, States, and Republics of the Known World, and of the United States in Particular.* Boston: Isaiah Thomas and Ebenezer T. Andrews, 1796.

Munck, Thomas. *The Enlightenment: A Comparative Social History 1721–1794.* New York: Oxford University Press, 2000.

Munzel, G. Felicitas. "Kant, Hegel, and the Rise of Pedagogical Science." In *A Companion to the Philosophy of Education,* ed. Randall Curren, 113–29. Malden, MA: Blackwell, 2003.

———. "Kant on Moral Education, or 'Enlightenment' and the Liberal Arts." *Review of Metaphysics* 57 (2003): 43–73.

Muthu, Sankar. *Enlightenment against Empire.* Princeton: Princeton University Press, 2003.

Nadler, Stephen. "Review Article: *Radical Enlightenment.*" *British Journal for the History of Philosophy* 10 (2002): 289–94.

Neier, Aryeh. *War Crimes: Brutality, Terror, and the Struggle for Justice.* New York: Times Books, 1998.

Neiman, Susan. *Evil in Modern Thought: An Alternative History of Philosophy.* Princeton: Princeton University Press, 2002.

Newman, John Henry. *The Idea of a University.* Introduction by George N. Shuster. New York: Image Books, 1959.

Niedermeier, Michael. "Campe als Direktor des Dessauer Philanthropins." In *Visionäre Lebensklugheit: Joachim Heinrich Campe in seiner Zeit*, ed. Hanno Schmidt, 45–66. Wiesbaden: Harrassowitz, 1996.

Nietzsche, Friedrich. *The Gay Science.* Edited by Bernard Williams. Translated by Josefine Nauckhoff. Cambridge, UK: Cambridge University Press, 2001.

———. *Twilight of the Idols.* Translated by Richard Polt. Indianapolis: Hackett, 1997.

———. *The Will to Power.* Translated by Walter Kaufmann and R. J. Hollingdale. New York: Vintage Books, 1968.

Norris, Christopher. "What Is Enlightenment? Kant and Foucault." In *The Cambridge Companion to Foucault*, ed. Gary Gutting, 159–96. New York: Cambridge University Press, 1994.

Nussbaum, Charles. *A Concise History of the Law of Nations.* Rev. ed. New York: Macmillan, 1954.

Nussbaum, Felicity, ed. *The Global Eighteenth Century.* Baltimore: Johns Hopkins University Press, 2003.

Nussbaum, Martha C. *Cultivating Humanity: A Classical Defense of Reform in Liberal Education.* Cambridge, MA: Harvard University Press, 1997.

O'Brien, George Dennis. *All the Essential Half-Truths about Higher Education.* Chicago: University of Chicago Press, 1998.

Ogden, Schubert M. *Is There Only One True Religion or Are There Many?* Dallas, TX: Southern Methodist University Press, 1992.

Ohmae, Kenichi. *The End of the Nation State: The Rise of Regional Economies.* New York: Free Press, 1995.

Oneal, John R., and Bruce M. Russett. "The Classical Liberals Were Right: Democracy, Interdependence, and Conflict, 1950–85." *International Studies Quarterly* 41 (1997): 267–94.

Otto, Rudolf. *The Idea of the Holy.* Translated by John W. Harvey. London: Oxford University Press, 1923.

Outka, Gene, and John P. Reeder Jr., eds. *The Many and the One: Religious and Secular Perspectives on Ethical Pluralism in the Modern World.* Princeton: Princeton University Press, 2002.

Outram, Dorinda. *The Enlightenment.* 2nd ed. New York: Cambridge University Press, 2005.

———. *The Enlightenment.* New York: Cambridge University Press, 1995.

The Oxford Classical Dictionary. Edited by N. G. L Hammond and H. H. Scullard. 2nd ed. Oxford: Clarendon Press, 1970.

Paine, Thomas. *Political Writings.* Edited by Bruce Kuklick. New York: Cambridge University Press, 1989.

———. *The Thomas Paine Reader.* Edited by Michael Foot and Isaac Kramnick. New York: Penguin, 1987.

———. *The Writings of Thomas Paine.* Edited by Moncure Daniel Conway. New York, 1902; reprint ed., New York: Burt Franklin, 1969.

Palmer, R. R. *The Improvement of Humanity: Education and the French Revolution.* Princeton: Princeton University Press, 1985.

Palmquist, Stephen R. "Kant's Critical Hermeneutic of Prayer." *Journal of Religion* 77 (1997): 584–604.

Pateman, Carole. *The Problem of Political Obligation: A Critical Analysis of Liberal Theory.* New York: Wiley, 1979.

Paulsen, Friedrich. *German Education Past and Present.* Translated by T. Lorenz. London: T. Fisher Unwin, 1908; reprint ed., New York: AMS Press, 1976.

Penelhum, Terence. "Hume's Criticisms of Natural Theology." In *In Defense of Natural Theology,* ed. James F. Sennett and Douglas Groothuis, 21–41. Downers Grove, IL: InterVarsity Press, 2005.

Penn, William. *An Essay towards the Present and Future Peace of Europe.* Washington, DC: American Peace Society, 1912.

Perkins, Merle L. *The Moral and Political Philosophy of the Abbé de Saint-Pierre.* Paris: Droz, 1959.

Pieterse, Jan Nederveen. *Globalization and Culture: Global Mélange.* Lanham, MD: Rowman & Littlefield, 2004.

Pittock, Murray G. H. "Historiography." In *The Cambridge Companion to the Scottish Enlightenment,* ed. Alexander Broadie, 258–79. New York: Cambridge University Press, 2003.

Plattner, Marc F. "Rousseau and the Origins of Nationalism." In *The Legacy of Rousseau,* ed. Clifford Orwin and Nathan Tarcov, 183–99. Chicago: University of Chicago Press, 1997.

Pocock, J. G. A. *Barbarism and Religion.* 2 vols. New York: Cambridge University Press, 1999.

———. *The Machiavellian Moment: Florentine Political Thought and the Atlantic Republican Tradition.* Princeton: Princeton University Press, 1975.

Pogge, Thomas W., ed. *Global Justice.* Malden, MA: Blackwell, 2001.

———. "Human Rights and Responsibilities." In *Global Justice and Transnational Politics: Essays on the Moral and Political Challenges of Globalization,* ed. Pablo De Greiff and Ciarin Cronin, 151–96. Cambridge, MA: MIT Press, 2002.

———. "Real World Justice." *Journal of Ethics* 9 (2005): 29–53.

———. *World Poverty and Human Rights: Cosmopolitan Responsibilities and Reforms.* Cambridge, MA: Polity, 2002.

Popper, Karl. *The Open Society and Its Enemies.* London: Routledge & Kegan Paul, 1945; reprint ed., New York: Harper & Row, 1963.

Porter, Roy. *The Creation of the Modern World: The Untold Story of the British Enlightenment.* New York: Norton, 2000.

Porter, Roy, and Macula Teach, eds. *The Enlightenment in National Context.* New York: Cambridge University Press, 1981.

Potter, David, David Goldblatt, Margaret Kiloh, and Paul Lewis, eds. *Democratization.* Malden, MA: Polity Press, 1996.

Powell, G. Bingham, Jr. *Contemporary Democracies: Participation, Stability, Violence.* Cambridge, MA: Harvard University Press, 1982.

Pufendorf, Samuel. *On the Law of Nature and Nations*. Translated by C. H. Oldfather and W. A. Oldfather. Oxford: Clarendon Press, 1934; reprint ed., New York: Oceana Publications, 1964.

Putnam, Hilary. *Ethics without Ontology*. Cambridge, MA: Harvard University Press, 2004.

Putnam, Robert D. *Bowling Alone: The Collapse and Revival of American Community*. New York: Simon & Schuster, 2000.

Quick, Robert Herbert. *Essays on Educational Reformers*. New York: Appleton, 1896.

Rachel, Samuel. *Dissertations on the Law of Nature and of Nations*. Translated by John Pawley Bate. Washington, DC: Carnegie Institution, 1916; reprint ed., New York: Oceana Publications, 1964.

Rahe, Paul A. *Republics Ancient and Modern: Classical Republicanism and the American Revolution*. Chapel Hill: University of North Carolina Press, 1992.

Rawls, John. *The Law of Peoples with "The Idea of Public Reason Revisited."* Cambridge, MA: Harvard University Press, 1999.

———. *Political Liberalism*. New York: Columbia University Press, 1993.

———. *A Theory of Justice*. Cambridge, MA: Harvard University Press, 1971.

Riem, Andreas. *On Enlightenment: Is It and Could It Be Dangerous to the State, to Religion, or Dangerous in General? A Word to be Heeded by Princes, Statesmen, and Clergy* (1788). In *What Is Enlightenment? Eighteenth-Century Answers and Twentieth-Century Questions*, ed. James Schmidt, 168–87. Berkeley: University of California Press, 1996.

Ringen, Stein. "Band of Hope: Players from the Past Whose Spirits Should Rule the G8." *TLS*, June 24, 2005, pp. 3–4.

Roberts, Adam, and Benedict Kingsbury, eds. *United Nations, Divided World: The UN's Role in International Relations*. 2nd ed. Oxford: Clarendon Press, 1993.

Robertson, Roland. *Global Theory and Global Culture*. London: Sage, 1992.

Roosevelt, Grace G. *Reading Rousseau in the Nuclear Age*. Philadelphia: Temple University Press, 1990.

Rorty, Richard. *Philosophy and Social Hope*. New York: Penguin, 1999.

Rorty, Richard, and Gianni Vattimo. *The Future of Religion*. Edited by Santiago Zabala. New York: Columbia University Press, 2005.

Rosemont, Henry, Jr. *Rationality and Religious Experience: The Continuing Relevance of the World's Spiritual Traditions*. Commentary by Huston Smith. Chicago: Open Court, 2001.

Rosen, Allen D. *Kant's Theory of Justice*. Ithaca, NY: Cornell University Press, 1993.

Rossiter, Clinton, ed. *The Federalist Papers*. New York: Mentor, 1961.

Rotberg, Robert I. "Failed States in a World of Terror." *Foreign Affairs* 81 (2002): 127–40.

Roth, Kenneth. "The Case for Universal Jurisdiction." *Foreign Affairs* 80 (2001): 150–54.

———. "The Court the U.S. Doesn't Want." *New York Review of Books*, 19 November 1998, 45. Reprinted in *International Human Rights in Context: Law, Politics, Morals*, ed. Henry J. Steiner and Philip Alston, 1198. 2nd ed. New York: Oxford University Press, 2000.

Rothschild, Emma. "Condorcet and Adam Smith on Education and Instruction." In *Philosophers on Education*, ed. Amélie Oksenberg Rorty, 209–26. New York: Routledge, 1998.

Rothschild, Emma. *Economic Sentiments: Adam Smith, Condorcet, and the Enlightenment.* Cambridge, MA: Harvard University Press, 2001.

Rousseau, Jean-Jacques. *The Confessions of Jean-Jacques Rousseau.* New York: Modern Library, n.d.

——. *Emile, or, On Education.* Translated by Allan Bloom. New York: Basic Books, 1979.

——. *On the Social Contract, Discourse on the Origin of Inequality, Discourse on Political Economy.* Translated by Donald A. Cress. Indianapolis: Hackett, 1983.

——. *The Political Writings of Jean-Jacques Rousseau.* Edited by C. E. Vaughan. Cambridge, UK: Cambridge University Press, 1915; reprint ed., New York: Wiley, 1962.

——. *Rousseau on International Relations.* Edited by Stanley Hoffmann and David P. Fidler. Oxford: Clarendon Press, 1991.

——. *The Social Contract.* Translated by Maurice Cranston. New York: Penguin, 1968.

Rousseau, Jean-Jacques, and Johann Gottfried Herder. *On the Origin of Language.* Translated by John H. Moran and Alexander Gode. New York: Frederick Unger, 1966.

Routledge Encyclopedia of Philosophy. Ed. Edward Craig. London: Routledge, 1998.

Rubin, Elizabeth. "If Not Peace, Then Justice." *New York Times Magazine*, April 2, 2006, pp. 42–75.

Ruddy, Francis Stephen. *International Law in the Enlightenment: The Background of Emmerich de Vattel's Le Droit des Gens.* Dobbs Ferry, NY: Oceana Publications, 1975.

Rudolph, Frederick. *The American College and University: A History.* New York: Vintage, 1962.

——, ed. *Essays on Education in the Early Republic.* Cambridge, MA: Belknap Press, 1965.

Russell, Ruth B. *A History of the United Nations Charter: The Role of the United States 1940–1945.* Washington, DC: Brookings Institution, 1958.

Rustow, Dankwart A. *A World of Nations: Problems of Political Modernization.* Washington, DC: Brookings Institution, 1967.

Ryan, Alan. *Liberal Anxieties and Liberal Education.* New York: Hill and Wang, 1998.

Sachs, Jeffrey. *The End of Poverty: Economic Possibilities for Our Time.* New York: Penguin, 2005.

Said, Edward. *Culture and Imperialism.* New York: Knopf, 1993.

Saint-Pierre, Charles Irénée Castal, Abbé de. *Selections from the Second Edition of the Abrege du Projet de Paix Perpetuelle.* Translated by H. Hale Bellot. Introduction by Paul Collinet. Grotius Society Publications. Texts for Students of International Relations, No. 5. London: Sweet & Maxwell, 1927.

Sands, Philippe. *Lawless World: America and the Making and Breaking of Global Rules from FDR's Atlantic Charter to George W. Bush's Illegal War.* New York: Viking, 2005.

Savelle, Max. "Nationalism and Other Loyalties in the American Revolution." *American Historical Review* 67 (1962): 918–32.

Schiller, Friedrich. *On the Aesthetic Education of Man in a Series of Letters.* Edited and translated by Elizabeth M. Wilkinson and L. A. Willoughby. Oxford: Clarendon Press, 1967.

Schlegel, Friedrich. *Essay on the Concept of Republicanism Occasioned by the Kantian Tract "Perpetual Peace."* In *The Early Political Writings of the German Romantics*, ed. Frederick C. Beiser, 93–112. Cambridge, UK: Cambridge University Press, 1996.

Schleiermacher, Friedrich. *Lectures on Philosophical Ethics.* Edited by Robert B. Louden. Cambridge, UK: Cambridge University Press, 2002.

———. *Occasional Thoughts on Universities in the German Sense.* Translated by Terrence N. Tice and Edwina Lawler. Lewiston, ME: Edwin Mellen Press, 1991.

———. *On Religion: Speeches to its Cultured Despisers.* Translated by Richard Crouter. Cambridge, UK: Cambridge University Press, 1988.

Schlereth, Thomas J. *The Cosmopolitan Ideal in Enlightenment Thought: Its Form and Function in the Ideas of Franklin, Hume, and Voltaire, 1694–1790.* Notre Dame, IN: University of Notre Dame Press, 1977.

Schmidt, James. "Introduction: What Is Enlightenment? A Question, Its Context, and Some Consequences." In *What Is Enlightenment? Eighteenth-Century Answers and Twentieth-Century Questions*, ed. James Schmidt, 1–44. Berkeley: University of California Press, 1996.

———. "Inventing the Enlightenment: Anti-Jacobians, British Hegelians, and the *Oxford English Dictionary*." *Journal of the History of Ideas* 64 (2003): 421–43.

Schmitter, Amy M., Nathan Tarcov, and Wendy Donner. "Enlightenment Liberalism." In *A Companion to the Philosophy of Education*, ed. Randall Curren, 73–93. Malden, MA: Blackwell, 2003.

Schneewind, J. B. *The Invention of Autonomy: A History of Modern Moral Philosophy.* New York: Cambridge University Press, 1998.

Schneiders, Werner. *Das Zeitalter der Aufklärung.* Munich: C. H. Beck, 1997.

Schumacher, Bernard. *A Philosophy of Hope: Josef Pieper and the Contemporary Debate on Hope.* Translated by D. C. Schindler. New York: Fordham University Press, 2003.

Schumpeter, Joseph A. *Capitalism, Socialism, and Democracy.* 3rd ed. New York: Harper Torchbooks, 1962.

Scott, George. *The Rise and Fall of the League of Nations.* London: Hutchinson, 1973.

Scott, James C. *Seeing Like a State: How Certain Schemes to Improve the Human Condition Have Failed.* New Haven: Yale University Press, 1998.

Searle, John. "Is There a Crisis in American Higher Education?" *Partisan Review* 60 (1993). Reprinted in *Classic and Contemporary Readings in the Philosophy of Education*, ed. Steven M. Cahn, 536–46. New York: McGraw-Hill, 1997.

Selle, Götz von. *Die Georg-August-Universität zu Göttingen 1737–1937.* Göttingen: Vanderhoeck und Ruprecht, 1937.

Sen, Amartya. *Development as Freedom.* New York: Anchor Books, 1999.

———. "Elements of a Theory of Human Rights." *Philosophy and Public Affairs* 32 (2004): 315–56.

Sengupta, Somini. "African Girls' Route to School Is Still Littered with Obstacles." *New York Times*, December 14, 2003, p. 1.

Sennett, James F., and Douglas Groothuis, eds. *In Defense of Natural Theology: A Post-Humean Assessment*. Downers Grove, IL: InterVarsity Press, 2005.

Sherman, Joel D., Steven D. Honegger, and Jennifer L. McGivern. *Comparative Indicators of Education in the United States and Other G-8 Countries: 2002*. Washington, DC: National Center for Education Statistics, U.S. Department of Education, Institute of Education Sciences, 2003.

Singer, Peter. *One World: The Ethics of Globalization*. New Haven: Yale University Press, 2002.

Smith, Adam. *An Inquiry into the Nature and Causes of the Wealth of Nations*. 2 vols. Edited by R. H. Campbell and A. S. Skinner. Oxford: Clarendon Press, 1976; reprint ed., Indianapolis: Liberty Fund, 1981.

———. *Lectures on Jurisprudence*. Edited by R. L. Meek, D. D. Raphael, and P. G. Stein. Oxford: Clarendon Press, 1978.

———. *The Theory of Moral Sentiments*. Edited by D. D. Raphael and A. L. Macfie. Oxford: Clarendon Press, 1977.

Smith, Anthony D. *The Antiquity of Nations*. Malden, MA: Polity Press, 2004.

Smith, Huston. *Why Religion Matters: The Fate of the Human Spirit in an Age of Disbelief*. San Francisco: Harper, 2001.

Snyder, Louis L., ed. *The Dynamics of Nationalism*. Princeton: D. Van Nostrand, 1964.

Sorkin, David. "Wilhelm von Humboldt: The Theory and Practice of Self-Formation (*Bildung*), 1791–1810." *Journal of the History of Ideas* 44 (1983): 55–73.

Souleyman, Elizabeth V. *The Vision of World Peace in Seventeenth and Eighteenth-Century France*. New York: G. P. Putnam's, 1941.

Steel, Ronald. "The Missionary." *New York Review of Books* 50, November 20, 2003, pp. 26–35.

Steiner, Henry J., and Philip Alston, eds. *International Human Rights in Context: Law, Politics, Morals*. 2nd ed. New York: Oxford University Press, 2000.

Stiglitz, Joseph E. *Globalization and Its Discontents*. New York: Norton, 2002.

Stone, Ralph A. *The Irreconcilables: The Fight against the League of Nations*. Lexington: University Press of Kentucky, 1970.

Suárez, Francisco. *Selections from Three Works*. Translated by Gwladys L. Williams. Oxford: Clarendon Press, 1944; reprint ed., New York: Oceana Publications, 1964.

Sully, Maximilien de Béthune, duc de. *Sully's Grand Design of Henry IV*. From the Memoirs of Maximilien de Béthune, duc de Sully. Introduction by David Ogg. Grotius Society Publications. Texts for Students of International Relations, No. 2. London: Sweet and Maxwell, 1921. Reprinted in *Peace Projects of the Seventeenth Century*. The Garland Library of War and Peace. Edited by Blanche Wiesen Cook, Sandi E. Cooper, and Charles Chatfield. New York: Garland, 1972.

Swatos, William H., Jr., ed. *A Future for Religion? New Paradigms for Social Analysis*. Newbury Park, CA: Sage, 1993.

Taylor, Charles. "Nationalism and Modernity." In *The Morality of Nationalism*, ed. Robert McKim and Jeff McMahan, 31–55. New York: Oxford University Press, 1997.

———. *Philosophical Arguments*. Cambridge, MA: Harvard University Press, 1995.

———. *Sources of the Self: The Making of the Modern Identity*. Cambridge, MA: Harvard University Press, 1989.

Terkel, Studs. *Hope Dies Last: Keeping Faith in Troubled Times*. New York: New Press, 2003.

Tieftrunk, Johann Heinrich. "On the Influence of Enlightenment on Revolutions." In *What Is Enlightenment? Eighteenth-Century Answers and Twentieth-Century Questions*, ed. James Schmidt, 217–24. Berkeley: University of California Press, 1996.

Tocqueville, Alexis de. *Democracy in America*. Edited by J. P. Meyer. Garden City, NJ: Anchor Books, 1969.

Todorov, Tzvetan. *Hope and Memory: Lessons from the Twentieth Century*. Translated by David Bellos. Princeton: Princeton University Press, 2003.

Tomlinson, John. *Globalization and Culture*. Chicago: University of Chicago Press, 1999.

Tuck, Richard. "The Making and Unmaking of Boundaries from the Natural Law Perspective." In *States, Nations, and Borders: The Ethics of Making Boundaries*, ed. Allen Buchanan and Margaret Moore, 143–70. New York: Cambridge University Press, 2003.

———. "The 'Modern' Theory of Natural Law." In *The Languages of Political Theory in Early-Modern Europe*, ed. Anthony Pagden, 99–119. New York: Cambridge University Press, 1987.

———. *Natural Rights Theories: Their Origin and Development*. New York: Cambridge University Press, 1979.

———. *The Rights of War and Peace: Political Thought and the International Order from Grotius to Kant*. New York: Oxford University Press, 1999.

Turner, R. Steven. "University Reformers and Professional Scholarship in Germany 1760–1806." In *The University in Society*, ed. Lawrence Stone, 2: 495–532. Princeton: Princeton University Press, 1974.

Tyack, David, and Larry Cuban. *Tinkering toward Utopia*. Cambridge, MA: Harvard University Press, 1995.

U.S. Bureau of the Census. *Historical Statistics of the United States: Colonial Times to 1970*. Washington, DC: U.S. Government Printing Office, 1975.

U.S. Department of State. "International Criminal Court: Letter to UN Secretary General Kofi Annan." Press statement. May 6, 2002.

Vassar, Rena L., ed. *Social History of American Education*. Vol. I. Chicago: Rand McNally, 1965.

Vattel, Emerich de. *The Law of Nations or Principles of Natural Law*. Translated by Charles G. Fenwick. Washington, DC: Carnegie Institution, 1916; reprint ed., New York: Oceana Publications, 1964.

Vincent, Andrew. *Nationalism and Particularity*. New York: Cambridge University Press, 2002.

Viner, Jacob. *The Long View and the Short: Studies in Economic Theory and Policy.* Glencoe, IL: Free Press, 1958.

Vogler, Candace. *Reasonably Vicious.* Cambridge, MA: Harvard University Press, 2002.

Voltaire. *Letters of Voltaire and Frederick the Great.* Translated by Richard Aldington. New York: Brentano's, 1927.

———. "Of the Different Races of Men." In *The Idea of Race*, ed. Robert Bernasconi and Tommy L. Lott, 5–7. Indianapolis: Hackett, 2000.

———. *Philosophical Dictionary.* Edited and translated by Theodore Besterman. Harmondsworth, UK: Penguin, 1971.

———. *Treatise on Toleration.* Edited by Simon Harvey. New York: Cambridge University Press, 2000.

Wagar, W. Warren. *The City of Man: Prophecies of a World Civilization in Twentieth-Century Thought.* Baltimore: Penguin, 1967.

Walker, David M., ed. *The Oxford Companion to Law.* New York: Oxford University Press, 1980.

Walters, F. P. *A History of the League of Nations.* Reprint ed. New York: Oxford University Press, 1965.

Waters, Malcolm. *Globalization.* London: Routledge, 1995.

Wattles, Jeffrey. *The Golden Rule.* New York: Oxford University Press, 1996.

Werhane, Patricia H. *Adam Smith and His Legacy for Modern Capitalism.* New York: Oxford University Press, 1991.

Weschler, Lawrence. "Exceptional Cases in Rome: The United States and the Struggle for an ICC." In *The United States and the International Criminal Court*, ed. Sarah B. Sewall and Carl Kaysen, 85–111. Lanham, MD: Rowman & Littlefield, 2000.

Willey, Basil. *The Eighteenth Century Background: Studies on the Idea of Nature in the Thought of the Period.* London: Chatto and Windus, 1940; reprint ed., Boston: Beacon Press, 1961.

Willey, Thomas E. "Kant and the German Theory of Education." *Studies on Voltaire and the Eighteenth Century* 67 (1977): 543–68.

Williams, Bernard. *Truth and Truthfulness: An Essay in Genealogy.* Princeton: Princeton University Press, 2002.

Williams, David., ed. *The Enlightenment.* New York: Cambridge University Press, 1999.

Williams, Howard. *Kant's Political Philosophy.* New York: St. Martin's, 1983.

Williams, Paul, ed. *The International Bill of Rights.* Introduction by Peter Meyer. Glen Ellen, CA: Entwhistle Books, 1981.

Wilson, Bryan. *Religion in Sociological Perspective.* New York: Oxford University Press, 1982.

Wokler, Robert. "The Enlightenment, the Nation-state and the Primal Patricide of Modernity." In *The Enlightenment and Modernity*, ed. Norman Geras and Robert Wokler, 161–83. New York: St. Martin's, 2000.

———. "Multiculturalism and Ethnic Cleansing in the Enlightenment." In *Toleration in Enlightenment Europe*, ed. Ole Peter Grell and Roy Porter, 69–85. New York: Cambridge University Press, 2000.

———. "Projecting the Enlightenment." In *After MacIntyre: Critical Perspectives on the Work of Alasdair MacIntyre*, ed. John Horton and Susan Mendus, 108–26. Notre Dame, IN: University of Notre Dame Press, 1994.

Wolf, Martin. *Why Globalization Works*. New Haven: Yale University Press, 2004.

Wolff, Christian. *The Law of Nations Treated According to a Scientific Method*. Translated by Joseph H. Drake. Introduction by Otfried Nippold. Oxford: Clarendon Press, 1934; reprint ed., New York: Oceana Publications, 1964.

Wollstonecraft, Mary. *The Vindications*. Edited by D. L. Macdonald and Kathleen Scherf. Orchard Park, NY: Broadview, 1997.

Wood, Allen W. *Kant's Ethical Thought*. New York: Cambridge University Press, 1999.

———. "Kant's Project for Perpetual Peace." In *Cosmopolitics: Thinking and Feeling beyond the Nation*, ed. Pheng Cheah and Bruce Robbins, 59–76. Minneapolis: University of Minnesota Press, 1998.

Wood, Gordon S. *The Creation of the American Republic 1776–1787*. Chapel Hill: University of North Carolina Press, 1969.

Wootton, David, ed. *Divine Right and Democracy: An Anthology of Political Writing in Stuart England*. New York: Penguin, 1986.

———, ed. *Republicanism, Liberty, and Commercial Society, 1649–1776*. Stanford: Stanford University Press, 1994.

Wordsworth, William. *The Prelude*. In *William Wordsworth*, ed. Stephen Gill, 375–590. Oxford: Oxford University Press, 1984.

World Bank. *Globalization, Growth, and Poverty: Building an Inclusive World Economy*. Policy research report. New York: Oxford University Press, 2002.

———. *World Development Report 1995*. New York: Oxford University Press, 1995.

Wright, Johnson Kent. " 'A Bright Clear Mirror': Cassirer's *The Philosophy of the Enlightenment*." In *What's Left of the Enlightenment? A Postmodern Question*, ed. Keith Michael Baker and Peter Hanns Reill, 71–101. Stanford: Stanford University Press, 2001.

Wright, Tom. "Annan Cautions Rights Council to Avoid Rifts." *New York Times*, June 20, 2006, p. A7.

Wynner, Edith, and Georgia Lloyd. *Searchlight on Peace Plans: Choose Your Road to World Government*. New York: E. P. Dutton, 1944.

Yasukata, Toshimasa. *Lessing's Philosophy of Religion and the German Enlightenment: Lessing on Christianity and Reason*. New York: Oxford University Press, 2002.

Zagorin, Perez. *How the Idea of Religious Toleration Came to the West*. Princeton: Princeton University Press, 2003.

Zakaria, Fareed. "Illiberal Democracy." *Foreign Affairs* 76 (1997): 22–43.

Zammito, John H. *Kant, Herder, and the Birth of Anthropology*. Chicago: University of Chicago Press, 2002.

Zouche, Richard. *An Exposition of Fecial Law and Procedure, or of Law between Nations, and Questions concerning the Same*. Translated by J. L. Brierly. Washington, DC: Carnegie Institution, 1911; reprint ed., New York: Oceana Publications, 1964.

Zuckert, Michael P. *The Natural Rights Republic: Studies in the Foundations of the American Political Tradition*. Notre Dame, IN: University of Notre Dame Press, 1996.

Web Sites

Center for the Study of Global Christianity. http://www.globalchristianity.org

Coalition for the International Criminal Court. http://www.iccnow.org

Freedom House. http://www.freedomhouse.org

———. http://www.freedomhouse.org/reports/century.html

Institute of Education Sciences National Center for Education Statistics. http://nces. ed.gov

International Association for the the Evaluation of Educational Acheivement. http://www.wam.umd.edu/~jtpurta/

Organisation for Economic Co-operation and Development. http://www. oecd.org

UNICEF. http://www.unicef.org

United Nations. http://www.un.org

———. http://www.un.org/Overview/unmember.html

Index